PLANUNG, ORGANISATION UND UNTERNEHMUNGSFÜHRUNG

Herausgegeben von Prof. Dr. Dr. h. c. Norbert Szyperski, Köln, Prof. Dr. Winfried Matthes, Wuppertal, Prof. Dr. Udo Winand, Kassel, Prof. (em.) Dr. Joachim Griese, Bern, Prof. Dr. Harald F. O. von Kortzfleisch, Koblenz, Prof. Dr. Ludwig Theuvsen, Göttingen, und Prof. Dr. Andreas Al-Laham, Kaiserslautern

Band 121
Caroline Merk
Cooperation among Airlines – A Transaction Cost Economic Perspective
Lohmar – Köln 2008 ◆ 278 S. ◆ € 48,- (D) ◆ ISBN 978-3-89936-692-1

Band 122
Frank P. Schmitz
Unterstützungsnetzwerke auslandschinesischer Unternehmungsgründungen
Lohmar – Köln 2008 ◆ 258 S. ◆ € 57,- (D) ◆ ISBN 978-3-89936-735-5

Band 123
Baris Calisan
Anbieterinitiiertes Outsourcing – Ein marktorientiertes Management-Konzept für strategische Unternehmenspartnerschaften, dargestellt am Beispiel der deutschen und türkischen Textil- und Bekleidungsindustrie
Lohmar – Köln 2009 ◆ 364 S. ◆ € 64,- (D) ◆ ISBN 978-3-89936-774-4

Band 124
Nicole Sodeik
Projektmanagement wertorientierter Mergers & Acquisitions
Lohmar – Köln 2009 ◆ 440 S. ◆ € 68,- (D) ◆ ISBN 978-3-89936-805-5

Band 125
Christoffer-Martin F. Seubert
Build, Ally or Acquire – Die strategische Entscheidung über den Entwicklungsweg
Lohmar – Köln 2010 ◆ 420 S. ◆ € 67,- (D) ◆ ISBN 978-3-89936-886-4

Band 126
Maren S. D. Breuer
Socio-Cognitive Dynamics in Strategic Processes
Lohmar – Köln 2010 ◆ 360 S. ◆ € 64,- (D) ◆ ISBN 978-3-89936-954-0

JOSEF EUL VERLAG

Reihe: Planung, Organisation und Unternehmungsführung · Band 126

Herausgegeben von Prof. Dr. Dr. h. c. Norbert Szyperski, Köln, Prof. Dr. Winfried Matthes, Wuppertal, Prof. Dr. Udo Winand, Kassel, Prof. (em.) Dr. Joachim Griese, Bern, Prof. Dr. Harald F. O. von Kortzfleisch, Koblenz, Prof. Dr. Ludwig Theuvsen, Göttingen, und Prof. Dr. Andreas Al-Laham, Kaiserslautern

Dr. Maren S. D. Breuer

Socio-Cognitive Dynamics in Strategic Processes

With a Foreword by Prof. Dr. Thomas Wrona, ESCP Europe Wirtschaftshochschule Berlin

Bibliografische Information der Deutschen Nationalbibliothek

Die Deutsche Nationalbibliothek verzeichnet diese Publikation in der Deutschen Nationalbibliografie; detaillierte bibliografische Daten sind im Internet über <http://dnb.d-nb.de> abrufbar.

Dissertation, ESCP Europe Wirtschaftshochschule Berlin, 2010

ISBN 978-3-89936-954-0
1. Auflage August 2010

© JOSEF EUL VERLAG GmbH, Lohmar – Köln, 2010
Alle Rechte vorbehalten

JOSEF EUL VERLAG GmbH
Brandsberg 6
53797 Lohmar
Tel.: 0 22 05 / 90 10 6-6
Fax: 0 22 05 / 90 10 6-88
E-Mail: info@eul-verlag.de
http://www.eul-verlag.de

Bei der Herstellung unserer Bücher möchten wir die Umwelt schonen. Dieses Buch ist daher auf säurefreiem, 100% chlorfrei gebleichtem, alterungsbeständigem Papier nach DIN 6738 gedruckt.

Foreword

The dissertation of Maren Breuer deals with the emergence of organizational strategies and makes a contribution to the process approaches in strategic management research. The author bases her work on a socio-cognitive perspective, i.e. she examines the role of the cognitive structures and cognitive processes of the involved actors. Although there are by now a number of noticeable empirical studies and conceptual contributions in the field of cognitive strategy research, the area of social interaction processes is at most dealt with marginally in these. With her dissertation Maren Breuer has thus entered virgin soil in different areas.

The work has two ambitious scientific objectives: Firstly, a conceptual examination of how strategies as shared strategic orientations develop in the course of the ongoing strategy processes is provided. Secondly, an empirical study is conducted, which uses the example of (fictitious) strategic decision making groups to examine the nature of social interactions and the role that these have for the development of organizational strategies.

The dissertation stands out both with its interdisciplinary theoretical foundations and with a number of interesting empirical results from the analysed experimental groups. With this, Maren Breuer puts forward an interesting and advancing work for the area of strategy research, which I wish an interested audience.

Berlin, July 2010   Univ.-Prof. Dr. Thomas Wrona

Preface

This work is inherently interdisciplinary in nature and as such its roots can be traced to the very beginnings of my academic life, i.e. my undergraduate studies in Integrated Social Sciences at Jacobs University Bremen. Besides my general interest in scientific research that was nurtured in this challenging international and interdisciplinary environment, also the more specific fascination with the interplay between cognition and different social and cultural contexts was created in such stimulating psychology courses like "Cross-cultural cognitions" as well as during my work as a student assistant in the university's social cognition lab group. The experiences I gained during my ensuing business master studies then both confirmed the high relevance of regarding cognitive issues also in the realm of international strategic management and my determination to continue my academic life at the PhD level. In line with the international focus that characterizes my entire educational life the ESCP Europe with its intriguing and challenging PhD programme and the simultaneous work as a research and teaching assistant at one of the school's chairs finally represented the ideal place for successfully pursuing my set objectives.

This book now represents the outcome of an intense three-and-a-half year period of research and work at the Berlin Campus of ESCP Europe at the Chair of Organisation & Empirical Management Research of Prof. Dr. Thomas Wrona. One of the main arguments I make in this work is that even though cognition is at its very basis something individual, it can only be fully understood by recognizing its close relation with the respective (social) context(s) that surround it. In a very similar way exactly this is also the case for the present dissertation, which I would not have been able to complete in isolation from a number of crucial others:

First to name in this respect is Prof. Dr. Thomas Wrona, who supervised my research and to whom I am grateful for the freedom he has given me to create a piece of work that is characterized by the individual notion I wished to give to it. My thanks also go to Prof. Dr. Jochen Koch for his time and efforts for providing the second constructive review of my work, and to Prof. Dr. Ulrich Pape as the chair of the review commission at ESCP Europe.

Apart from the concrete academic context, a much more indispensible imprint on my work and especially my life during the PhD derives from the social contexts that surrounded me and from those precious people that were there already before, those who entered newly into my life, and those who left during those years. The eternal Bremer group of friends constitutes the first of these, and is complemented by a special colleague from ESCP with whom I could share both the usual sorrows of doing a PhD and the pleasures gained from exploring the city's culturally diverse and exciting culinary venues.

The most essential and influential "gain" from this time, however, is Nils Horch. With him I not only consistently shared a wall between our offices at ESCP during the three years, was able to exchange and debate all the 'socio-cognitive' issues I was dealing with at work, but also to advance both his and my cooking skills and to make an entrance to the German wine tasting society. No words can truly express the amount of gratitude I have for his constant emotional support, the stimulating intellectual challenges, and especially the indispensible strength he needed as a continuously more integrated member of the Breuer family.

Exactly this family, i.e. my parents and my grandma, finally is to whom I owe everything I have been able to do and to achieve in my work and personal life to date. These three have and will always be the most precious people for me and I am sure that my mum agrees with me that I dedicate this work to those that have physically left but in my heart will always be with me: my beloved father Willi R. Breuer and my grandma Gertrud Winkler.

Maren S. D. Breuer

Berlin/ Jakarta, July 2010

Table of contents

Foreword v

Preface vii

Table of contents ix

List of tables xv

List of figures xvii

List of abbreviations xix

1 Introduction 1
   1.1 Positioning and overall research objective 1
   1.2 Derivation of research questions 2
   1.3 Structure of the work 7

2 Strategic management 11
   2.1 Foundations of the field 11
   2.2 Conceptions of "strategy" and own conception in this work 14
   2.3 Traditional and dominant theoretical perspectives 19
       2.3.1 Economic approaches 20
       2.3.2 From economic theories to organisation studies 23
       2.3.3 Further theoretical approaches 26
   2.4 The cognitive perspective on strategic management 26
       2.4.1 Origins of the managerial and organizational cognition perspective (MOC) 28
       2.4.2 Basic principles 30
       2.4.3 Perspectives in MOC research 30
           2.4.3.1 The computational perspective 31
           2.4.3.2 The interpretive perspective 35
           2.4.3.3 Integrating the two perspectives 39
       2.4.4 The "landscape" of cognitive strategy research 41
       2.4.5 Value of adopting a cognitive approach to strategy research 48
       2.4.6 Deriving a socio-cognitive research framework 50

3 Strategic processes ... 55

3.1 Introducing strategy process research ... 55
3.2 Major theoretical approaches and perspectives in strategy process research ... 57
- 3.2.1 Rational-decision oriented approaches ... 57
- 3.2.2 Incremental approaches ... 59
- 3.2.3 Evolutionary approaches ... 59
- 3.2.4 Political approaches ... 60
- 3.2.5 Cognitive approaches ... 61
- 3.2.6 The "micro" perspective ... 63

3.3 Theory spanning perspectives on strategy processes ... 67
- 3.3.1 Strategy "formation" according to Mintzberg ... 68
- 3.3.2 The "genesis" of strategies according to Kirsch ... 72

3.4 Towards an own – socio-cognitive – view on strategic processes ... 76
- 3.4.1 Dimensions of strategic processes ... 80
  - 3.4.1.1 Nature of the basic process ... 82
  - 3.4.1.2 Actors ... 83
  - 3.4.1.3 (Strategic) Activities ... 85
  - 3.4.1.4 Content ... 95
  - 3.4.1.5 Context ... 95
- 3.4.2 Implications for the parallelization of strategic orientations ... 96

4 From *intra-* to *inter*individual cognition in strategic processes ... 99

4.1 Knowledge ... 101
- 4.1.1 Conception(s) and categories of knowledge ... 101
  - 4.1.1.1 Tacit and explicit knowledge ... 103
  - 4.1.1.2 Declarative and procedural knowledge ... 103
  - 4.1.1.3 The relationship between knowledge and information ... 104
- 4.1.2 (Managerial) knowledge structures and strategic knowledge ... 106

4.2 Knowledge representation in the human mind ... 108
- 4.2.1 Schema-based theories ... 108
  - 4.2.1.1 Characteristics of schemata ... 109
  - 4.2.1.2 Functional aspects ... 111
  - 4.2.1.3 Acquisition and change of schemata ... 114
- 4.2.2 Network theories ... 115
- 4.2.3 Interim summary ... 117

4.3 Situated cognition ... 119
4.4 Socially shared cognition and collective knowledge in organisations ... 123
4.5 Synthesis 1: A socio-cognitive perspective (SCP) on strategic processes ... 128

	4.6	Towards examining the socio-cognitive processes in decision making teams	135
	4.7	Collective information processing	136

5 Social interaction processes in (small) groups 141

    5.1 A general framework for the study of groups 142

    5.2 Process research on group decision making 144

        5.2.1 Factors in group interaction processes and conditions for successful cooperation, knowledge sharing and growth 146

        5.2.2 Phases and temporal patterns in group processes 149

        5.2.3 Evidence from processes of group learning 151

            5.2.3.1 Sharing knowledge 152

            5.2.3.2 Generating new knowledge 153

            5.2.3.3 Evaluating knowledge 154

            5.2.3.4 Combining knowledge 155

            5.2.3.5 Potential impediments to group learning 157

            5.2.3.6 The relationship between group learning and organisational learning 159

        5.2.4 Forms and functions of social interaction 160

    5.3 Synthesis 2: A socio-cognitive model of strategic decision making processes 162

        5.3.1 Towards an integrated view on strategic decision making processes 165

            5.3.1.1 Processing objective 166

            5.3.1.2 Accumulation 168

            5.3.1.3 Storage 169

            5.3.1.4 Retrieval 172

            5.3.1.5 Examination 173

            5.3.1.6 Accommodation 173

            5.3.1.7 Interim summary and specifics of the model's "centrepiece" 175

            5.3.1.8 Outcomes and "products" of group interaction processes 178

        5.3.2 General meaning and implications of the socio-cognitive perspective on group (decision making) processes 179

        5.3.3 Towards examining the empirical reality of socio-cognitive dynamics 181

6 Empirical study of social interaction processes in decision making groups 185

    6.1 Rationale of the empirical study 185

    6.2 A multi-level and multi-functional process analysis 188

        6.2.1 Group decision making on complex tasks 188

        6.2.2 Interests and specific questions in the empirical investigation 191

    6.3 Methodological approach 195

    6.4 Data collection 199

	6.4.1	Simulations 199
	6.4.2	Free simulation of a complex strategic decision task 202
	6.4.3	Concrete scenario 203
	6.4.4	Realisation of the simulation 205
	6.4.5	Research participants 206
	6.4.6	Instructions to the participants 207
	6.4.7	Data preparation 209
6.5	Data analysis 209
	6.5.1	Functional content analysis of small group interactions 210
	6.5.2	Qualitative content analysis 211
		6.5.2.1 Towards the final category system 213
		6.5.2.2 The specific coding system 216
	6.5.3	'Suggestions' part 223
	6.5.4	Behavioural analysis – Process management and team climate 225
6.6	Quality criteria 226
	6.6.1	Inter-subject comprehensibility 229
	6.6.2	Indication of the research process 229
	6.6.3	Empirical foundation 230
	6.6.4	Limitation 231
6.7	Results and discussion 232
	6.7.1	Group level communication at the macro level of action areas 233
	6.7.2	Group level results at the micro level of the content dimension 236
		6.7.2.1 Group 1 236
		6.7.2.2 Group 2 237
		6.7.2.3 Group 3 237
		6.7.2.4 Cross-case analyses and considerations 237
	6.7.3	Results concerning the 'suggestions' 242
		6.7.3.1 Group 1 243
		6.7.3.2 Group 2 249
		6.7.3.3 Group 3 254
		6.7.3.4 General and comparative discussion 259
	6.7.4	Micro level results for group process management and team 'climate' 262
		6.7.4.1 Group process management 262
		6.7.4.2 Group 'climate' 265
	6.7.5	Within-group results: Individual member profiles 269
		6.7.5.1 Group 1 269
		6.7.5.2 Group 2 273
		6.7.5.3 Group 3 276
		6.7.5.4 Comparative discussion of the within-group results and implications 278

		6.7.6	Interaction processes and learning from the participants' views	279

- 6.8 Evaluation and general implications of the empirical study 281
    - 6.8.1 Limitations 282
    - 6.8.2 Summary and implications for the strategic reality 283

7 Final summary and conclusions 287
- 7.1 Overall goal and research questions 287
- 7.2 Theoretical contributions and value added of the overall work 293
- 7.3 Future research directions 300

Appendix 303
Questionnaire administered to the participants 303

Bibliography 313

List of tables

Table 1: Selected definitions of strategic management 13
Table 2: Selected research topics and exemplary studies according to levels of 'strategic cognitions' 44
Table 3: Mintzberg's grass-roots model of strategy formation 70
Table 4: Summary description of Mintzberg's strategy types 71
Table 5: Strategy development modes with approximate correspondences 83
Table 6: Selected strategy-making process models 89
Table 7: Overview of specific questions in the empirical investigation 195
Table 8: Overview of compositional characteristics of research participants 207
Table 9: The categories of the "conference coding" according to Fisch (1994) 216
Table 10: Own coding system 217
Table 11: Detailed descriptions and empirical examples for the individual codes 218
Table 12: Relative importance of the three functional areas of social interaction according to groups 233
Table 13: Detailed results for the content-oriented dimension – all groups 236
Table 14: One-way ANOVA - 'V' and 'Ke' 240
Table 15: t-test statistics – 'V' and 'Ke' 240
Table 16: Numerical overview of the suggestions in Group 1 244
Table 17: Information overview of suggestions in Group 1 244
Table 18: Final strategic concept of Group 1 247
Table 19: Numerical overview of the suggestions in Group 2 249
Table 20: Suggestion information Group 2 249
Table 21: Final strategic concept of Group 2 252
Table 22: Numerical overview of the suggestions in Group 3 254
Table 23: Suggestion information Group 3 254
Table 24: Final strategic concept of Group 3 258
Table 25: Detailed results for the process-directing dimension – all groups 263
Table 26: Detailed results for the relationship-oriented dimension – all groups 266
Table 27: Individual member details Group 1 270
Table 28: Individual member details Group 2 273
Table 29: Individual member details Group 3 276

List of figures

Figure 1: Deliberate and emergent strategies according to Mintzberg 16
Figure 2: Strategies as action orientations and real behavioural patterns 18
Figure 3: Outline of a generic information-processing model 33
Figure 4: "MOC-landscape" 43
Figure 5: Example of a taxonomic knowledge structure 47
Figure 6: Research framework depicting the emergence of 'organisational strategies' from a socio-cognitive perspective 52
Figure 7: Overview of the strategic issue management process 63
Figure 8: Process categories of strategy 'genesis' in its context 75
Figure 9: Components of a framework for strategic processes 81
Figure 10: Own framework for analysing strategic processes with corresponding dimensions and exemplary variables 81
Figure 11: An integrated framework of strategic decision processes 87
Figure 12: Example for a cognitive map of a bank CEO 117
Figure 13: A general conceptual framework for the study of groups 143
Figure 14: Own socio-cognitive model of group decision making 163
Figure 15: Flow-chart of procedures for qualitative content analysis with the example of inductive category formation 212
Figure 16: Exemplary screenshot of the video analysis with *ELAN* 214
Figure 17: Between-group comparison of the means of the relative proportion of 'Vs' across all individual codes 239
Figure 18: Between-group comparison of the means of the relative proportion of 'Ke' across all individual codes 239

List of abbreviations

a.o.	and others
cf.	confer
e.g.	for example
etc.	et cetera
IPA	interaction process analysis
KBV	knowledge-based view
MOC	Managerial and Organizational Cognition
RBV	resource-based view
SCP	socio-cognitive perspective
TMT	top management team

1 Introduction

1.1 Positioning and overall research objective

In an important article published in the *Strategic Management Journal*, Levinthal and March (1993) conclude that **strategic management is** the art of dealing intelligently with three grand problems of decision making: (1) Ignorance, i.e., uncertainty about the future and the past and the causal structure of the world; (2) ambiguity, i.e., complexity, instability, and endogeneity in preferences and identities; and (3) conflict, i.e., inconsistent preferences and identities of multiple nested actors confronting multiple nested time perspectives (Levinthal & March, 1993, p. 109).

In line with this observation, whereas rational-analytical considerations and economic theories for long dominated the thinking in strategic management, like Levinthal and March, an increasing number of scholars in the field by now clearly recognize that the kinds of problems and challenges facing strategic actors are essentially the result of both *cognitive* and *social* impediments (Ginsberg, 1994, p. 156). As a consequence, the discipline is today a truly **multi-paradigm area** wherein especially two perspectives have come to the fore in recent years, i.e. the **cognitive stream** on the one hand, and so-called **"micro"** or **"practice" approaches** on the other (Hutzschenreuter & Kleindienst, 2006, p. 702 f.).

Concerning the former of these, works in this area most centrally draw on the concept of **knowledge structures**, which is here used synonymously with the terms **cognitive structures** or **schemata**. Knowledge structures order an information environment in a way that enables subsequent interpretation and action, are built on past experience, and represent a person's organized knowledge about a given concept or type of stimulus (Walsh, 1995, p. 281). In line with this, a fundamental assumption of all cognitive strategy research is that knowledge structures provide a set of lenses for strategists to make sense of their firms' strategic predispositions, competitive position, and internal capabilities. These lenses thus are essentially cognitive filters that admit certain bits of information into the strategizing process while excluding others. From this perspective, strategic processes then are regarded as **cognitive processes**, i.e. processes of perception, filtering, selection, interpretation, abstraction, and the development of firm strategies is said to occur in the strategist's own mind, i.e. it is a **mental process** (Bamberger & Wrona, 2004, p. 71).

As regards the latter perspective, also here the main concern is not with the *content* of concrete and observable strategic plans or strategies as something an *organization has,* but interest lies more in what its *members do* (Jarzabkowski & Seidl, 2008, p. 1391). In line with hence conceptualizing strategy as a **social 'practice'** (Whittington, 1996, p. 731), adherents of this perspective then focus specifically on the *process* of strategic management and point to the myriad of micro activities of managers and others in organizations, both at the centre as well as at the periphery.

Following from these outlines and regarding them together, it becomes obvious that even though an actor's knowledge and his cognitive processes are situated inside his own mind, at the same time they are clearly not isolated from the surrounding context, especially the social interactions with others that managers engage in while performing strategic activities. Here then, despite the close interlinkage between the cognitive and the social dimensions, and their respective individual valuation and treatment by strategy scholars, no real connection between the two has so far been achieved in the strategic management literature. In recognition of this deficiency, the **overall aim and contribution** of the present work is to fill exactly this gap. For this, the research builds on the cognitive stream in strategy research and extends it with the explicit integration and deepening of the social dimension in order to finally **develop a socio-cognitive perspective on strategic processes**. With this, a more adequate and comprehensive view of the emergence of organizational strategies is provided, which also points other researchers to the many elements of the overall process that are worth further investigation. Since the approach is truly interdisciplinary and integrates insights from diverse (scholarly) fields, it enlarges the pool of knowledge in the discipline of strategic management both content-wise and also method(olog)ically with the innovative research approach adopted in the empirical investigation. Practical contributions are provided by specifying in detail the different dimensions of strategic processes and hence sensitizing managers to important factors that need to be taken into account for careful overall process designs. At the micro level, concrete suggestions are derived for composing and instructing strategy teams in such a way as to allow for efficient interchanges during the discussions themselves, as well as to enable the effectiveness of these efforts beyond the specific group context and for the performance of the wider organisation.

1.2 Derivation of research questions

Following from the above outlines, the present work is clearly situated in the area of research on the ***process* of strategic management**. Here, whereas in the overall discipline of strategic management for long a rather sharp division was made between strategy *content* and strategy *process* research, the conception by now is that these issues are intrinsically linked (e.g.

Chakravarthy & White, 2002; Huff & Reger, 1987; Ketchen Jr, Thomas, & McDaniel Jr, 1996). In line with this, among the variety of strategy *process* issues, it is the **emergence of firm strategies** that is a central theme and of great importance in strategic management today. The scholarly interest thus is on investigating how strategies *(content)* develop in strategic processes *(process)*.

Regarding the *content* part, there are in fact a variety of different **conceptions of** *what* **strategies** actually are. One of the most widely followed approaches is to focus on some concrete strategic manoeuvres, for instance a market entry or an acquisition, or on the *outcome* of firms' past actions as expressed e.g. in the type and degree of diversification or internationalisation. Besides such interests in *real behavioural patterns* (e.g. Mintzberg, Ahlstrand, & Lampel, 2007, p. 23 ff.), another approach is to regard strategies as *action orientations* or action programmes, which, in the sense of intentions, are supposed to guide future behaviour. In this perspective, strategies are then often equalized with concrete *plans* that have been authorized officially and are explicitly written down in the organization (Bamberger & Wrona, 2004, p. 108). The clear difference between these two approaches is that while in the former it is *ex post* considerations of strategies, in the latter an *ex ante* view is adopted. Still, common to both of these perspectives is that they regard strategies as something quite tangible and in principle *observable*. Here then, however, particularly the equalisation between models of future behaviour and openly formulated strategy plans is not compulsory because often there are in fact no concrete written down action programmes existing in an organisation (Bamberger & Wrona, 2004, p. 108). Nevertheless, in line with the cognitive perspective taken here, which clearly emphasizes the importance of cognition in the strategy context, i.e. of both managerial knowledge structures and their cognitive processes (e.g. Daniels, Johnson, & de Chernatony, 1994; Gavetti & Rivkin, 2007; Johnson & Hoopes, 2003; Sparrow, 1999; Walsh, 1995), in these cases strategies in the sense of action orientations or strategic orientations[1] may still exist, namely in a purely cognitive form, i.e. in the minds of the individual actors involved. A firm can thus also "have" a strategy when an organisation's major decision makers *share* knowledge about the action principles of their organisation (Wrona & Breuer, 2008, p. 3).

Considering these different conceptions of what strategies can be, it is obvious that in the first case the focus is clearly on some concrete strategic *outcome*, thereby largely ignoring questions concerning *how* a certain action or behavioural pattern occurred in the first place.

---

[1] "Action orientation" is the verbatim translation of the original German term "Handlungsorientierung". Because there is no truly equivalent concept in the English language, for a better comprehension in the present work the term "strategic orientation" will be used interchangeably with "action orientation".

Research on strategies in the form of concrete *plans* or on specific planning *activities* against that often suffers from the fact that even though such action programmes may have been authorized officially this still does not necessarily mean that these public intentions also truly materialize into strategic actions. In contrast to these possible strategy conceptualisations, since humans' underlying cognitive structures are generally quite stable and change only slowly (Eysenck & Keane, 2005, p. 385), strategies in the form of shared strategic orientations usually outlive several decision or planning episodes and can thus be attested a particularly high degree of direction guiding power. In this context then, also the link between the *content* of strategies and the *process* of their development is most obvious and crucial. Specifically, while each individual actor clearly always predisposes of certain ideas and beliefs concerning the future development of his organisation, in order to also attest for the existence of *organisational strategies* there must clearly be more than those idiosyncratic knowledge structures or *individual strategies* of the actors involved. In recognition of the usually quite large number of diverse individuals in organisations, and consequently also the plurality of different knowledge, beliefs, and perceptions, truly understanding the strategic management process and the nature of strategies as shared strategic orientations is hence centrally concerned with explaining *how* these diverse frames of reference are reconciled within organizations, and *how* parallelized knowledge structures develop among key actors (Hodgkinson & Johnson, 1994, p. 531). Here then, findings from cognitive strategy researchers have already yielded a number of valuable results on issues regarding *cognition* in organisations, which include both insights on cognitive structures as the sets of managerial beliefs, orientations and knowledge, as well as on the intrinsically related cognitive processes. Still, despite their merits, most of these studies adopt a quite static focus on the individual managerial level and even forgo any considerations of the respective contexts their investigations are situated in (e.g. Calori, Johnson, & Sarnin, 1994; Reger & Palmer, 1996; Waller, Huber, & Glick, 1995).

Drawing on the above, and moving with this concretely to the ***processual side*** of strategy research, in line with the many and diverse social practices that strategic actors engage in during their daily work and that especially the "micro" researchers have pointed to (e.g. Hodgkinson, Whittington, Johnson, & Schwarz, 2006; Jarzabkowski & Seidl, 2008; Whittington, Molloy, Mayer, & Smith, 2006), it is also clear that the process of strategic management entails not only formulating or deciding on concrete strategy plans. Exactly this, however, is the traditional view of *process* approaches according to which strategic actions are determined through strategic decisions, and strategic processes are then equalized with (strategic) decision processes (e.g. Huff & Reger, 1987; Rajagopalan, Rasheed, & Datta,

1993). As a consequence, a large part of the existing works in the field is primarily concerned with the characteristics of decision or planning processes and has not really differentiated the *continuous* process of strategy formation. Different from this mainstream narrow focus, others already take a broader perspective and regard **strategic processes** as including not only all those decisions but also other actions and interactions that significantly affect an organization's potential for success or its organizational capabilities (e.g. Bamberger & Wrona, 2004, p. 336 ff.). In line with this, strategic processes thus not merely include decision making activities, but these rather merely constitute one element or "episode" within the overall process (e.g. Hendry & Seidl, 2003, p. 180 ff.; Kirsch, 1991, p. 131 ff.). As a consequence, it is clear that there are in fact many different occasions for managers to interact and exchange their knowledge and views on strategic issues. As may be intuitively comprehended, also the cognitive processes and implications will then clearly vary, whereby some of these "forums" in which interactions take place may provide more or better opportunities and conditions for parallelisation in *strategic* knowledge structures[2] to occur than others.

Now, following from the above outlines, it has been clearly established that there are different conceptions concerning the most central *object* of strategic management, i.e. what strategies are. Even though each of the described perspectives clearly has its value, in most works in the field the focus then is either predominantly static on some specific strategic outcome(s), or, if processual considerations are included, they remain largely focused on specific planning or decision making activities. Strategies considered from an ex ante view and defined as shared knowledge among some key actors about the action principles of their organisation, however, can, but clearly must not be the result of some conscious planning circles or retrospective observations of specific realized action structures (Bamberger & Wrona, 2004, p. 108). Instead, these shared strategic orientations are more emergent in nature, and are influenced to considerable degrees by the **social interactions**, i.e. direct face-to-face exchanges and communications through other channels (e.g. email or telephone), that a plurality of different organisational actors engages in during their daily strategy work.

In light of these outlines now, investigating the development of such knowledge structures in the ongoing strategic processes is then clearly not only important because of their high behavioural relevance and hence their close link to actual organisational outcomes and effectiveness (Hambrick & Mason, 1984, p. 193), but also because these more enduring and deeply rooted orientations may in fact be considered an organisation's very strategy itself. To better

---

[2] In this work "*strategic* knowledge structures" are defined as knowledge structures with strategically relevant content (cf. 4.1.2). These strategic knowledge structures constitute the basis for the individual's strategic orientation.

understand the strategic management process and illuminate on the emergence of organizational strategies, the central research question of the present work therefore asks:

- **How (and to what extent) do shared or parallelized strategic knowledge structures (among key decision makers) develop in strategic processes?**

Moreover, in the derivation of this overarching question, which is to guide the first *conceptual* part of the research, the importance of social interactions has already been implied. In fact, apart from a number of commonly experienced but rather passive influences on managerial cognitions (i.e., both cognitive structures and cognitive processes), that result from participation and work in the similar general strategic environment and organisational context, it is argued that this cognitive convergence process depends essentially on the social interactions and activities wherein organisational members discuss about and collectively reflect on their individual views concerning the future development of their organisation (e.g. Kirsch, 1992, p. 82 ff., 1996, p. 123 ff.). The basic assumption is that through their interactions group or organisational members share knowledge and process information, which finally *contributes* to the development of shared knowledge structures or reconciliation in strategic orientations. The degree to which such a parallelisation happens, however, will depend on the different characteristics, the conditions, the forms, etc., of the specific social activities and processes in which the interactions occur. Here then, even though a lot of such interchanges may occur rather informally or "on the fly", much of the strategy work done in today's organisations is essentially teamwork that is assigned to specific groups of managers (e.g. Guzzo & Salas, 1995; Paroutis & Pettigrew, 2007; Simons, Pelled, & Smith, 1999). In this context then, despite the myriad of possible collective activities strategists engage in, decision making and discussions in small groups or selected teams still constitute the core "forum" in which managers exchange knowledge and information on concrete strategic issues. Whereas especially here recourse is then also often made in the existing strategy literature to the essential role of social interaction processes (e.g. Amason, 1996; Knight et al., 1999; Smith et al., 1994), what exactly these entail is almost nowhere differentiated in more detail. In line with this and to fill this void, the second part of the overall work looks more specifically into this kind of "micro" context and asks:

- **What is the *nature* of social interactions in strategic decision making groups and what is the *role* of these interactions for the (non-) development and change of shared knowledge structures?**

Apart from investigating this question firstly on a conceptual basis, this micro level finally also constitutes the setting for the own *empirical* study, which is specifically aimed at opening up the 'black box' of group processes (e.g. Lawrence, 1997; Pelled, Eisenhardt, & Xin, 1999) and with this to contribute to the often called for, but not yet thoroughly established, true *process view* on strategic decision making.

1.3 Structure of the work

Based on the positioning and the overall research aims and questions, the argument will be developed as follows:

Following the (present) introduction, **Chapter 2** sets out with the **foundations of the discipline** of strategic management (2.1) and a more detailed outline of the different existing **conceptions of 'strategy'**, including the own conception adopted in this work (2.2). Having briefly outlined the traditional and dominant **theoretical perspectives** in the field (2.3), an in-depth consideration of the **cognitive perspective** on strategic management is provided (2.4). In this regard, even though (or possibly because) cognitive strategy research has by now become a quite prominent approach, the overall field is in fact quite vast and not yet systematically developed. Since it is essentially the cognitive perspective on which the entire research here is based, a first major contribution is made by providing a **structuring schema** for the 'landscape' of research on managerial and organisational cognition (MOC), which is based on an own comprehensive review of more than 100 (empirical) studies in the field (2.4.4). A discussion of the concrete value that can be derived from insights into the cognitive processes and structures of individuals, groups of managers, or organizations, complements this section (2.4.5). Finally, following from these insights, but also from the deficits identified in MOC research, at the end of Chapter 2 the essential issues to be considered for the development of a truly processual *socio*-cognitive approach to strategic processes are derived. In this context, a corresponding framework is presented that is able to remedy the existing deficiencies and hence allows for a more adequate and comprehensive view of the overall phenomenon at hand, i.e. the emergence of organisational strategies. Apart from enabling other researchers to draw on this and to investigate different elements of the framework in more detail themselves, it also serves as the general ordering frame for the entire work at hand (2.4.6).

Subsequent to the developmental and theoretical basics of the overall discipline, **Chapter 3** deals with one of the core 'objects' of the research, i.e. **strategic processes**. From the outline of the traditional views and existing theoretical perspectives in the area, the complexity of such processes and hence the need for more comprehensive and integrative approaches to strategic processes will have become clear. In recognition of this and for further developing the own perspective, **dimensions** of strategic processes are derived and discussed, which allow for a characterization of the individual strategic processes occurring in different organisations (3.4.1). Of particular importance here is the detailed discussion of the variety of different strategic activities managers (may) engage in, which hence also points to the plurality of "forums" in which social interactions among the actors involved in the process occur. Having recognized that depending on the specific values of all these dimensions also the socio-cognitive dynamics vary, finally certain tentative implications for the parallelisation of strategic knowledge structures and orientations are discussed (3.4.2).

The second core element of the research is the *socio-cognitive dynamics*, which by definition consists of essentially two parts, i.e. the cognitive and the social dimensions. For illuminating on the former and in order to finally move successfully from the *intra-* to the *inter*individual cognitive level, **Chapter 4** sets out by first focusing on the individual level and presenting concepts and theories from **traditional cognitive psychology**, which provide insights on concrete cognitive 'contents' (i.e. "knowledge") (4.1) and issues regarding cognitive structures generally (4.2). Besides, the second major stream in the field is considered, i.e. **situated cognition**, which complements the original works by broadening the focus to include social factors and considerations of the wider context surrounding the individual (4.3). Here then, not only is this actually a quite innovative approach for management and strategy research, but by proceeding in this way a step is also made forward to overcome the still prevailing divide between the computational and the interpretive perspectives on human cognition. Moreover, because concepts from both the cognitivistic and the situated perspectives still primarily aim at explaining cognition at the level of the individual actor, a third theoretical element is outlined which contains approaches that deal specifically with questions regarding the development of **socially shared cognitions**. In this context then, since the overall interest is essentially in cognitive developments and changes, which are obviously closely linked to *learning* issues, at this point a brief discussion of approaches to collective knowledge and learning in organisations finally complements this section (4.4). In the **first synthesis** of the work, an integration of all the preceding is made, which leads to the presentation of an **own socio-cognitive perspective on strategic processes** and allows to answer the first overarching research question (4.5). One of the major conclusions here is that the development of shared strategic orientations clearly depends on the nature of the specific strategic processes in an organisation, which are in turn highly influenced by a number of social factors. Besides the resulting need to generally consider the dimensions of the strategic process(es) and their respective values, it is thus even more important to also differentiate carefully between the different strategy "forums" and activities wherein social interactions occur. In line with this, the last part of Chapter 4 finally prepares the ground for moving from the rather general "macro"-view on the overall ongoing process to one such concrete micro-setting, i.e. decision making groups. For this, section 4.7 focuses on the cognitive side of the socio-cognitive dynamics taking place in this specific kind of forum for strategic activity.

Chapter 5 then deals with the social dimension and dwells on **social interaction processes in (small) groups**. For this, valuable insights are gained by drawing on research from other disciplines and fields and transferring these to the present strategic context. In a **second synthesis**, the cognitive concepts and findings outlined in the latter part of the preceding chapter are brought together with the social issues discussed here in order to finally suggest an **own socio-cognitive model of group decision making** (5.3). The particular value of this model is manifold: I.e., it opens up the "black box" of the actual group processes, which has seldom been investigated so far, and provides a detailed account of the different cognitive operations and process phases, as well as social factors at work in this context. Also, thanks to the truly interdisciplinary approach, a bridge is built between two rarely connected areas, i.e. the small group area and the strategic decision making area. In addition, regarding specifically its cognitive foundations, by integrating explicitly ideas from both traditional cognitivistic information processing theories and situated cognition, it is shown that these are actually complementary rather than (as still widely believed) opposed to each other. Finally, with all this not only researchers but also managers are sensitized to the importance of truly considering the *inside* of such processes if they want to be able to understand and to evaluate the immediate *outcomes* of collective efforts, or want to assess their respective developments and implications for the future.

Having seen the importance and the value that lies in adopting a processual approach to group decision making and differentiating in detail the social interactions occurring therein, exactly this is lastly done in an **own empirical study**, which is presented in **Chapter 6**. By means of a creative and innovative research approach the focus here is specifically set on illuminating more thoroughly on the first part of the second research question and investigating the **nature** and the functions **of social interactions** in three simulated decision making teams, tracing the groups' argumentative developments over time, and deriving individual behavioural patterns. In addition, while the conceptual outlines in the preceding chapters have revealed that truly deep and lasting cognitive changes occur mostly only slowly and that they are subject to a variety of diverse influences, these empirical data still allow to establish links to the underlying cognitive thought processes and to derive indications for the degree of cognitive developments at both the individual and the respective group levels. Whereas certain hints for better process designs and team composition were already made at various points in the conceptual parts of the work, the own empirical findings then finally also lead to some concrete suggestions as regards factors to keep in mind in the context of composing and organizing teams that are supposed to work collectively on a complex strategic decision task.

In **Chapter 7**, a final **summary and conclusions** regarding the overall research goals and questions is followed by considerations of the **theoretical contributions** and **value added** with the research, before the work finally closes with a variety of ideas for **future research directions**.

Overall then, with this structure the present work complies with the requirements for scientific contributions outlined by Whetten (1989). According to him, it should be clarified why the work is relevant and which concrete aspects and factors are included in the analysis. In addition, links between the outlined elements should be made and the findings derived be critically reflected (Whetten, 1989, p. 490 f.). In line with this, the relevance and overall contribution of the present research have already been clarified at the very outset of the present introduction. They will be reiterated at various points throughout the work. In order to narrow down the different elements, in Chapters 2 and 3 the discipline of strategic management generally and strategic processes in particular are discussed, respectively. Chapter 4 substantiates the essential psychological basics (both for the individual and the collective levels), and the own socio-cognitive perspective developed there from then integrates these different elements, clearly shows the interlinkages between the various parts, and also allows to answer the first research question. Moving from the rather macro-level to considerations of the socio-cognitive dynamics in a concrete micro-context, insights from the relevant literatures concerning the cognitive and the social dimensions are discussed separately first (Chapters 4 and 5), before by integrating them an own conceptual model for the researched group context is derived. The outlines of this second synthesis together with the insights from the own empirical study (Chapter 6) answer the second research question. A critical reflection of all the findings and results and of the contributions made with the present work is finally presented in the concluding Chapter 7.

2 Strategic management

2.1 Foundations of the field

As an applied area of study, the discipline of strategic management has its roots in practice. Indeed, many of the seminal works in the field, such as Igor Ansoff's (1965) *"Corporate strategy"* and Alfred Sloan's (1972) *"My years with General Motors"* were contributed not by academics but by practicing managers that wished to reflect on and to expand what they had learned during long tenures as corporate executives (Floyd & Wooldridge, 2000).

Academically, the origins of the strategic management discipline can be traced to such defining landmark works as Chandler's (1962) *"Strategy and structure"*, Ansoff's (1965) *"Corporate strategy"*, and Andrew's (1971) *"The concept of corporate strategy"*. Particularly through these fundamental works and the practical need felt by their authors and many others to better understand the reasons for success and failure among organisations the field of strategic management started to develop into an own discipline in the 1960s. Here then, the incipiencies were dominated by the search for a consciously designed process, with which the internal strengths and weaknesses and the external opportunities and threats could be set into the best possible relation for an organisation, and by the question how exactly this process has to be structured and secured. Following these times and its reconceptualization and relabeling from 'Business Policy' by Schendel and Hofer (1979), in the 1970s and 1980s the strategic thinking was primarily oriented at the competition, accompanied by the development and implementation of numerous tools like the model for competitor analysis (five-forces-model) and the value chain model by Porter (1980; 1985). Strategic thinking and acting was geared to achieving the optimal position(ing) in the competitive environment. The assumption underlying this strategic orientation is that the structure of the market largely determines both the strategic behaviour as well as an organisation's performance. It is thus primarily external forces that are regarded as determinants for strategic behaviour.

Towards the end of the 1980s the perspective started to change. Due to an increasingly dynamic environment, new concepts became necessary. Instead of the externally oriented look towards the competitive environment, the focus turned to the inside, i.e. towards the value potentials within the organisation itself. Long-term success is now said to depend on the organisation's internal material and immaterial assets and resources. Since these cannot be easily exchanged between or imitated by other firms, they are seen as the strategic capital which can lead to sustained competitive advantage(s) (Gomez, 1993, p. 21 f.). A sustained competitive advantage is here understood as an organisation's ability to implement a value enhancing strategy. Such a strategy must not be currently pursued by any of the firm's competitors, and must also be inimitable for any present and future competitors because the required knowledge and internal resources are firm-specific (Barney, 1991, p. 102 ff.).

The first of the above described perspectives is today generally subsumed under the term 'market-based-view'; the second one is (widely) called 'resource-based-view'. These two broad "categories" shall be taken up again in more detail in the context of discussing theoretical perspectives in strategic management (2.3).

This short, rather chronological sketch, about how strategic concepts, main ideas and the instruments deduced from these have developed over time, in no way means that theorists and practitioners advance a consistent view. On the contrary, the literature dealing with strategic management is by now extremely vast and almost unmanageable; no "unified" area of strategy research that would be built on one 'cohesive' concept can really be discerned. In this regard, a categorization that has dominated the field for many years was the distinction between *content* and *process* research in strategic management. Strategy research characterized as *content research* has focused on the subject of the strategic decision itself or on content-related descriptions of potential organizational strategies and the explanation of their use. *Process research* against that has been defined as primarily focused on the actions that lead to, and that support strategy (cf. e.g. Chakravarthy & Doz, 1992, p. 5ff.; Fahey & Christensen, 1986, p. 167 ff.; Huff & Reger, 1987, p. 211 ff.). Whereas this formal distinction has tended to divide research in the area for long (and still does to certain extents), today it is increasingly recognized that the process of strategic management and the content of strategy are clearly intrinsically linked, and researchers thus call for ceasing to see the two as separate 'entities'.[3] Moreover, another reason for the absence of a 'cohesive' concept or lack of unity in the area, is due to the fact that the discipline's subjects of interest actually overlap with several other important fields, including economics, sociology, marketing, finance, and psychology, and its participant members have often been trained in widely varying traditions, i.e. some in economics departments, some in strategic management departments, some in organizational behaviour, some in marketing, and so on (Nag, Hambrick, & Chen, 2007, p. 935). In line with this, it is little surprising then, that the published, espoused definitions of strategic management vary. In this regard, some scholars refer to general managers (e.g. Fredrickson, 1990; Jemison, 1981; Schendel & Cool, 1988), while others do not. Some indi-

---

[3] This is also the view advanced in the present work.

cate the overall organization or firm as the relevant unit of analysis (e.g. Learned, Christensen, Andrews, & Guth, 1965), while others do not. Some refer to the importance of organizational performance or success (e.g. Bowman, Singh, & Thomas, 2002; Rumelt, Schendel, & Teece, 1994; Schendel & Hofer, 1979), some to external environments (e.g. Bracker, 1980; Jemison, 1981), some to internal resources (e.g. Bracker, 1980; Jemison, 1981), some to strategy implementation (van Cauwenbergh & Cool, 1982), and others refer to none of these (e.g. Smircich & Stubbart, 1985).[4] Table 1 provides an outline of selected definitions of strategic management.

Table 1: Selected definitions of strategic management (adapted from Nag et al., 2007, p. 954 f.)

Author	Definition
Learned et al. (1965)	[This definition is of business policy, the precursor of strategic management.] Policy is the study of the functions and responsibilities of general management and the problems which affect the character and success of the total enterprise
Schendel and Hofer (1979)	Strategic management is a process that deals with the entrepreneurial work of the organization, with organizational renewal and growth, and, more particularly, with developing and utilizing the strategy which is to guide the organization's operations
Bracker (1980)	Strategic management entails the analysis of internal and external environments of firms to maximize the utilization of resources in relation to objectives
Jemison (1981)	Strategic management is the process by which general managers of complex organizations develop and use a strategy to co-align their organization's competences and the opportunities and constraints in the environment
Van Cauwenbergh and Cool (1982)	Strategic management deals with the formulation aspects (policy) and the implementation aspects (organization) of calculated behaviour in new situations and is the basis for future administration when repetition of circumstances occur
Smircich and Stubbart (1985)	Strategic management is organization making—to create and maintain systems of shared meanings that facilitate organized action
Schendel and Cool (1988)	Strategic management is essentially work associated with the term entrepreneur and his function of starting and (given the infinite life of corporations) renewing organizations
Fredrickson (1990)	Strategic management is concerned with those issues faced by managers who run entire organizations, or their multifunctional units
Teece (1990)	Strategic management can be defined as the formulation, implementation, and evaluation of managerial actions that enhance the value of a business enterprise
Rumelt, Schendel, and Teece (1994)	Strategic management is about the direction of organizations, most often, business firms. It includes those subjects of primary concern to senior management, or to anyone seeking reasons for success and failure among organizations
Bowman, Singh, and Thomas (2002)	The strategic management field can be conceptualized as one centred on problems relating to the creation and sustainability of competitive advantage, or the pursuit of rents

In light of the above sketched wide range of varying definitions found in the literature, the question "What is strategic management, really?" arises. Exactly this question was taken up by three prominent scholars in the field in a recent study (cf. Nag et al., 2007). In line with the authors' prior assumptions, the results of their empirical investigations showed that even though there is no unified, formally espoused definition of the field, there nevertheless seems

---
[4] See also Mintzberg et al. who identified "Ten schools of thought" in strategic management (Mintzberg et al., 2007).

to be an implicit, widely shared understanding among strategic management scholars regarding the essence of their discipline. More concretely, the multistep process Nag et al. (2007) adopted in their investigation led the authors to the following definition of strategic management: "The field of strategic management deals with (a) the major *intended and emergent initiatives* (b) *taken by general managers on behalf of owners*, (c) involving *utilization of resources* (d) to enhance the *performance* (e) of *firms* (f) in their *external environments*" (Nag et al., 2007, p. 942). Apart from these six elements derived inductively from the distinctive lexicon of the field, their subsequent examination of explicit definitions made the authors include a seventh element, the *internal organisation*.

Moreover, in line with the fact that there is also a considerable number of so-called 'boundary-spanners' (i.e., scholars whose major affiliation is in adjacent disciplines like marketing, economics, sociology) who are active in the field of strategic management, particularly through these, diverse but complementary conceptual lenses and tools are brought to the study of strategic management issues. Overall, it may thus be concluded that the discipline's apparent weakness seems to be its actual strength: I.e., despite varied theoretical and methodological approaches, and despite a lack of any agreed-upon extant definition, strategic management benefits from the combination of a basic consensus about the meaning of the field *and* substantial variety in how strategy issues are framed and explored (Nag et al., 2007, p. 950). One of the distinctive competences of the field might then be seen as its ability – and willingness – to broker, reconcile, and integrate the works of multiple other fields. "Its amorphous boundaries and inherent pluralism act as a common ground for scholars to thrive as a community, without being constrained by a dominant theoretical or methodological straitjacket" (Nag et al., 2007, p. 952).

2.2 Conceptions of "strategy" and own conception in this work

In line with the existing diversity and plurality as regards the field's general definition, central ideas and perspectives, similarly numerous are also the diverse views concerning what a 'strategy' actually is. Agreement exists that the adjective 'strategic' generally means "critical for achieving sustained success". Considered as **'strategic'** are all issues that impact significantly on an organisation's capabilities, touch strongly on the firm's position, and which are thus essential for securing the existence and survival of the firm (Krüger, 2002, p. 13). As regards the central 'object' (i.e. 'strategy'), however, how it has to be defined, and how a strategy is or should be generated and implemented, the existing notions vary widely. Therefore, in the following, the different conceptions of 'strategy' (and their development over time) shall be outlined and discussed briefly. Subsequent to this, the concrete conception underlying the present work is presented.

In the most classical conceptions of strategy, strategies are regarded as the result of formal, rational planning processes designed and executed exclusively at the organisation's top level (cf. e.g. Chaffee, 1985; Welge & Al-Laham, 1999). In response to growing frustrations with 'elite' planning systems, however, the 1970s soon gave rise to a variety of efforts designed to advance the traditional practice of planning within large corporations. Writers of that period wrote books and articles describing what they believed to be exemplary corporate planning and advancing their own notions of best practice (e.g. Lorange & Vancil, 1977; Steiner, 1970; Vancil, 1976). Even though prescientific, these writings represent the field's first "process" literature and provide early hints that strategy occurs (or should occur) at multiple levels in organisations (Floyd & Wooldridge, 2000, p. 8). In addition, following from a key insight of this literature, i.e. that plans produced by staff planners without involvement of line managers were often rather ineffective, growing scepticism developed among many concerning the idea of strict rational planning. In line with this, extended definitions of 'strategy' emerged whose authors started to move away slightly from the concept of planning ability. In this regard, although Michael E. **Porter** must clearly still be counted into the pool of the 'traditional' strategy researchers, also for him it is not concrete long-term *planning* anymore that is relevant, but rather the ability to develop a competitive advantage on the basis of a more general long-term *approach* that rests on clearly distinctive criteria (Porter, 1980).

A truly different and new conception of strategy, however, was then brought forward by Henry **Mintzberg**. According to him, multiple definitions of strategy can be distinguished and have to be recognized (Mintzberg, 1987).[5] Here then, most importantly, while Mintzberg

---

[5] Specifically, Mintzberg provides five definitions of strategy: i.e. strategy as 'plan', 'ploy', 'pattern', 'position', or 'perspective' (cf. Mintzberg, 1987, p. 11 ff. for details on these different strategy types):
Plan: Strategy is a plan, i.e. some sort of consciously intended course of action, a guideline (or set of guidelines) to deal with a situation. By this definition strategies have two essential characteristics: They are made in advance of the actions to which they apply, and they are developed consciously and purposefully.
Ploy: As plan, a strategy can be a ploy too, i.e. really just a specific manoeuvre intended to outwit an opponent or competitor.
Pattern: If strategies can be intended (whether as general plans or specific ploys), they can also be realised. In other words, defining strategy as plan is not sufficient; a definition is also needed that encompasses the resulting behaviour: Strategy is a pattern – specifically, a pattern in a stream of actions. Strategy is consistency in behaviour, whether or not intended.
Position: Strategy is a position – specifically a means of locating an organisation in an "environment". By this definition strategy becomes the mediating force, or "match", between organisation and environment, i.e., between the internal and the external context – *Positioning of an organisation in its environment.*
Perspective: Strategy is a perspective – its content consisting not just of a chosen position, but of an ingrained way of perceiving the world. Strategy in this respect is to the organisation what personality is to the individual. What is of key importance is that strategy is a perspective shared by members of an organisation,

acknowledges the rational planning of strategies, he adds explicitly the possibility for emergent strategies. These are strategies that have not been written down anywhere but that have developed from inside the organisation. Moreover and in line with this, in Mintzberg's system of concepts he then specifically distinguishes between **intended, unrealised, deliberate, emergent** and **realized** strategies. **Intended** strategies include plans that are supposed to serve as confinements and guidelines for future behaviour. The term **realized** strategy is related to real action structures. Mintzberg talks about strategies in the sense of *patterns*. These behavioural patterns unfold only ex post as a kind of structure within a stream of decisions or actions. Intended strategies must not necessarily become realized. Realized strategies can be based on concrete plans; they may, however, also develop in an 'emergent' manner. Mintzberg characterizes these different strategies and their relations in the following way (Mintzberg et al., 2007, p. 23 ff.):

- Intended strategies that are realized are called **deliberate** strategies.
- Intended strategies that cannot be realized during strategy implementation e.g. because of unrealistic expectations, misjudgements about environmental developments or changes in the environment, are called **unrealized** strategies.
- Realized strategies that were not intended, e.g. because a strategy was initially perhaps not projected or because it was discarded in the meantime, are called **emergent** strategies.

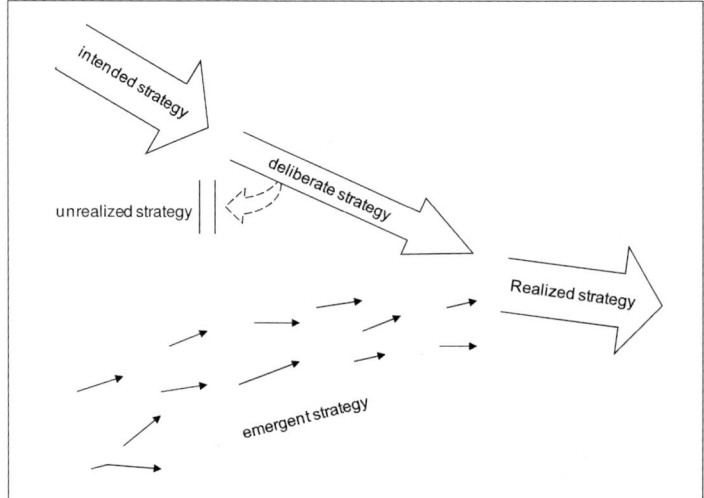

Figure 1: Deliberate and emergent strategies according to Mintzberg (Mintzberg et al., 2007, p. 26)

through their intentions and by their actions. In effect, when talking of strategy in this context, one is entering the realm of the collective mind - individuals united by common thinking and behaviour.

In a similar way like Mintzberg, also the German scholar Werner **Kirsch** distinguishes between **formulated** (i.e. put down explicitly in written form) and **formed** (i.e. developed of its own volition) strategy. For Kirsch every strategy is ex definitione a formed strategy with a strongly evolutionary character. Formulations are only one part of it, which attempt to interfere with rational control (cf. for the original works e.g. Kirsch, 1970; Kirsch, 1971, 1991, 1992; and Kirsch, 1996, p. 107 ff.) (see also 3.3.2).[6]

The above outlines have shown that the term 'strategy' can and is used quite differently in the scientific world and in practice. Here then, however, it can be asserted that the diversity of strategy definitions is in fact not due to fundamental disagreements, but rather that it is actually different 'strategy phenomena' each of the conceptualizations refers to. In line with this, and following particularly from Mintzberg's systematization, an important criterion for differentiation regarding the usage of the term 'strategy' may thus be seen in whether 'strategy' is related to action orientations (ex ante examination) or to real behavioural patterns (ex post considerations) (cf. Bamberger & Wrona, 2004, p. 108):

➢ As action orientations, strategies constitute action programmes which, in the sense of intentions, are supposed to describe ex ante global activities and to guide future behaviours and actions. In this perspective, strategies are *ex ante* models of future behaviour and are thus often equalised with **plans**. This equalisation, however, is not compulsory because strategic orientations can also 'emerge' in an unscheduled manner. Coherent with this perspective is that although strategies as action orientations can be expressed publicly, they exist often in a purely **cognitive form**, i.e. in the minds of the strategic actors involved. If they are expressed in public, they can be formalized, i.e. put down in written form. Strategies as action orientations can, but must not, be subject to decisions or acts of authorization.

➢ Strategies as **real behavioural patterns** comprise *ex post* considerations and are, in contrast to action orientations, in principle observable. This behaviourally oriented strategy definition can be used in two variants:
  - The first notion refers to individual strategic actions or "**manoeuvres**" like e.g. a concrete market entry, an acquisition or a specific pricing policy or act.
  - The second one considers strategies as real action structures or **behavioural patterns**. Strategic behavioural patterns are outcome or result of preceding decisions and actions; they signify an organisation's strategic behaviour or position at a specific

---

[6] A related position could already be found with Harry Igor Ansoff (1965) where he talks about "planned learning".

point in time. This kind of strategy is meant when the discussion is e.g. about an organisation's degree or type of diversification, its internationalisation or extent of vertical integration (see Figure 2).

Ex-ante consideration: Strategies as action orientations	Ex-post consideration: Strategies as real behavioural patterns	

Models of future behaviour which outlive several decision episodes and unfold direction guiding power
 	
• either formulated officially (formulated strategy plans) *or*
• in the form of **cognitive orientations**
	Manoeuvre
	• strategically relevant actions, like e.g.
	  • market entry
	  • acquisition
	  • and the like
		Action structures
		• outcome of past actions
		• expressed e.g. in
		  • type and degree of diversification or of internationalisation

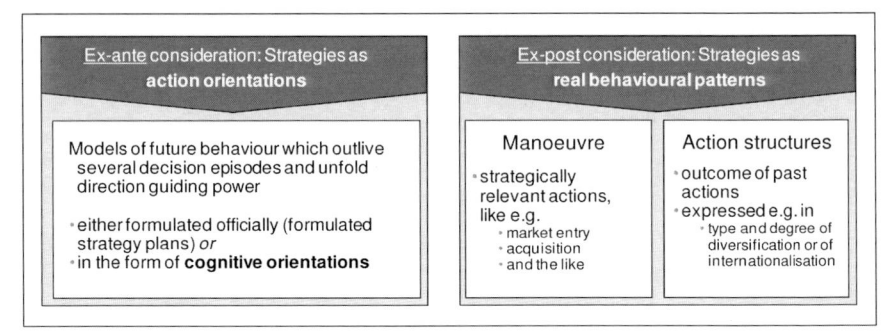

Figure 2: Strategies as action orientations and real behavioural patterns (Bamberger & Wrona, 2004, p. 108)

Overall then, being conscious of the different ways of looking at 'strategy' is clearly important and helpful to manoeuvre successfully through the field of strategic management. Since the specific kind of conceptualization a researcher adopts certainly depends on what exactly is to be explored, clarity must then be assured as regards the particular kind of 'strategy phenomenon' of interest in a given research project.[7] Here then, traditionally and still by the majority, strategy research (especially research concerned with the *content* of strategy) has centred on the investigation of real behavioural patterns and strategy outcomes, or on examining the authorized strategic plans with which organizations formally document their action orientations. In contrast to these more or less observable phenomena, the underlying cognitive orientations of the strategic actors involved are clearly much more difficult to investigate and have consequently for long been widely neglected or at least under researched in empirical strategy research. This negligence is particularly unfortunate since it may even be argued that the plurality of initially existing strategic orientations in fact constitute the very basis for the (few) actual manoeuvres and behavioural patterns an organisation finally displays.

Following from the above, in the present research now, the outlined *ex ante* viewpoint on 'strategy' is taken. Here then, apart from when there are formerly written down strategy plans

---

[7] In this regard, however, it must of course also be recognized that the different types of strategies are clearly interlinked. Investigating exactly these relations would thus be another interesting and valuable research endeavour. Questions here could for example be: In how far or to what degree do explicit plans or implicit ex ante orientations result in real strategic behaviours? Can observable manoeuvres truly be traced to concrete plans? Why has a planned strategy not been realized? Was a realized strategy really intended?

according to which actors (potentially) behave, a firm can also be said to "have" a strategy when an organisation's major decision makers share knowledge about the action principles of their organisation (and consequently act on the basis of this commonly held knowledge or these common strategic orientations) (Wrona & Breuer, 2008, p. 3). In line with this, it is thus specifically the rather concealed strategic orientations of strategic actors which are of focal interest.[8] One of the central questions for strategy researchers then is (or should be): How or under which conditions does shared strategic knowledge develop in groups of managers?

Investigating this kind of issue clearly calls for the adoption of a cognitive perspective. In addition, however, social interactions play an important role in this context, too. Consequently, considerations taking into account the social (and political) dimension must clearly also be included. The specific theoretical lens(es) serving as the starting point here are thus already implied in the very research questions themselves. Still, in order to underline the appropriateness of the choices made and to emphasize the novelty and added-value of the own socio-cognitive approach to be developed, a brief sketch of some of the other existing perspectives on strategic management shall be provided first. Here then, it is clearly recognized that especially the most influential strategic management directions of the last decades, i.e. the industrial organisation (IO) based strategy perspective (e.g. Porter, 1981, 1985), and the resource-based view (e.g. Bamberger & Wrona, 1996b; Barney, 1986, 1991; Wernerfelt, 1984), are primarily concerned with explaining competitive advantages once these have been recognized explicitly, and thus have rather little to say about the origins of new strategies or the process of strategic management (Regnér, 2005, p. 23). However, apart from acknowledging the interlinkage between content and process issues in strategic management (cf. 2.1) and hence also the interdependence and close relations between content and process approaches (Bamberger & Wrona, 2004, p. 28), the other even more compelling reason for still including these perspectives in the present research context is the intention to point out thereby where already in these traditional approaches links to the importance and value of investigating managerial cognitions can be identified.

2.3 Traditional and dominant theoretical perspectives

Already in Section 2.1 the variety of theoretical perspectives and approaches existing in the overall field of strategic management was mentioned. In fact, there is no consistent theory of strategic management, but the discipline can be described as a multi-paradigm research area (Wrona & Breuer, 2008, p. 4). Here then, the partially quite different streams choose or offer

---

[8] In Mintzberg's terminology the interest here thus is in strategy as 'perspective'.

partly very diverse approaches to the ‚object' strategic management. By doing so, other views are necessarily blanked out and certain perspectives allow for investigating (only) specific issues at the expense of others.[9]

In line with this diversity of theoretical approaches, in the literature there is also a plurality of classifications, summaries, and overviews regarding the different theories or perspectives that exist and are used in the discipline (cf. e.g. Bamberger & Wrona, 2004; Mintzberg, 1990; Mintzberg et al., 2007; Welge & Al-Laham, 1999). Broadly seen, in the current strategic management mainstream one often finds the distinction between two approaches, i.e. the market-based paradigm and the resource-based approaches. This contrast, however, merely signifies whether the organisation (or the researcher himself) focuses or believes more in the importance of external factors versus that of internal factors as determinants of the firm's strategic position and fate. Despite this focal difference, concerning their disciplinary affiliation, both perspectives have their roots in the field of economics. Apart from these, however, in line with the fact that there are many scholars who are not only active in research on strategic management, theories and approaches from adjacent disciplines have been brought into the field, too. Thanks to this 'import' strategic management can be considered a truly interdisciplinary area of research (Nag et al., 2007, p. 935 ff.). An appropriate overview of the field's theoretical 'pool' of available theories therefore clearly needs to go beyond the market- versus resource-based dichotomy. In this regard, with his "10 schools of thought" Mintzberg has provided one of the most encompassing systematizations (Mintzberg, 1990). However, his different strategy schools are not entirely mutually exclusive, seem to be partially incomplete, and new developments have also led to different emphasises (Welge & Al-Laham, 1999, p. 21 f.). A better orientation may therefore be achieved by ordering the theoretical approaches according to the respective disciplines they derive from originally.

2.3.1 Economic approaches

Historically, the fields of business and management were dominated by the discipline of economics. Economic theories have thus traditionally been strongly influential also in the area of strategic management. Different sub-streams are subsumed among these and may be distinguished.

---

[9] Choosing one or a few particular theories or approaches for a specific research project must thus clearly not mean ignorance of other perspectives. In line with this, the purpose here is not to contrast or truly criticize any of the approaches. Instead it is acknowledged that they all make certain contributions and are hence valuable for examining different research questions and specific aspects of the strategic management process.

Industrial organization

The first and most central approach to be mentioned here is the research in industrial organization (IO), which is based on the so called "*structure-conduct-performance paradigm*" originally developed by Mason (1939) and Bain (1959). In their classical paradigm, organisational performance (e.g. rents) is considered as largely determined by the characteristics of the firm's industry. The structure of the industry (*structure*) influences the behaviour of firms in an industry (*conduct*), and this behaviour in turn influences organisational outcomes (*performance*).

Initially, the early research in this tradition received little attention in the strategy literature, particularly because of its strong determinism and the 'black-box character' it ascribed to decision makers (Welge & Al-Laham, 1999, p. 39). Influenced by certain such deficiencies, conceptual refinements were undertaken that led to the development of the new IO approaches. This stream turns away from the strong industry determinism towards a more dynamic concept of industry competition. Here then, the assumption is no longer that organisational performance can be traced solely to the structural conditions within the market or that strategic management is merely about positioning the firm in a given environment. Instead, it is the strategic decisions and actions that the individual firms – each of them embedded in a certain competitive environment – take for maximizing their profits, which come more to the fore (Knyphausen-Aufseß, 1995, p. 24 and 67). The three variables of the original paradigm are seen as interdependent, such that industry structure not only determines behaviour, but also firms' strategies and market performance influence industries, e.g. by creating barriers to entry or augmenting market attractiveness which may in turn lead to either less or more rivalry in an industry. The first complete and nowadays widely applied concept describing this refined industry construct and outlining an industry's 'driving forces' is Porter's "*five-forces model*" (Porter, 1975, 1985).

Overall, a common thread running through all the approaches from industrial organization is that they emphasize the impact of the environment on the design and success of strategic initiatives. The environment is seen as the primary source of competitive advantages.

Regarding the concrete making or formulation of strategy and the solving of strategic problems, generally, strategies are here commonly conceptualized as the result of a formal, analytical planning process accounted for by the top management. This process is said to comprise the following phases: Systematic environmental analysis, assessment of internal strengths and weaknesses, explicit goal setting, evaluation of alternative courses of action, and strategy evaluation and selection as well as strategy implementation (e.g. Andrews, 1971; Ansoff, 1965; Hofer & Schendel, 1978; Porter, 1980; Welge & Al-Laham, 1999).

Here then, even though the IO approaches do not explain these very processes themselves, a first hint concerning the importance of cognitions in the context of strategic management and strategic processes can nevertheless be found by looking at the described phases of strategy making. As remarked already by Stubbart (1989) "[The] ... steps [of the planning process] require managers to envision, contemplate, prioritize, use knowledge, direct their attention, anticipate, engage in problem solving, use logic, perceive, make conscious judgements." While cognitions, especially the capacities and constraints characterizing executives' thinking, are thus implied, any detailed considerations of 'micro' strategic activities and cognitions at the individual managerial level are left out or "passed over in silence" (Stubbart, 1989, p. 328).

Taken together, with their identification of a suitable process for successful strategy making as well as the provision of tools to be utilized during the different phases of strategic planning, the approaches from industrial organisation have a strongly normative character.[10] Apart from this, the focus is clearly on externally oriented ('macro') factors, specifically industry or market structure, demand conditions, or the kind of technology relevant in the particular industry. In addition, with the particular contribution they also make for explaining different kinds of strategies, they are finally also normative in so far as Porter for example suggests certain specific strategy types (e.g. cost leader, differentiation) for organisations in certain external/ industry environments (cf. Porter, 1997, p. 62 ff.).

Regarding the second major influential stream in strategic management from economics, i.e. **new institutional economics** (NIE),[11] a detailed discussion of this perspective and its substreams (i.e., transaction cost theory, principal agent theory, property-rights theory) shall be forgone here (for details cf. e.g. Göbel, 2002; Ménard & Shirley, 2005). In light of the present research focus in this work, this omission is regarded as justified since these merely deepen or

---

[10] An overview of different planning instruments and methods is provided in Homburg (1998, p. 55 ff.) or in Welge & Al Laham (1992, p. 51 ff.).

[11] NIE is an economic perspective that attempts to extend economics by focusing on the social and legal norms and rules that underlie economic activity. It is about the impact or effect of institutions on economic entities (private households, firms, etc.) Whereas the term "new institutional economics" was originally coined by Oliver Williamson in 1975, other major scholars associated with this school include e.g. Ronald Coase, Avner Greif, or Douglass North.

complement[12] the new industrial organization approach in a way that is not relevant for identifying links to a cognitive perspective (Rogers-Wynands, 2002, pp. 10-11).

2.3.2 From economic theories to organisation studies

Traditionally, in economic theories the view is clearly oriented towards the market and the organisation itself is largely treated as a 'black box'. With time, however, also in economics organisational topics and issues started to be recognized and an increasing preoccupation with intra-organisational phenomena led to the development of ideas that were also interesting and important for scholars in strategic management. In this regard, even prior to a conclusion by Williamson (1991) that "strategy ... begins at home", other empirical research investigating the relevance of organisational variables found that such 'internal' variables (e.g. human resources) explained at least the same amount of performance variance as 'economic' factors (e.g. industry profitability, market share, firm size) (e.g. Hansen & Wernerfelt, 1989; Powell, 1990). Statements compatible with this observation can be found with Chandler, who uses explicitly the term 'organisational capabilities' and makes it even into the leading term for his analyses (Chandler, 1990, 1992a, 1992b). While a small behaviourally oriented stream has always existed in strategic management, the perspective then started to shift to the firm's inside on a much larger scale and strategy scholars increasingly converged on 'organisational capabilities' as a key construct in strategy (e.g. Eisenhardt & Martin, 2000; Nelson & Winter, 1982; Winter, 2003; Zollo & Winter, 2002). Even though, overall, a variety of specific individual approaches can by now be distinguished here, the unifying, fundamental assumption is that superior profits of organisations result from resources that the firms possess. Resources or "organisational capabilities" are thus regarded as the most important basis for sustained competitive advantage. Concerning its basic theoretical roots, the overall stream takes a kind of bridging position because it is rooted both in economic theory but at the same time it makes a connection to the socio-scientific oriented approaches in organisational theory (Knyphausen-Aufseß, 1995, p. 88 ff.).

Resource- and knowledge-based approaches

The economic roots of capabilities-based works are then represented by the **resource-based view** (RBV), which has been mentioned above already. This approach, which has been in-

---

[12] It is argued that game theoretical approaches basically only make available a new *formal* set of instruments for the newer approaches from industrial economics in strategic management, whereas transaction cost economics constitute a complementary, rather than an opposing model (cf. Knyphausen-Aufseß, 1995, p. 67 ff. and 78 ff., and for game theory Camerer, 1991, p. 137 ff.).

creasingly popular in strategic management since the 1990s, substitutes the causal chain of the structure-conduct-performance paradigm with the idea of *"resource-conduct-performance"* and thus attempts to explain organisational performance and success with the existence of unique firm specific resources (cf. e.g. Bamberger & Wrona, 1996a, p. 386 ff., 1996b, p. 130 ff.; Wernerfelt, 1984, p. 171 ff.). Such resources, which are often called "core competences", have to fulfil four conditions in order to allow for a sustained competitive advantage, i.e. they must be *valuable, rare, inimitable* and *not substitutable* (Barney, 1991, p. 105 f.).

By differentiating in detail different kinds of resources, the resource-based view already points to the importance of intangible resources, e.g. skills like an organisation's learning aptitude, its responsiveness, or the organisational culture. A clear link to the cognitive approaches, however, is then only made in the **knowledge-based approaches**. Even though these approaches are originally affiliated more with organisation theory than with economics, they clearly draw on the resource-based view and follow its basic reasoning (but they go beyond the RBV). Also like the RBV they include a dynamic component in that they explicitly address the importance of the *process* of resource (or knowledge) acquisition (cf. e.g. Bamberger & Wrona, 1996b; Barney, 1991) or the historical development of organisations (cf. e.g. Eisenhardt & Santos, 2002; Nelson & Winter, 1982; Zack, 2003). While among the knowledge-based approaches, too, there are different streams, their commonality is that they centre knowledge and focus especially on the role and importance as well as the development of knowledge as the basis for the achievement of competitive advantages.[13]

In line with the above, generally then, organisational capabilities are not any kind of abilities, but they refer to such ones that are related to the deep structure of the system, i.e. the intangible or invisible parts of the surface structure. In addition, they comprise of a dynamic component. Here then, as *the* central capability the learning aptitude is emphasized. In this regard, in the theory of organisational learning, learning is conceptualized as a collective process that extends from the accumulation of knowledge, its processing, to the storage of knowledge (keyword "knowledge management" in recent years) (cf. e.g. Huber, 1991; Schreyögg & Noss, 1995, p. 89 f.; Schüppel, 1996, p. 177). In line with this, learning is seen as a reconstruction or a change of the organisational knowledge base. Often, the learning aptitude is attributed the status of a meta-capability which accounts for the existence of other abilities.

---

[13] A specific approach here is the so-called "knowledge-based theory" most prominently associated with Nonaka and Takeuchi (1995). As its name suggests, in this theory it is knowledge that is considered as the most strategically significant resource of a firm. Whether or not the knowledge-based theory of the firm actually constitutes a *theory*, however, has been the subject of considerable debate. According to Grant (2002), one notable proponent of the knowledge-based view of the firm (KBV), "the emerging knowledge-based view of the firm is not a theory of the firm in any formal sense" (Grant, 2002, p. 135).

This reflects a tendency in the literature to call fundamental abilities *organisational capabilities* (cf. e.g. Knyphausen-Aufseß, 1995, p. 95 ff.; Müser, 2000, p. 84 f.; Rasche, 1994, p. 159). Concerning the question what exactly constitutes the organisational knowledge base, there are different views. Put simply, two broad conceptions exist: I.e., some authors understand as the organisational knowledge base primarily that kind of knowledge which is stored independently from individual people in certain rule systems like standard procedures, handbooks or specialized data bases (e.g. Schneider, 1996, p. 18 f.; Schüppel, 1996, p. 188; Willke, 1996, p. 281 f.). Others against that rather emphasize those knowledge and thought patterns that have been gained through experience and are shared by all or some organisational members (e.g. Nonaka, 2005, p. 374 ff.; Nonaka & Konno, 1998, p. 40 ff.; Schreyögg & Noss, 1995, p. 170 ff.). In the capability-based works the first of these views plays at most a secondary role because it refers to explicitly formulated, superficial knowledge that does not meet the criterion of deep structure characteristics of organisational capabilities (Rogers-Wynands, 2002, p. 18).

Taken together, following from the emphasis on firm internal resources (i.e. especially the deep structure and the other characteristics of organisational capabilities) as originators of competitive advantages, all these approaches clearly imply a different process of strategy making compared to the IO approaches: Strategies or the solving of strategic problems is no longer conceptualized as (only) the result of an analytical planning process accounted for exclusively by the top management, but instead as emergent products of an ongoing process which consists of many small, locally taken decisions and other activities, and which consequently takes place on all levels of the organisation (cf. e.g. Kirsch, 1997b, p. 474 ff.; Mintzberg, 1994, p. 25). With this, the importance of collective knowledge and cognitions, and the link to the different strategy conceptions outlined above, especially strategies as shared action orientations, is apparent. In addition, with the specific research focus here on how *changes* in these orientations come about, proximity clearly also exists to the above mentioned learning processes. In this regard, the overall area of organizational learning is in fact a very broad field, in which both in terms of 'carriers' and types of organisational knowledge issues are considered that go beyond the specific research focus here, which is on the development of *strategic* knowledge structures among *key strategic* actors. Nevertheless, at later points in the work recurrences will be made to some of these particular ideas and insights in order to properly classify the present research within the wider literature (cf. 4.4 and 5.2.3).

2.3.3 Further theoretical approaches

Apart from the above outlined approaches coming from economics and increasingly also from organisational studies, there are a number of further theoretical perspectives from other disciplines that are influential specifically in research on processual issues in strategic management. In this regard, it is especially theories and ideas from the discipline of sociology which have been increasingly expanded into the strategy field,[14] in particular **systems-theoretical approaches** (e.g. Luhmann, 1984) and, even more recently, Gidden's **structuration theory** (e.g. Giddens, 1979, 1984). In addition, although the **evolutionary approaches** take their basic ideas from evolutionary biology, they are still closely connected to systems theory. In the strategy context, an explicit separation between the two is thus hardly possible. Besides these, further prevalent approaches to be emphasized are the **rational-decision-oriented perspectives** and **political approaches**.

Together, all of these clearly constitute very different approaches to research in the area of strategic management. What they have in common, however, is that they become important especially through the contributions they make for the description and explanation of strategy *process* issues. In line with this, since strategic processes are at the centre of the present work these are treated separately in an own chapter (Chapter 3). In this context then also the decision-oriented, evolutionary and political approaches will be taken up again and discussed in more detail (cf. 3.2.1, 3.2.2, 3.2.4, respectively).

2.4 The cognitive perspective on strategic management

The above discussion of some of the most prominent theoretical approaches to the study of strategic management has demonstrated the variety of perspectives researchers may adopt for their work in the field. However, despite there being an increasing openness in terms of theoretical lenses employed, the dominant framework of the classical strategic management still relies and draws heavily on assumptions and insights from economic and rational-analytical models. Even though, as has been shown, links to cognitive issues and their importance were implicitly contained already in the early economic approaches, in the traditional strategic paradigm intuition and feelings still have no place and the human factor with his specific *cognitive* characteristics is largely neglected (cf. e.g. Hambrick & Mason, 1984; Walsh, 1995).

An entirely different stance towards investigating the strategic management process is now being taken by a stream of research that has been increasingly proliferating in recent years and which has come to be called the *cognitive perspective in strategic management and strategic*

---

[14] This expansion actually took place via the wider field of organisation studies.

decision making (Schwenk, 1995, p. 472).[15] As will be discussed in detail below, also here there are in fact a variety of quite heterogeneous approaches that are generally subsumed under this theoretical label. One central and unifying assumption of cognitive organizational theory, however, is that an individual's behaviour toward external stimuli is mediated by his or her cognitive representations of those stimuli (Dill, 1958, p. 410 ff.). For the strategy context, the most fundamental and distinguishing characteristic of this perspective therefore is that organizational processes and especially strategic processes are regarded as cognitive processes: The development of firm strategies occurs in the mind of the strategist, i.e. it is a mental process (Bamberger & Wrona, 2004, p. 71). An understanding of how organizations respond to their environments (whether internal, competitive, or external) consequently requires understanding the 'mental models' of key decision makers, who must interpret and understand these environments and eventually make critical strategic choices. As firm strategies are accordingly seen as cognitive constructs, perspectives or action orientations (Bamberger & Wrona, 2004, p. 71), the focus of interest in this perspective thus explicitly concerns the **human being** and the question **how he perceives his environment**. In line with this, theorists stressing the cognitive foundations of competitive strategy have specifically examined the ways in which managers interpret and analyze competitive environments (Porac & Thomas, 1990) and situations (Zajac & Bazerman, 1991), the way they develop their own rules and guidelines to strategic problems, the personal and organizational characteristics that influence this process, and the way these rules influence their own decision making (Hodgkinson, 2001b; Schwenk, 1995). Implicit in these studies is the assumption that organizational actions depend heavily on factors that influence the **interpretation** of strategic issues (Dutton & Jackson, 1987; Ginsberg & Venkatraman, 1992). The adaptation of a cognitive perspective on strategic management thus shifts the focus of analysis away from the objective characteristics of firms, industries and markets, to consider the subjective and the inter-subjective worlds of individuals and groups (Hodgkinson & Sparrow, 2002, p. 316). In doing so, this perspective challenges two of the core assumptions of the neo-classical economics (e.g. Coase, 1937; Williamson, 1975, 1985) – namely that all firms have equal access to information about the market-place, and that they will invariably respond to such information in similar ways. As a clear counter to the tendency of economic approaches to view competitive environments as objective phenomena, it is postulated that competitive industry structures are socially constructed through processes of interaction and learning (e.g. Burgelman, 1988; Davis & Luthans, 1980; Maitlis, 2005).

---

[15] This perspective is in fact by no means exclusive for strategy research. The focus here, however, shall be on what is most essential in the present research context.

Overall, what the cognitive viewpoint does with its emphasis on managers as the driving force in competitive landscapes is to bring out the psychological details of the less argued aspects of competitive environments (Porac, Thomas, & Baden-Fuller, 1989, p. 401 and 412 ff.). As research from the cognitive perspective is consequently most significantly distinguished by its application of cognitive psychological concepts, theories and techniques to the field of strategic management, it may thus generally be described as the "analysis of the strategic management process from a psychological perspective" (Hodgkinson & Sparrow, 2002, p. 3).

2.4.1 Origins of the managerial and organizational cognition perspective (MOC)

The foundations of what is today called the "managerial and organizational cognition perspective" (MOC)[16] in strategic management were originally laid with the development of **cognitive psychology** as a major sub-field of study within academic psychology. In an attempt to render psychology a truly scientific endeavour, behaviourists (e.g. Mowrer, 1947; Skinner, 1938) argued that concepts relating to 'under the skin phenomena', such as 'perception', 'attention' and 'memory', should be shunned in favour of the analysis of stimulus → response (S → R) connections, on the grounds that the latter could be readily subjected to direct observation and measurement. In practice, however, it became increasingly difficult to account for anything apart from the simplest behaviours without recourse to cognitive terms. As a result, **rejecting the central tenets of behaviourism**, cognitive psychologists thus started focusing on the **analysis of the various intervening mental processes that mediate responses to the environment**.

Even though compared to these long-established roots, the recurrence and application of psychological concepts and cognitive theory to managers and organizations is still a relatively recent phenomenon (cf. Hodgkinson & Sparrow, 2002, p. 8 ff.), implicit hints for a need for a cognitive approach to analysing managerial and organizational issues may nevertheless already be found in a number of the earlier, classical works on strategy and organization theory, such as those by Hofer and Schendel (1978) and Andrews (1971). Irrespective of these, however, the work that is generally acknowledged as having laid the main foundations of modern cognitive theory and research in organizational settings is Simon's (1947) classic work "*Administrative behaviour*". Simon introduces the notion of **"bounded rationality"**, which suggests that actors are constrained by **fundamental information processing limitations** and

---

[16] Since MOC research is basically equal to research conducted from the cognitive perspective on (strategic) management, the two terms will be used interchangeably in the following.

thus are unable to take decisions in a completely rational manner. Nevertheless, they strive for rationality within the limits of their cognitive capacities (Simon, 1947).

In line with these early thoughts, a decade later, March and Simon (1958) further elaborated and stressed the **centrality of individual knowledge representations** as the basis of organizing. Like that, together with their colleagues (see also Cyert and March, 1963), these authors pioneered a cognitive stance in both organization theory and the social sciences as a whole. Their emphasis on processes of "bounded rationality" clearly countered the view that decision processes were intendedly rational – rather, individual decision makers are more likely to simplify reality and to use subjectively created models (Cyert & March, 1963; March & Simon, 1958).

Still, although the conceptual roots for developing cognitive perspectives in organizational and management theory may thus be traced back at least to the Carnegie school's work in the 1950s, for a long time the strategy field nevertheless continued to be dominated by the largely unquestioned assumption that the strategy process is an inherently rational phenomenon.[17] Drawing on theory and research from a variety of interrelated fields, especially cognitive and organizational psychology, social cognition and organizational sociology, it is only over the last 20-25 years that the managerial and organizational cognition perspective has truly matured and developed into an own research stream. Based on the important foundations laid by this interdisciplinary body of work, an increasing number of academics and practitioners started to call into **question a number of key assumptions of rational theories**[18] which have hitherto underpinned the field of strategic management. Indeed, following Eden and Spencer (1998), *the* defining question for the field of managerial and organizational cognition is based upon a negative assertion – that the existing body of knowledge about managerial decision making is inadequate, as are the theories of rational expectations and strategic choice that dominate business school syllabi (Eden & Spender, 1998, p. 2). The cognitive approach to strategic management therefore differs from previous traditions in that it focuses specifically "on the models that drive actual managerial actions, rather than on abstract, rational models" (Hodgkinson & Sparrow, 2002, p. 10).

---

[17] Although for notable exceptions see e.g. Chaffee (1985), Johnson (1987), Mintzberg (1994), Mintzberg et al. (2007).

[18] As observed by March (1999), rational theories are characterized by four common assumptions: 1. that the decision maker has knowledge of the alternatives for action; 2. that he has knowledge of the consequences of the alternative actions (at least to the point of being able to derive a probability distribution); 3. that there is a consistent preference ordering, or set of values, by which alternative courses of action can be compared; and 4. that there is a decision rule by which single, alternative actions can be selected.

2.4.2 Basic principles

The focus of interest here concerns the most central tenets and contributions that the cognitive perspective can make to the field of strategic management. However, in line with the interdisciplinary foundations from which the psychological analysis of the strategic management process has emerged, it is evident that what is today generally subsumed under the "managerial and organizational cognition umbrella" is in fact a quite broad area, within which a number of disciplines have developed language systems and constructs that are all heavily laced with cognitive connotations.[19] As a result, a rich diversity of complex terms (as well as diversity in questions and topics) are today used in the field that are each highly similar on the surface, but which actually have very different connotations within the respective fields from which they have ultimately originated (Meindl, Stubbart, & Porac, 1994, p. 290). Nevertheless, even though the overall field is clearly cross-disciplinary in nature and cognitive approaches are by now means exclusive to the study of strategic management and strategic decision making, the basic principles of the perspective can be summarized as follows (cf. Hodgkinson & Sparrow, 2002, p. 11):

- **Individuals are limited** in their ability to process the rich variety of stimuli contained in the external world – stimuli, which are exceedingly complex in nature.
- Consequently, they employ a variety of strategies in order to reduce the burden of information processing that would otherwise ensue.
- This culminates in the development of a **simplified understanding of reality** which is encoded within the mind of the individual.
- Once formulated, these 'mental representations' act as **filters** through which incoming information is subsequently processed, which in turn can lead to **biased and inappropriate decisions**.

2.4.3 Perspectives in MOC research

As mentioned above, research in the managerial and organizational cognition tradition is not exclusively concerned with strategic questions, but with managerial knowledge representations and the influence of cognition on organizational activity generally. The field's most basic interest thus lies in the cognitive characteristics and cognitive processes of organizational

---

[19] As observed by Hodgkinson and Sparrow (2002), industrial economists have for example examined how the behaviour of industries and firms is dependent on the way in which managers combine information on costs, demands, competitors and profits, while sociologists have given importance to the norms and taken-for-granted beliefs that shape organization practice.

actors. Here then, strategy researchers specifically ask how managers perceive and process information and especially how and why certain information is attributed strategic importance from which strategic actions are then derived. Coherent with these fundamental interests, what all enquiries that take a cognitive approach have in common, is that they draw on the same fundamental models from cognitive psychology[20] as the basis for their research.

Apart from this unity, however, MOC research can and is in fact approached in different ways, influenced by different assumptions about the world (ontology) and what we know about it (epistemology) (Huff, 2005, p. 344 f.). In line with this, the role of cognition in organizations has been seen differently, depending on whether organizations are viewed as **systems of** *information* or as **systems of** *meaning*. As a result, within the overall body of work on managerial and organizational cognition two major perspectives may be discerned, i.e. the so-called **computational perspective** and the **interpretive perspective** (Lant, 2002, pp. 344-345). Here then, even though both streams trace their roots to an open system, information-processing view of the firm (e.g. Cyert & March, 1963; March & Simon, 1958), each of them is clearly based on a **distinct epistemological position**, i.e. a positivistic stance on the one hand, and a (social) constructivist on the other. The specific goals, attentional priorities, as well specific research approaches and methods used within each perspective therefore differ significantly.[21] Here then, even though taking a clear epistemological positioning seems oftentimes warranted, it must nevertheless be stressed that in order to develop adequate theoretical accounts of the ways in which strategic competence is developed and utilized in organisations, ***both* perspectives are required**. Researchers in the MOC field are therefore increasingly called upon to stop asking *if* apparently paradoxical cognitive processes coexist, and instead begin asking *how* and *when* they occur (e.g. Fiol, 2002, p. 134 f.; Hodgkinson & Sparrow, 2002, p. 27; Lant, 2002, p. 360). In line with this, in order to be finally able to provide some hints as to how and why the computational and interpretive perspectives may indeed be usefully combined, in the next two sections, each of the two streams will be discussed in turn.

2.4.3.1 The computational perspective

The computational perspective on managerial and organizational cognition, which is most clearly exemplified by the work of March and Simon (1958) and behavioural decision re-

---

[20] More details on these psychological basics are outlined in Chapter 4.
[21] For the fundamental assumptions and differences between these two basic epistemological stances in the overall scientific community cf. e.g. Popper (2002) versus Berger & Luckmann (1969). This philosophical distinction will also be met and detailed again in the context of discussing the different conceptions of "knowledge" in 4.1.1.

searchers, originates primarily from the field of experimental cognitive psychology. Following March and Simon, in this perspective, **organizations are viewed as information processing systems** that consist of embedded routines through which information is stored and enacted. The principal contribution this approach has made is to draw attention to the fundamental information processing limitations of organizational actors and the strategies they employ in an effort to overcome these limitations (March & Simon, 1958; Simon, 1957). More specifically, supplementing initial research efforts focused on the scanning and search activity of firms, a concern emerged later for how information from the environment is perceived and interpreted by managers. As with this attention eventually turned to addressing the **phenomenon of subjective perception**, a significant step was made in that the subjectivity of perceptions in the processing of information by organizations was recognized for the first time. In addition to this initially new idea that the information which is available can and is in fact perceived and interpreted differently by different individuals and groups, research in this tradition further argues for the **critical role that managers play** in positioning their organizations within their environment through strategic choice. In line with the primacy of the dominant coalition construct developed by Cyert and March (1963), it thus are firms' top-level managers who are regarded as the key mechanisms of organizational interpretations and hence ultimately also of firm strategies. Following from this, the most central concern characterising research enquiries conducted from a computational perspective are their attempts to develop a set of propositions for why managers actually do see strategic issues differently.

To gain a better understanding of the individual mechanisms that for example cause managers to *mis*interpret their environments, research in this positivistic cognitive strategy school heavily draws from work on individual level cognition on problem sensing, scanning, noticing and interpreting stimuli (e.g. Kiesler & Sproull, 1982). In line with this, the most important theory underlying this research perspective is the so-called **information processing theory**, which is the dominant approach in cognitive psychology (cf. e.g. Anderson, 2005, pp. 11-13; Eysenck & Keane, 2005, p. 174 ff.; Neisser, 1976, pp. 15-18). In this regard, even though over time various models and information processing approaches have been developed,[22] they all are generally based on some common agreed on principles (i.e. limited capacity, control mechanism, two-way information flow) and thus also include similar elements.[23] An example

---

[22] For example: Atkinson & Shiffrin's (1968) "**stage theory**"; the "**levels-of-processing**" theory by Craik & Lockhart (1972); or the **parallel-distributed processing model** by Rumelhart & McClelland (1986).

[23] I.e., classic information-processing models describe individual human cognition in terms of a long-term memory store, a short-term working memory, basic memory processes that filter, transform, combine, and store information, and executive processes that control memory operation (cf. e.g. Hinsz et al., 1997, p. 44 f.;

of a generic information-processing model, which specifies in detail the different stages of the entire processing, is depicted in Figure 3.

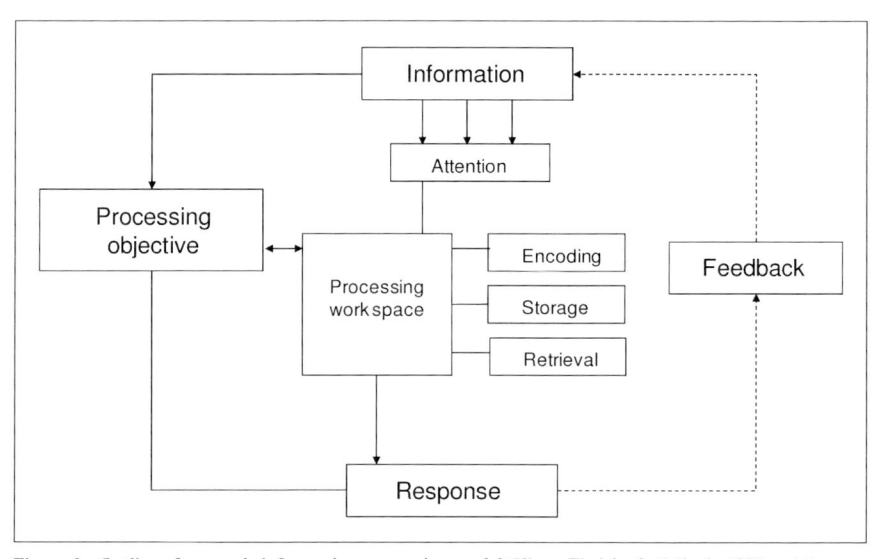

Figure 3: Outline of a generic information-processing model (Hinsz, Tindale, & Vollrath, 1997, p. 44)

Initially, an individual acquires information from interactions with the world. This information is embedded within a context that provides a processing objective for the information. The attention phase of information processing consists of the perception of the information. The encoding process involves the structure, evaluation, interpretation, and transformation of the information into a representation. Information then enters memory through the storage process and is accessed and brought out of storage through retrieval processes. Retrieval and attention enable information to enter awareness to process on the basis of an objective. In the processing work space, information integration and schematic processing occur on the basis of many different rules, strategies, and procedures. After the information is processed on the basis of objectives, the individual generally makes a response, such as a choice among alternatives (decision making), conclusion based on premises (inference), evaluative judgment (opinion), or solution (problem solving). Finally, the response or output may lead to feedback about changes in the situation (cf. Hinsz et al., 1997, p. 44).

Smith, 1994, pp. 110-119). Although long-term memory capacity is virtually unlimited, all information input to it must first pass through limited capacity attentional and other working memory processes which serve as a bottleneck for acquiring new knowledge (Derry, DuRussel, & O'Donnell, 1998, p. 29).

Of particular significance in the information processing approach now is that it explains human behaviour – like for example a manager's strategic decisions or actions – not as a direct reaction to the objective environment, but with reference to the subjective interpretation or construction of this environment as it is reflected in his **knowledge structures**. Besides being **subjective** as they are in part shaped by past experiences and learning, these mental representations are also **incomplete** due to the individuals' limited information processing capacity which only allows people to map a complex environment in a simplified, abstract way (Simon, 1957).

Drawing on this, often, in an effort to reduce the amount of cognitive activity required, past experience, stored in long-term memory, is influential in determining an individual's responses to current stimuli; actions that worked in the past are routinely applied to the present so as to free up mental capacity. Here then, concerning the conversion of information, this process is assumed to take place either predominantly **theory-driven,** i.e. **"top-down"**, or **data-driven,** i.e. **"bottom-up"** (Nisbett & Ross, 1980). The latter activity occurs when incoming stimuli influence actors' cognitions and actions directly, without reference to past memories. In the top-down modus against that, it is the manager's idiosyncratic knowledge structures which direct the entire information conversion. This kind of process already starts with the knowledge structures influencing what kind of information is attended to in the first place (scanning, perception), and continues with them determining the way in which the incoming information is to be interpreted and which conclusions are to be drawn from it.

At a given point in time, information processing may be affected by what an individual brings to the task at hand (e.g. prior expectations, influenced by previous experience and contexts) and key features of the stimuli present in the current task environment. In practice, the balance between stimuli-driven and conceptually-driven information processing strategies is clearly likely to vary across tasks and situations. However, because strategic decision making is regarded as a typical example for a situation involving complex problems and a complex reality (cf. e.g. Bamberger & Wrona, 2004, p. 376; Kirsch, 1998, p. 139 ff.; Kirsch & Mayer, 1976, p. 99 ff.), in the contexts in which senior managers operate, the latter approach is assumed to predominate (cf. Walsh, 1995 for why this is the case). As a consequence, in line with regarding managerial knowledge structures as one of the most central influencing factors for strategic decisions and actions, strategy research conducted from a computational perspective has thus generally focused on a similar set of top-down or schema-driven information-processing constructs (Fiol, 2002, p. 121). Even though subjective perception and interpretation of environmental stimuli are recognized in this paradigm, the computational approach nevertheless implies that there is an environment that exists independently of the perceiving subject, and the reason subjective differences in perception occur is because the objective environment can only be partially comprehended due to limited processing capacity ('bounded rationality'). The reference point in this perspective thus remains an **objective reality** and the centre of research interests is on individual managers as computing devices rather than on their interactions and their role as social entities.

2.4.3.2 The interpretive perspective

The second key foundation or major perspective within cognitive strategy research has been laid by the work of Weick through his development of the interrelated notions of *enactment*, *sensemaking* and the *enacted environment* (cf. e.g. Weick, 1979; Weick, 1995). Overall, the so-called interpretive perspective is not inconsistent with the information processing view of organizations, but it offers a different view of the interpretation process at work. What it shares with the computational approach is the open systems view and its allowance for varying interpretations of the environment. However, rather than implying that the environment is an objective entity and conceiving of organizations as systems of information, here, organizations are seen as *systems of meaning*. In line with this, Weick's work challenges the limited view of the environment, arguing that theories stressing the notion that reality is selectively perceived overemphasize the *object* → *subject relationship* at the expense of the idea that often the subject itself exerts considerable influence on the object. In fact, "there is a reciprocal influence between subjects and objects, not a one-sided influence such as implied by the idea that a stimulus triggers a response" (Weick, 1979, p. 164 f.). Following this argument, the most central aim of the distinct stream of research that Weick's early work encouraged thus is to disentangle the mechanisms through which strategic reality is itself constructed through the cognitive processes of the individuals interacting in an organizational context. In line with this, underlying this overall objective, a number of **critical assumptions** can be discerned that are characteristic of interpretive studies:[24]

Firstly, concerning the rationale for why managerial interpretations of stimuli differ, it is suggested that they do so because all organisations fundamentally face different environments. Environments differ because they are *enacted*, not interpreted. While the term *interpretation* implies that a phenomenon that is being perceived also exists in some objective sense, the term *enactment* implies that the phenomenon being interpreted by the perceiver is also created by the perceiver. Coherent with this distinction, the interpretive perspective thus suggests that

---

[24] Cf. for the following arguments also Hodgkinson & Sparrow (2002, p. 25 f.), Isabella (1990, p. 9 f.), Lant (2002, pp. 351-355).

organizational members actively create, or *enact*, the reality they inhabit (e.g. Berger & Luckmann, 1969; Weick, 1979). They create a "material and symbolic record" (Smircich & Stubbart, 1985, p. 726) upon which they predicate future action. In line with this conception, adherents of the Weickian paradigm therefore emphasize the 'upstream process of sensemaking' in contrast to the predominance of schema-based studies in the computational perspective. In this context, regarding the particular notion of 'sensemaking' as introduced by Weick, it is important to recognize that sensemaking is more than an interpretation of reality based on conceptual schemata (Floyd & Wooldridge, 2000, p. 73). In fact, sensemaking includes the creation of the schema itself, i.e. it provides a rich description of the processes that lead to the creation of individual and organizational cognitive frameworks. According to Weick (1995), sensemaking is "about authoring as well as reading"; it is about "creation as well as discovery" (Weick, 1995, pp. 7-8). Knowledge is constructed by organizing sensory perceptions within a conceptual framework, and the truth of beliefs is judged by their consistency with the framework. Sensemaking thus is about the construction of knowledge.

Furthermore, a second assumption in the interpretive perspective is that managers' individual frames of reference can be shared and that they thus exist within a collectivity (e.g. Axelrod, 1976; Daft & Weick, 1984; Weick & Bougon, 1986). Created through **social interchange** or **negotiated** over time (e.g. Burrell & Morgan, 1979; Walsh & Fahey, 1986), this cognitive consensuality (Gioia & Sims, 1986, p. 7) represents the **dominant logic** or dominant reality of a group (e.g. Bettis & Prahalad, 1995; Prahalad & Bettis, 1986). According to Prahalad & Bettis, this dominant logic is pictured as a funnel through which 'relevant' data are filtered by an organisation's or a group's respective logic and by the analytic procedures managers use to aid strategy development. These 'filtered' data are then incorporated into the strategy, systems, values, expectations, and reinforced behaviour of the organization (Bettis & Prahalad, 1995, p. 7). In line with this, inherent in this argument and of particular significance in the context of the present research is the view that in order to understand how strategic decisions actually come about, it therefore clearly does not suffice to consider managers' idiosyncratic knowledge structures as static constructs in isolation from the respective social context they are part of. Instead, **context** is an integral part of cognition as both cognitive processes and the development of cognitive structures happen to large extents through social interaction (Lant, 2002, p. 356 f.; Pea, 1993, pp. 48-49).

Following logically from the above argument, a third crucial assumption interpretive studies draw on is that the views of **managers as a collective** are especially salient because managers appear to be at the heart of the cognitive shifts that occur during organizational change

(Isabella, 1990; Kiesler & Sproull, 1982). This accentuation of the importance of managers' interpretive activities is found similarly in studies conducted from the computational perspective. The basic idea here, however, is that managers ultimately *use* their interpretations of organizational events to frame meaning for other organizational participants (Daft & Weick, 1984; Gioia, 1986; Gray, Bougon, & Donnellon, 1985) and like that to *influence* the construed realities of others (Daft & Weick, 1984; Gray et al., 1985). In addition, while subjective perceptions and interpretations clearly are at the centre of research interests in both of the streams underlying cognitive strategy research, what is significantly different in the Weickian tradition is the departure from the focus on top managers as the most important "interpreters" in the organization. In line with viewing the way in which "reality" is constructed as a **social interaction process**, strategic interpretation thus is not seen to occur merely within the heads of top managers, but rather as a social process that occurs through interaction throughout the entire organization. This conception has important implications for strategy research in that it calls for broadening the traditional focus on the upper echelons perspective (cf. Hambrick & Mason, 1984 and also 3.4.1.2) to include the contributions of other organizational actors, particularly the middle management (cf. e.g. Floyd & Wooldridge, 2000), when examining the strategic direction of corporations

Taken together, by drawing attention to the fact that the environmental constraints and opportunities faced by organizations are actively constructed by the actions of particular individuals and groups, the notions of enactment and the enacted environment inherent in interpretive studies have laid an important conceptual foundation for understanding the strategic management process (see e.g. Smircich & Stubbart, 1985). In contrast to the computational model of informational processing, within a Weickian framework choices are not seen as being correct or incorrect as judged against an abstract mathematical equation. Instead, reality within organizations, and thus also strategic decisions, are relative. The 'correctness' of a decision is dependent upon the point of view that is being used to evaluate it (Hodgkinson & Sparrow, 2002, p. 26).

Moreover, sensemaking is partially dependent on the perceptions of what Weick calls *'communities of believer'* who have their own 'local rationalities' or 'interpretive stances' (Weick, 1995). These local rationalities are in turn embedded in larger 'systems of meaning' – some of which are individual and some of which are shared by the group. Consequently, if we are to explain organizational choice, these rationalities have to be unpacked (Hodgkinson & Sparrow, 2002, p. 26).

Here then, drawing on these last arguments, certain important links to the specific questions as well as the relevance of the present research can be established: Firstly, in order to understand how within a particular organization certain strategic decisions and actions come about, a critical look is needed at the particular **group context** and the **interactive dynamics** that predominate at the time the decision is made. Even though such a focus on what might be termed the specific 'micro system of meaning' within strategic management teams is increasingly called for, attempts to genuinely integrate insights from the literature on group processes into MOC research have so far been largely absent. To fill this void, in the later parts of the present work an own chapter (Chapter 5) will be dedicated specifically to a discussion of research on social interaction processes and to linking these insights with the assumptions and findings of cognitive studies on strategic management.

Furthermore, in the context of dealing with strategic processes in globally operating and distributed organizations, further attention seems necessary to the fact that there might indeed be several different 'systems of meaning' prevailing simultaneously within the same organisation due the diversity of individuals' cultural backgrounds and experiences, as well as due to the different country locations in which the firm's units are based. Following from this, coherent with the basic assumptions made here that reality and especially knowledge and strategic interpretations are subjective and will vary depending on the social (and cultural) context within which they are observed, the phenomenon at hand thus clearly calls for a phenomenological, case study approach that allows paying particular attention to and taking into account the peculiarities of the context these processes are embedded in.

Here then, exactly this concern with the specific **method of investigation** used can be seen as a final crucial distinction between MOC studies conducted from the information processing perspective and those from the enactment perspective: Studies conducted from a computational perspective largely tend to elicit individual responses to questionnaires or scenarios. Even though the stimulus used to trigger responses is organizational, the interpretations are individual (Wrona & Breuer, 2009, p. 83). In contrast, interpretive studies investigate collective beliefs and actions predominantly by using case studies, direct observation of interactions, and linguistic analysis. An implicit distinction between these two perspectives is consequently "where the action" is. Whereas in the former positivistic perspective the cognitive action takes place in the heads of individuals, in the social constructivist perspective the cognitive action takes place among individuals engaged in collective activity (Lant, 2002, p. 355).

2.4.3.3 Integrating the two perspectives

Now, in the preceding two sections each of the distinct perspectives underlying cognitive strategy research has been outlined and their origins, basic principles and respective contributions have been discussed. While conceptually the basic distinction between the *downstream* choice or calculation process associated with decision making and the *upstream* process of sensemaking clearly is important, in reality, an adequate understanding of the role of cognition in the strategy process requires an acknowledgement of both elements of organizations (Lant, 2002, p. 359). In line with this, even though research continues today that is consistent with either the information processing view or the meaning creation view, there is nevertheless growing recognition that organizations are both systems that process information and systems that create meaning. As March (1997) noted, decision making in organizations can be viewed at times as rational and computational in nature, and as retrospective sensemaking processes at other times (March, 1997). While schema-based studies for example neglect social context, other research, however, has shown that computational cognition is in fact facilitated or inhibited depending on the particular social context (i.e., enactment processes influence the boundaries and categories that determine what is computed and what is not; what is important and what is not).

Coherent with the argument above, since organizational behaviour involves the simultaneous coordination of activities at many levels, the cognitive processes going on during the accomplishment of some tasks may thus include both automatic and controlled processes simultaneously. Strategic decision makers, for example, may utilize controlled and centralized cognitive processes to retrieve well-learned schemata of their environment as threat- or opportunity-filled. An unexpected antagonistic competitor move, however, may cause them to revise the schemata in ways that may not relate to the original schemata, and without their conscious awareness that they are doing so (Fiol, 2002, p. 130). Consequently, regarded more specifically at the individual level, instead of defining managers solely as computing devices, researchers are beginning to define them as actors who proactively make sense of and invent their own decision possibilities. In line with this, recently a number of works of prominent organizational researchers have appeared that are good exemplars for scholars' growing recognition of the complementary, rather than competing, nature of the different approaches to (intra-) organizational cognition and interpretation research (see for example Eden & Spencer, 1998; Weick, 1995; and the works listed in Fiol, 2002). In these works, each of the authors continues to rely on some aspects of top-down schema-based theories, while at the same time the focus is also on active and real-time sensemaking and pattern matching.

Moreover, even though in the overall field of MOC research studies are often differentiated according to whether they examine or focus on cognition at the individual, the organizational, or the interorganizational level, the general paradigm debate described here in fact pervades each one of these different levels in a similar way.[25] As a result, representatives of the different research areas come to similar conclusions regarding the future of these two paradigm debates as they concurrently argue against an either/ or determination, and encourage a recognition that both paradigms are simultaneously correct. More specifically, Fiol (2002, p. 126) suggests that the two cognitive architectures that are used to describe cognition at the individual level, i.e. connectionist and symbolic, operate at different levels of brain activity. Similarly, concerning organizational cognition, Lant et al. (2002) argue that organizations are both systems of information processing and systems of meaning creation depending on the type of activity. Following Bougon's suggestion (1992, p. 381) that "there is no underlying or deeper reality to be discovered" but that the "socially constructed reality of a system of cognitive maps...is the social reality", the authors take the position that social reality is constructed, but also that the symbolic representation of basic rules and mechanisms is important. Symbolic representation and meaning creation are thus interdependent, not mutually exclusive (Lant & Shapira, 2000, p. 369).

Taken together, whether at the group, the organization, or the industry levels of analysis, it consequently seems clear that cognitions (as cognitive *structures*) emerge from the interplay of bottom-up inference processes and top-down influences and constraints over time. Also, in order to gain a deeper understanding of the role of cognition for strategic decision making and strategic processes, particular attention has to be paid to understanding the relationships between cognition and social interaction. Here then, in the context of the present research, exactly this recognition of the existence of mixed cognitive architectures as well as the importance of the social context within which cognitive strategy research is conducted, constitute some of the most important tenets underlying this work. Each of these aspects will therefore be picked up again and discussed in detail in Chapters 4 and 5, respectively.

---

[25] In this context, cf. also Fiol's (2002) discussion of the two paradigms of individual cognition – symbolic and connectionist – which in fact parallels the paradigms discussed here, i.e. computational/ information processing versus meaning creation. The perspective of organizations as information processing systems is based on the individual level models of symbolic processing in which individuals interpret stimuli by using pre-existing knowledge structures. The perspective of organizations as systems of meaning creation share the same assumptions as connectionist models of individual cognition, in which the interactions among actors are the key process by which interpretations are made and meaning is created.

2.4.4 The "landscape" of cognitive strategy research

The discussion of the cognitive perspective to strategy research has so far focused on the foundations of this approach and the central tenets and underlying epistemological stances. In this context it was already implied that there are a variety of research approaches that are generally subsumed under the label "cognitive perspective". In line with this, as stated above, cognitive strategy research can in fact be seen as a subarea of the overall field of "Managerial and Organizational Cognition" (MOC). In order to now give a more detailed overview of the specific kinds of **topics and questions** dealt with and the **methods** applied in the field, in this section an attempt shall be made to systematize this quite wide and so far only sparsely structured approach to management and organizational research. Following this, the value of adopting a cognitive perspective shall be discussed, and finally an own framework for the present research is derived and presented.

A concise overview over the concrete contents and the specific research methods applied in cognitive strategy research is now already problematic because a clear separation between MOC works with purely strategic questions and those that deal rather generally with the influence of cognitions on organizational behaviour is difficult to make. In line with this, a consistent definition of what is to be understood under "MOC", and which theories are subsumed under this label, does not yet exist. Instead, the MOC field is not only a rather broad approach but it is also an area in which there actually is no consistent use of language or terms (cf. e.g. Walsh, 1995 for the complexity and variety of terms used). A systematization of the cognitive "landscape" is further complicated by the fact that a large part of the immense amount of works in the field exists isolated and without reference to one another (Walsh, 1995, p. 284). In this context, a crucial reason for the difficulty of systematizing the overall approach may be seen in the fact that MOC is actually composed of two different research streams, i.e. **Managerial Cognition (MC)** on the one hand and **Organizational Cognition (OC)** on the other. Even though in the literature one often finds the composite term "Managerial and Organizational Cognition", underneath the labels "MC" and "OC" quite divergent theoretical approaches are in fact concealed. Concerning **Managerial Cognition**, research in this area takes a more individualistic perspective, assuming that organizational action can be understood by examining the mental models of influential managers (Floyd & Wooldridge, 2000, p. 72). According to this approach, it is primarily the individual manager, particularly the top manager, who is responsible for the interpretation of strategic and operative questions. These are then adopted by the organization as a whole (Daft & Weick, 1984; Hambrick & Mason,

1984). The more sociologically based research in the area of **Organizational Cognition** against that takes a more social constructivist or even systems theoretical perspective, in which cognitions at the organisational level proceed differently than the sum of cognitions taking place at the individual level. Accordingly, studies in this area deal with the way perceptions in the organization as a whole, and not only among individual organizational members develop, and how these are conveyed through the organization's structure (e.g. Gioia & Sims, 1986; Lant & Shapira, 2000).

Conditional on the above outlined classification difficulties, only few attempts have been made to systematize the existing works dealing with cognition in a managerial and organizational context. Even though two central *concepts* in cognition research are **cognitive processes** and **cognitive structures** (cf. 1.1 and also 4.2), a simple division of the field into works that deal with either of these would certainly be too abridging (Ginsberg, 1990, p. 517). So far, to the author's knowledge, merely four works may be named that provide hints as to what dimensions might offer some ordering help in the MOC landscape, i.e. Hodgkinson & Sparrow (2002),[26] Porac & Thomas (2002),[27] Schneider & Angelmar (1993),[28] and Walsh (1995).[29] Still, even though each of these approaches clearly has its merits, merely following one of these would be only limitedly useful in the present research context. Therefore, an own *systematization scheme*[30] shall be presented here. Although this scheme is not aimed at providing a complete overview of studies in the field, it nevertheless allows for a more comprehensive and clearer orientation and location of the different existing studies as well as the own present work in the overall "MOC-landscape" (see Figure 4).

---

[26] Book; its chapter outline may be considered as a kind of systematization outlining the different topic areas covered by researchers taking a cognitive perspective.
[27] Handbook chapter; systematization according to levels of analysis, i.e. individual, group, organization, industry.
[28] Journal article in *Organization Studies*; systematization according to cognitive structure, process, and style.
[29] Landmark meta-analysis in *Organization Studies*; systematization according to the content and structure of knowledge structures, four levels of analysis, and theoretical & empirical works.
[30] The systematization is based on an own comprehensive review of 139 empirical studies in the area of cognitive strategy research (cf. Wrona & Breuer, 2008, p. 8 ff.).

2 – Strategic management

Level of analysis		Topic areas	Methods	Study types
MC	Managerial Cognition — Individual (Manager)	• Strategy (process, performance) • Strategic change (learning) • (Strategic) decision making • Cognitive biases, heuristics, etc. • Strategic cognitions in TMTs • Scanning, perception, interpretation • Strategic groups	*Data collection* • Interviews (unstructured, semi structured, structured) • Structured questionnaire • Scenario technique • Observation (field notes) • Published documents • Repertory Grid • Visual card sorting • Cognitive Mapping *Data analysis* • Cognitive mapping • Content analysis (quantitative, qualitative) • MDS • Grounded Theory	• Cross-sectional study • Longitudinal study • Case study/ studies • Large scale analyses • Experiment • (Business-) Simulation(s) • (Management) Workshop(s)
	Managerial Cognition — Group (TMT)			
OC	Organizational Cognition — Organization			
	Organizational Cognition — Industry			

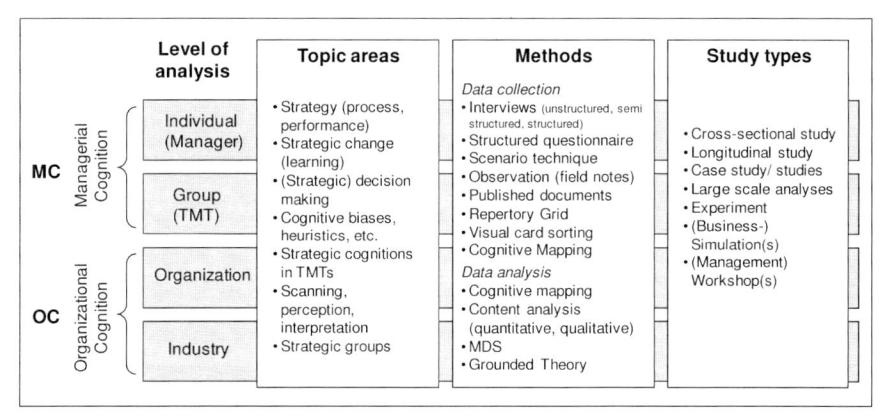

Figure 4: "MOC-landscape" (adopted and translated from Wrona & Breuer, 2009, p. 77)

If one starts by looking at the content dimension of the collectivity of published MOC works, (thereby) including both empirical and conceptual contributions, the diversity of **topics** investigated from a cognitive perspective becomes obvious. Central content categories are for example the strategy process and firm performance; strategic and organizational change; decision making; cognitive biases[31], heuristics[32] and limitations inherent in the process of judgment and choice; and issues like scanning, perception, and interpretation behaviours.[33] Even though overlaps between these different subjects may often be found within individual studies, these listed topic areas nevertheless provide a first useful insight into the field's complexity but also, positively seen, the breadth of research questions for which the adaptation of a cognitive perspective can be fruitful.

Moreover, for strategy researchers the most central interest clearly lies in examining the linkages between cognitive processes, cognitive structures and decision processes in strategic management with regard to strategy formulation and implementation. In line with this, the central element within the works concerned with the contents of the so called managerial 'black box' is the cognitive structures (models) used by senior/ top managers in the strategy process, i.e. beliefs about the environment, about strategy and about the business portfolio and

---

[31] The term "**cognitive bias**" is generally used to refer to a person's tendency to make judgmental errors. A large number of such different biases have by now been identified and are well-documented in the literature (for the strategy context cf. e.g. Das & Teng, 1999, p. 760 ff.; Lyles & Thomas, 1988, p. 132 ff.).

[32] In psychology, **heuristics** refer to so-called 'rules of thumb' which people apply to help them in problem solving, learning and discovery. Although under most circumstances these simple but hard-coded rules work well, in some cases they may also introduce cognitive biases that can lead to severe and systematic errors in decision making (Kahneman, Slovic, & Tversky, 1982).

[33] Apart from these, another specific stream in the area is the extensive methodological literature, which specifies a variety of techniques for eliciting cognitive maps and structures from individuals as well as approaches to mapping 'collective cognition' (cf. e.g. Huff, 1990; Brown, 1992; Clarkson & Hodgkinson, 2005; Daniels, Chernatony de, & Johnson, 1995; Hodgkinson, Maule, & Brown, 2004; Markoczy & Goldberg, 1995).

state of the organization. In this respect, even though the debate about the concrete 'locus' of cognition still continues (Lant, 2002, p. 355 f.), general agreement nevertheless exists concerning the assumption that strategic cognitions can be found and described at both the individual managerial level as well as at the collective level. Accordingly, inquiries into the interrelationships between cognition and strategy take place at four different **levels of analysis**: The individual level (i.e. mostly the top manager), the group (i.e. mostly the top management team, i.e. 'TMT'), the organization, or the level of the industry or the collectivity of TMTs within an industry (so called "cognitive communities") (Porac & Thomas, 2002).

Systematizing the existing works in the MOC field according to their particular level of analysis is also in so far quite useful as such a differentiation further allows for a broad attribution of central research issues to these different levels of analysis. Table 2 provides a listing of selected research topics and issues sorted according to the respective levels at which strategic cognitions are investigated.

Table 2: Selected research topics and exemplary studies according to levels of 'strategic cognitions'

	Topics	Exemplary studies
Individual (Manager)	- Content and origin of managerial cognitions - Mental models, cognitive maps - Individual cognitive processes (esp. cognitive biases, use of heuristics, a.o.) - Managers' cognitive style - Individual decision making	Reger & Huff, 1993 Waller, Huber, & Glick, 1995 Lant, Milliken, & Batra, 1992 Tyler & Steensma, 1998 Calori, Johnson, & Sarnin, 1994 Chattopadhyay, Glick, Miller, & Huber, 1999 Daniels, Johnson, & de Chernatony, 2002 Gavetti, Levinthal, & Rivkin, 2005 Sutcliffe & Huber, 1998
Group (TMT)	- Group composition, structure, (social) processes - Existence or degree of cognitive consensus in TMTs; diversity effects ➢ these variables are largely used to ultimately establish a connection to performance or organizational strategy	Pelled, 1996 Jackson, 1992 Ambrosini & Bowman, 2005 Simons, Pelled, & Smith, 1999 Fiol, 1994 Iaquinto & Friedrickson, 1997 Kilduff, Angelmar, & Mehra, 2000 Knight et al., 1999 Walsh, Henderson, & Deighton, 1988
Organization/ Firm	- Organizations as interpretation systems (in contrast to individuals as interpretation systems)	Daft & Weick, 1984 Lyles & Schwenk, 1992 Virany, Tushman, & Romanelli, 1992 Nadkarni & Narayanan, 2007b Barr, Stimpert, & Huff, 1992 Bartunek, 1984 Elenkov, 1997 Thomas, Clark, & Gioia, 1993

Industry	- "Industry belief systems", i.e.
	  - industry recipes
	  - beliefs about the boundaries of markets and competitive interactions
	- Cognitive foundation(s) of industry communities
		Porac, Thomas, & Baden-Fuller, 1989
		Porac et al., 1995
		Abrahamson & Fairchild, 1999
		Benjamin & Podolny, 1999
		Nadkarni & Narayanan, 2007a
		Benjamin & Podolny, 1999
		Greve, 1998
		Johnson & Hoopes, 2003

Moving now subsequent to the description of the contents and the levels of cognitive strategy research on to the examination of the **methodological question**, it is not surprising to see that the above outlined dichotomy of the MOC field in terms of its disciplinary and theoretical foundations (i.e. MC and OC) is similarly reflected here. What is firstly obvious is the fact that in the area of Organizational Cognition a significantly larger amount of works can be found that deal primarily conceptually with the topic. This makes intuitively sense since already the empirical investigation of individuals' cognitions exposes the researcher to considerable problems. The question how or whether it is possible at all to study collective or supra-individual structures and processes is consequently all the more difficult.

Generally, a first huge challenge for empirical studies in cognitive strategy research derives from the fact that the central research 'object', i.e. cognitive structures and processes, is by definition of a non-observable nature. In addition, the question what 'strategic knowledge' really is still remains open.[34] As a result, empirical research in the area continues to be strongly exploratory and to follow an own, rather pragmatically oriented way that is coined by almost the entire methodical spectrum for data collection and analysis. Starting from repertory grid to in-depth interviews to the classic questionnaire and from cluster analysis to multidimensional scaling to qualitative or quantitative content analyses and even grounded theory approaches, the most diverse methods can be found. Not unusual is also the simultaneous or consecutive application of different methods within a single research project. Even though, overall, cognitive mapping (i.e., the creation of cognitive maps in different variations) as a methodical approach is found quite often, there still is no method that could be called a standard in the field. This claim may be substantiated by the above outlined variety of topics that is being investigated from a cognitive perspective.

In accordance with the above, also the **type of empirical studies** is very diverse. An overwhelming majority here are large scale and thus usually quantitative cross- sectional designs (e.g. Calori et al., 1994; Fombrun & Shanley, 1990; Iaquinto & Friedrickson, 1997; Waller et al., 1995). Apart from these, however, there still is a notable amount of longitudinal studies that can partially be classified as quantitative, partially as qualitative, or as so called 'mix methods' studies (e.g. Barr & Huff, 1997; Haleblian & Finkelstein, 1993; Papadakis, Lioukas, & Chambers, 1998). A further category, even though it indeed partly but not always overlaps with the previous one, is case study research. Especially in the area of Organizational Cognition a number of in-depth and sometimes long-lived examinations of individual organizations or business units can be found. Apart from these rather ‚common' study types, there are also

---

[34] A detailed discussion about *knowledge*, particularly the own conception of *strategic knowledge* followed in the present research context, is provided in 4.1.

experiments, simulations, and studies or interventions that have been conducted in the context or with the help of management workshops (e.g. Bowman & Johnson, 1992; Bukszar & Connolly, 1988; Haley & Stumpf, 1989; Langfield-Smith, 1992).

Even though a clear-cut classification of concrete methods to specific research questions or study types is not possible, a useful help for orientation nevertheless results if one systematizes the methods used in the studies according to the particular level of analysis on which the empirical work is focused. In this respect, where the interest concerns the examination and analysis of **individual knowledge structures**, mapping methods are often used. Here then, the corresponding empirical works can be grouped according to whether they measure and map such knowledge structures by means of quantitative or with qualitative methods (Rogers-Wynands, 2002, p. 29). Works that can be characterized as rather quantitatively oriented try to assess individual knowledge structures by using e.g. standardized questionnaires or the repertory grid technique to collect "knowledge data" and then solidify these data into "knowledge structures" (in the form of cognitive maps) by means of cluster analyses, multi-dimensional scaling or factor analyses. Appendant to this category are also works which use documentary analysis to establish causal relations between certain concepts found e.g. in letters to shareholders, or studies where participants themselves are asked to establish causal links between certain concepts deemed relevant by the researcher („causal cognitive mapping") (e.g. Daniels et al., 1994; Daniels, Johnson, & de Chernatony, 2002; Reger & Huff, 1993; Reger & Palmer, 1996; Spencer, Peyrefitte, & Churchman, 2003). In the comparatively small number of qualitative individual level studies, the investigation of knowledge structures mostly takes place in the form of unstructured or semi-structured oral interrogations. Like this the researcher aims to ensure that it is truly the knowledge structures of the managers themselves and not the researchers' own, or prior existing, beliefs that are being assessed (e.g. Hodgkinson & Johnson, 1994).

Concerning the investigation of **collective cognitions** at the **industry level**, here mostly the cognitions of individuals (e.g. those of the CEO or other powerful organizational actors) are being used to ultimately deduce the respective dominant industry recipe(s), perceptions of industry boundaries or reputation orderings in a particular industry (e.g. Calori, Johnson, & Sarnin, 1992; Calori et al., 1994). Accordingly, similar to the individual level, quite often mapping methods are used, especially to construct cognitive taxonomies (cf. Figure 5). Even though apart from using structured questionnaires to collect data, partially also non standardized interviews or secondary data analyses (e.g. company reports) are thus used, altogether also here quantitative methods clearly dominate.

2 – Strategic management   47

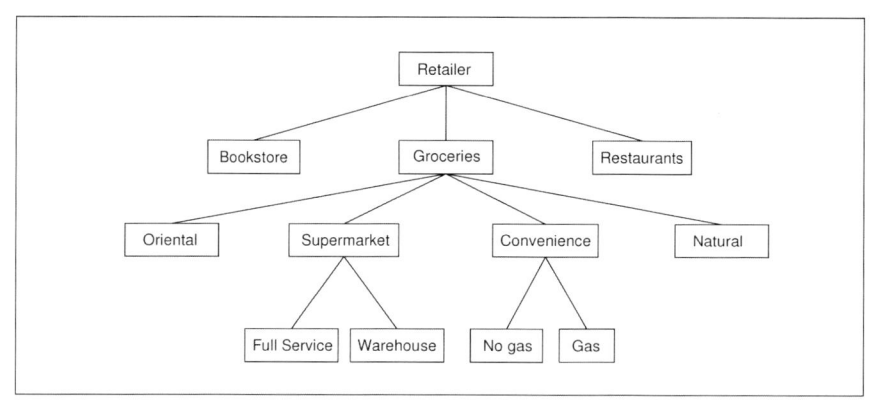

```
                              ┌──────────┐
                              │ Retailer │
                              └──────────┘
                    ┌──────────────┼──────────────┐
              ┌──────────┐   ┌──────────┐   ┌─────────────┐
              │ Bookstore│   │ Groceries│   │ Restaurants │
              └──────────┘   └──────────┘   └─────────────┘
          ┌─────────┬──────────┴──────────┬──────────┐
     ┌─────────┐ ┌───────────┐    ┌─────────────┐ ┌─────────┐
     │ Oriental│ │Supermarket│    │ Convenience │ │ Natural │
     └─────────┘ └───────────┘    └─────────────┘ └─────────┘
                   ┌────┴────┐        ┌────┴────┐
           ┌────────────┐ ┌──────────┐ ┌────────┐ ┌─────┐
           │Full Service│ │ Warehouse│ │ No gas │ │ Gas │
           └────────────┘ └──────────┘ └────────┘ └─────┘
```

Figure 5: Example of a taxonomic knowledge structure (Porac & Thomas, 1994, p. 57)

Much more diverse is the methodical and methodological picture where the aim is to assess and understand **cognitions at the organizational level**. Roughly seen, two methodical approaches may be differentiated. One of these simply aggregates the individually measurable cognitive structures, processes or styles[35]. The other tries to find variables that represent the collective cognitions existing in an organization (e.g. Schneider & Angelmar, 1993). Possibilities for the latter are for example afforded by the analysis of an organization's communication channels (top-down or bottom-up), ways of communicating (open, covered, hierarchical, etc.), or the analysis of the respective organizational identity and culture (e.g. Bartunek, 1984; Bougon, Weick, & Binkhorst, 1977). While the former approach is accordingly reflected in predominantly large scale quantitative analyses, there are also case studies and interpretive approaches in the area of Organizational Cognition. In the latter cases researchers often combine different data collection methods (e.g. unstructured or semi-structured interviews, participant observation, field notes), and then analyse these data using either qualitative or quantitative content analyses (e.g. Bougon et al., 1977; Dutton & Dukerich, 1991; Fiol, 1994; Gioia, Thomas, Clark, & Chittipeddi, 1994).

Finally, as regards **group cognitions**, a major impediment to empirical research here is the fact that strategy researchers only rarely or merely limitedly have access to (such) teams of high level managers. Hence it is not surprising that a large part of studies in the so called 'upper echelons tradition' (e.g. Finkelstein, 1992; Hambrick & Mason, 1984) uses demographic

---

[35] **Cognitive style** is a person's *preferred* way of gathering, processing, and evaluating information (Hayes & Allinson, 1998, p. 850). Considered as a valuable indicator for predicating and classifying people's behaviour, cognitive style has been typically used in studies of information processing in order to develop decision-making systems. The relevant literature defines four different cognitive styles: ST (sensation-thinking), SF (sensation-feeling), NT (intuition-thinking) and NF (intuition-feeling) (e.g. Gallen, 1997, p. 543 ff.).

data (such as e.g. age, tenure, education, function) as proxies for the cognitive structures and processes of the respective team members (e.g. Bantel & Jackson, 1989; Hambrick, Cho, & Chen, 1996; Wiersema & Bantel, 1992). Still, due to increasing criticisms against this kind of methodical procedures, several newer approaches have emerged in recent times from which better research results are expected. One such an approach is the direct measurement of cognitions at the TMT level. For this purpose, in the majority of studies large scale surveys and quantitative analyses are conducted (e.g. Hitt, Dacin, Tyler, & Park, 1997; Knight et al., 1999). Yet, both theoretically and methodically this procedure appears problematic: While the argument in these studies is at the team level, the underlying data is mostly collected on an individual basis and is merely aggregated post hoc by the researcher himself to form the shared perception or knowledge of the group. In addition, especially in the context of conducting research on collective cognition in teams of managers, social interaction processes clearly play a major role. Nevertheless, despite various calls to pay attention to such interactions and to conduct more direct, in-depth and process-oriented research (e.g. Hutzschenreuter & Kleindienst, 2006), only very few studies may be named in which methods better suited to explicitly incorporate and take into account interactive processes have been applied (see for an exception Ambrosini & Bowman, 2001; Ambrosini & Bowman, 2005).

Taken together, the above discussion has shown that the "landscape" of cognitive strategy research is both in terms of content and methods a very diverse and little coherent field. In line with the initial description of strategic management as a multi-paradigm research area, this conception is thus again clearly reflected in the "micro-structure" of individual theoretical approaches like the cognitive perspective to strategy research discussed here.

2.4.5 Value of adopting a cognitive approach to strategy research

In the preceding section the cognitive perspective on strategic management has been characterized as a very heterogeneous and in fact still quite unstructured approach within the overall area of management and organizational research. Despite this diversity, however, widespread agreement exists among the different scholars in the field as regards the **value** that can be derived from insights into the cognitive processes and structures of individuals, groups of managers, or organizations.

Concerning first of all the *individual managerial level*, it is recognized that top managers' understanding of their competitive systems influences their decisions and actions, which in turn shape their environments (Calori et al., 1992, p. 75). One major *practical* value of the cognitive approach thus is that it provides a useful basis to understand the dynamics of indus-

2 – Strategic management

tries from a managerial viewpoint. Even more importantly, research on **cognitive heuristics and biases** gives insights into the ways decision makers with limited cognitive capacities comprehend and solve complex strategic problems (Schwenk, 1988, pp. 43-44). In this context, because misjudgements of internal or external opportunities and risks are often seen as a crucial cause for the failure or absence of strategic action (cf. e.g. Prahalad & Bettis, 1986; Walsh, 1995), cognitive analyses are particularly valued for the possibilities they afford to identify patterns of 'retracted' thoughts. In line with this, the surfacing of managerial frames of reference and their explanation, in narrative form or by mapping, can provide a useful basis for feedback to managers. Beneficial for management development, the resulting findings and maps[36] can for example be used to demonstrate to managers the implicit structure of their thinking and the extent to which it corresponds to or differs from colleagues or others in their industry (c.f. e.g. Eden & Radford, 1990, p. 190 ff.). In this context, as firms become more and more international, uncovering commonalities and differences between countries at the cognitive level also appears as a **powerful training or consulting approach** both for future expatriates as well as for managers already operating in intercultural work environments. Ultimately, a better understanding of strategists' cognitive structures and processes thus provides a basis for better recommendations for **improving strategic decision making**, and **decision aids** may be developed that allow for reducing important biases once these have been identified (cf. e.g. Swan, 1995, p. 1266 f.).

Moreover, moving beyond the individual level focus, since strategic decision making is increasingly a collective activity, one way to conceptualize 'organizational strategies' is to regard them as shared knowledge among a firm's key actors (cf. 2.2). In line with this, also *group cognitions* and knowledge structures that are shared by a collective are of high interest. Here then, in a similar way as with individual cognitions, also for the collective counterpart partially negative consequences are assumed. On the one hand, shared knowledge structures foster stability and effective communications within the group in the first place and allow for a better handling of complexity. On the other hand, however, an existing 'dominant logic' can at the same time cause 'groupthink' (Janis, 1972) and act as a kind of perception filter, thereby promoting stereotypical interpretations and ultimately suboptimal group results. This negative effect may be counteracted by surfacing the collective knowledge structures and like that exposing them to **explicit reflection**. In addition, by exploring and disclosing collective

---

[36] **Cognitive maps**: In general, cognitive maps and models serve to: (1) help managers structure issues by focusing attention and triggering memory; (2) improve issue resolution by revealing gaps in information; and (3) facilitate creative problem solving by highlighting key factors and supplying missing information (Fiol and Huff, 1992, p. 275 f.).

knowledge structures, "dormant" knowledge can be unlocked, which in turn may lead to a better **utilization of a firm's knowledge base** and like that possibly to an accruement of sustainable competitive advantages. Taken together, cognitive analyses thus give valuable support both to the individual manager through a reflectance of the knowledge he uses in the context of strategic decision making, as well as to the management team, insofar as the individual knowledge structures of its members are made transparent in a **comparative juxtaposition**. Based on these insights and the open pooling of individuals' knowledge, the group is then able to work out a common perception and like that to make the most of its prevailing cognitive diversity.[37]

Finally, and apart from its primarily practical implications in the area of Managerial Cognition, also on the *organizational level* the cognitive focus is valuable, specifically in studying and managing **organizational and strategic change** (Isabella, 1990, p. 7 ff.; Rajagopalan & Spreitzer, 1997, p. 70 ff.). In this context, some authors have for example suggested that understanding the cognitive basis for responding to change would enhance the effectiveness of **organizational responses** (e.g. Gioia, 1986). Related to this, taken as an enrichment to the 'traditional' rational lens in strategy research, the cognitive lens provides additional value because it helps researchers to understand why different firms respond differently to a similar context (i.e. because of different cognitions and actions) (Rajagopalan & Spreitzer, 1997, p. 70). Also, variation in beliefs across an industry might help explain sustained competitive differences between close competitors ('competitive heterogeneity'). In line with the 'raison d'être' of strategic management, i.e. ensuring the sustained existence and profitability of organizations (cf. 2.1), it may thus be asserted that a better understanding of top managers' cognitions will ultimately also lead to a better understanding of **organizational performance**.

2.4.6 Deriving a socio-cognitive research framework

Managerial and organizational cognition has now been shown to be an important topic in strategic management. At the same time, however, and despite the general benefits and value of adopting a cognitive perspective, the discussion of the cognitive "landscape" has also revealed a common **deficit** in MOC research: I.e., how cognitions at the individual level and the

---

[37] In recognition of the value that the surfacing of managerial cognitions has, especially also in group contexts, different kinds of specific interactive map-making tools have been developed over time. As enumerated by Eden (1992, p. 805), these facilitate behavioural integration and heedful interrelating in a number of ways: (1) they facilitate negotiation among team members; (2) provide teams with an efficient use of their time; (3) develop consensus, rather than compromise, within the team; (4) develop a commitment to act, rather than commitment to a plan; (5) reduce the possibility of 'groupthink'; (6) give members of the team the belief that they are developing a more intelligent and thoughtful strategy; and (7) create an effective organizational memory and transitional object to influence the implementation of strategy.

collective level differ from each other, how they interrelate, and how they influence each other. In the context of strategy research this may be said to correspond to the question concerning the 'translation' of "individual strategies" into "organizational strategies" (Kirsch, 1996, p. 117 ff.) (cf. also 3.3.2). In addition, although it is in fact both cognitive *structures* and cognitive *processes* that matter if insights are to be gained into *how* strategies actually emerge and to explain *why* there is a certain (strategic) outcome, a large part of MOC research still has a quite predominant focus on the *content* side (i.e. on cognitive structures), thereby neglecting *processual* issues. Exactly for the latter then, and as argued already above, the *social contexts* in which strategic activities take place and strategy research is conducted are clearly of high importance. Consequently, in order to gain a deeper understanding of the role of cognition in strategic processes specific considerations of the interactions between the cognitive and the social dimensions have to be included, too.

In recognition of these deficits now, and in light of the specific research interests and questions at hand, it thus seems clear that a more encompassing approach is needed, which is able to remedy these very deficiencies. Here then, a first important aspect to be considered is to acknowledge explicitly the *inseparability of the individual and the collective levels*: The system (i.e., organization, society) socializes its members, who interact within it, and influences their perceptions and actions. Organizations are thus no objectively given entities. Instead, they are based on the cognitions of their members and these people's interaction partners, which are in turn at least partially determined by the operating modes, i.e. the routines and rules, of the system itself. The members, however, have the opportunity or are at least partially able to comprehend and critically reflect upon the functioning of the system (Hoffmann-Ripken, 2003, p. 155). Following from these arguments, even though the transition between the different levels of analysis is clearly not straightforward, it is still obvious that the different levels cannot be regarded in isolation from each other. Hence, the overall perspective clearly needs to consider the *different levels of analysis* involved: The individual manager(s), the team(s), and the organizational, social and cultural context, i.e. the organization as a whole or the respective business unit within which the individuals' thinking and acting are embedded ("context").

Secondly, as emphasized above, a common deficit in the MOC literature so far concerns the missing considerations given to the *transitions* between the different levels at which cognitions are seen to exist. Here then, in line with the repeated, though still only implicit hints from other researchers (cf. e.g. Fiol, 2002, p. 130 ff.; Huff, 2005, p. 346 ff.; Lant, 2002, p. 356

ff.), *social interactions* are regarded as the most crucial *mediators* between the different levels of analysis. Social interactions processes are thus the central element in the overall approach.

Thirdly, rather than assuming a one-directional process starting with "individual strategies" and resulting in what may be termed "organizational strategies", strategies and their (potential) development are seen to be embedded within an *ongoing process* of decisions, actions and interactions (cf. Chapter 3). Apart from thus having to acknowledge *dynamic interactions* and *feedback loops* between cognitions at the individual and the collective levels, mutual influences also exist between this overall process and the different kinds of contexts (i.e., organisational, political, institutional, cultural, historical), it is situated in.

Following from all the above, as well as drawing on some related, fundamental outlines by Bamberger & Wrona (2004, p. 366 ff.), a research framework that incorporates exactly these central elements is now presented in Figure 6.

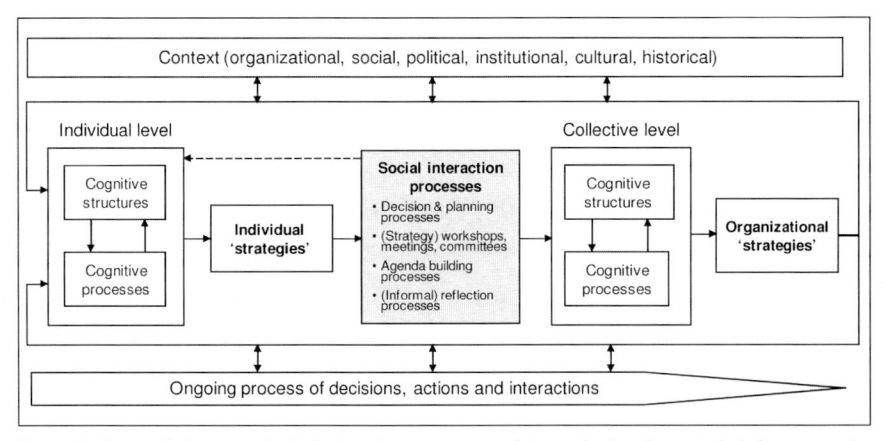

Figure 6: Research framework depicting the emergence of 'organisational strategies' from a socio-cognitive perspective (adopted and modified from Wrona & Breuer, 2008, p. 15)

While depicted in a more simplified way than the descriptive outlines above, the figure clearly answers the call to explicitly include the different levels of analysis that need to be considered for understanding the phenomenon at hand. In addition, the inseparability of the individual and the collective levels is visualized by means of the different lines and arrows connecting these. Here then, concerning specifically the relationship between individual level cognitions[38] and individual 'strategies', there are in fact two perspectives that have to be

---

[38] As mentioned previously (cf. 1.2) cognitive structures and cognitive processes are regarded as intrinsically interlinked. This issue will be considered in the context of a more thorough discussion of the psychological basics involved in the present research (cf. 4.2).

considered (Bamberger & Wrona, 2004, p. 366). On the one hand, individual strategic orientations can be regarded as being based on the person's different knowledge structures (cf. 1.2). At the same time, strategies as action orientations (cf. 2.2) can also be components of knowledge structures. Exactly this is likely to be the case for 'organisational strategies', which may have been formally decided on, officially communicated across the organisation, and like that feed back to the individual cognitive level.

Moreover, in line with the outlined importance of social interactions as central mediators in the ongoing process, these thus constitute the very centre of the framework. In this regard, as demonstrated exemplarily here, there clearly is a variety of occasions for interactions between actors, e.g. in the context of concrete planning processes, workshops, or rather informal reflections at some dinner party. Here then, on the one hand, individual knowledge structures and 'strategies' can be regarded as *input* to these interactions. On the other hand, they are also produced and reproduced by these (the latter is signified by the dotted line in the figure). Finally, apart from these feedback loops and dynamic interactions, the framework also clearly visualizes the mutual influences between this overall process and the different kinds of contexts it is embedded in.

Overall now, following from these outlines, it seems clear that the framework thus presented and roughly described finally visualizes what may be considered a more adequate, comprehensive, and especially truly *processual* approach to the emergence of organisational strategies. In line with this, the diverse insights and research areas that hence have to be considered and aligned in order to finally present a coherent *socio-cognitive perspective* on strategic processes will now be each discussed in the subsequent chapters.

3 Strategic processes

The purpose of the preceding chapter was to establish the basis for the present research project. For this, it has provided an outline of the overall field of strategic management and of the work's underlying conception of "strategy", as well as a discussion of the major theoretical perspectives in the discipline, followed by a detailed focus on the cognitive perspective on strategic management as the primary theoretical lens in the research at hand. In the present chapter now, the emphasis is set on strategic *processes*, i.e. on how strategies are actually formed, implemented and changed. These are the questions that "strategy process research" attempts to address. As will be shown, like the overall discipline of strategic management also the specific area of process research is in fact a complex and large field in itself with a variety of different perspectives on the various issues.

The chapter will proceed as follows: First, an outline of the origins of strategy process research is provided. Then, the major existing theoretical approaches and perspectives are illustrated, including two more encompassing approaches to strategy process phenomena. Finally, the own view on strategic processes (including their dimensions) and strategy formation developed in the present work is presented and the implications of adopting such a perspective are discussed.

3.1 Introducing strategy process research

The history of strategy as *process* can at least be traced back to the early 1960s when three of the discipline's landmark books by Adam Chandler (1962), Igor Ansoff (1965), and Kenneth Andrews (1971) were published. These books were actually among the first to propose formally the distinction between the *process* of strategic management and the *content* of strategy (cf. 2.1). By doing so, a new research focus was initiated that led scholars to start considering process aspects rather than seeing strategy merely as a fixed formula or policy.

In this context, strategy process research attempts to address the difficult question of how strategies are formed, implemented and changed. Embedded in this work is the assumption that managers aspire to, and firms realize, something that can be called a "strategy" (cf. 2.2). What constitutes effective strategy is addressed in the work of 'strategy content' researchers. Content research describes attractive destinations, but without explaining how to get there. The getting there, the journey, is the task of strategy process researchers (Chakravarthy & White, 2002, p. 182).

In line with this general outline of "strategy process research", the majority of approaches that can be classified as belonging to this area are based on an *action oriented understanding* of such processes (Bamberger & Wrona, 2004, p. 336). This means, rather than investigating the change of strategic objects or specific strategy contents over time, the focus is on questions concerning how strategic issues (especially strategies) as objects or result of cognitive, decision or planning processes, emerge, are realized or become implemented. Following this conception, **strategic processes** are thus considered as a plurality of activities involving decisions, actions and interactions, which generate specific strategic issues (Bamberger & Wrona, 2004, p. 327).[39] Concerning what qualifies as "strategic", as outlined in Chapter 2, the perspective taken here is that *strategic* is related to success potentials or to organisational capabilities. Strategic actions then are all those individual and collective activities which have a significant influence on the development, preservation or change of (organizational) success potentials (Bamberger & Wrona, 2004, p. 358).

This definition of strategic processes already implies their complex nature, the many different issues inherently involved, as well as the different dimensions of such processes. Most importantly, however, different from the traditional view in which strategic processes were largely equated with (strategic) decision making,[40] the conception followed here is clearly broader: While concrete decisions on strategic plans or other strategically relevant issues are certainly an important *element* within the overall strategy process (i.e. within the ongoing process), such a decision is nevertheless only one step (or "episode") in a long sequence of decisions and actions that all together culminate in a strategy (e.g. Bamberger & Wrona, 2004, p. 355 ff.; Kirsch, 1991, p. 131 ff.). Also, irrespective of whether conceptualized as strategic orientations, manoeuvres, or structures, "strategies" are not always the result of or the object of decision processes.[41] In addition, decisions and actions need not follow an orderly precedence, and what may appear to be a decision made by the top management may have its origins in a process that was in parts intuitive, social and political (Chakravarthy & White, 2002, p. 183).

In line with the above and as a consequence of a number of studies and empirical findings which have confirmed these assertions, a visible shift in focus has occurred in strategy

---

[39] In this context, a strategically relevant issue can, but must not be a concrete strategy (in the sense of a kind of plan or manoeuvre).
[40] In fact, exactly this is often quite confusing in the existing literature since often, at least terminologically, no real distinction is made between "strategic(/y) processes" and "strategic decision making (processes)"; instead authors use these terms interchangeably even though they may actually be focusing merely on decision making.
[41] Instead, the existence of different strategy making modes including planning and emergence is today widely recognized (cf. 2.2).

3 – Strategic processes

process research over the years. Having recognized the need to complement the traditionally dominant rational perspective on strategic processes with social, political and evolutionary perspectives, the field may today be described as a truly multi-perspective area. While decisions are of course still important and studies from the rational-mechanistic perspective continue to flourish, in a recent extensive review of strategy process research Hutzschenreuter & Kleindienst (2006) identify six main perspectives of strategy process research representing the current intellectual structure of the field: rational-mechanistic, cognitive, upper-echelon, middle management, organic, and micro perspective (Hutzschenreuter & Kleindienst, 2006, p. 701 ff.). Without denying any of these perspectives their respective valuable contributions, it is clearly recognized that each of them builds on varying base disciplines and underlying assumptions, and hence offers somewhat different insights into the strategy process phenomenon.

Following from this diversity, to enable a better understanding and overview of the field, and to justify and underline the usefulness of the particular 'lens' taken for investigating the specific phenomenon at hand, below an outline of the field's overall development and major perspectives shall be provided first. What will be seen from this is that even though the existence of many perspectives is clearly valuable, a unified theory, however, is still missing because little cross-fertilization really occurs. Nevertheless, two more integrative approaches exist, authored by Mintzberg and Kirsch, which will be outlined at the end of the next section.

3.2 Major theoretical approaches and perspectives in strategy process research[42]

3.2.1 Rational-decision oriented approaches

In line with the traditional view that strategic actions, and thus strategies, are largely determined by, or even equal to, (strategic) decisions made by firms' top managers, a major influence on the development of process research came from different streams in the area of decision theory. In this context, the starting point for most research on strategic decision processes was for a long time the **rational choice model** developed in these theories. Based on the view that decision makers are rational actors, the model assumes that (even complex) decision problems can be solved in an all-embracing process. In this deterministic understanding of the classical, often also called "**synoptic**", models of decision behaviour (e.g. Andrews, 1971;

---

[42] The following sections (3.2.1 – 3.2.4) roughly follow the structure that Bamberger & Wrona (2004, pp. 337-341) use to outline the developmental lines of strategy process research.

Ansoff, 1965), strategy processes then represent sequential, rational, and analytical activities in which managers must analyse both their external and their internal environments. Strategy then is the alignment of internal strengths or weaknesses with external opportunities and threats.

Coherent with these assumptions, in its early times research concerned with strategy as process was clearly characterized by its strong focus on planning issues, both descriptively and prescriptively, with attention directed towards the effectiveness of alternative means for generating and implementing strategy. In this context, the 'ideal' model of decision behaviour found its practically oriented value particularly in the early (normative) **models of planning behaviour**. The planning actor is said to act with foresight and systematically, and is characterized by his extensive search for information and his comprehensive processing capacities. As systematic planning involves a sequence of activities, the planning process thus consists of different, **distinct phases** (cf. also 2.3.1).

In line with this sequential view or phase orientation, a further important vestige from the early works in the field is Andrew's (1965) famous and enduring distinction between the process of **strategy formulation** (deciding what to do), and the process of **strategy implementation** (achieving results). Since then, several researchers have been concerned with how the overall strategy process can be divided into different steps or phases. One of the broadest perspectives on strategy process phases offered comes from Schendel and Hofer (1979) who propose six basic tasks in the strategic management process:

1. Establishing a set of overall organizational goals
2. Considering the environment and possible changes in environmental conditions
3. Formulating strategy
4. Evaluating past strategies and assessing future strategy
5. Implementing strategy
6. Controlling strategy

Even though the authors themselves point out that these tasks should not be seen as strictly sequential, rather "in practice [these steps] are interactive, recycle and repeat themselves and do not move forward in sequence as neatly as described here" (Schendel & Hofer, 1979, p. 14), this (quite rigid) formulation-implementation framework still today remains a dominant classification scheme for works in the area (cf. Floyd & Wooldridge, 2000, pp. 10-13).

Over time, as these models became increasingly criticized, their basic assumptions were partially relaxed, leading particularly to the recognition and inclusion of the idea of *bounded rationality* (Simon, 1947) on the side of the strategic actors. Today, there exists a quite differentiated spectrum of models and streams such that even within this specific area one can now differentiate between different perspectives researchers take on these decision processes. In this regard, whereas the rational decision-oriented approaches remain predominantly *normative*, it is in the *descriptive* approaches to strategic decision making where first subtle links to a cognitive perspective can be identified (Bamberger & Wrona, 2004, p. 59). Overall, however, regardless of whether normative or descriptive, the primary research object is decisions, and the traditional top-down focus remains the dominant perspective taken here.

3.2.2 Incremental approaches

Despite relaxed assumptions concerning the logic of strictly rational decision making and planning, scholars increasingly recognized that even the orderly decision processes and the phases implied by procedural rationality are not always (some would contend, not often) observed in practice. In line with this, a first opposition to the synoptic models of decision making and planning was contained in different **'incremental' approaches**. According to these (descriptively-oriented) approaches complex problems, such as strategic problems usually are, are not really solved with foresight in a single encompassing decision process. Instead, the actors proceed more reactively and in small, consecutive steps. In addition, in the organizational context interdependent decisions may also be taken in a decentralized and at the same time possibly even unmatched manner. As a consequence, organizational behaviour and development are considered as the result of a plurality of insufficiently coordinated, single decisions. The incremental models thus portray a picture of (strategic) decision processes as a sequence of reactive, successive, short-term, small, and possibly even "disjointed" steps.[43]

3.2.3 Evolutionary approaches

Following the incremental ideas, **evolutionary approaches** to strategy process issues then represented a further development in the field. In this regard, generally, based on evolutionary biology, evolutionary theories describe the actions of and in organisations as an evolutionary process.[44] The assumption is that firms evolve into an unknown and open future, and that they are highly complex. Accordingly, their development cannot, or only in a limited way, be deliberately influenced by the management (cf. e.g. Malik & Probst, 1981; Ulrich, 1984). With

---

[43] For specific exemplary models cf. e.g. the models of "disjointed incrementalism" (e.g. Lindblom, 1959) and "logical incrementalism" (e.g. Quinn, 1980).

[44] Since evolution theoretical propositions concerning the emergence and development of organisations (social systems) are closely connected to systems theory, an explicit separation between them is not possible. Readers interested in details on systems theory may consult e.g. Seiffert (2001), Willke (2006).

this, evolutionary theories thus stand in opposition specifically to the economic theories of organisations, which act on the assumption that actors behave in a more or less rational and intentional way and that in principle organisations can be designed and controlled deliberately (Bamberger & Wrona, 2004, p. 78).

In line with these general assumptions then, like in the incremental approaches, also here strategic processes are regarded as emergent and non-teleological. Different, however, is the explicit move away from the focus on concrete decisions and planning, i.e. while planning processes are still considered important, they do not to really 'create' strategy (cf. e.g. Burgelman, 1983; Cohen, March, & Olsen, 1972; Mintzberg & McHugh, 1985; Weick, 1979). Implied in this then also is that the focus is no longer solely or primarily top-down oriented. Instead, these approaches recognize that initiatives and activities from below in the organisation matter as well, and that it is especially middle managers who, besides actors at the top management level, are involved in and impact on the whole strategy process. Strategic processes can thus not be fully understood by just studying decision making processes or the actions of the top management team (cf. e.g. Floyd & Wooldridge, 2000, p. 21 ff.).

3.2.4 Political approaches

Even though political perspectives are today taken for the analysis of a variety of phenomena in strategic management, they become important especially through the description and explanation of strategic processes (cf. e.g. Bamberger & Wrona, 2004, p. 341). Here then, like in the above sketched evolutionary approaches, adherents also refrain explicitly from equating strategic processes with decision processes. Instead, in line with their starting point, which is to transfer terms from the political sciences to issues concerning the management of organisations, strategic processes are interpreted as political processes, i.e. as processes imprinted by power, conflict and negotiations. Since political processes contain "power plays", strategic management can thus be characterized as a plurality of such successive and parallel power plays in which different actors or groups of actors with divergent interests, roles, resources, values, etc., participate (cf. e.g. Easton, 1965; Lindblom, 1959, 1964; Narayanan & Fahey, 1982; Sandner, 1992). These different actors address objectives and problems (requests) to the political system, which in turn selects certain of these. Strategic issues and planning problems are thus not obvious as such, but they go through „bargaining processes". The core of the political process then is the transformation of requests and support into authorized decisions (Bamberger & Wrona, 2004, pp. 61-66).

3 – Strategic processes   61

Overall, by explicitly taking into account the existence of diversity in interests, objectives, values, etc., and hence pointing to the importance of such issues like conflict, power, processes of negotiation and coalition building, and use of micro-political tactics, the political perspective clearly allows for a more 'real' description of strategic processes than the normative decision theories. Especially in the present research context the approach makes a valuable contribution as political processes (thus) also constitute an important mechanism for the transformation of views at the individual level to perspectives at the higher level of social systems (e.g. organisations) (Bamberger & Wrona, 2004, p. 398). Nevertheless, since the social interactions among the actors involved must clearly not always be of a political or conflict-laden nature, political processes finally constitute merely one element of the more general *social* dimension of strategic processes (cf. also 3.4).

3.2.5 Cognitive approaches

In the context of dealing in detail with the cognitive perspective on strategic management in 2.4, it was already outlined that cognitive approaches can by now be found in diverse corners of the overall field of management and organisation research. The very beginnings of the inflow of ideas and theories from cognitive psychology to strategy research, however, may be traced back to when researchers interested in strategic decision making became increasingly dissatisfied with the traditional rational models. Here then, in line with extending the rational model with *bounded* rationality (Simon, 1947) and examining specifically the cognitive processes and structures of the actors involved in decision processes, this stream can thus be regarded as a kind of distinctive sub stream in the overall area of research on strategic decision processes. One of its major merits in the present context of strategic processes then is that the cognitive approach points to the path dependency of decision making, i.e. decisions reflect the cognitive model of the decision maker that was developed over time but which is also subject to change. In line with identifying knowledge structures as the essential filters through which incoming information is subsequently processed, which in turn can lead to biased and inappropriate decisions, the major topics dealt with by researchers in this context concern **biases** in decision making, e.g. selective perception, heuristics, escalating commitments, a.o. (cf. e.g. Schwenk, 1995 for an overview of issues in this context and for further references).

Here then, whereas the majority of research in this specific area is primarily concerned with investigating the concrete cognitive 'maps' and predispositions of influential individuals in the process, i.e. the so-called 'upper echelons' (Hambrick & Mason, 1984), another interesting stream that involves cognitive aspects is research on **strategic issue diagnosis**. Originally, the concept of 'strategic issue' was introduced by Igor Ansoff.[45] However, the work by Dutton and her colleagues has been essential in advancing the concept and its cognitive linkages (cf. e.g. Dutton & Duncan, 1987; Dutton, Fahey, & Narayanan, 1983; Dutton & Jackson, 1987). Specifically, these researchers argue that no issue is inherently strategic. Rather, an issue is first categorized as strategic when the top management believes that this issue might have a future impact on the organisational performance. By focusing on beliefs, the role of interpretations and subjectivity in strategic processes is highlighted. The two step process of triggering and interpreting strategic issues is then called *strategic issue diagnosis* (Dutton & Duncan, 1987, p. 281 ff.). Two different assessments are central elements for the interpretation, i.e. the perceived urgency of taking action regarding the issue, and the organisational feasibility for taking necessary action (Dutton & Jackson, 1987, p. 85 ff.). The *strategic agenda* then is the total set of issues to which the top management mainly allocate their time and attention (Dutton, 1997, p. 81 ff.). Since both strategic issue diagnosis and agenda building essentially are critical top management activities, also here it is top managers who are in the focus. Nevertheless, recent research has also emphasized the possible role of middle managers in these processes. I.e., as at the middle management level possible strategic issues are continuously recognized and diagnosed, if these managers see any new issues as strategically relevant, they will tend to influence the top management's attention and understanding of these issues. This behaviour towards affecting the organisation's strategic agenda is called *issue selling* (Dutton & Ashford, 1993, p. 398). Figure 7 illustrates the major elements of the strategic issue management process.

Lastly, although not incorporated in the below illustration, a final finding that has emerged from empirical research in this tradition and that is worth mentioning here, is the strong linkage pointed to between **issue interpretation** and **context** (Thomas & McDaniel, 1990, p. 299 ff.). In this sense, even though 'context' is not differentiated in any true details, the context-dependant nature of strategic decisions is still recognized.

---

[45] Ansoff defines a strategic issue as "... a forthcoming development, either inside or outside the organisation, which is likely to have an important impact on the ability of the enterprise to meet its objectives" (Ansoff, 1980).

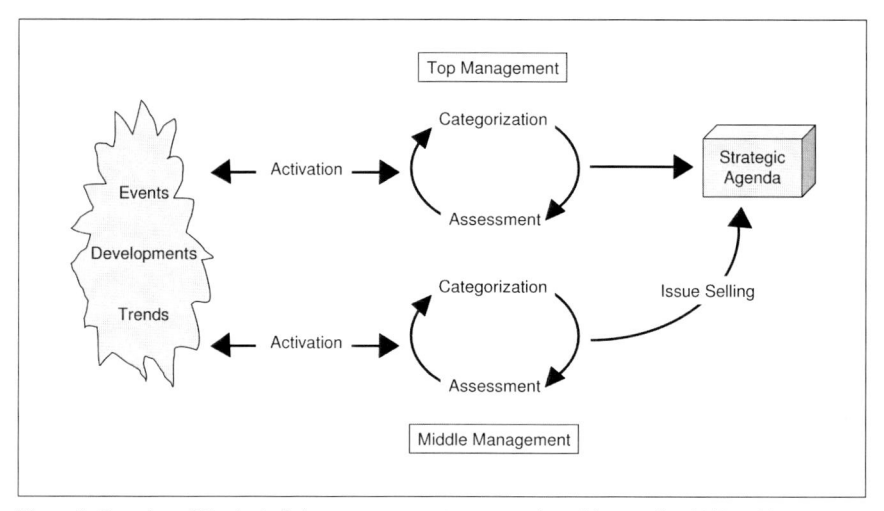

Figure 7: **Overview of the strategic issue management process** (adopted from Aadne, 2000, p. 24)

3.2.6 The "micro" perspective

In the preceding sections the major theoretical approaches to strategy process research have been outlined. Here then, in light of the currently existing six perspectives in the field identified by Hutzschenreuter & Kleindienst (2006) (cf. 3.1), it is in fact only the rational-mechanistic and the cognitive perspectives which are clearly based on some of these particular theories. In line with this, even though like the others (i.e., the upper-echelon, middle management, and organic), also the micro perspective seems to represent more a 'community' of scholars rather than a singular theoretical approach in its own, due to the fact that it is actually the newest and currently most 'active' perspective in the field, it still merits to be treated in a separate section here.

In this regard, the original term, "activity based view", used by Johnson et al. (2003), has by now been subsumed within the broader research agenda for what has generally come to be known under the label of "strategy-as-practice". Here then, 'practice' refers both to the situated doings of the individual human beings (micro) and to the different socially defined practices (macro) that the individuals are drawing upon in these doings (Jarzabkowski, Balogun, & Seidl, 2007, pp. 6-7).

Many indicators clearly attest for the recent rapid growth in the number of scholars subscribing to this perspective, e.g. popular conference tracks at major conferences worldwide,[46] five

---

[46] See summaries of conferences and workshops over the past years (i.e. since 2002) under 'News and Events' on www.strategy-as-practice.org.

special journal editions published focusing explicitly 's-as-p' research,[47] books,[48] an official website (www.strategy-as-practice.org), and a fast growing virtual community of over 2800 members,[49] as well a growing number of top-tier journal publications.

Regarding its origins, this stream started to emerge from a general unease with the way that strategy research had developed over the last three decades, especially from the fact that it had 'lost sight of human beings'. Even though it is recognized that process researchers have made important contributions, most work remains on the macro level, i.e. on investigating strategic developments and change processes of the organisation as a whole. In order to understand human agency in the construction and enactment of strategy, scholars increasingly deem it necessary to re-focus research on the actions and interactions of strategy practitioners, i.e. to look at the micro activities. This reinstatement of agency in strategic action is located within the wider 'practice turn' (e.g. Orlikowski, 1992, 2000; Schatzki, Knorr-Cetina, & Savigny, 2001) or 'linguistic turn' (e.g. Alvesson & Karreman, 2000; Grant, Hardy, Oswick, & Putnam, 2003) in the social sciences, which has arisen in response to a general dissatisfaction with the prescriptive models and frameworks arising from normal science modes of research. Strategy-as-practice may thus be seen as "part of a broader concern to humanize management and organization research" (Jarzabkowski et al., 2007, p. 6).

Scholars taking up this perspective then are not mainly concerned with the content of strategies as something an *organization has,* but interest lies more with what its *members do* (Jarzabkowski & Seidl, 2008, p. 1391). Strategy is thus conceptualized as a **social 'practice'** (Whittington, 1996, p. 731). In line with this, strategy-as-practice starts from the proposition that value lies increasingly in the micro activities of managers and others in organizations, both at the centre as well as the periphery. Concerns therefore focus on the consequential details of organizational work and practice (e.g. Whittington, 2003), and on understanding the myriad micro activities that make up strategy and strategizing, i.e. the devising or planning of strategies, in practice. Researchers go deep inside organizations, their strategies and their processes, to investigate what is actually done and by whom, i.e. emphasis is set on "the detailed processes and practices which constitute the day-to-day activities of organizational life *and* which relate to strategic outcomes" (Johnson et al., 2003, p. 3).

---

[47] I.e. *European Management Review* (McKiernan & Carter, 2004); *Human Relations* (Balogun, Jarzabkowski, & Seidl, 2007b); *Long Range Planning* (Whittington & Cailluet, 2008); *Journal of Management Studies* (Johnson, Melin, & Whittington, 2003); *Revue Francaise de Gestion* (Rouleau, Allard-Poesi, & Warnier, 2007)

[48] There are four foundation books that set out key characteristics, as well as methodological and philosophical implications of this so-called s-as-p perspective, i.e. Golsorkhi (2006), Jarzabkowski (2005), Johnson et al. (2007), Golsorkhi et al. (2009).

[49] Numbers as of April 2009.

Although researchers in this perspective still share much with the earlier works on strategic processes, i.e. like all process research they dig inside the 'black box' of the internal dynamics of organizations, the micro perspective wishes to delve even further into it. Micro strategy and strategizing is concerned with the same strategic issues (e.g. diversification, competitive advantage, organizational performance, etc.) but in terms of the organizational activities and practices which are at their fabric. Their agenda is distinct in that it is concerned with the enduring issues in strategy that come from the bottom-up, from the activities that constitute the substance of strategic management. With all this, one of its explicit aims is then also to overcome the traditional divide between *content* and *process* issues that has existed for so long in the strategy field (cf. 2.1).

Furthermore, while the most distinguishing characteristic of research in this tradition is its particular sensitivity to specific strategic practices and activities, at the same time it clearly recognizes that these micro activities need to be understood in their **social context**: Actors are not acting in isolation but they draw upon the regular, socially defined modes of acting that arise from the plural social institutions to which they belong in order to ensure that their actions and interactions are meaningful to others (e.g. Balogun, Jarzabkowski, & Seidl, 2007a; Chia & MacKay, 2007; Whittington, 2006; Wilson & Jarzabkowski, 2004). One must thus look to those social structures, such as tools, technologies and discourses, through which micro actions are constructed and which, in turn, construct the possibilities for action (Jarzabkowski & Seidl, 2008, p. 1391). In line with this, much of this social infrastructure through which micro-actions are constructed has macro, institutionalized properties that enable its transmission within and between contexts, whilst being adopted and adapted differently within micro-contexts (e.g. Seidl, 2007; Wilson & Jarzabkowski, 2004). The strategy-as-practice approach thus emphasizes explicit links between micro- and macro perspectives on strategy as a social practice (e.g. Jarzabkowski, 2004; Whittington, 2006).

Overall, the strategy-as-practice literature treats **strategy as a situated, socially accomplished activity**; focussing upon the unfolding nature of strategy as interplay between wider social practices and the micro-level of **situated actions**, interactions and negotiations, as actors draw upon these practices to accomplish that strategic activity (e.g. Jarzabkowski et al., 2007; Johnson et al., 2003; Whittington, 2006). As such, strategy-as-practice agendas call for empirical studies into the way that social practices, such as tools, technologies or discourses, are implicated in situated strategizing activities (Jarzabkowski & Seidl, 2008, p. 1416). To this end, several studies have been initiated including research into e.g. the successes and failures in strategizing processes (Maitlis & Lawrence, 2003); the construction of social order and the use of language and discourse in shaping strategic direction (Samra-Fredericks, 2004); a longitudinal case study into an engineering firm, which found that evolutionary processes were driven by a recombination of core micro-strategies, micro-processes and microbehaviours (Salvato, 2003); and, the development of specific skills and the career patterns of strategy practitioners (Hendry & Seidl, 2003).

Taken together, the micro perspective or "strategy-as-practice" can be considered a valuable addition to the existing approaches to research on strategic processes. Particularly, in line with their concern with the effectiveness of strategists rather than organisations, these contributions reflect the call for a more "innovative and multidisciplinary approach for the study of everyday [strategic] practice" (Samra-Fredericks, 2003, p. 167). Here then, while sensitivity to contextual factors and micro-level considerations are clearly nothing entirely new in research on strategic processes, it seems to be especially the strong focus on empirical, especially qualitative in-depth, projects, which makes this kind of research distinctive. With the change of focus, methods,[50] and in many cases also unit of analysis initiated by these studies, also the discourse by which strategy research is explained and communicated is today increasingly being transformed (e.g. Chia & MacKay, 2007).

Finally, regarding their theoretical foundations, the widely perceived lack of any explicit theoretical roots is often voiced as a point of critique against research from this 'school'. To certain extents this scepticism seems justified because as mentioned at the outset here already, in comparison to the other approaches presented before, the micro perspective seems to represent more a 'community' of scholars rather than a new theoretical approach in its own. In line with this impression, adherents of this perspective, however, actually emphasize themselves that practice research is in fact not confined to one theoretical lens, but instead it can and does draw on a variety of different theoretical foundations (Jarzabkowski et al., 2007, p. 19 f.). In line with the fact that there is generally no shortage of theoretical perspectives upon which researchers in strategic management can build (cf. 2.3), practice scholars thus draw e.g. on structuration theory, institutional theory, script theory, or on concepts and ideas from social psychology, and they apply these exiting lenses to illuminate on different phenomena in the strategy process.

---

[50] Methodologically the discipline of strategic management has been traditionally dominated by quantitative approaches and methods. In line with the specific nature of their 'objects' of interest and study, practice researchers against that employ a large spectrum of qualitative methods that are often even quite 'innovative' (at least for research in business studies).

In conclusion, the above outlined propositions and assumptions underlying and characterizing the practice approach to strategy research are clearly largely in line with the own conceptualization of strategic processes advanced initially: I.e., strategies and strategic issues are seen as the outcome of or subject to a plurality of situated, socially accomplished activities that take place in the context of continuously unfolding strategic processes. Of particular interest and value in the present research context is then also their recognition and discussion of the various kinds and occasions where these strategic activities (can) take place in organisations. Referring to the existing works on e.g. strategy workshops, board meetings, committees, awaydays, etc., all of these point to the existence of many different 'forums' in which social actions and interactions important for strategizing, and thus for strategic outcomes, occur.

Here then, despite these benefits and the commonalities with the own present view, however, with their emphasis on overt social practices in strategizing, any explicit discussions or considerations of the cognitive implications or underlying cognitive processes among the actors involved is forgone. Also, even though a link between the micro and the macro level is explicitly attempted, the specific focus on the micro activities still results in a quite focused research agenda, which thus again (like in the other perspectives), allows investigating in-depth only a fragment of the entire strategic processes, leaving out other elements.

Drawing on the latter argument, in the following now, two more comprehensive conceptualizations of strategic processes shall be presented. The own specific socio-cognitive view on strategic processes developed and discussed in detail in the final sections of this chapter then draws on and integrates the various insights outlined up to that point.

3.3 Theory spanning perspectives on strategy processes

From the above outline of the different theoretical approaches and perspectives in strategy process research it has become clear that the field is truly multi-perspective. Each of the different streams looks at specific aspects or issues and all are certainly noteworthy for their respective contributions. The result is an amazing set of partly competing, partly overlapping models (cf. Hutzschenreuter & Kleindienst, 2006, p. 674 ff.). On the one hand, such diversity is of course valuable since different perspectives and disciplinary contributions provide far more insights into the strategy process phenomenon than a single perspective could do. On the other hand, however, the proliferation of concepts and frameworks fosters a complexity in which it is easy to get lost. This is also problematic because research from each of the perspectives is basically only concerned with certain specific aspects of the whole. Different empirical studies thus find support for these seemingly disparate views of the strategy process.

Like the proverbial blind man describing different parts of an elephant, each perspective thus provides a different description of the beast unconnected with the others (cf. Mintzberg et al., 2007, p. 15 ff.).

Even though a unifying theory that can reconcile these multiple perspectives is still lacking (Chakravarthy & White, 2002, p. 182), there are, however, a few approaches that have attempted to provide a more comprehensive theory. In this context, two of the most important examples of such more broadly conceptualized approaches, which integrate and extend several of the existing contributions to strategy process research, are the conceptions on strategy formation and strategy 'genesis' by Mintzberg and by Kirsch et al., respectively. At present, these are among the most encompassing and differentiated perspectives on the emergence of strategic phenomena (Bamberger & Wrona, 2004, p. 341). Because each of these perspectives, however, is based on a different conception of strategy, they also refer to different, even though often in many ways connected, areas of interest. Taking up again the above introduced distinction between strategies as *ex ante* orientations or plans and *ex post* observed manoeuvres or patterns (cf. 2.2), Mintzberg chooses structures or manoeuvres as the central focus in his works. Kirsch's research against that is centred on strategies as strategic orientations. Even though, as stated in 2.2, the specific conception of strategy that is of interest in the present research corresponds largely to that of Kirsch's **ex ante orientations**, in his works Kirsch himself refers explicitly to Mintzberg. As these two approaches can thus be seen as complementary rather than competing, both of them will be outlined briefly in the following. Subsequent to this, based on the entirety of outlines thus far in this chapter, it will be shown that there are in fact different dimensions for describing and characterising strategic processes. These dimensions and variables (i.e. activities, process types, actors, content, context) will then be described in order to finally present an own socio-cognitive view on strategic processes.

3.3.1 Strategy "formation" according to Mintzberg[51]

Few people have had as much influence on the field of strategic management and on strategy process research in particular, as Henry Mintzberg. Overall, with his numerous works in which he has attempted to draw a holistic picture of organizations and to classify them, Mintzberg has made significant contributions to the field, both as regards theoretical and empirical achievements. In 1985, he and James Waters published "Of strategies, deliberate and

---

[51] This summary of Mintzberg's work draws on a similar compilation provided by Bamberger & Wrona (2004, pp. 342-350).

emergent", which reflected the findings of several research studies conducted over a period of years (Mintzberg, 1973, 1978; Mintzberg & Waters, 1982, 1984). It could be argued that Mintzberg's work, based on a distinctive system of concepts, created a paradigm shift in the way scholars think about strategy.

At the core of Mintzberg's research is his definition of "strategy" as a pattern that emerges over time from the decisions and actions taken by the members of an organization (Mintzberg & McHugh, 1985, p. 161; Mintzberg & Waters, 1985, p. 257). In contrast to the early decision-oriented works in the field, which defined strategies in terms of openly formulated plans, Mintzberg considers such a restriction to **formulation processes** as too narrow or limiting. Instead, in his view, strategies can 'form up' through different decisions both internal and external to the organization, even if they have not been deliberately developed (**formation processes**). Strategies thus are historical patterns in organizational behaviour that can be "isolated…and identified as…consistencies" over time (Mintzberg & Waters, 1985, p. 257). A particular significance of this definition is that by suggesting that strategy results, over time, from the different kinds of activities of multiple organizational actors, it clearly broadens the view of strategy to encompass more than top management decision making.

Based on this conceptual view, Mintzberg and his colleagues' empirical research is consequently also designed more broadly compared to the traditional, decision and planning focused, approaches. Specifically, they investigate the relations between managerial intentions or the plans they develop, and firms' actual behaviour. According to them, all strategies are at least somewhat intentional because without intention it is unlikely that there would be a pattern or consistency to behaviour. Another component of strategy, however, is emergent. **Emergent strategy** is a pattern that is realized without intentions, without being anticipated in the thinking of top management, or perhaps, *despite* it. Thus, the concept of realized strategy can be broken down into intentions that lead to **deliberate strategy**, intentions that lead to **unrealized strategy** (i.e. ideas that fail to be implemented), and **emergent strategies** that develop as part of a pattern but without being intentional a priori (cf. also 2.2 specifically on Mintzberg's different conceptions of 'strategy').

In line with these conceptual distinctions, Mintzberg basically assumes that firms' observable behaviour never comes about only in a completely emergent manner or in a completely intended manner. Intended strategies on the one hand, and emergent strategies on the other, merely represent the idealized end points of a **continuum**. An organization's real strategy formation takes place somewhere between these two poles. It is determined by the interplay of environmental influences, firm internal forces and the organization's leadership (Mintzberg, 1978, p. 941).

Following from the empirical observations Mintzberg made based on these theoretical considerations, one of his central conclusions is that the synoptic ideal of an intended and then also implemented strategy is only one possibility for how strategies can develop. The phenomenon of emergent strategies clearly shows that in reality the assumptions of perfect information on the side of the planer and a stable environment are normally not given. Planned strategies change during the course of implementation such that the result of strategy formation possibly diverges quite substantially from the intentions formulated before. In addition, the relationship between emergent and intended strategies does not only have to be unilateral, but it is also reciprocal. The management transforms an unplanned pattern ex post into an intended strategy and like that rationalizes the firm's behaviour. The development of strategies thus usually does not happen in one big shot as the result of formalised planning processes, but the process may also have strong incremental traits. Following from this, Mintzberg contrasts the (phase-) models of rational decision behaviour (cf. 3.2.1) with his own **"grass-roots model"** of strategy formation (see Table 3).

Table 3: **Mintzberg's grass-roots model of strategy formation** (summarized from Mintzberg & McHugh, 1985, pp. 194-196)

1.	Strategies grow initially like weeds in a garden and they are not cultivated like tomatoes in a hothouse. The process of strategy formation can be overmanaged; sometimes it is more important to let patterns emerge than to force an artificial consistency upon an organization prematurely. The hothouse, if needed, can come later.
2.	These strategies can take root in all kinds of places, virtually wherever people have the capacity to learn and the resources to support that capacity. ... Neither where the strategies will emerge, nor the strategies themselves can be entirely planned or controlled. Instead, strategies can develop 'accidentally' within the mind of a single person, in a group, or through influences from the external environment.
3.	Such strategies become organizational when they become collective, that is, when the patterns proliferate, to pervade the behaviour of the organization at large. What looked like weed initially becomes the favoured plant in the garden. The emerging strategy can sometimes replace the existing one.
4.	The process of proliferation may be conscious and may be managed, or may be left to itself. In the latter case, patterns can emerge through collective actions. Once the strategies are recognized as valuable, the process of proliferation can be managed.
5.	The pervasion of new strategies, which themselves may be emerging continuously, tends to occur during distinct periods of divergence that punctuate distinct periods of convergence of established, prevalent strategies, in which organisations rely on existing strategies.
6.	To manage this process is not to preconceive strategies but to recognize their emergence and intervene when appropriate. To manage in this context is to create the climate within which a wide variety of strategies can grow.

Mintzberg emphasizes, however, that an encompassing theory of strategic processes has to incorporate ideas from both these models. Neither one of them is able to fully explain real strategy processes. Similarly, also real strategies develop neither purely intentionally nor purely emergent. Besides thus calling for respecting both approaches, he also points to the importance of taking situational factors into account such as e.g. environmental complexity and dynamics, managerial experiences, or an organization's general willingness to transform intended into realized strategies (Mintzberg & McHugh, 1985).

In line with these outlines, for showing how such positions on a continuum between the two (ideal) models of strategy formation may look like, Mintzberg and Waters (1985) identified eight **strategy types** which correspond to firms' real behaviour (see Table 4). These types then not only represent various combinations of deliberate and emergent components, but they also differ in terms of:
- Environmental characteristics,
- Design, role or importance of management systems,
- Activities and impact of leadership.

Table 4: Summary description of Mintzberg's strategy types (Mintzberg & Waters, 1985, p. 270)

Strategy	Major features
Planned	Strategies originate in formal plans: precise intentions exist, formulated and articulated by central leadership, backed up by formal controls to ensure surprise-free implementation in benign, controllable or predictable environment; strategies most deliberate
Entrepreneurial	Strategies originate in central vision: intentions exist as personal, unarticulated vision of single leader, and so adaptable to new opportunities; organization under personal control of leader and located in protected niche environment; strategies relatively deliberate but can emerge
Ideological	Strategies originate in shared beliefs: intentions exist as collective vision of all actors, in inspirational form and relatively immutable, controlled normatively through indoctrination and/or socialization; organization often proactive, vis-á-vis environment; strategies rather deliberate
Umbrella	Strategies originate in constraints: leadership, in partial control of organizational actions, defines strategic boundaries or targets within which other actors respond to own forces or to complex, perhaps also unpredictable environment; strategies partly deliberate. Partly emergent and deliberately emergent
Process	Strategies originate in process: leadership controls process aspects of strategy (hiring, structure, etc.), leaving content aspects to other actors; strategies partly deliberate, partly emergent (and, again, deliberately emergent)
Unconnected	Strategies originate in enclaves: actor(s) loosely coupled to rest of organization produce(s) patterns in own actions in absence of, or in direct contradiction to, central or common intentions: strategies organizationally emergent whether or not deliberate for actor(s)
Consensus	Strategies originate in consensus: through mutual adjustment, actors converge on patterns that become pervasive in absence of central or common intentions; strategies rather emergent
Imposed	Strategies originate in environment: environment dictates patterns in actions either through direct imposition or through implicitly pre-empting or bounding organizational choice; strategies most emergent, although may be internalized by organization and made deliberate

Concerning these different strategy types it is finally important to note that all eight represent "mixed modes". Purely deliberate and purely emergent forms, while conceivable, are impossible as a practical matter.

In conclusion, even though a number of critiques have been voiced against his works, Mintzberg can nevertheless be accredited for having developed a quite differentiated framework for the description of strategies and strategic processes, which is based on a wide theoretical and empirical foundation (Bamberger & Wrona, 2004, p. 349). Overall, Mintzberg's works are indeed innovative and clearly stand out from the mainstream in strategic management research. As a consequence, his ideas have and are still giving a number of impulses for management research in general and works on strategy formation in particular. His research also had a great influence on the works by Kirsch and his colleagues.

3.3.2 The "genesis" of strategies according to Kirsch[52]

The works of Kirsch and his colleagues, also called the "Munich school" or "Munich approach" to evolutionary management, constitute the most comprehensive theoretical framework of ideas on strategic management in the German-speaking area. It consists of terminological, conceptual, and methodological basics for the analysis of management phenomena, particularly issues in strategic management (cf. e.g. Kirsch, 1970, 1971, 1991, 1992, 1996, 1997a, 1997b; Kirsch, Esser, & Gabele, 1979; Kirsch & Maaßen, 1990; Kirsch & Trux, 1989).

Already early on Kirsch made considerable contributions and added to progress in the area of action-oriented process research. Specifically, he is accredited for having worked on and extended the ideas of incrementalism by Braybrooke & Lindblom (1963) and Lindblom (1965), the information processing approach to decision behaviour, for his early emphasis on political processes in strategic management, as well as for the integration of strategic planning into the broader field of strategic management. From these works a well differentiated account of the formation and implementation of strategies has resulted. In this context, Kirsch's aim is to present directions for the development of action-oriented management research which goes beyond the decision-oriented approaches to strategic processes, and which also extends Mintzberg's works, or research on the cognitive perspective (cf. for this particularly Broich, 1994; Kirsch, 1997c).

---

[52] The following concise summary of Kirsch's works has been adopted and translated from Bamberger & Wrona, 2004, p. 350-355.

Kirsch's overall conception is based on assumptions of "**moderate voluntarism**"[53]. According to this view, organisational development is neither predetermined (determinism), nor does it proceed entirely in line with the intentions of the organization's key 'designers' (voluntarism). While organisations are thus generally changeable on intent, due to deficits in knowledge and resistances to change, the well- directed management of change is nevertheless seen sceptically. As a result, strategic issues and especially strategies in the form of strategic orientations can develop even in the absence of any such management intentions (Kirsch et al., 1979, p. 232 f.).

Whereas Mintzberg uses the term "strategy formation" for his discussion of the development of organizational strategies, Kirsch uses "genesis" for his analyses. A crucial distinction, which is of particular importance in the context of the present research, is Kirsch's view on the central concept of "strategy". While Mintzberg focuses on 'observable' issues, Kirsch differentiates explicitly between **"individual strategies"** (*Individualstrategien*), **"strategies for the organization"** (*Strategien für die Organisation*), and **"organizational strategies"** (*Strategien der Organisation*). Concerning the first of these, the assumption is that different actors also have different interests, which they aim to realize through their (strategic) activities. These interests can have the character of *strategies* and then constitute 'individual strategies' related to the organisation. In cases where such individual claims or interests become openly addressed to the organisation's key actors with the aim of having them officially approved, they become 'strategies for the organisation'. 'Organisational strategies' finally are those of the former requests that have been authorized officially through the political system (cf. fundamentally Kirsch, 1969; Kirsch, 1971; and Kirsch, 1996, p. 117 ff.).

For Kirsch it remains an empirical question whether there are really decision processes in an organization through which the heterogeneous individual strategies or strategies for the organization are transformed into authorized organizational strategies (Kirsch, 1996, p. 119). Especially for political decisions, with repercussions on the distribution of power in the political system, a renunciation on explicit organizational strategies seems feasible.

Related to this, and similar to Mintzberg, is the relativasation of the importance of explicitly formulated strategies for strategy formation. Even though there are certainly explicit strategy formulations, e.g. in the context of strategic planning processes, these constitute, however, merely 'episodes' within the "Ongoing Process", i.e. the ongoing flow of decisions, actions and interactions in organizations. Strategies can also emerge along different paths outside of

---

[53] The moderate voluntarism can be traced back to the works of Klages (1971), Mannheim (1958), Popper (1965), Lindblom (1965), and Etzioni (1968).

such episodes, i.e. they can '**form up**'.[54] In line with this, Kirsch thus focuses on the ongoing process, and not on concrete decision episodes that are oriented towards the adoption of strategic plans. As a consequence, organizational strategies are conceived of as always being '**ex definitione formed up**'. Strategy formulations against that are merely considered as special cases or partial episodes within the ongoing process. The task here is to investigate in how far they influence the formation process.

To characterize his 'formed up' organizational strategies, Kirsch derives four specific criteria[55] (Kirsch 1996, p. 127 f.):

- Action orientations in the form of principles exist, because only like this a certain generalization of the action orientation can be assumed.
- These principles get attributed a political will.
- The principles bear reference to organizational success potentials.
- The involved persons have shared knowledge about these principles.

In order to explain how these kinds of strategies develop, it is exactly these above outlined characteristics which constitute the starting point for the analysis. Questions here may for example be: How do strategic orientations obtain the character of principles? How does shared knowledge about these develop among the involved actors?

For Kirsch, the answer to these questions has to be found in the ongoing organizational processes. A central thesis here is that reflections, i.e. non-incidental discussions or communications, about the ongoing process and strategy related issues foster strategy formation. This kind of "basic process of strategy formation" is an integral part of the ongoing process (cf. Figure 8). It does not necessarily have to take place in the context of isolated decision processes, and in extreme cases it does not even have to be influenced by such processes. Instead, it may take place on the fringes of 'formal' organizational processes. Informal talks and interactions between organizational members in situations where there is no pressure to produce any specific results (e.g. in the context of chimney conversations, company parties, informal lunches, etc.) would be examples of such opportunities. The more of such reflections about actions and principles occur, the more shared knowledge will finally develop about them.

---

[54] An example of such a formed up organizational strategy would be that individual manoeuvres are oriented repeatedly towards a particular pattern, even if no explicit authorisations exist for this.

[55] These criteria were originally formulated by Kirsch in an internal working paper (cf. Kirsch, 1993, p. 151 as cited by Broich, 1994, p. 17).

3 – Strategic processes

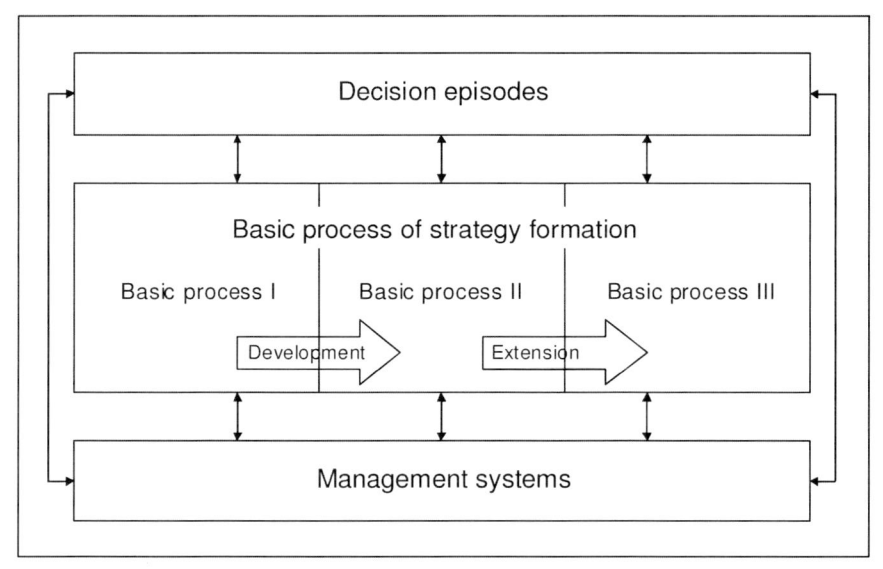

Figure 8: Process categories of strategy 'genesis' in its context (Broich, 1994, p. 26)

As illustrated in Figure 8, the basic process of strategy formation can take place on three successive, but content-wise and procedurally different, levels of development.

1. The first level (basic process I) corresponds to the ongoing process. Here, organizational actors follow, reproduce, and at the same time further the development of the rules or orientations of the organizational "environment" (*Lebenswelt*).
2. The second level (basic process II) is reached when, in the context of their activities and interactions, organizational members start to think intentionally about whether and how (parts of) organisational processes can be traced back to maxims or are directed by these.
3. A third level is reached (basic process III) when reflections address explicitly the capabilities or potentials of the organization.

Even though Kirsch's focus for explaining strategy formation is clearly on the ongoing process, apart from this, he nevertheless also includes the possibility that explicit **decision processes** exist from which strategies emerge. Reflections may for example occur in the basic process that initiate or influence episodes of political decision processes. The explicit and authorized strategy formulations elaborated in these processes can then in turn have a significant influence on the basic process of strategy formation.

In addition to these decision episodes, the model further includes the role of **management systems**[56] in the ongoing process. In this context, planning and information systems, for example, constitute a method for the professional observation of strategic manoeuvres, the own organization, or the environment. As such they thus further reflection processes (Kirsch, 1996, p. 138 ff.). In addition, in line with their implementation function, management systems also have an important indirect influence on all the factors relevant for the genesis of strategies.

Finally, Kirsch discusses the relationship between **organizational strategies** and **strategic manoeuvres**. Here, a strategic manoeuvre is the concrete strategic behaviour which can be observed from persons external to the organization. While in much of the research on strategic processes manoeuvres follow the strategies that have (been) developed before (i.e. strategies as 'strategic orientations' or ex ante 'plans'), Kirsch also considers the opposite case as possible. I.e., observing the strategic behaviour of the organization from an outsider perspective may initiate or influence activities of strategy genesis, and like that impact more or less strongly on the formation of new strategies. In such cases then, strategies follow manoeuvres.

3.4 Towards an own – socio-cognitive – view on strategic processes

Now, in the above outline of the development of research on process issues in strategic management it was shown that there are indeed different conceptualizations and views on what strategic processes really are and thus also on how these processes are to be explained. As the overall field is quite complex and diverse, researchers approach it from various perspectives and usually focus on different particular aspects within the whole. Clearly, all this is also closely connected to the specific conceptualization or view on 'strategy' adopted in a concrete research context (cf. 2.2).

Typically then, the research on strategic processes is pursued from a single perspective (e.g. the rational, evolutionary, cognitive, political, or micro perspective), the choice of which often depends on the disciplinary bias of the researcher. Despite their individual merits, unfortunately each of these approaches only provides a partial understanding of a complex process. Also, only rarely are these studies contextually and historically situated. Strategic processes, however, span long periods of time and traverse multiple levels (multi-level process). In fact, they bridge the cognitive processes of individual decision makers, the social

---

[56] Management systems actually represent a huge research area in themselves. In the present research they shall thus not be discussed in more detail. Instead, management systems are rather considered as part of the 'internal context' (cf. 3.4.1.5).

psychological and political processes within groups of individuals, the organizational rules and routines that guide and constrain the decisions and actions of organizational members, and ecological considerations that affect the survival and success of firms (Chakravarthy & White, 2002, p. 183). In addition, regarding their most central object, 'strategies' can be both intended and emergent and they result from action taking that may or may not be preceded by concrete decision making.

In line with all this, as observed by Chakravarthy & White (2002, 184 ff.), a large part of the difficulty of providing more comprehensive and adequate accounts of strategic processes is due to the nested and inter-related nature of these processes. A process of **variation-selection-retention** occurs at the individual cognitive level (e.g. Neisser, 1976), the group/social level (e.g. Weick, 1979, 1995), the organizational level (e.g. Nelson & Winter, 1982) and has been extended to the population of firms (e.g. Hannan & Freeman, 1989). Importantly, what occurs at one level affects the other levels. The process at one level creates the context for the next level. Both external selection and internal selection, together, determine the fates of organizations. Meaningful process research thus requires rich linkages through time and across levels. As it is clear that better integrated perspectives have to be forged, the field urgently needs a few ambitious multidisciplinary research programs. Only through such it is possible to arrive at the broader and more encompassing view that scholars increasingly call for.

Following from the above, the theory that would be needed here should take more of a systems view of the process and accommodate dynamic interactions between context, process and outcomes (Chakravarthy & White, 2002, p. 199). Even though this theory in its complete form does not yet exist, the works by Mintzberg and Kirsch outlined before are two examples that have already done a lot into such a direction. In this regard, in the present work it is clearly neither possible nor the goal to develop a real 'theory' like this. Nevertheless, the socio-cognitive perspective to be developed here still aims at making at least a small contribution, thanks to its (by definition) openly interdisciplinary approach which leads to the inclusion of different focal areas and recognizes process issues at multiple levels. Especially through considering in detail both the cognitive and the social dimensions of strategic processes, respectively, and trying to integrate them, the call for a less narrow-minded and singular view on strategic processes is clearly taken up.

Here then, in line with the concrete research foci at hand, Kirsch's conceptualization of strategic processes is seen as providing the right starting point: I.e., the basis of the socio-cognitive perspective is the conceptualization of **strategic processes as a continuous process** that is embedded in the organization's ongoing process. Strategic processes are made up of decisions, actions and interactions. At their core, strategic processes are then seen as containing cognitive processes as well as social interaction processes. Besides, regarding the specific 'object' of the process, as stated already in Chapter 2, the concern in the present work is on how **'strategies' as shared strategic orientations**, i.e. ex ante mental representations or knowledge structures about the future strategic development of the organization, develop. As mentioned before, shared knowledge about action guiding principles is an important characteristic of 'formed' organizational strategies. In this sense then, shared strategic orientations or knowledge structures can be seen as both *precursors* and *outcome* of actually executed strategic manoeuvres and openly formulated strategy plans. Regarding the first of these, (strategic) cognitions *underlie* and *drive* actors' individual behaviours, which in turn and taken in their totality later accumulate into an organisation's observable 'pattern' of strategic behaviour (i.e. 'organisational strategies' in Kirsch's terminology). Also, especially in many smaller organisations often no formal and written down strategic plans exist but some shared knowledge or orientations must be there as the basis on which the key persons (inter)act (Wrona & Breuer, 2008, p. 2). At the same time, however, commonalities in mental orientations or convergence of knowledge on strategic issues may of course also result from similar experiences and observations that organisational members make by *looking back* at the strategic actions they themselves or others have taken. Altogether then, regarding strategies as shared strategic knowledge structures among the organisation's key actors and examining their development can hence be seen as a valuable and revealing endeavour, which also allows for a better understanding of other kinds of 'strategy phenomena' like e.g. formal strategy plans, concrete manoeuvres or real action structures (cf. 2.2).

Following these basic conceptualisations now, for an adequate analysis of strategic processes (in the outlined sense) an interdisciplinary approach, which forges more integration between the cognitive and social dimensions and issues, is clearly needed. In this context, even though both of these aspects have already been implied in Kirsch's own works, neither of them is treated truly in depth therein. Even more importantly, there is nowhere a discussion of the concrete interrelations between cognitive and social interactive processes (i.e. the "socio-cognitive dynamics"). Whereas the existence of different kinds of strategic **activities** (e.g. planning, decision making, business dinners, etc.) as well as various **occasions** for social interactions among strategic actors (e.g. chimney conversations, conferences, meetings, etc.) is acknowledged, there is no detailed differentiation regarding the implications that the specific characteristics of different strategic processes and occasions ('forums') in which social inter-

3 – Strategic processes 79

actions take place have for the convergence of strategic orientations. Doing this is therefore exactly the aim and the value of the socio-cognitive view developed here.

More concretely, in line with the present conceptualisations, the knowledge structures and individual 'strategies' related to the organisation of the strategically relevant actors are the starting point for the analysis of strategic processes in the present perspective. However, cognition is and must not be seen as isolated inside the minds of individuals (cf. Chapter 4), but the social context is clearly equally important to consider. In fact, it is the interactions taking place and the social factors in the ongoing process which can be regarded as central mediators between the individual and the collective levels (cf. 2.4.6). Acknowledging this, the purely cognitive perspective is thus here extended by explicitly adding the social component and by paying attention to social interaction processes.

In this regard, already Kirsch and others have pointed to the importance of reflection processes and especially **political processes** in the context of strategic processes (cf. e.g. Lindblom, 1964; Pettigrew, 1987; Sandner, 1992). While these are of course also recognized in the present work, rather than picking out merely political processes, the socio-cognitive approach integrates such (political) behaviours into the more comprehensive category of social interaction processes (SIPs). I.e., "social interaction processes" is a broader term which subsumes processes or interactions that may, but must not, be of a political nature. Here then, while there have been numerous studies that highlight the emergent nature of strategy and generally the importance of social interactions in this context, there have been very few studies that really differentiate the different **'forums'** in which such social interaction processes associated with the strategic process(es) (can) occur. Instead of superficially emphasizing the essential role of interactive processes, a second important aspect here is therefore to point explicitly to the different 'forums'. Exactly this differentiated attention and the recognition of the fact that the respective kinds of interactions and hence socio-cognitive dynamics clearly vary according to the different characteristics of the specific occasions for interchange (the 'environment'), is thus of utmost importance with regard to the central research question at hand: I.e., differences concerning how (or to what extent) shared or parallel (strategic) knowledge structures develop in strategic processes are clearly likely to be observed when comparing e.g. the behaviour in and outcome of informal meetings versus formal decision processes.

Finally, as strategic processes are seen as ongoing and as involving many different activities (that are strategically relevant, or that deal with strategically relevant contents), they are clearly not equated with strategic *decision making processes* here (cf. also Bamberger &

Wrona, 2004, p. 327). Nevertheless, the latter still constitute an important element within the overall process. Most notably because decision making (both on specific strategic plans and on other strategically relevant issues) provides a particularly important 'forum' in which managers interact, thereby displaying distinctive socio-cognitive dynamics, a specific consideration shall be given to these kinds of processes. In this context, like can be assumed for any other forum, too, it may then be suggested that depending on the specific values of the dimensions of the decision processes (i.e. formalized, highly political, etc.) also the degree of or possibility for the development of shared knowledge structures varies accordingly.

In line with the latter point, and reflecting now back on all of the above, strategic processes can obviously be quite different in nature so that it is not possible to speak about *the* strategy process. To characterize or describe an organisation's individual strategic processes, different variables can be looked at or dimensions along which these may vary. Even more importantly in the present context, it is then exactly such differences in the characteristics of the strategic processes that clearly also have important implications for the respective socio-cognitive dynamics occurring in them. How and to what extent shared strategic orientations develop thus depends on the specific type of process, i.e. the characteristics of its dimensions.

3.4.1 Dimensions of strategic processes

Having argued for the importance of considering the different dimensions by which individual strategic processes may be described and characterized, an own general framework for analysing strategic processes shall be introduced and discussed here first, which includes such different dimensions. From there, assumptions will then be derived concerning what can be expected in terms of knowledge structure convergence, e.g. where it is most pronounced, how the development in specific cases is, etc. In this regard, at this stage all the assertions to be made remain only tentative. These shall then be developed further in the following chapters, which deal specifically with individual and 'social' cognition (Chapter 4) and with social interaction processes (Chapter 5), respectively.

A useful starting point for developing such a framework and for deriving dimensions is to look at the existing perspectives and works in the field, especially empirical research on strategy process issues. In addition, one particularly valuable conceptual contribution resorted to in this context is the integrative framework outlined by Bamberger & Wrona (2004, p. 355 ff.). These authors suggest conceptualizing strategic processes on the basis of four components. Figure 9 represents their approach.

3 – Strategic processes

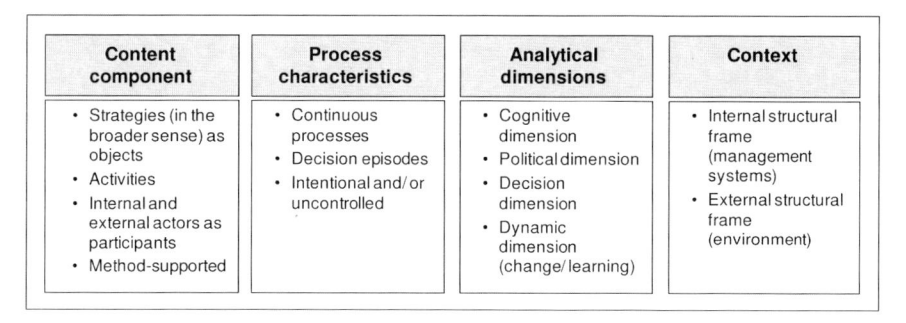

Content component	Process characteristics	Analytical dimensions	Context
• Strategies (in the broader sense) as objects • Activities • Internal and external actors as participants • Method-supported	• Continuous processes • Decision episodes • Intentional and/or uncontrolled	• Cognitive dimension • Political dimension • Decision dimension • Dynamic dimension (change/learning)	• Internal structural frame (management systems) • External structural frame (environment)

Figure 9: Components of a framework for strategic processes (translated from Bamberger & Wrona, 2004, p. 356)

On the basis of a synthesis of these existing conceptual thoughts and the variety of other views and approaches in the field, the own framework for describing and analysing strategic processes in the present context finally consists of five broad dimensions, which each include several sub dimensions (see Figure 10). The dimensions are regarded as suitable as they allow classifying the most important aspects of strategic processes identified in the preceding sections of this chapter. Also, some of the other streams in strategy process research discussed before, which each concentrate (only) on specific aspects or topics under one of the headings here, can be subsumed within this framework.

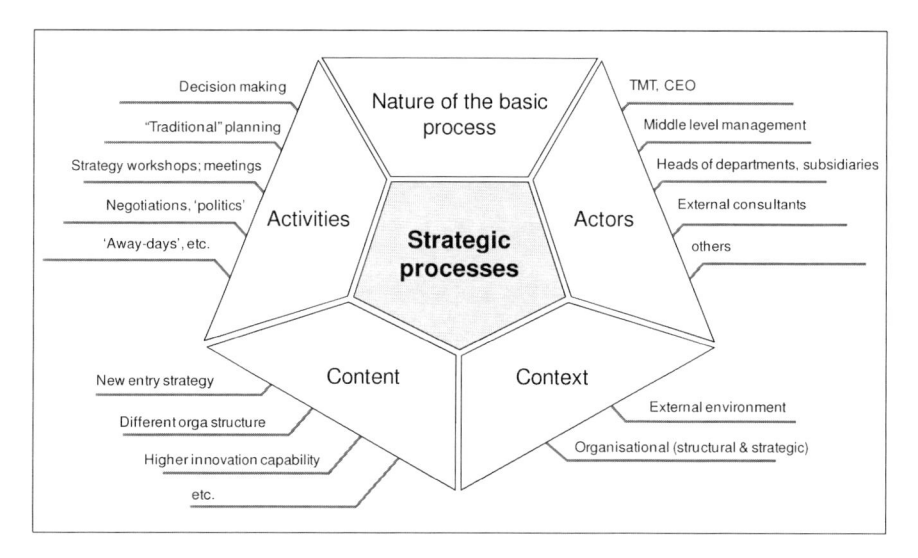

Figure 10: Own framework for analysing strategic processes with corresponding dimensions and exemplary variables

While clearly recognizing their partial interrelatedness, the five dimensions identified are the following:
- the nature of the basic process (synoptic, incremental, etc.),
- the actors involved,
- the activities accomplished,
- the context both external and internal, and
- the specific strategic content (e.g. is it about strategy at the corporate level, the business unit level, or the functional/ departmental level; or about other strategic issues like the organisational structure, its innovation capability, etc.).

Here in fact, depending on the specific perspective taken on strategic processes, clearly different views exist on these issues. In line with the rather broad definition in the present research context, however, the conception is that strategic processes involve diverse actors, (may) proceed in different paces (regarded over the entire evolution of the organisation), and include more than merely decision making activities. In addition, the context in which such processes take place is crucial to consider, particularly the internal environment because it is largely inside the organisation where it is determined how many and what kinds of 'forums' exist in which social interactions take place.

In the following, each of these dimensions is now discussed in more detail.

3.4.1.1 Nature of the basic process

The first dimension is the **nature of the basic process of strategy formation.** Generally, strategic processes, as components of the ongoing process and thus tightly interwoven with the daily "operative" processes, are continuous processes over time. As such they can be either directed intentionally, i.e. be rather deliberate, or proceed without explicit steering, i.e. be rather emergent. In this context, as has been argued before, much strategy practice is said to be *episodic* in nature (Hendry & Seidl, 2003, p. 176 ff.). In line with this, within the overall continuous process different decision and planning episodes may be delineated that are related to generating specific strategic manoeuvres or implementing strategic plans. Here then, within the entire population of organizations, firms' strategic processes clearly vary in terms of e.g. the frequency of such distinctive occurrences (e.g. hardly ever, occasionally, often, regularly), their extent, or the formal versus informal way in which the activities underlying them are carried out. Accordingly, while the progressive form of some strategic processes may thus be described as incremental, smooth or stable, others are more episodic or synoptic (cf. 3.2.2).

A critical determinant or influence on this general process form is related to the particular strategy-making mode or decision making style an organisation uses (see Table 5). While most organisations certainly employ a combination of several different of such 'ideal' styles, some firms will be using a rather huge variety depending on the specific strategy-type in question (e.g. corporate, competitive, market, etc.), whereas others may be quite consistent, thus displaying a more unitary process pattern. Strategy making processes can thus clearly make a difference for the nature of the overall strategic process as they determine for example whether strategy formation is piecemeal or quantum, incremental or revolutionary, or a process of gradual learning versus rapid insight. The different styles also affect which kinds of concrete activities are carried out and by whom, i.e. the role that different organisational members play (cf. e.g. Hart, 1992).

Table 5: Strategy development modes with approximate correspondences (Balabanis & Spyropoulou, 2007, p. 47)

Miller (1987)	Hart (1992)	Dess, Lumpkin and Covin (1997)	Mintzberg and Lamped (1999)	Bailey, Johnson and Daniels (2000)
Rationality	Rational		Design Planning Positioning Environmental	Planning Enforced choice
Interaction	Transactive	Participative Adaptive	Power Learning Cultural	Political Incremental Cultural
	Symbolic Command	Simplistic		Command
Assertive	Generative	Entrepreneurial	Entrepreneurial Cognitive Configurational	

Note: Earlier typologies of strategy development modes have been reviewed and systematically integrated by Hart (1992, p. 336).

3.4.1.2 Actors

The traditional view is that strategy work is and should be the province of top management, and a critical aspect of their ordinary work (Ansoff, 1965; Schendel & Hofer, 1979). Other levels of managers, and particularly middle managers, are merely supposed to play the role as suppliers of necessary information for the strategy process, and instrumental in the process of implementing the decisions made by the top management. A specific research stream in which this focus on top management teams (TMTs) is still today at the centre, is one of the perspectives identified by Hutzschenreuter & Kleindienst (2006, p. 702), i.e. the **upper echelons perspective**. Here, the main message from researchers like Hambrick and his colleagues is that organizational strategies and performance are reflections of the firm's top management: "Organizational outcomes, both strategies and effectiveness, are viewed as reflections of the values and *cognitive bases* of powerful actors in the organization" (Hambrick & Mason, 1984, p. 193). In line with these assumptions, researchers in this tradition look specifically at the cognitive dispositions and properties of top managers and senior executives. Here then, on the one hand, this focus supports the importance given to (shared) knowledge structures in the present research context. On the other hand, however, with "powerful actors" the emphasis is explicitly on firms' TMTs (not on middle managers or other organisational actors). Also, to gain empirical insights into these cognitive structures, the majority of upper echelon studies typically draw on certain observable or easy to measure managerial characteristics (such as age, tenure, educational or functional background, etc.) as indicators or 'proxies' for the subjects' covert cognitive processes and structures. Both, the focus on TMTs and the rather superficial large scale quantitative research approaches, however, are rejected in the present research context: If at all meaningful, demographics are merely weak indicators of managerial cognitions; and, as has been recognized clearly, there are more actors than only an organization's TMT that are involved in or impact on strategic processes.

In support of these assertions, and specifically in line with the latter argument, over time, there has been increasing opposition against the exclusive focus on top managers, which finally led to the development of the **middle management view**, most clearly elaborated in the works of Floyd & Wooldridge (cf. e.g. Floyd & Wooldridge, 2000). These authors point to the importance of other levels of managers and their impact on the process.[57] In line with this, there exists today a growing amount of empirical evidence which clearly shows that it is in fact different groups of participants in strategic debates that can be distinguished (cf. e.g. Schwarz & Nandhakumar, 2002).

Overall thus, in light of these views now, in the socio-cognitive perspective developed here it is therefore clearly recognized that influential actors in strategic processes can not only be organizational members from different, in fact possibly all, levels, but often also **external stakeholders** have an impact or interfere. The relative importance or influence of different stakeholder groups then depends on certain additional factors such as e.g. the size of the organisation, its business or industry context, its culture, the relevant legal system, etc. In any cases, however, it is crucial to recognize that the participants each have different knowledge and expertise in the business, and have different personalities, which are expressed in their beliefs, values and interests. Also the respective communication styles of and among the ac-

---

[57] A similar stance is taken by researchers advancing the *strategic issue diagnosis* view (cf. 3.2.5).

tors vary accordingly. As a result, as observed e.g. by Schwarz & Nandhakumar (2002, p. 77 ff.), the interactions between the different groups of stakeholders or organisational actors are then (often) shaped by different interests and powers. In meetings with senior managers, for example, politics and interests of each senior manager and his organizational unit play an essential role during the discussion. Since it is the actors participating in and contributing to strategic debates that can be said to represent the essential source out of which strategic ideas are generated, to also understand how or to what extent shared strategic orientations develop, it is thus clearly crucial to examine closely who is actually involved in the process(es) and who exactly interacts with whom.

3.4.1.3 (Strategic) Activities

The conceptualization of strategic processes taken here is deliberately wide, thereby including all those decisions, activities and interactions that deal with and generate strategic issues. Strategy is thus clearly connected with a variety of particular types of practices, such as strategic planning, annual reviews, strategy workshops and budget cycles. However, these kinds of activities are often overlooked as the *mundane* practices of strategy (Jarzabkowski & Seidl, 2008, p. 1392). Regarding them merely as a means to an end neglects the way that these routine, institutionalized, and often taken-for granted practices socially structure strategic outcomes (Whittington, 1996, 2003). More recently, research has shown how a study of micro routines and practices can illuminate the way that strategists act and interact and the strategic outcomes that they produce. For example, Sturdy et al. (2006) illustrate how the routinized social structures underpinning *business dinners* are consequential for the way senior consultants construct their business, while Jarzabkowski (2003, p. 51) explains how the recurrent *annual cycles* of formal administrative procedures shape patterns of stability and change in strategic activity over time. Especially thanks to such researchers from the still young 'practice school' (cf. 3.2.6), it is now increasingly widely recognized that there is a multitude of different activities strategists carry out in their strategic reality. In the literature so far, however, the focus is most often on the 'making' of strategies as such and on decisions, i.e. deciding on or implementing certain concrete, formulated strategy concepts. In this context then, strategic processes are even equated with strategic decision making processes (cf. 3.1). While the conception here is clearly broader, decisions (both on specific strategies but also on other strategic issues like e.g. a new organizational structure or configuration) remain of course an important element. Thus, to start with, the decision making line of research and its insights shall be discussed first. In fact, as will be seen, the phases and dimensions often outlined for describing and characterizing strategic decision making processes are in many respects similar or can at least be generalized to strategic processes. As such, strategic processes can thus be seen as subsuming the phases in strategic decision making processes, and the latter can be seen as adding aspects to the former at a more specific level.

(Strategic) Decision-making

Strategic decision making processes were largely and for long regarded as *the* core 'forum' for how strategies are determined. Since accordingly a huge amount of research has been conducted in this area, the examination of strategic decision making processes can be seen as the 'mainstream' in research on strategic processes.

Making decisions is one of the most important managerial activities and generally there are of course many different kinds of decisions taken all the time in organizations. In this context, however, it is crucial to clearly distinguish strategic decisions from decisions which are more of an operational nature.[58] Strategic problems are seen as problems which are highly complex, ill-defined and tainted with high uncertainty. Due to their ill-structuredness and the lack of any clear right- or wrong-solutions they may also be described as 'multi-context' or 'political' problems (Bamberger & Wrona, 2004, p. 376). In line with these characteristics, synthesizing from the relevant literature (cf. also Roberto, 2004, p. 630), strategic decisions can be defined as important choices that:

- have a significant expected impact on future firm performance (e.g. Bourgeois & Eisenhardt, 1988; Mintzberg, Raisinghani, & Théorêt, 1976),
- involve multiple functional organizations (e.g. Bourgeois & Eisenhardt, 1988),
- represent a significant commitment of financial, physical, or human resources (e.g. Bower, 1970; Mintzberg et al., 1976), and
- exhibit high complexity (e.g. Schweiger, Sandberg, & Ragan, 1986).

Moreover, in line with the central importance of the overall field in research on strategic management, a number of different streams and subareas of interest have developed here.[59] At the centre of all of these, however, is the question how, i.e. through which specific processes, strategic decisions are being taken (Rajagopalan et al., 1993, p. 350). Clearly, strategic decisions can be made in quite different ways and thus they cannot be mapped onto a single model like for example an encompassing, systematic planning process. Also, since decision

---

[58] Even though the lines between the two are often blurred.
[59] In line with the truly vast amount of works specifically on strategic decision making (processes), a number of efforts have been undertaken to date that have attempted to classify and work up the existing literature and insights in the field. Among some of the most popular overviews are the following: Eisenhardt & Zbaracki (1992), Huff & Reger (1987), Papadakis et al. (1998), Rajagopalan et al. (1993), Schwenk (1995).

processes are influenced by a number of different factors, it is quite obvious that even within a single organisation, different types or modes will apply for different decision situations. However, based on a comprehensive and critical review of a large amount of works in the area, Rajagopalan et al. (1993) developed a good general model mapping the different influencing factors in strategic decision processes in an integrated framework.[60] Decision processes are accordingly influenced significantly by three major factors (cf. Figure 11):

- external environmental conditions
- organizational factors (e.g. internal structures, power distribution, past strategies and results), and
- situational characteristics of each decision candidate (e.g. threat/ crisis, uncertainty, novelty, and time pressure) (cf. e.g. Dutton & Jackson, 1987; Hickson, Butler, Cray, Mallory, & Wilson, 1986; Mintzberg et al., 1976; Papadakis et al., 1998).

Environmental factors
- Uncertainty
- Complexity
- Munificence

Organizational factors
- Past performance
- Past strategies
- Organization structure
- Power distribution
- Organization size
- Organizational slack
- TMT characteristics

Decision process characteristics
- Comprehensiveness
- Decision rationality
- Degree of political activity
- Participation/ involvement
- Duration/ length
- Extent/ type of conflict

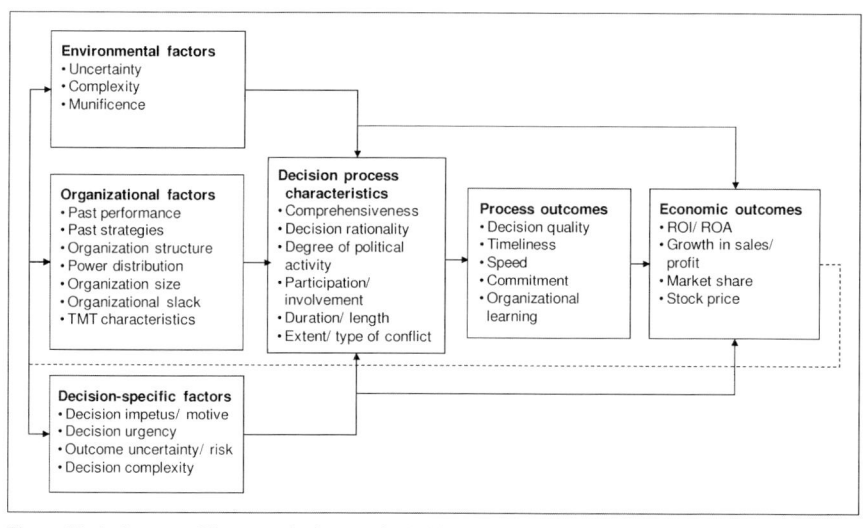

Process outcomes
- Decision quality
- Timeliness
- Speed
- Commitment
- Organizational learning

Economic outcomes
- ROI/ ROA
- Growth in sales/ profit
- Market share
- Stock price

Decision-specific factors
- Decision impetus/ motive
- Decision urgency
- Outcome uncertainty/ risk
- Decision complexity

Figure 11: An integrated framework of strategic decision processes (adopted from Rajagopalan et al., 1993, p. 352)

Besides identifying such **influencing factors**, another crucial question concerns the concrete **process characteristics** or dimensions by which different decision processes may be characterized or described. In this context, both Rajagopalan et al. (1993) as well as other, especially empirical studies, have made important contributions by focusing on and delineating a num-

---

[60] For readers interested in more details see the article in which Rajagopalan et al. give a good overview of the different works that have dealt with the direct or indirect influence of the three influencing factors (environment, organisation, and decision situation) on the decision process.

ber of variables or dimensions, whose different and combined values then allow for mapping quite diverse process forms (cf. e.g. Eisenhardt & Zbaracki, 1992; Papadakis et al., 1998; Rajagopalan et al., 1993). Among some of the most important variables in this context are the following (Bamberger & Wrona, 2004, pp. 377-378):

- type and sequence of activities executed, as well as the respective length of these individual activities and of the overall process
- actors involved
- rationality (also termed *comprehensiveness*, i.e. intensity/ depth of information gathering)
- 'politisation' (refers to the extent of negotiation processes, coalition building, the use of political tactics or the opposition of the actors involved)
- degree of process formalization or standardization
- division of labour (includes e.g. also hierarchical centralization versus decentralization, participation)
- extent and type of conflicts
- methods employed (e.g. SWOT, five-forces, scenario technique, brainstorming, a.o.)

As shall be discussed in more detail at a later point in this work (cf. particularly the empirical results and discussion in Chapter 6), depending on the different values a particular decision process assumes on these different dimensions, crucial implications may be derived regarding the resultant opportunities for individual cognitive activities as well as for social interactions to take place. These in turn determine the degree to which shared or parallelised knowledge structures or strategic orientations are likely to develop from the process.

Furthermore, while such 'dimensional' approaches allow for a very differentiated and fine-grained analysis and description of individual decision processes, another, more simplistic approach to capture or classify such processes is in the form of certain general typologies or models of strategies decision processes (Bamberger & Wrona, 2004, pp. 378-379). In this context, due to the variety of existent research streams, there is also quite a large number of such different, primarily 'ideal' categorisations (see Table 6).

3 – Strategic processes

Table 6: Selected strategy-making process models (Hart & Banbury, 1994, p. 253)

Allison (1971) - rational - organizational - bureaucratic	Mintzberg (1973) - entrepreneurial - planning - adaptive	Chaffee (1985) - linear - adaptive - interpretive	Nonaka (1988) - deductive - compressive - inductive
Ansoff (1987) - systematic - ad hoc - reactive - organic	Bourgeois & Broodwin (1984) - commander - change - cultural - collaborative - crescive	Grandori (1984) - optimizing - satisficing - incremental - cybernetic - random	Mintzberg (1987) - plan - position - ploy - perspective - pattern
	Mintzberg & Waters (1985) - entrepreneurial - planned - ideological - umbrella	- process - consensus - unconnected - imposed	

A detailed description of these individual typologies and an outline of the distinctive characteristics of the different process modes shall be foregone here.[61] Nevertheless, what is important to emphasize in the present research context is that even though in these typologies different process types are outlined and distinguished from each other (theoretically), in reality, strategic decision processes will hardly ever fit entirely into any one of these specific 'ideal' categories. Also, instead of regarding different process modes as mutually exclusive, the conception followed here is that within a particular organization and even within a concrete decision process, different types or modes may coexist and may be combined with each other, thereby allowing for a highly complex and differentiated interplay between individual cognitive activities (and structures) and collective social interactions.

Drawing on the above, on a more general level again, from the socio-cognitive perspective taken here, strategic decisions are on the one hand conceived of as the result of the cognitions (i.e. cognitive structures and cognitive processes) of the individual organisational members. On the other hand, they are the result of or are deeply embedded in the social interactions taking place in the specific context: Each individual searches and perceives certain stimuli in the environment. From this a certain opinion or decision develops first of all (Simons & Thompson, 1998, p. 18 f.). This process, however, does not take place in a social vacuum but is influenced in many ways by the social context in which the individual acts. Within this

---

[61] For a detailed discussion of such typologies of strategic decision processes cf. e.g. the article by Hart & Banbury (1994).

context, the individual interpretations are being exchanged, shared and changed through different communication mechanisms, which are in turn reflected in routines and rules until a shared perception of reality materializes on the basis of which a decision is then taken. Reality is thus not comprehended objectively, but it is constructed by means of this individual and social process. The possible strategic decisions thus depend on the perceived action reality, which can either be designed deliberately with the help of a top-town approach to management decisions, or it can emerge through certain incidents in the organization. In any case, however, strategic actions develop largely through the help of communication and interpretation mechanisms in an organization, which constitute at the same time the instruments through which organisational reality is constructed (Hoffmann-Ripken, 2003, p. 90).

Other 'forums' for strategic activities

As outlined above, the conception of strategic processes taken here regards decision making activities as constituting merely one type of 'forum' in which strategic activities take place within the ongoing process. Hence, apart from concrete decision making episodes, there are of course a number of other forums that provide occasions for individual learning and social interactions to take place, and consequently for shared orientations concerning strategic issues to develop. Among these, a further useful distinction can be made between occasions or episodes that are rather tightly embedded in the regular (formal) strategy development process, e.g. (recurring) formal planning processes, and those that are more loosely coupled, i.e. which are less institutionalized and thus occur sometimes often, or over long periods not at all. In the latter, the interactions and procedures are then usually also less rule-guided, e.g. in strategy workshops or rather casual meetings.

(Traditional) planning processes

As regards the former, besides decision making (strategic) **planning processes** certainly constitute the second major area of interest for researchers interested in strategic activities. Consequently, also here a vast amount of literature can be found on the topic. In the present context, however, the aim is not to outline in detail the different characteristics, progressive forms or methods used in strategic planning.[62] Instead, the focus shall be confined to establishing formal planning processes as another kind of important 'forum' contributing to the parallelisation of actors' strategic orientations. Here then, even though planning processes can also be regarded as a certain kind of decision process, what makes them distinct is the fact that in

---

[62] For a good overview and discussion of the planning literature see e.g. Hahn & Hungenberg (2001), Hahn & Taylor (2006), Simons (1995), Ansoff (1976).

planning the search for problem solutions is distinctively anticipative and systematic (Bamberger & Wrona, 2004, p. 381). The high degree of procedural rationality characteristic of planning activities implies a high intensity of information search and processing, as well as the usage of (scientific) analytical methods (cf. e.g. Flamholtz, 1996). Thanks to this, the potential for information gathering and knowledge creation is particularly high. Nevertheless, the rather formal nature of such processes seems to suggest that often the unhampered and pressure-less exchange and deliberation of divergent views that is generally regarded as conducive to successful collective information processing and learning (cf. Chapter 5) might be rather limited in these contexts. Similar arguments might be brought forward concerning activities of operative planning as well as the control activities associated with these. Also the formal activities of *operative planning* (cf. e.g. Hahn & Hungenberg, 2001), which are in the literature usually discussed in the area of "implementation" (cf. e.g. Ansoff, 1976), generate strategically relevant topics and problems and can therefore lead to changes in the knowledge structures and perceptions concerning the organization's strategies. In how far, however, such potential cognitive changes truly materialize, endure, and finally also become visible in the firm's observable pattern of strategic behaviour, again depends on a variety of boundary conditions and factors. These will be the subject of detailed discussion in the following Chapters 4 and 5.

Towards less institutionalized or less regular activities

(Strategy) workshops

While highly formalized planning systems or activities were for long considered an essential element of strategy development processes, for some time already such formal and elitist strategic planning practices have widely been seen as in decline (e.g. Hamel & Prahalad, 1994; Mintzberg, 1994). However, instead of postulating an abandonment of formal approaches and practices altogether, it is rather suggested that formal strategy-making may now be developing new roles, including softer ones such as communications and coordination (Hodgkinson et al., 2006, p. 480; Whittington & Cailluet, 2008, p. 242). In line with this, there are clearly a number of other occasions that provide additional crucial 'forums' for individual reflections and social interactions and exchanges of strategic information and knowledge among key actors. Here then, strategy workshops (e.g. in the form of away-days) are important forums for discussion and constitute a wide-spread practice in strategic processes (Hodgkinson et al., 2006, p. 486).[63] In this context, in a recent study conducted among a large number of UK businesses, Hodgkinson et al. (2006) provide a detailed discussion of the characteristics, purposes and implications associated with the conduct and results of specific, episodically conducted, strategy workshops:

Overall, even though their official status still remains for formal strategy design, both their purposes and conduct are much less formal. I.e., little information gathering and analysis occur in preparation for them, and also during their conduct the focus is rarely on new research and analysis, as evidenced by the little use of analytically demanding tools. Instead, strategy workshops function largely as forums for debate in which it is the existing experiences of managers that is brought to bear on issues. In line with this, the role of workshops can be seen more as a vehicle for general communication, coordination or achieving buy-in of strategy. Workshops have benefits in terms of a general vision or mission, a better understanding of business processes and a better understanding of corporate values (Whittington et al., 2006, p. 619 f.). Consequently, thanks to their function as intensive episodes of strategy debate, they thus provide valuable opportunities for more open, informal discussion and exchange of knowledge and information. In addition, even though strategy workshops still showed to be mostly confined to senior managers, this potential 'exclusiveness-drawback' nevertheless does not contradict the concept of emergent strategy. On the contrary, the fact that workshops may be primarily forums for debate does not mean that more formal analysis does not take place elsewhere in the organisation and then feeds into workshop deliberations. Like this, strategy workshops could thus be "the very forums in which such emergent strategy is thought through, translating, perhaps even legitimising and formalising, that which has its origins lower down the organisation" (Hodgkinson et al., 2006, p. 488).

Taken together, since strategy workshops are primarily forums for the socialising of strategy, the reconciliation of different views, and might be seen as 'channels' through which issues from lower levels get to the key actors and are discussed among them in a more informal and pressure-less surrounding, they can be considered as a very fruitful forum for the development of shared strategic orientations (and thus potentially for the development of organizational strategies).[64]

---

[63] Strategy workshops can also be regarded as 'agenda building events' (cf. 3.2.5 and the references provided there).

[64] Caution is needed here, however, since there is clearly still an important difference between the formulation and the implementation of strategies. Also the effectiveness of such workshops is clearly not always guaranteed and it remains to be seen in how far the ideas and concepts developed in this context are also considered again or developed further later on (Johnson, 2008, pp. 3-5).

Overall then, strategy workshops can be seen as part of a changing practice of formal strategy making. As such, this is in line with the growing importance of what Grant (2003) calls the 'softer' roles in practice, thereby referring to this new kind of strategic planning as 'planned emergence'. Here then, workshops constitute an effective bridge between formal (institutionalized) design and informal emergence (Grant, 2003, p. 514). Similarly, even longer ago, also Mintzberg already advocated a less formal type of strategic planning, urging new and more diverse roles for planners as catalysts, communicators and co-coordinators (cf. Mintzberg, 1994). In line with this, it thus seems appropriate to move towards defining strategic planning more widely, and to include not just the responsibilities of some designated strategic planning department, but formal strategy-making in all its manifestations, whether undertaken by strategic planners, managers or strategy consultants, or happening in boardrooms, strategy awaydays, or virtually through electronic communications (Whittington & Cailluet, 2008, p. 242).

These assertions then support the observation made in previous parts of this work in the context of describing the recent practice turn in strategic management research (cf. 3.2.6). Researchers in this tradition now really go into organizations and look at what strategists actually *do* during their daily work. By doing so they have gotten closer to strategic reality and make us conscious of the plurality of forms that strategy activity can, and in fact does, take in different contexts, as well as the more diverse roles and multiple tasks strategists fulfill today.

(Strategy) meetings

Drawing on the above, a final typically occurring activity ('social practice') in strategic processes that shall be emphasized here is strategy meetings. Similarly as workshops, meetings are very important and even much more typically occurring events in strategic processes. Still, despite their importance and frequency, in the classical organization studies literature meetings are largely perceived uncritically as tools for accomplishing specific tasks, such as decisions (Jarzabkowski & Seidl, 2008, p. 1393). In contrast to this instrumental view, recent studies, especially research coming from political studies, however, have shown meetings as important for setting agendas (e.g. Tepper, 2004), building commitment, and providing information to policy makers (e.g. Adams, 2004), rather than for generating policy decisions as such.

In line with this, also among strategy researchers increasing attention is now being paid to such practices as they are clearly conspicuous events in strategic processes. Here then, on the one hand, meetings are scheduled routinely; for example in the annual strategic planning cycle. However, they are also turned to during critical strategic incidents; for example, calling a meeting whenever an important strategic issue arises. Meetings are thus part of the ongoing flow of organizational activities and can be understood as focal points for the strategic activities of organisational members (Jarzabkowski & Seidl, 2008, p. 1393). With these functions and characteristics meetings are clearly distinct from casual encounters. Instead, by definition, all meetings are regarded as formal, to the extent that they are planned gatherings for a purpose, bracketing in some actors and issues during a particular space and time, whilst bracketing out others. Within this classification, however, and in the context of strategic processes, meetings may vary in the degree of formality in their approach, depending e.g. on planning or management issues such as the role of agendas or chairing (cf. e.g. Kieffer, 1989; Volkema & Niederman, 1996).

Explicit support for these arguments, which point to the centrality of meeting practices as another crucial forum for strategic activities, comes from the empirical findings reported in a recent paper by Jarzabkowski & Seidl (2008). On the basis of an extensive qualitative analysis of more than 50 strategy meetings in three UK universities, the authors underline the influential role that such strategy meetings have in shaping strategic stability and change. More specifically, particular meeting practices, such as administrative discussion and restricted discussion, were associated with stabilization of existing strategic orientations, while others, such as working groups and free discussion, were associated with a destabilization tendency. Nevertheless, rather than truly leaving observable strategic traces on their own, it was shown that it is only the particular combination of practices in a series of meetings over time that is finally related to consequential strategic outcomes. Thus, similar as the cautioning in the previous section, one always needs to bear in mind that even where strategic orientations are either confirmed or changed *within* a strategic episode, this also needs to be fed into the wider organisation. Not only the effect of a meeting but those of many other strategic activities, plans or decisions as well, therefore depend on the receptiveness that its outcomes meet within the wider organization (cf. Jarzabkowski & Seidl, 2008, p. 1395 f.; and also Hodgkinson et al., 2006).

Finally, apart from all these more formal or 'stereotypical' activities, it is clearly recognized that there are also many more **informal activities** or occasions for interaction and communication that contribute to shaping the strategic process. Examples are lunch meetings, after-work gatherings, exchanges over coffee, leisure weekends, etc. In addition, there are also the interactions and conversations taking place before meetings or workshops, i.e. 'on the way', during lunches and dinners on such days, or as by-products of conversations held for other purposes. Hence, what has to be kept in mind is that many critical interactions occur outside or well before any formal discussions held for the purpose of finding a problem solution or making a strategic plan in institutionalized activity contexts (McGrath, 1991, p. 147 ff.).

Taken together then, in this section it was shown that the array of activities in strategic processes clearly goes far beyond ('classical') decision making episodes. Since all these activities have different characteristics, together with the other dimensions and their respective values (e.g. who the actors involved are, what the content and the concrete micro-context is, etc.), there are then different and important implications for the parallelisation of strategic orientations.

3.4.1.4 Content

The major 'object' of strategic processes is clearly 'strategy'. Here, however, it has to be noted that strategies can emerge on or be developed for different, though interrelated, levels of abstractions. In this regard, according to the classical strategy literature, three organisational levels can be distinguished for which strategies can be formulated, and which can thus be dealt with in strategic processes: Corporate level strategies, business (unit) level strategies, and functional or departmental level strategies (Mintzberg et al., 2007; Schendel & Hofer, 1979).

Besides such concrete strategies, there are also other contents dealt with in the context of strategic processes that are strategically relevant. For example, changes of the organisational structure, its culture, approaches to strengthen the firm's innovation capability, large investments in new (production) technology, or similar issues that are clearly of high (and thus 'strategic') importance. In addition, in line with the conceptualization of strategies as 'shared strategic orientations' and thus the rather broad definition of 'strategy' taken here, also goals, principles and norms are counted to the *content* dimension of strategic processes.

3.4.1.5 Context

As the fifth dimension and of course very crucial to consider, is finally the context in which the entire strategic process is embedded. Strategic processes take place within a structural frame. Here, structure is meant to refer not only to physical and immaterial resource constellations, but specifically to systems of **rules** (Bamberger & Wrona, 2004, p. 362). Both the internal and the external context have to be considered for this.

As regards the **internal** context, the broader term **'organisational context'** shall be used here, instead of 'structural' and 'strategic' contexts. Included within this is the purpose of the organisation, the organisational structure, its management systems and informal organisation, as well as particularly also its culture. Both formal rule systems as well as informal norms can be important. Parts of the rules can be directly related to the execution of strategic processes (e.g. institutionalized planning cycles). Together, all of these help shape the decision and action premises of an organization. Senior executives in a firm are not only decision-makers and actors in the strategy process, but they are also the architects and managers of the organizational context that shapes these decisions and actions (Chakravarthy & White, 2002, p. 194).

Apart from the concrete internal context, strategic processes are of course also influenced by **external** factors, i.e. the broader environment which includes the social, political, cultural, national, etc. context they are embedded in. Here, the environment can be regarded as the external structural frame in which strategic processes take place. In this, the environment derives its impact specifically from the perceptions and interpretations that the strategic actors take from external stimuli and 'carry' inside the organisation (cf. e.g. Dill, 1958; Elenkov, 1997; Kiesler & Sproull, 1982; Sutcliffe & Huber, 1998).

Overall, whereas both internal and external contexts clearly influence the strategic processes, at the same time the strategic processes also influence the environment, i.e. it is a reciprocal relationship with feedback loops.

3.4.2 Implications for the parallelization of strategic orientations

The here outlined framework consists of several dimensions (and sub dimensions) for the analysis of strategic processes. By examining, in combination, the characteristics of the different variables, quite diverse processes can be described. The characterisation of a specific strategic process results from the totality of values of the dimensions regarded.

The nature of (a) specific strategic process(es) then clearly also has implications for the development of shared strategic orientations among an organisation's key actors. In this regard, particularly high differences in terms of the respective *socio-cognitive dynamics* occurring must be expected between the different **'forums'** in which strategic activities take place. For example, in the context of a strategic planning session, the overall process (and consequently the social interactions) is clearly much more rule-guided compared to more informal gatherings for the purpose of e.g. collective brainstorming on a topical issue. Whereas good process management might be beneficial to not get lost in irrelevant details, at the same time, however, too many restrictions and rules hamper creative thinking and the unconstrained exchange of knowledge and information. Consequently, it is clearly crucial and interesting to examine the different **activities** that are executed in strategic processes, because depending on the specific tasks also more or less exchange and social interactions occur.

Influential for the interactive dynamics is also who exactly the **actors** involved in the processes are. As mentioned before, individuals as well as different groups of participants often have quite divergent communication styles, knowledge, preferences and interests. All these aspects influence the social and cognitive dynamics. In this context, apart from who exactly interacts inside a specific 'forum', also more generally it is interesting and important to consider who the relevant strategic actors in an organisation are in the first place. Here, drawing on a quite common distinction found in the literature, organisations vary in terms of whether their decision and strategy processes can be described as 'top-down'- or more 'bottom-up'-oriented. In the former 'elitist' case then, middle and lower level managers will not really be given a chance to be involved in the strategic processes. As there are hence no or only few opportunities for exchange and communication between these organisational members and the firm's decision makers, the strategic cognitions of the latter are also little likely to be impacted by such influences from 'below'. Also in these cases, it can be assumed that there are quite few forums where different organisational members interchange on strategic issues. Alternatively, even if there are such occasions, it remains questionable how much of the results of these interactions would then actually be successfully fed into the wider organisation and truly impact on the key actors' views, and hence on strategic outcomes.

Generally again, further important aspects refer to the overall quantity of opportunities for interactions as well as to whether the wider organisational context provides systems or rules that might foster the convergence of knowledge structures even in the absence of direct interactions among the actors. Regarding the former, it has been repeatedly suggested that the greater the interaction (both among top executives themselves but especially across levels), the richer are the strategic alternatives which are considered (cf. e.g. Bower, 1970; Burgelman, 1983). As high interaction is thus crucial for exploration, in cases where there is constant exchange between the actors involved, rather than merely occasional or seasonal updates, there then clearly is also more room for the parallelisation of strategic orientations. In addition, also management systems, as examples of the internal environment (Bamberger & Wrona, 2004, p. 362), help foster the convergence of strategic knowledge structures.

Taken together, in light of these examples, it seems clear that it is the **quantity** of the interactions and their **quality**, i.e. the specific characteristics of the social exchanges themselves, as well as the **surrounding context**, which matter. Basically, more interactions are beneficial. However, if these interactions are e.g. too conflict-laden, or driven by political interests, it seems questionable whether they really contribute to sharedness in terms of the participants' strategic orientations. What exactly can be regarded as a good or appropriate process design then ultimately depends on the requirements of the individual organisation. In highly dynamic environments, for example, strategic issues usually have to be dealt with at a high(er) pace, leaving little place for extensive involvement of all managerial levels in the decisions the top management takes. On the other hand, however, diverse insights and safeguards against 'myopia' or stale dominant logic are clearly important, too, in order for the organisation to retain its flexibility and adoptability. An adequate balance between these conditions seems therefore warranted.

Drawing on the above now, with the socio-cognitive approach developed here, valuable insights regarding the dynamics of strategic processes and their implications for the development of shared strategic orientations have already been gained. In order to substantiate the assertions made so far, however, it is clearly imperative to provide more detailed and scientifically deeper considerations from cognitive psychology as well as from research on social interactions and group processes. Hence, the following Chapter 4 deals specifically with cognition, thereby progressing from the individual to the 'socially shared' levels. In Chapter 5 the focus is set on social interaction processes. Here, the emphasis will be on small group interactions, particularly in the context of decision making tasks. These different insights are finally discussed together and integrated into an own socio-cognitive model of strategic decision making in Section 5.3. By thus developing the socio-cognitive perspective in depth, the claim to present a truly integrative and interdisciplinary approach to the analysis of strategic processes will finally be justified.

4 From *intra-* to *inter*individual cognition in strategic processes

The work's central research question, i.e. how shared strategic knowledge develops or knowledge structures change in the context of strategic processes, clearly requires a dynamic view and has to consider both the individual and the collective levels. Having focused on strategic processes in the previous chapter, in order to finally move successfully from the intra- to the interindividual cognitive level, a detailed outline concerning the central issues of "knowledge" and "cognition" is now imperative. In this regard, in the context of presenting the cognitive perspective on strategic management in 2.4, certain ideas and concepts from the discipline of cognitive psychology have already been mentioned and touched on. The focus and explicit aim there, however, was to analyse the status quo of how ideas from cognitive psychology are generally used and applied to illuminate on phenomena of interest to strategic management scholars. The value of adopting such a *cognitive* perspective was clearly outlined in this context (2.4.5). At the same time, however, in light of the specific interests at hand in the present work, also a number of deficiencies were identified in the current cognitive strategy literature (cf. 2.4.6). Apart from the need derived from this analysis to include more specific considerations concerning the impact of social factors on managerial cognitions, also the often rather superficial treatment or insufficient expertise of the variety of relevant concepts and theories from the field of cognitive psychology was observed. Therefore, in the present chapter now, one of the first aims is to give the required more differentiated and deeper look and description of the central **cognitive foundations** involved in the specific research focus. In this respect, generally, regarding the overall issue of "human cognition", in psychology two different streams exist that deal with this topic: I.e., the traditional **cognitivist view** which focuses on the 'inside' of the individual mind (e.g. Anderson, 2005; Neisser, 1976); and the 'newer' approaches that recognize explicitly the **situated** nature of knowledge and thus emphasize the (social) context (e.g. Greeno, 1998; Kirshner & Whitson, 1997b; Lave & Wenger, 1991). Here then, especially in the management and organisation literature, a similar split as the one seen before between the computational and the interpretive streams in MOC research (cf. 2.4) is often found between these two perspectives. In psychology, however, this divide and mutual non-recognition is in fact not the case. Instead, it is rather a question of 'history' or focus: I.e., the cognitivist perspective represents the original or historically first approach to the study of human cognition. Its roots and the majority of its central concepts and assertions can thus be traced to the times when not much was yet known about the brain's structure and functioning. The central and exclusive occupation with the individual mind can hence be comprehended. Over time, however, as more and more became and is today known about the brain's 'infrastructure', a development away from the sole focus on the inside of the individual mind has occurred. I.e., more researchers now look explicitly beyond the individual and e.g. to the social context, the situation, etc. Consequently, instead of postulating any one of these streams as right or wrong, it is clearly both that are needed if one is to understand the phenomenon in its entirety.

Exactly this recognition then also constitutes the starting point of the outlines to be presented in the following. The overall aim is to finally thoroughly derive a *socio-cognitive* perspective on the phenomenon at hand. For this, the present chapter sets out by first focusing on the individual level and defining the underlying conception(s) and kind(s) of **knowledge**, particularly 'strategic knowledge', dealt with here. Then, a number of concrete insights from the **cognitivist view** are outlined, which go much deeper than cognitive strategy researchers usually do. This approach is particularly valuable because it provides the theoretical basis for questions concerning how knowledge is organised, stored, categorized, as well as processed in the individual's mind. Subsequently, in line with the research question at hand, i.e. how shared knowledge structures develop in the context of strategic processes, the **situated cognition** perspective is considered. As this approach broadens the focus to include social factors and considerations of the wider context surrounding the individual, it is a fruitful approach for illuminating the overall phenomenon at hand. Here then, not only is this perspective actually a quite 'innovative' approach in the area of management and strategy research, but by progressing in this way a step is also made forward to overcome the still prevailing divide between the symbolic (computational) and the connectionist (interpretive) perspectives. Why and how the two are in fact rather complementary and should be combined, instead of regarded as opposing each other, will become obvious.

Furthermore, because both the cognitivistic and the situated perspectives still are approaches that are primarily meant to explain cognition at the level of the individual actor, to proceed to issues beyond the individual's 'inside', a third theoretical element is outlined which contains approaches that deal specifically with questions regarding the development of **socially *shared* cognitions**. In this context then, since the overall interest is essentially with cognitive developments and changes, which are obviously closely linked to *learning* issues, at this point a brief discussion of approaches to collective knowledge and learning in organisations finally complements this section.

Following this, an integration of all the preceding is then made that cumulates in the presentation of the own socio-cognitive perspective on strategic processes. The closing sections of the present chapter finally prepare the ground for moving from the rather general macro-view on the overall ongoing process to one specific micro-setting ("forum" for strategic activity), i.e. decision making groups, which allows for a more detailed examination of the socio-cognitive dynamics taking place therein.

4.1 Knowledge

The nature of knowledge may be one of the most complex and controversial issues facing not only management researchers but researchers from all kinds of different disciplines. In line with recognizing 'knowledge' as one or even *the* core resource and thus essential source of competitive advantages (cf. 2.3.2), in management, there is in fact by now an entire research community of its own that is concerned with issues like 'knowledge management', 'knowledge transfer', or 'organisational knowledge' (cf. the handbook edited by Easterby-Smith & Lyles, 2006 for a comprehensive overview of the field). Already here it is thus clear that it is not only different *types* of knowledge that may be distinguished, but that there are also different *levels* at which knowledge topics can and are examined. A comprehensive overview of this by now truly vast literature would clearly be beyond the scope of the present work. Also, even though the research question here includes the notions of "sharedness" and "group", and the different levels are of course not independent from each other, the specific 'cognitive' interest still remains in the strategy schemata that are held in the individuals' minds. The following discussion will therefore centre on knowledge at the individual level and on *managerial* knowledge structures (as compared to organisational knowledge and cognition).

4.1.1 Conception(s) and categories of knowledge

Most scholars in the management area would agree that knowledge is "created and organized by the...flow of information" (Nonaka, 1994, p. 15). Besides, however, due to the great diversity in the literature, no consistent and complete definition of the term 'knowledge' exists. One of the major reasons for the near impossibility to derive a uniform definition is the fact that a researcher's conception of knowledge is clearly dependent on the respective philosophical position he takes. In this regard, the discussion about the nature of knowledge is currently dominated by two fundamentally different approaches, i.e. the *cognitivistic* and the *constructivistic* conceptions of knowledge.[65]

Regarding the latter of these, the **constructivistic perspective** regards knowledge as the individual's construction of the surrounding world based on his or her perception. Because knowledge resides in people's bodies and is closely related to their senses and previous experiences, individuals come to create the world in ways that are unique to themselves. As a consequence, there is no objective reality given and knowledge thus has to be regarded as inherently subjective in nature (e.g. Berger & Luckmann, 1966; Glasersfeld, 1995; Schütz, 1962).

The most fundamental assumption in the **cognitivistic perspective** against that is that there is a reality that is given objectively. Even though the involvement of individual actors as information processors is recognized here (cf. 2.4.3.1), the human brain is said to take over the task of producing a representation of this reality as accurately as possible. Knowledge then is considered to be "representations of the world that consist of a number of objects or events" (Krogh, 1998, p. 134). In this perspective, knowledge is generally seen as explicit and codifyable.

Even though these two conceptions appear clearly opposed to each other, like with all other definitions of knowledge, none of these can be said to be right or wrong. Instead they are only suited more or less, respectively, to a specific problem or research question. Here then, in line with the present interests and the overall position taken in this research, the constructivistic conception is followed in this work. This conception is particularly valuable in the present context as it clearly recognizes person and context specifics.

Moreover, apart from regarding general philosophical positions on knowledge, the term can be further conceptualized and differentiated by introducing *categories* of knowledge (Spelsiek, 2005, p. 15). In this regard, in the literature there are in fact diverse approaches to classify knowledge into different categories depending on its respective characteristics.[66] However, in the following only those types of knowledge shall be outlined which are of concrete relevance in light of the present research interests. In particular, these are the categories of **tacit** and **explicit** knowledge, and **declarative** (theoretical – 'that') versus **procedural** (practical – 'how') knowledge.[67] Since these two are in fact the most common and widely

---

[65] These opposing conceptions correspond largely to the distinct epistemological positions that underlie the two major perspectives in MOC research outlined in 2.4.3.

[66] Cf. for classifications of knowledge types e.g. Blackler (1993; 1995), Krogh & Venzin (1995, p. 421 ff.).

[67] Besides **procedural** and **declarative** knowledge, some authors further distinguish a third category here, i.e. **causal** knowledge ('describing why things happen') (cf. e.g. Zack, 1999).

accepted distinctions found in the literature, they also frame the general discussion in the field.

4.1.1.1 Tacit and explicit knowledge

A common and probably the most 'famous' classification in the knowledge literature is the difference between *explicit* and *implicit* knowledge, i.e. knowledge that can be articulated and knowledge that cannot be articulated but that is still known in some sense. This distinction can be traced to Polanyi. He basically recognized that "we know more than we are able to say", and denotes this kind of knowledge as implicit or tacit knowledge (Polanyi, 1967). An often used definition of implicit knowledge has been provided by Nonaka: "Tacit knowledge is personal, context-specific, and therefore hard to formalize and communicate". Explicit or 'codified' knowledge against that refers to "knowledge that is transmittable in formal, systematic language" (Nonaka & Takeuchi, 1995, p. 59).

Often, especially in the management literature, the terms "explicit" and "implicit" are treated as two distinct concepts; knowledge is either clearly explicit or, in all other cases, implicit. In the constructionist literature, however, both terms are conceived of as opposite points of a continuum (e.g. Nonaka & Takeuchi, 1995, p. 57 ff.). In the strategy context then, it is especially tacit knowledge which is considered important because it is knowledge that is difficult – if not impossible – to imitate (Ambrosini & Bowman, 2001).

Overall, the notion of tacitness complicates the question of what constitutes knowledge because it suggests that people know more than they consciously believe. In line with what has been argued at several points before, this difficulty goes away, however, if one recognizes action over articulation as the measure of belief. Assuming that knowledge in one form or the other causes human behaviour, then one can tell what people know by observing their actions as well as their assertions (Floyd & Wooldridge, 2000, p. 70). Exactly this is also a premise of most philosophy, namely that people's beliefs about things, issue or other people can be observed directly from their behaviour.

4.1.1.2 Declarative and procedural knowledge

The distinction between theoretical and practical knowledge is often traced to the types of knowledge introduced by the philosopher Gilbert Ryle, who distinguishes between "knowledge that" and "knowledge how" (Ryle, 1949). Concerning the former, "knowledge that" signifies theoretical or abstract knowledge of facts or data; usually knowledge an individual has about himself or his environment. Examples for this kind of knowledge in the strategy context can be knowledge about the organisation's closest competitors, or about legal regulations in one's industry.

Practical knowledge, i.e. "knowledge how", against that refers particularly to the cognitive and motor abilities an individual has acquired, and that have proven useful in his or her interactions with the surrounding world (Thiel, 2002, p. 17). Examples for practical knowledge in the strategy context may be the ability to motivate one's members of staff, or to subtly influence others in a discussion such that one's own position finally gets through.

Ryle's assumption that "knowledge that" and "knowledge how" denote two fundamentally different kinds of knowledge has been supported by neurophysiological research. In line with this, a today established taxonomy of the human memory distinguishes between a declarative and a procedural part of the brain. "Declarative memory is memory that is directly accessible to conscious recollection. It can be declared. It deals with the facts and data that are acquired through learning and it is impaired in amnesia. In contrast, procedural memory is not accessible as specific facts, data, or time-and-place events. Procedural memory is memory that is contained within learned skills or modifiable cognitive operations. It is spared in amnesia" (Squire, 1987, p. 152). Declarative knowledge corresponds to Ryle's theoretical knowledge; procedural knowledge is the counterpart to Ryle's practical knowledge.

4.1.1.3 The relationship between knowledge and information

Besides differentiating between different types of knowledge (categories), another issue that is particularly crucial in the present research context concerns the need to clarify the distinction between "knowledge" and "information", which is often not done accurately in the management literature.

According to Picot, *information* is data put into a specific problem context where it can be used for a particular purpose (Picot, Reichwald, & Wigand, 2001, p. 91). In the strategy context, information is data that serves the preparation of decisions and actions. As such it is thus relevant for the receiver. Information can lead to a new perception when interpreting events or relationships, and hence to new insights. A prerequisite for this is the preoccupation with or processing of information. In this sense, information constitutes the raw material for knowledge, i.e. "information ... enables knowledge creation" (Krogh & Roos, 1995, p. 133).

Nevertheless, knowledge must not be understood as a trivial collection of information (Thiel, 2002, p. 15). In contrast to information, knowledge *enables* action (Picot & Scheuble, 2000, p. 22). Moreover, in line with the earlier outlines, knowledge can be regarded as a very complex and frequently loose pattern, whose parts are connected in various ways by ties that are of varying degrees of strength. This structure is also called the *knowledge base*. Information constitutes the building blocks of knowledge and influences the structure in different ways (cf. e.g. Boulding, 1956, p. 204): Firstly, information can *complement* a knowledge structure (schema) by substantiating existing knowledge and like that becoming part of the structure. Secondly, information can *reinforce* the credibility of a knowledge structure (or of parts of it) and like that strengthen the belief in its correctness or feed doubts regarding the schema. And finally, information can *lead to a revision* of the existing knowledge structure, for example by creating new areas of knowledge (in the sense of "learning"), or by radically modifying or reducing existing areas. Modifications or reduction become necessary when the credibility of parts of the knowledge structure is lost. This may e.g. be the case when a message hits the structure which is inconsistent with the basic pattern of the cognitive structure, but which is of a nature that cannot be disbelieved. The structure is then forced to undergo a complete reorganization.

The above outlines have shown that information can in fact be regarded as the very building blocks of knowledge. As it is thus basically the exchange of 'information' which is crucial for the potential development or modification of individual knowledge structures, information, and particularly its exchange between actors is hence also of crucial importance in the context of examining the (potential) parallelisation of strategic knowledge structures among different organisational key actors (cf. Chapter 6).

Overall now, in light of all of the above, the definition of knowledge to be used here clearly needs to be tailored to the present research focus. For this, a **wide definition** of knowledge is regarded appropriate, which includes different types of the construct: Knowledge that describes *what* something is (i.e., declarative knowledge), knowledge that describes *how* something is (i.e., procedural knowledge), and knowledge that describes *why* something happens (i.e., causal knowledge) (Zack, 1999, p. 46). Here then, in line with acknowledging the subjective nature of knowledge, knowledge is not merely objective data but it is considered as information that is combined with individuals' conscious and unconscious experiences, interpretation and reflection, and that is embedded within a context.[68]

---

[68] This wide definition of knowledge is in fact closely in line with how other management and strategy scholars view the issue. In this context, Hodgkinson & Sparrow (2002) for example use the broad term "mental material" to refer to the entirety of managers' knowledge, and they also discuss different forms of thought employed and the varying ways in which these different kinds of mental material are processed (cf. Hodgkinson & Sparrow, 2002, p. 249 ff.).

In line with this conception, as regards the **sources** of knowledge, this knowledge then is accumulated as individual members encounter information, interpret it, and interact with one another in the process of pursuing their collective interests. What individuals in organisations believe to be known is based on the information that is available to them in the form of prior beliefs (conscious or subconscious), objective data, (boundedly) rational thinking, and, importantly, ideas communicated in the words and deeds of others (Floyd & Wooldridge, 2000, p. 72).

4.1.2 (Managerial) knowledge structures and strategic knowledge

Now, as implied above and to be detailed more in 4.2.1, according to schema theories, all the different kinds of knowledge are stored in knowledge structures or schemata. While there are specific schemata for different areas of information, generally, important elements of these include factual knowledge, assumptions about relations in reality, technological knowledge, knowledge of concepts, values, goals, motivations, norms, and attitudes (Rumelhart, 1984, p. 163 and 169). In line with this, managerial knowledge structures clearly contain a large variety of different elements, and the mental models employed by managers are thus not unitary representations. Rather, they are the product of multiple representations of knowledge (Hodgkinson & Sparrow, 2002, p. 251).

Here then, regarded in their entirety, managers' cognitive structures certainly comprise of much more than merely strategy or organisation related contents. Nevertheless, in the present context the focus is on *strategic* knowledge structures, i.e. knowledge structures with strategically relevant content. In order to investigate what these (might) look like and what may be regarded as "strategically relevant content", there thus is a need to clarify and define more specifically what "strategic knowledge" is.

Strategic knowledge

Since there is no theory of managerial knowledge that would describe which memory contents managers resort to in the context of specific kinds of strategic decisions or actions, one way to still approach a definition of strategic knowledge is to consider typical **characteristics of the situation(s)** in which this kind of knowledge is applied. In this respect, strategy making or the solving of strategic problems take place in an environment that can generally be characterized as complex, highly dynamic, and in parts unknown or non-transparent (cf. 2.1). As a consequence, it is obvious that strategists must predispose of and apply quite a large amount of different knowledge in order to accomplish their tasks successfully. In line with recognizing that curtailing an account of strategic knowledge would thus make little sense, different suggestions can be found in the literature: Floyd and Wooldridge (2000), for example, focused on the external environment and argued that knowledge in this domain includes a sense of the competitive scene or broader institutional context in which an organization is embedded. Dutton et al. (2001) on the other hand look more to the inside and state that "strategic knowledge includes an understanding of the organization's goals, plans, and priorities" (Dutton, Ashford, O'Neill, & Lawrence, 2001, p. 728). Phrased generally, it is thus clearly about what managers know about their competitive situation, including both internal and external elements. I.e.: Who are we? What is important to us? What do we do? What don't we do? Who are our competitors?

Moreover, further indicators for what strategic knowledge is may then also be derived from what researchers in the field actually "map", for example 'identity', 'threats' and 'opportunities', or 'causality', i.e. positions, routes and projected outcomes (Fiol & Huff, 1992). Finally, apart from these different, largely explicit and 'factual' types of knowledge, especially in strategy it is also tacit and procedural knowledge that are important, i.e. knowledge about how to behave in their environment(s), how to approach competitors, or how to win the internal political battles in order to get one's strategic issues or concepts through (cf. e.g. Ambrosini & Bowman, 2001; Bennett III, 1998).

Overall, what follows from the above outlines is that strategic knowledge must clearly be defined in a wide sense. As such, it could thus be said that strategic knowledge comprises those stocks of information stored permanently in a manager's memory which are relevant in the context of strategy making and the solving of strategic problems. In other words, individual strategic knowledge can be defined as that kind of knowledge on which decisions are based and carried out that aim at the development or extension of competitive advantages for securing the long-term existence and profitability of the organisation. In line with this, strategic knowledge then comprises both knowledge about concrete strategies, as well as other strategically relevant knowledge, i.e. knowledge which can lead to competitive advantages. Finally, as knowledge that is strategically relevant can thus clearly vary (e.g. depending on what the specific strategic decision or issue at stake is, the internal context, the external environment and the person(s) involved) the particular advantage of such an open and wide definition hence is that it accommodates exactly this situation and person specificity of strategic knowledge.

Taken together and referring back to the different categories of knowledge outlined previously, knowledge that is strategically relevant in a specific case may then be of a 'declarative', 'procedural' and 'causal' nature, it comprises facts and concrete data, as well as perhaps most importantly, tacit knowledge.

4.2 Knowledge representation in the human mind

Having now outlined the most important issues concerning *what* is considered as knowledge, the following sections focus on questions regarding *how* knowledge is organized and represented in the human mind. In this regard, in cognitive psychology there are in fact various approaches to this question. While it is still not really known how exactly knowledge is stored, the most widely used theory in this context, however, are schema-based approaches. To start with, in the following subsections the basic ideas of these approaches will be outlined, including notes on characteristics of schemata, structural and functional aspects, and schema acquisition and change.[69]

4.2.1 Schema-based theories

The term *schema* was first used by Jean Piaget[70] in 1926 (Piaget, 1926). Its prominence in the context of cognitive psychology research, however, can be traced back to the experimental works of Bartlett (1932) on memories and prose narration. Bartlett describes a schema as "an active organization of past reactions, or of past experiences, which must be supposed to be operating in any well-adapted organic response". With this he conceived of schemata as "organized knowledge units" in memory, in which knowledge and experiences are represented in a systematic manner (Bartlett, 1932, p. 201). Since that time the term schema has been taken up by a plurality of researchers – particularly in cognitive psychology – as a descriptive and explanatory construct.[71] Even though there thus is not a single schema theory, but rather a variety of schema-based theories, wide agreement nevertheless exists concerning the most basic tenets underlying all of these approaches. In this regard, closely mirroring Bartlett's original conception, the term schema is generally used to refer to a way of mentally representing knowledge (Fiske & Linville, 1980, p. 543). The task of schemas is the organization

---

[69] While, as has been seen, in the literature on strategic management it is the terms "knowledge structures" or "cognitive structures" that are most commonly used, in cognitive psychology it is the term "schema" which is most widely employed. In line with this, in outlining insights from the field of cognitive psychology in the following, the original term is thus kept. Since conceptually, however, the three terms basically denote the same underlying construct, they are used interchangeably in the overall work.

[70] Jean Piaget (August 9, 1896 - September 16, 1980), a professor of psychology at the University of Geneva from 1929 to 1954, was a French Swiss developmental psychologist who is most well known for organizing cognitive development into a series of stages. According to Ernst von Glasersfeld (1982), Jean Piaget is "the great pioneer of the constructivist theory of knowing."

[71] Among these it was Richard C. Anderson, a prominent educational psychologist, who developed the so called "schema theory of learning" (cf. e.g. Anderson, 1977).

of knowledge at different levels of abstraction. By means of such organization schematic representations bring order to the chaos of a lifetime of myriad experiences through the coding of the commonalities and regularities of those experiences and the representation of them in the mind. For example, a *meeting schema* would code generic features of meetings and participation in meetings, as a function of many individual meeting experiences in a person's history. Schemas then are parsimonious mental representations that serve as models of aspects of the world, the self and other people. Consequently, the existence of schemas "obviates the need to mentally reinvent the wheel with each new experience by providing a blueprint against which that experience can be fitted" (Dalgleish, 2004, p. 232). They provide a preexisting representational structure against which all incoming information can be compared and through which that information can be filtered (Fiske & Linville, 1980, p. 552).

4.2.1.1 Characteristics of schemata

In line with the fact that there are different schema approaches, in the various works also different outlines of the attributes or characteristics are used to define "schema" more specifically. Based on a review of several of the most prominent conceptions (i.e. Anderson & Pearson, 1984; Brewer & Nakamura, 1984; Neisser, 1976; Norman, 1982; Rumelhart, 1980; Schank & Abelson, 1977), however, the most essential characteristics of schemata can be summarized as follows:

- A schema is an „*organized knowledge structure*" that consists of different knowledge elements or component parts. Largely in line with Bartlett's original ideas, these knowledge units are seen to have both structured relationships and to be convoluted and cross-linked with each other. Each schema consists of subschemata, which can again be described as configurations of subschemata. They represent conceptual knowledge about objects, situations, events, consequences of events, actions and consequences of actions. In addition, schemata also have empty slots or can be filled with different variables into which newly incoming information becomes integrated.
- A schema is "*unspecific*", i.e. it consists of generic experiences (knowledge) that a person has made with objects or events. Schemata represent typical relations within a "stimulus domain". Schematic knowledge is thus said to be made up of variables and of the knowledge about relationships between variables. Brewer and Nakamura (1984), for example, talk about „higher order cognitive structures" in contrast to concrete episodic information (Brewer & Nakamura, 1984, p. 120). In this sense, schemata are *abstract* as

they contain summary information and prototypical categories rather than details about a specific case.
- Schemata are *"modular"*, i.e. for different cognitive domains, schemata with different structural and functional characteristics can be imagined, e.g. motor schemata, perceptive schemata, action schemata (general action sequences), or pure knowledge schemata. Hastie (1981, p. 40 f.), for example, distinguishes between three **kinds of schemata**: (a) „central tendency schemata" (meaning the „prototype"-construct), (b) "template schemata" (meaning a template like "filling system" for the classification, storage, and coordination of incoming sensory information), and (c) "procedural schemata".[72] This assumption of modularity is particularly important since it allows calling all kinds of knowledge representations a schema. With this, an integrative concept thus exists for a variety of cognitive psychological models.

The knowledge gained through schemata can be represented on all kinds of different levels of abstraction. On the one hand, schemata can represent very concrete objects (like e.g. a specific product or a person's face). On the other hand, however, they are also able to cognitively represent abstract relations (e.g. theories). Besides purely generic knowledge, schemata may also contain episodic knowledge. Like this, action sequences and procedures are cognitively processed and stored in a so called "action" or "process schema", or a "script" (Schank & Abelson, 1977, p. 36 ff.).
- Schemata are *active* and *dynamic* structures, i.e. they interact with the incoming sensory information and have the ability to change and develop. Neisser's (1976) conception makes this aspect particularly clear: "A schema is that portion of the entire perceptual cycle which is internal to the perceiver, modifiable by experience, and somehow specific to what is being perceived. The schema accepts information as it becomes available at sensory surfaces and is changed by that information; it directs movements and exploratory activities that make more information available, by which it is further modified" (Neisser, 1976, p. 54). Also Rumelhart (1980, p. 38) characterizes schemata as „active processes", that are seen as similar to „procedures" or „computer programmes". Inseparably related to this defining component is then the following aspect:
- Schemata have a *process component* (Rumelhart, 1980, p. 41 ff.); thus they are conceived of as both structures and processes. Schemata are actively acquired through experiences

---

[72] Largely drawing on these fundamental works from cognitive psychology, Elsbach et al. (2005) identify and discuss some other forms of specific cognitive schemas that are of particular relevance in the organisational/ managerial context. These are: event schemas (understanding about how a process is likely to unfold); self-schemas (perceptions of personal or social identities); rule schemas (understanding about how key variables are related) (Elsbach, Barr, & Hargadon, 2005, p. 425).

and are applied in different situations. People's knowledge structure processes the incoming information. By applying an existing schema to a given environmental configuration people are for example able to organize and structure information. This schema characteristic of being both a kind of structure and a process is also called the "dual character". A good example for a definition emphasizing particularly the structural and functional aspects can be found in Taylor and Crocker's (1981) conception of schemata. According to the authors a schema is a cognitive structure that consists in part of the representation of some defined stimulus domain (Taylor & Crocker, 1981, p. 91). The schema contains general knowledge about that domain, including a specification of the relationships among its attributes, as well as specific examples or instances of the stimulus domain. As such, the schema provides hypotheses about incoming stimuli, which include plans for interpreting and gathering schema related information. It may also "provide a basis for activating actual behaviour sequences or expectations of specific behaviour sequences, i.e. scripts for how an individual behaves in a social situation" (Schank & Abelson, 1977, p. 91).

- Furthermore, schemata are *stable* memory representations in so far as they contain unspecific generic experiences. This aspect implies that once they have been built, schemata are relatively resistant to change.
- Finally, schemata are *instruments for perception* whose instantiation aims at the best possible match with the information that has to be processed in order to enable (its) comprehension (Rumelhart, 1980, p. 46). With this, schemata are thus of central importance in the acquisition of new knowledge.

4.2.1.2 Functional aspects

The above outline of the most central characteristics of schemata has clearly exemplified that schemata play a key role in many cognitive processes. In this context, following from the structural aspects of a schema, two basic processes derive for describing the interaction between existing schemata and a given environmental and stimuli configuration. One of these 'mechanisms' is called "top-down processing" or "conceptually-driven processing". Here, an activated schema directs the acquisition and processing of information. In this case, the information available in the environment is selected, structured, analysed, interpreted and integrated in light of the currently active schema. "Data-driven processing" or "bottom-up processing" on the other hand takes place when certain stimuli in the environment activate an existing schema (Eysenck & Keane, 2005, p. 289).

These two processes, however, are not mutually exclusive but alternate constantly. Newly incoming information, for example, is aimed at being related to a schema that best fits the available information environment ("data matching"). Once a schema gets activated it directs the further information processing and search (e.g. Rumelhart, 1984, p. 170 f.). If no adequate schema is found this may cause the creation of a new schema. If an activated schema is not able to accommodate the currently available data and no assimilation to the existing structure of the schema takes place (e.g. in the case of events that are discrepant to expectations), a transition to "data-driven" processing will take place again.

Many studies conducted by schema theorists in cognitive psychology have shown this interaction between knowledge structures and the currently available information offer, as well as the two basic processing types. In line with this, the most central functions schemata are thus said to have are to *direct attention* in perceptual processes, to *categorize and interpret* existing and incoming information, and to *support knowledge integration* and memory (Fiske & Linville, 1980, p. 552). To more specifically distinguish between these different kinds of functions, in the literature these processes are often referred to as 'selection', 'abstraction' and 'reconstruction' processes. Each process that is given such a label then stands for a specific kind of interaction between environmental information and cognitive structure (cf. e.g. Anderson, 2005, p. 157 f.; Brewer & Nakamura, 1984, p. 152 f.).

Like the two basic mechanisms described above, also these different processes are of course not mutually exclusive, but merely constitute different functional approaches. The integration of information into an existing schema, for example, is often accompanied by a selection process. While a number of such processes thus often occur simultaneously, in the following some of the most important processes schema researchers distinguish shall be outlined in order to further underscore the broad areas of application of the schema construct (for more comprehensive overviews see e.g. Brewer & Nakamura, 1984, p. 119 ff.; Hastie, 1981, p. 39 ff.; Taylor & Crocker, 1981, p. 89 ff.).

Attention processes: In order to perceive objects in the environment certain schemata get activated. These structure the perceived in a way that it can be cognitively processed. For this reason, the respective context in which parts of an object are perceived is crucial for their interpretation. At the same time, individuals' attention is directed selectively through the instantiation of schemata. Schemata thus influence the degree of attention that is given to different kinds of information. These relations, however, are not uniform since schema-related information is not always attributed more attention. Important mediators in this context are the relevance and the consistency vs. inconsistency of schema-related information (Brewer & Nakamura, 1984, p. 144 and 153 f.).

Selection processes: In so far as schemata for a certain information environment exist and are activated ("availability and accessibility"), incoming information is processed "selectively", i.e. information that fits the schema will be 'kept' (bound), unsuitable or irrelevant information is discarded.

Structuring and organizing processes: If a certain stimulus configuration can be related to a schema ("matching"), then the elements of the stimulus get arranged in such a way as to fit the structure of the schema. Schemata also allow to connect individual classes of observation and to order them in different ways (e.g. in linear or in hierarchical order).

Abstraction processes: Schemata also function to reduce the information environment by means of abstraction, i.e. surface level information of selected information is neglected during integration into the schema. Primarily schema-related information about meanings is encoded and stored. In addition, redundancies are eliminated ("editing-hypothesis"). This process occurs especially in cases of particularly rich information environments (Fiske & Linville, 1980, p. 544).

Interpretation processes: In cases where the information offer concerning an activated schema is limited, schemata can "fill in" the missing data of a particular stimulus configuration. This process can occur in different forms. On the one hand, a better fit between data and schema can be reached by means of an active search for missing information. If a manager for example arrives at a scheduled meeting place and sees no one else, then he will wonder where everybody is, and will possibly look for them. On the other hand, a better fit can be reached by means of an addition of the missing values on the basis of the given information and their mutual relations (e.g. Rumelhart 1984, p. 170 ff.). In the latter case, variables that have not been filled in are clogged with so called "default values" (Rumelhart & Ortony, 1977, p. 105) or "default assignments" (Minsky, 1975, p. 212 f. and 228 f.).[73]

Integration processes: Schemata interact with the incoming episodic information and thereby produce a memory trace. This memory trace is a combination of general schematic informa-

---

[73] If a friend tells me, for example, that he hurt himself while trying to put a nail into the wall to place a picture there, I will assume, based on the given information, that he hurt himself with a hammer.

tion and new episodic information (Brewer & Nakamura, 1984, p. 144). A piece of episodic information has become fully integrated into the "generic" schema if in later memory and recognition processes it cannot be discriminated against by other schema-related information.

Memory and reconstruction processes: The hypothesis that active schemata can direct the search for schema-related episodic information predicts higher memory performance for schema-related information (e.g. Andersen & Pichert, 1978, p. 10 f.; Bransford & Johnson, 1972, p. 720 ff.). Generally, schemata thus support the integration and memory of knowledge. In this context, schema research has shown that information which is instanced into a schema is recalled and remembered better than information which cannot be integrated in any schema. Also the degree of elaboration of a schema is essential for the integration of new knowledge (Brewer & Nakamura, 1984, p. 142 ff.). This integration is facilitated by the application of cognitively accessible schemata. Moreover, information is processed and recalled in a schema-consistent manner. At the same time this means that schema inconsistent information cannot be recalled or at least not correctly because no adequate schema will be applied (Fiske & Linville, 1980, p. 544).

4.2.1.3 Acquisition and change of schemata

In the context of outlining the most important characteristics of schemata it was already mentioned that such knowledge structures are generally relatively stable and enduring over time. In this respect, research indicates that information processing is biased in favour of maintaining the status quo with respect to schema content. For example, people are relatively better at remembering schema-consistent information (e.g. Swann & Read, 1981, investigations I and III), tend to make mnemonic errors in a schema-consistent pattern, and interpret new information so as to support pre-existing schemata (cf. e.g. Cantor & Mischel, 1977, p. 43 ff.). For these reasons schematic knowledge is very resistant to change and schematic change takes place only slowly (Eysenck & Keane, 2005, p. 385).

Even though the entirety of a person's cognitive contents thus changes only slowly, its different component parts, i.e. schemata, nevertheless are in a constant state of change as people encounter new experiences and new information that shape their schemata. To explain the acquisition and change of schemata and the effects that new knowledge can have on the structures of the mind, Rumelhart (1980, pp. 52-54) and Rumelhart & Norman (1978, p. 37 ff.) identified three different kinds of processes: *Knowledge* **accretion**, **tuning**, and **restructuring**. In *accretion* the existing schema is not changed, but rather its empty slots are enriched with additional information. If new information thus fits into a slot in an existing schema, it may be quickly comprehended. *Tuning* involves a modification or development of an existing schema by means of structural changes. New information may be used to "tune" an existing schema so it is more accurate, complete, or useful. New schemata then can be acquired by means of *restructuring*. This process takes place by means of pattern matching as well as schema induction. In case of pattern matching new information will be represented on an already existing schema. In schema induction, i.e. the actual acquisition of a schema, a schema is created based on a specific meaningful configuration that has already been perceived several times. Hereby learning takes place through contiguity, i.e. the perception of issues that often occur together leads to the development of new schemata or to the restructuring of old schemata (Mandl, Friedrich, & Hron, 1988, p. 127 f.).

Drawing on the above, the activities described there are in fact essentially the same as the categories of **assimilation, accommodation** and **equilibrium** outlined already very early on by the famous child psychologist and educationalist Piaget. Here then, it is the concepts of assimilation and accommodation which have been used to describe slow schematic change (Piaget, 1952). New information is assimilated into schematic structures by being selectively processed and stored in a schema-congruent manner. In addition, schema representations are themselves altered by small degrees by the accumulation of a critical mass of schema-inconsistent information. It has been argued that such conservatism regarding schema change is a function of an evolutionary need for existential stability and coherence in higher order meaning structures (Nisbett & Ross, 1980, p. 188 ff.). However, schema change is not viewed as a uniformly slow process. Piaget made the seminal proposition that slow schematic change occurs up to a point when the existing schemas become untenable as valid representations of the experienced world (Piaget, 1952, p. 236 ff.). At this juncture (or "developmental stage", as Piaget referred to it), old schemas are abandoned and new schemas instantiated. Other authors have proposed rapid schema change processes under different circumstances. For example, Rothbart (1981) argued for a relatively abrupt change mechanism when schemas are faced with a minimal number of salient, highly incongruent critical instances.

4.2.2 Network theories

As mentioned at the outset, schema-based approaches represent not the only attempts to explaining human cognition and knowledge. In this regard, network theories provide a different view of how knowledge is stored in individuals' heads. Even though network theories and schema theories are in fact compatible and are even often used together, the latter present a more creative, goal-oriented view of mental activity. Network theories against that tend to present a somewhat mechanistic view of mind, modelled after the interconnections of computer memory. Whereas the strength of schema theories is the organization of abstracted knowledge, the primary advantage of a network theory is the connectivity between different representations. Network theory thus gives the theorist a representation of how disparate pieces of information can activate each other and lead to the generation of affect (e.g. Bower, 1981, p. 130 ff.).

In the **network model** then, knowledge is stored in a network of interrelated propositions (cf. e.g. Eysenck & Keane, 2005, p. 13 f.). The network consists of elementary or neuron-like units or nodes connected together so that a single unit has many links to other units. The individual "node-link" structures are quite simple but they can be related in complex ways. A network can be thought of as a collection of contents ("propositions") which are interconnected in very specific ways that reveal important relationships among them. The network as a whole then is characterized by the properties of the units that make it up, by the way they are connected together, and by the rules used to change the connections among units. It is the connections among nodes which give information meaning and make it accessible. A similar analysis of knowledge structure is widely used in research on artificial intelligence. In the network model, connections, meaning, and learning are intertwined concepts. As a consequence of this, when no meaning (i.e., no connections) can be created, nothing is learned (Gagné, 1985, p. 79).

Exactly this conception of the human memory as a propositional network composed of node-link structures then also constitutes the starting point for the variety of mapping approaches and cognitive maps that have become so popular especially in strategy research (cf. 2.4). Figure 12 shows an example of such a cognitive map.

Clearly comprehensible is that such kinds of maps merely picture a fragment or a simplified version of the person's actual cognitive structures. In line with this, there are different kinds of maps depending on what exactly is to be assessed or described with them. In this regard, Huff (1990) distinguishes three 'generic families': Maps that assess attention and importance of concepts (family 1), maps that show dimensions of categories and cognitive taxonomies (family 2), and maps that show influence, causality and system dynamics (family 3). What is depicted in the below figure then corresponds to the latter of these kinds and shows the perceptions of one particular manager, a bank CEO, of the dynamics of his industry. Here, after the researchers used content analysis on the respective interview transcripts, the text elements in the figure correspond to the *concepts* describing the industry dynamics from the participant's view. In addition, *links* between these concepts are visualized with arrows. In the present example, these are drawn according to three different categories, i.e. proximity (represented by the *length* of the respective arrow), equivalence ("="), and causality (positive: "+" or negative: "-") (Calori et al., 1994, p. 444 ff.).

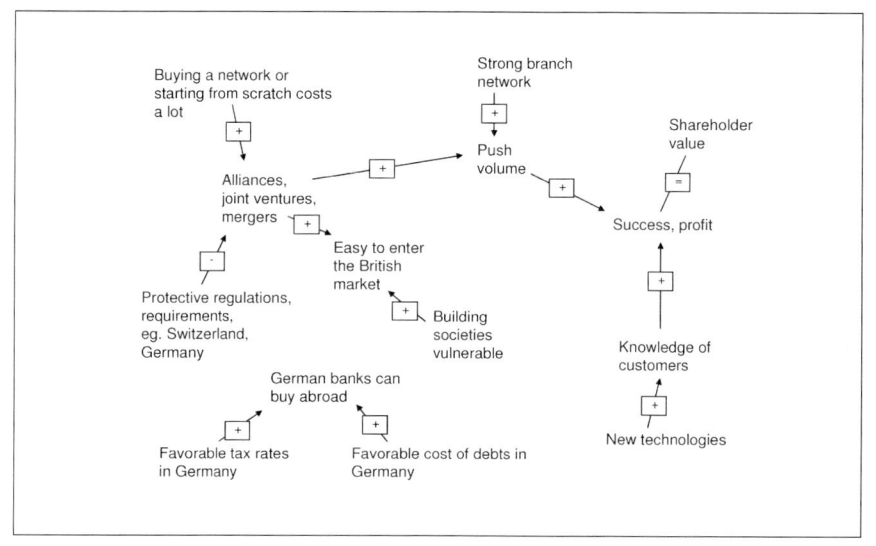

Figure 12: **Example for a cognitive map of a bank CEO** (adopted from Calori, Johnson, & Sarnin, 1994, p. 447)

Compared to the map depicted here, there can of course be much more complex representations. What is generally not shown in any such cognitive maps, however, is the many other links that radiate from each of the different elements in the memory network to other areas of the person's entire cognitive contents.

4.2.3 Interim summary

Having outlined the most essential cognitive foundations of knowledge representation in the human mind, the question now concerns the value (or implications) that the schema construct and network theories have with regard to strategic processes. Essentially, and of particular importance in the present research context, schemas deliver two very powerful explanatory principles concerning the organization of knowledge, including acquisition and change. The first is the idea that regularities of past experience, represented at different levels of abstraction, act as filters through which all new experiences are processed. In this way, a strategist's current and past sense of reality is organized in a schema-consistent manner. This idea allows the possibility of individual differences in the content and nature of schematic representations as a function of past experience, and it also follows that dysfunctional schematic representations can have a potentially profoundly disabling effect on moment-to-moment psychological processing. The second explanatory principle is that new experiences or information that are significantly inconsistent with schematic representations are disruptive and lead schemas to either assimilate, to organize them in some way, or to become changed by them (accommodation).[74]

Schema approaches concentrate on providing an account of generic, abstracted representations of the self, the world, and others rather than on just e.g. the strategic issue. The positioning and integration of the issue into these abstracted meaning structures is what does the theoretical work. In contrast, network approaches are relatively more issue or topic centric, and it is the connectivity between information, centred around the core strategic experience or knowledge, that is the driving force of the theory (Dalgleish, 2004, p. 239). What is valuable, therefore, is that two very different unirepresentational approaches can provide quite robust accounts of the acquisition, storage and change of managerial cognitive structures generally, as well as of strategic orientations more specifically. What is more, as stated before already, the two approaches seem in fact to be complementary rather than mutually exclusive. This complementarity indicates that any gaps left by either approach might potentially be filled by models that combine more than one representational format.

Overall now, taken together from the above sections, cognitivistic approaches to human cognition and knowledge have clearly yielded a number of crucial research insights, models and explanations for some of the basics of the phenomenon at hand in the present research context. In summary of these arguments, schema and information processing models (cf. 2.4.3.1) have been shown to depend heavily upon the premise that knowledge exists in the mind (i.e., stored figuratively in schemata and literally in the brain's synapses), and that it is abstract and symbolic, thus decontextualized (cf. e.g. Anderson, 2005, p. 11 ff.). A common metaphor for this type of knowledge is a computer; people (like computers) are said to process information sequentially in a number of steps or stages. They selectively input information from the environment and then allow for some of that information to be reflected on and acted on (Wilson & Madsen Meyers, 2000, p. 63). In line with all this, the unit of analysis for these approaches is clearly the individual and his/ her 'isolated' mind. What is or occurs outside the head is

---

[74] For example, if a manger hears some completely new information about a certain competitor, or if he interacts with someone that advances an entirely different view on the present strategic situation, these inputs may lead to small changes in the actor's own cognitive structures.

consequently not dealt with herein. Since contextual or social factors are exempted from discussion, in the present research context there is thus clearly a need to still go beyond the insights presented so far and to draw on other theories and from other fields as well. This will be done in the following sections.

4.3 Situated cognition

The theories and insights on human cognition outlined in the preceding sections all can be classified as belonging to the tradition on which cognitive psychology was founded, namely that of *symbolic processing*. While mainstream psychology has for many years been characterized and paradigmized through this kind of cognitivist lens,[75] more recently, another approach has emerged in response to the increasing recognition of the limitations inherent in the traditional theories.[76] This approach, which is variously called *situated action*, *situation cognition*, or *situativity theory* (cf. e.g. Greeno, 1998; Kirshner & Whitson, 1997b; Lave & Wenger, 1991), breaks with cognitivistic views concerning knowledge acquisition and change, and assumes that knowledge is situated and is acquired in **social exchanges**. For cognitivists action is inside the head, yielding a distinction between the "stuff out there" and the processing taking place "inside here". Because cognitive processing occurs within the heads of individuals, one must understand the internal mental processes and the nature of the input-output transformation of individuals. A situated action approach to cognition in contrast considers these traditional individualistic cognitive theories as *not enough* because they widely ignore the essentially social and situated nature of human cognition. Human knowledge and interaction cannot be divorced from the world: "To do so is to study a disembodied intelligence, one that is artificial, unreal, and uncharacteristic of actual behaviour" (Norman, 1993, p. 4). What really matters is the situation and the parts that people play. In line with this fundamentally *constructionist* conception, rather than focusing entirely on the inside of individuals' heads,[77] adherents of situated cognition emphasize the role of the environment, the context, social interaction, culture, and the situation in which actors find themselves, and they minimize the importance of internal cognition (Norman, 1993, p. 4).

Moreover, similar to the cognitivistic tradition, also research emphasizing the situated aspects of cognition is varied in character and can be seen as comprising an evolving family of related

---

[75] I.e. for long, information processing models of cognition, studies of symbolic representation, and what has been called the representation of knowledge problem have dominated the fields of cognitive psychology and social psychology.

[76] Norman (1993) cited three factors that present particular problems for the symbolic representation approach, i.e. dense information, the complexity of the world, and the impossibility of observing all the relevant aspects of human cognition (cf. Norman, 1993, p. 1-6).

[77] I.e. the processing structures of the brain and the symbolic representations of mind

approaches. Also, even though situated cognition is in fact itself still in the development and thus not an established theory (yet), a common theme uniting the many different contributions is a shift in the way the relationship between person and environment is conceived. "Rather than viewing a person as being 'in' an environment, the activities of person and environment are viewed as parts of a mutually constructed whole" (Bredo, 1994, p. 28). The inside-outside relationship between person and environment, which is generally presupposed in a symbol-processing view, is thus replaced by a 'part-whole' relationship.

In line with these assertions, while traditional cognitive psychology conceives of cognition intrapsychically, the most critical requirement for an emerging situated cognition theory is to shift the focus from the individual as the unit of analysis toward the **sociocultural setting** in which the activities are embedded (Kirshner & Whitson, 1997a, p. 5). To achieve such a breaking out of the focus on individuals, situated cognitionists have developed complementary means; i.e. they focus on the structures and interrelations within activity systems; and they link the community of practice to broader categories of social and political analysis. Sociocultural theory pursues this first agenda by examining appropriation of knowledge within the "zone of proximal development" (ZPD). The ZPD "refers to an interactive system within which people work on a problem which at least one of them could not, alone, work on effectively. ...The zone is considered both in terms of an individual's developmental history and in terms of the support structure created by other people and cultural tools in the setting" (Newman, Griffin, & Cole, 1989, p. 61). The second agenda is pursued in Lave's (1988) critical anthropology, as informed by Bourdieu (1977; 1984). Here, activity (locally conceived) is linked to broader social and political institutions by distinguishing *arenas* from *settings* and relating these to each other.[78] Both of these strategies signal important attempts to break from "the hegemony of individual psychology" (Kirshner & Whitson, 1997a, p. 6).

Furthermore, as indicated above, seen over the history of cognitive science, situated cognition is still a rather 'new' approach to the study of human cognition. While it is today recognized generally and finds adherents among the entire discipline of psychology and beyond, it is particularly well suited and valuable for the study of learning issues, specifically in the context of schooling and apprenticeship. In line with this, the most robust theoretical and practical contributions to our understanding of situated cognition have been made within the field of edu-

---

[78] The organization or specific company (for example) as 'arena' is the product of patterns of capital formation and political economy. It is not negotiable directly by the individual. It is outside of, yet encompasses the individual (organisational member), providing a higher-order institutional framework within which 'setting' is constituted. At the same time, for individual organisational members, the organization is a repeatedly experienced, personally ordered and edited version of the arena. In this respect it may be termed a "setting" for activity (Lave 1988, p. 151).

cational psychology. From there, beginning in the 1990s, empirical research began to demonstrate how 'rule bound' approaches to understanding and explicating thinking (i.e. schema theories) were inadequate at describing the complex ways human learning takes place in the real world.[79] Rather than taking place offline and mainly in our heads, empirical results support the notion that learning happens as human beings interact with the living world (i.e. with both the artefacts and other people that are found in the respective situation), with learners (agents) possessing specific intentions, and in response to specific affordances of the learning environment. Thus, in the situativity theory of cognition learning and thinking are considered as mainly "on the fly" and "in the moment" (e.g. Greeno, 1998; Lave & Wenger, 1991). In line with this assumption that learning occurs perpetually with ongoing activity, an actor's neural connections are seen to be composed, changed, or reinforced with each act of coordination, whether physical, mental or linguistic. It is through this learning process then that knowledge is created, and can become embedded not just in an actor's mind, but also in how the actor's environment becomes structured as a result of this activity. Consequently, knowledge is here regarded as distributed across time and space, i.e. not just within individual minds but residing in people, practices, artefacts, and symbols. These components then constitute organisations as well as society at large (Lant, 2002, p. 357).

Drawing on the above now, despite the important insights studies investigating cognition *in situ* have yielded by now, the concrete application and reference to such situativity frameworks has so far been largely confined to specific educational issues and has not often been taken up in management and organisation research. Even though it is thus rarely found explicitly in the strategic management literature, the importance of the context, specifically as regards artefacts and tools as well as situational coactors, however, is also obvious in organizational settings. Here then, situated cognition would suggest that basic cognitive activities like e.g. strategic problem recognition or the evaluation of strategic alternatives are in close interaction with the respective organisational context, i.e. they are influenced by the context and in turn retroact on it (Wrona, 2008, p. 67). Following this, and taking this centrality of the context serious, then actually constitutes a challenge to the widely held traditional cognitivistic conception that individuals do or should apply the same decision rules or cogni-

---

[79] At first sight, all the above outlined assertions and assumptions seem to suggest that situated cognition stands in opposition to the traditional cognitivistic approaches. In fact, however, situated cognition researchers do by no means aim at proving the traditional theories wrong. Instead, this newer approach should rather be conceived of as an extension of the cognitivistic approach. The merits of the established theories are clearly recognized, but situated cognition aims to go beyond this. By seeking different paradigms and methods that might bypass the apparent block to the progress of cognitivism, 'richer' explanations for human thinking and cognitive change may be provided.

tive schemata across different situations in order to make rational choices. Instead, the schemata individuals apply or the cognitive processes occurring are not uniform all the time or across all situations. As articulated by Pea (1993), our own knowledge cannot be separated from the contextual knowledge that frames it: "Knowledge is commonly socially constructed, through collaborative efforts toward shared objectives or by dialogues and challenges brought about by differences in persons' perspectives" (Pea, 1993, p. 48 f.). Here then, in light of the present research focus on strategic processes, this seemingly clear context dependence of cognitive structures and operations underlines the above outlined importance of carefully differentiating between the different 'forums' in which strategic activities are carried out in the ongoing process (cf. Chapter 3). Moreover, these outlines also substantiate what has been hinted at in the context of discussing some (tentative) implications of taking a socio-cognitive perspective on strategic processes in Section 3.4.2: I.e., since the different activities and respective forums can each be characterized by describing them along the values they have along different dimensions in analogy to those of the overall strategic process, merely at a 'lower' level (i.e. the specific content, different actors), managers then also apply context-specific schemata. This means, comparing for example a planning context to a strategy workshop, as the former is more 'rational' and formal, the creative mind may not be stimulated or activated that much here. Also the tools actually used or available in the different contexts are different. Whereas in workshops mostly tools are used that are less analytically demanding (cf. 3.4.1.3), in traditional planning cycles against that more demanding methods are utilized which thus also stimulate managers' thinking more. On the other side, however, less 'thinking out of the box' can be assumed in the latter context.

Overall then, since situated cognition explicitly allows for dynamic interactions between context, process and outcomes, incorporating its arguments here thus clearly contributes to the development of the broader systems view of strategic processes that was called for in Chapter 3. Apart from this, the above explicated thesis of the contexuality of knowledge then finally also has crucial **methodological implications**. I.e., if according to the theory knowledge structures cannot be examined without situating them in their specific context, then the large-scale studies that various scholars call for (cf. e.g. Hodgkinson, 2001a) are not appropriate for investigating the phenomena at hand. Because relevant context variables cannot be specified and controlled ex ante, qualitative research designs therefore appear more suitable here (Wrona, 2008, p. 68). These apply idiographic methods (i.e., methods that allow for describing the unique) and thus capture the research object in its entire variety. In addition, also the mutual relations among the object's different characteristics as well as its context are taken into account (cf. e.g. Denzin & Lincoln, 2005; Flick, Kardorff, & Steinke, 2004a; Wrona, 2005). Exactly this has been recognized in the present research and will be taken up and discussed in detail in Chapter 6, which presents the own empirical study.

4.4 Socially shared cognition and collective knowledge in organisations

The situated cognition approach has clearly pointed to the importance of considering the context in which cognition occurs or is examined; specifically the **artefacts** and tools as well as the **co-actors** that are present. As has been shown, overall, the approach thus offers a more general framing in which significant aspects of (cognitive) activity evolve in processes of construction and negotiation between participants and other systems in situation (Greeno, 1998, p. 14). Even though questions of how elements of cognitive structures can actually become shared or parallelised between individual actors are thus implicitly contained (i.e., since they are in the same context and interact), these situativity approaches are generally not focused on explaining cognition beyond the individual. Instead, like basically all research on group processes in psychology has done for decades, also here the focus is nearly exclusively on individual-level phenomena (i.e., the individual as the 'proper' focus of investigation). In line with this, although in 'situated cognition' direct social interactions are indeed pointed to since they are part of the situation, the idea of how *shared* knowledge or *collective* meaning evolve is not dealt with explicitly. Individual-level processes are clearly necessary, but they are not sufficient to explain fully how this sharedness develops in the end. Hence, what is needed in the present research context is something still beyond situated cognition.

Here then, regarding the idea of 'socially shared cognition', in the literature many terms and definitions can be found and also different models or approaches for explaining how things (can) become shared between two or more individuals exist. In this respect, tracing the collective meaning approach to its origins, it is most closely associated with the **symbolic interactionist approach** as elaborated within sociology (cf. e.g. Blumer, 1969; as well as the works of the early American pragmatists James, Dewey, Peirce and Mead). As expressed by Blumer (1969), the social interactionist perspective contends that social meaning develops from and then is modified through interaction among social actors. The collective meaning approach is not antagonistic toward individual models of cognition but cognition is here only regarded as one component of a more complex social process in understanding behaviour. Mental models, shared mental representations, and distributed cognition thus presumably *re-*

sult from **social interaction**. In line with this emphasis on direct interactions among social actors, the research focus consequently is on interacting dyads or larger groups as the key content of analysis. Groups are then not seen as static entities but should properly be conceived of as '**arenas**' or '**forums**' in which collective interpretations of reality develop. Social interaction thus is the engine that drives the creation of collective meaning with individuals converging, diverging, or remaining unchanged as a consequence of their interaction with others (Ickes & Gonzalez, 1994, p. 306 ff.).

While the social interactionist perspective can be considered as the classical or original approach within the collective meaning tradition, from this different conceptions and advancements have (been) developed over time. Despite certain differences among these, overall, the models are complementary rather than truly distinct from each other, specifically since they all incorporate constructionist/ interactionist bodies of thought (cf. e.g. Berger & Luckmann, 1969; Blumer, 1969). One particular theoretical modification that has elaborated the interactionist approach and that is worth mentioning here is the **social constructionist approach**. This approach had its most profound and influential depiction in Berger & Luckmann's 1966 classic "The social construction of reality". Operating from a sociology of knowledge perspective and indebted to their mentor, the social phenomenologist Schütz, Berger & Luckmann argued that social actors develop intersubjective realities, incorporating the external, objective reality into a collective, subjective one (Berger & Luckmann, 1969; Schütz, 1960). Through collective construction of meaning society is constructed in ways that depend on the interaction of its members. With this, the authors do not deny the existence of an objective reality, but they deprivilege it as the proximal cause of action. Although constructionism is most often used by interactionists to address the institutional formulation of social problems, it is by no means limited to the examination of social problems but applies more broadly to the creation of all social life (Thompson & Fine, 1999, p. 293).

Drawing on this, a compatible perspective, labelled **neo-institutionalism**, has been developed by organizational theorists. Also these scholars recognize the central role of the lived experience of being in organizations and the effects of interaction, generating collective meaning in organizational life (cf. e.g. Ouchi & Wilkins, 1985; Pfeffer, 1981). In this context and in a similar vein, some organizational theorists argue that organisations are characterized by loosely coupled systems (e.g. Weick, 1976), are fundamentally anarchic (e.g Cohen et al., 1972), and have recognizable cultures (e.g. Kamens, 1977; Zucker, 1977). Here then, the fact that actors are corporate in that they represent positions or agencies does not mean that the interactionist perspective on social action is irrelevant. Instead, interaction is still considered as the means by which people come to understand their situations. In fact, *that* organizations are symbolic persons makes the constructionist perspective only more powerful, if it admits that these actors are motivated by corporate impression management and limited by organizational structures (Thompson & Fine, 1999, p. 294).

Furthermore, following from the above assertions concerning the essential role scholars from a variety of different disciplines attribute to social interactions, it thus seems clear that shared cognition is most centrally related to **communication**. Specifically, communication plays an integral role in the development of shared cognition, with it being both a process and a product of shared cognition. Therefore, shared cognition and communication have a dynamic relation in which shared cognition improves communication and communication in turn improves the extent and quality of shared cognition (Roloff & Van Swol, 2007, p. 172).

In this context, a good example for the role of communication in shared cognition in organizations is Weick's (1993) work on **sensemaking** in organizational groups (Weick, 1993a, 1993b; Weick & Roberts, 1993). He argued that much of the decision making and work within an organization is done through the medium of groups of individuals communicating to make sense of a chaotic situation and to create a shared meaning. In particular, Weick states that "organizations become important because they can provide meaning and order in the face of environments that impose ill-defined, contradictory demands" (Weick, 1993a, p. 632).

Another example of the role of communication in creating shared cognition is research on **transactive memory** (cf. e.g. Wegner, 1987; Wegner, Erber, & Raymond, 1991). Through a process of communication and interaction, individuals in a group learn about each other's areas of expertise and learn what information is stored externally in the memories of fellow group members. This information about what others in the group have in their memories allows members access to this external memory, and in this way, the transactive memory system then offers "a group memory that is more than its individual components" (Wegner, 1987, p. 190).

Taken together, the outlines so far have provided a number of assertions and examples of insights and research approaches that all agree on the crucial role that social interactions and communication play for understanding the emergence of shared cognitions and the existence of socially shared reality. Here then, while in these approaches the overall focus is in fact more generally on the creation of collective meaning in societies at large or in different kinds of collectives, rather than specifically in organisations, these ideas and related concepts are also drawn on and applied by scholars conducting research on knowledge and learning in organisations. In analogy to the preceding outlines, a central interest here then concerns how individual knowledge is or can be transformed into knowledge that is shared by more than merely one organisational actor, and how changes or developments in knowledge structures at the individual level are related to learning at the collective, specifically the organisational, level. Along with this, for the own specific research interest in how shared strategic knowledge structures develop in the context of strategic processes, further valuable insights may thus be drawn from the wider literature on **organisational learning**.

Drawing on the above, in line with the importance ascribed to *knowledge* as a core resource in organisations (cf. 2.3.2), the corresponding literature on organisational learning is in fact by now a quite vast and complex field in itself such that a thorough treatment and discussion of the variety of different views and approaches to the issue would clearly be beyond the scope and the purposes of the present work (for comprehensive overviews cf. e.g. Argote, 1999; Argyris, 1999; Easterby-Smith & Lyles, 2006). In light of the specific research interests at hand, however, what is of particular value is that also in the most dominant perspective to organisational learning, i.e. the knowledge-based approaches, the central role of social interactions and communication among organisational members is emphasized (e.g. Brown & Duguid, 1991; Cohen & Levinthal, 1990; Elkjaer, 2003; Klimecki, Probst, & Eberl, 1994). More specifically, while generally different ways and possibilities have been outlined through which uses, changes and developments of an organisation's stocks of knowledge (can) occur (cf. e.g. Kogut & Zander, 1992; Nonaka, 1994; Nonaka, Krogh, & Voelpel, 2006), according to this perspective the starting point of it all are the individual organisational participants. Since organisational learning is considered to take place through individuals and their interactions, individual level cognition and knowledge are hence clearly important. However, the learning of a social system is not equal to the sum of individual learning processes even though these are an important basis for it (Fiol & Lyles, 1985, p. 804). The organisation learns as individuals 'put' knowledge into it. At the same time these individuals themselves draw on the knowledge stored in the organisation and hence learn in turn. In line with this, organisations can thus have more or less knowledge than their individual members, i.e. *more* because a variety of knowledge from different individuals is stored in the organisation's systems and structures, and *less* because not all the individual parts are accessible for the organisation (e.g. Argyris & Schön, 1978, p. 9; Hedberg, 1981, p. 6). Also, through the individuals' interactions and mutual relations a changed whole is finally created. The difference between knowledge and learning at the individual and the organisational level consequently stems from the

reciprocity between the individual organisational members and the organisation. Similar as in current models of socially shared cognition, which postulate a fluid and dynamic conception of shared understanding, also in organisational learning it is thus active persons that shape the collective nature of shared understanding and knowledge and in turn it shapes them (Thompson & Fine, 1999, p. 296).

Furthermore, along with the recognition that there are different ways through which organizational knowledge can develop, a particular emphasis in the literature on organisational learning is put on the **variety of contexts** that further these learning processes. Among these, strategy development and strategic planning constitute important occasions for such developments in knowledge to occur (cf. e.g. Probst & Büchel, 1994, p. 93 ff.). In line with this, Mintzberg et al. for example even explicitly state that strategic processes contain essentially learning processes (Mintzberg et al., 2007, p. 203 ff.).

Moreover, apart from but closely related to recognizing the variety of contexts and consequently also the number of (potential) **carriers** of collective knowledge, what is finally crucial to be able to truly speak of *organisational* knowledge, is that all these insights derived or produced in specific contexts are also stored independently from the individual or the group and hence become really integrated in the organisation. A variety of storage mediums may be imagined for this. In this regard, a large part of organizational knowledge about how to do things is stored in the form of standard operating procedures, routines, and scripts (Huber, 1991, p. 105), as well as in increasingly sophisticated computer-based knowledge management systems. The reciprocity outlined above between individual cognition and the overall organisation and its structures is apparent here again then. I.e., on the one hand it is in such systems where the knowledge openly shared and further developed through communication in a particular context is stored. On the other hand, by storing the knowledge in different mediums the results of such learning are made transparent and accessible for other members in the organisation, which (potentially) contributes to further sharedness in knowledge among a wider range of people.

Now, considering all the above outlines together, both in the general models of socially shared cognition and in approaches to collective knowledge and learning in organisations, the central role of interactions and communication is stressed. Here then, whereas situated cognition already points to the importance of considering cognition and knowledge in context (cf. 4.3), the approaches here clearly go beyond the individual actor and explicitly stress that knowledge is socially constructed from living and specifically working practices. To understand how socially shared meaning and collective knowledge develop, the focus thus needs to be on those 'communities of practice' where people interact and share knowledge through collaborative mechanisms such as narration and joint work (Brown & Duguid, 1991, p. 40 ff.). In line with the crucial role that especially groups as *carriers* of (organisational) knowledge and *context* for (organisational) learning are hence generally ascribed, also for the own specific interest in how shared *strategic* knowledge structures emerge among key actors in strategic processes, it is thus finally the investigation of the interactive behaviours in a specific group context, i.e. in strategic decision making groups, which appears most valuable. Before moving to this concrete 'micro'-context, however, an integration of all that has been discussed so far shall be provided now to show what exactly the *socio-cognitive perspective* on strategic processes means generally, and especially in comparison to the traditional cognitive perspective. With this, also the first overarching research question of the present work is finally answered.

4.5 Synthesis 1: A socio-cognitive perspective (SCP) on strategic processes

In this section, an integration of the insights discussed in the previous parts of this work is presented. With this, the essentials of a socio-cognitive perspective on strategic processes are outlined. Adopting such a socio-cognitive approach will be shown to allow for a more holistic view on the development of organisational strategies in the ongoing process of strategy formation. Finally, with all this, also an answer to the first, overarching, research question is provided at the end of this first synthesis.

Taking together the variety of theoretical accounts and details on human cognition presented so far (as well as referring back specifically to the outline of the cognitive perspective on strategic management in 2.4), it seems clear that the cognitive approach truly offers new and important insights on organizational life. The cognitive 'basics' discussed, like e.g. schemata and information processing models, are essential for illuminating and understanding cognitive phenomena at the level of individuals.

However, as seen in the preceding sections, cognition is not only an intra-individual process and structure but it is highly influenced by elements that are fundamentally social. It is contextualized and often has a social end, in particular when it is expressed in discourse: "Our knowledge is socially structured and transmitted from the first days of our life and they are coloured by the values, motivations and norms of our social environment in adulthood"

(Forgas, 1981, p. 2). Also, if individuals continually construct and reconstruct their schemata, they do not only do it in interactions with artefacts and other tools in their environment, but in social interactions with others. Empirical works on the cognitive development of children (e.g. Piaget, 1952) on the one hand, and on the systems of representation in group situations (e.g. Abric, 1984; Codol, 1974, 1984) on the other, clearly demonstrate this permeability of the social and cognitive dimensions. As cognitive phenomena cannot be reduced to intra-individual processes and inversely, interactions are influenced by the representations held by group (or organisational) members, a **collective representation** or schema thus appears to be inseparable from social interactions (Allard-Poesi, 1998, p. 401). These interactions have to be understood as the process and the result of the social construction of reality (Berger & Luckmann, 1966). Such a conceptualization hence leads to the examination of shared orientations not as a phenomenon in itself, but as something "always in the making, in the context of interrelations and actions ... that are themselves always in the making" (Moscovici, 1988, p. 219). In this context then, **communication** is an essential element because through the influence processes it activates, it enables individual representations to converge and something individual to become social (Moscovici, 1988).

In line with these arguments, it now seems clear that despite its merits, overall, the purely cognitive approach is not well-suited for explaining phenomena that are more complex and especially dynamic. It thus does little to account for the emergence and the properties of shared orientations in strategic processes. Specifically in light of the present research concerns then, the cognitive perspective therefore clearly falls short because it neither appreciates the role of the general context or strategic situation, nor that strategists do not act in isolation but that it is actually groups or collectives that have a pivotal role in today's organizations, and that hence need to be examined. In a similar vein, already Gioia and Sims (1986), in their seminal book *"The thinking organization"* have stated that studying cognition and social interactions separately is a sterile approach in modern organizations. The authors noted that no phenomenon in organizations is more strongly influenced by the social setting than cognitive processing, and vice versa (Gioia & Sims, 1986, p. 4).

Thus, following from the above, to address the dynamic and collective aspects of strategic processes not adequately canvassed by individual cognitive theory, and to provide an answer to the first research question, a multi-level representation of cognition is required, which takes account of the cognitive processes and structures, the (inter-)actions of individuals, their organizational culture and routines, as well as the prevailing structures and management systems (Allard-Poesi, 1998, p. 411; Schneider & Angelmar, 1993, p. 362). For this, it is considered fruitful to extend the traditional cognitive perspective by adding explicitly the social element, stating clearly what such a *socio*-cognitive approach implies, and like that linking existing theoretical concepts and models in this extended perspective. As will be shown, this socio-cognitive view then actually provides a valuable bridge towards overcoming the still widespread and often criticized "either/ or"-stances and to achieving more integration between the computational and the interpretive perspectives (cf. 2.4.3.1 and 2.4.3.2).

Considered at the **general level**, the most central and distinguishing characteristic of the socio-cognitive perspective (SCP) is that it highlights the **mutually permeable character** of the cognitive and the social fields (Allard-Poesi, 1998, p. 406). The premise is that knowledge structures affect an understanding of social interactions. These knowledge structures, however, are **developed through interactions** with others as individuals communicate their knowledge to the larger community as they become part of the culture. In turn, that culture has a **reciprocal effect** on individual actions and knowledge structures (Kahlbaugh, 1993, p. 80 ff.). In the strategy context the perspective thus argues that strategic orientations are an outcome of reciprocal interactions of socio-cognitive constructs linked by organizational culture. Individuals are recognized as both the source and the target of influence in strategic processes (Akgün, Lynn, & Byrne, 2003, p. 840). **Socialization processes** and managers' symbolic actions, which more specifically activate these influence processes, are then crucial to the development and maintenance of **shared mental models** in organizations (e.g. Beyer, 1981; Louis, 1980; Nystrom & Starbuck, 1984; Sproull, 1981). Consequently, shared strategic orientations have to be understood as expressed and constructed in and through interactions between an organization's key actors.

In line with this, although the SCP must not be conceived of as being in opposition to the purely cognitive approach or to socio-political approaches, these are regarded as too restrictive (Allard-Poesi, 1998, p. 407). Specifically, such approaches tend to consider strategy making as an outcome of *either* cognitive *or* socio-political variables. Even in cases where both cognitive and political dimensions are taken into account they are then envisaged in terms of sets of variables that influence each other causally and diachronically (see e.g. Schwenk, 1989; Walsh, Henderson, & Deighton, 1988; Ward & Reingen, 1990). The SCP thus clearly goes beyond how such approaches would explain the overall process by explicitly considering that social, specifically political, and cognitive dimensions **interact during the process itself**.

By incorporating socio-political aspects, the socio-cognitive perspective allows recognizing that especially in the context of everyday strategy life involved actors do not necessarily mention their opinion (*individual strategies*), do change their views, do influence each other, and do continually reconstruct their orientations. Such an approach to cognition not only gives a more accurate picture of organizational life generally and strategic processes in particular, but it also sheds new light on change and learning. Additionally, it also helps to understand more about why e.g. some innovative ideas are diffused and implemented while others are not (Allard-Poesi, 1998, p. 409); why in some organisations there is a relatively persistent 'dominant logic' (i.e. for example when it is always only the same TMT members that have a final say on strategic issues); or why some firms display action patterns that suggest more cognitive diversity and flexibility than others (e.g. where participation of multiple actors is encouraged and their respective views are truly taken into account rather than choking them down in political power plays).

Furthermore, the view of the traditional cognitive perspective is that managers learn because people learn and that, because these cognitive processes take place in an organizational setting, managerial cognition is essentially an analysis of the cognitive processes and structures of an organization (Nicolini, 1999, p. 833). Managerial and organizational cognition then is said to: (1) influence the learning process in an organization, (2) is constituted by the common knowledge shared by people (especially symbolic representations), and (3) is slow and difficult to change. In contrast, the SCP developed here emphasizes the *dynamic* nature of the **learning process** in organizations. Because people (including managers/ strategic actors) are not isolated in organizations, they are a part of a knowledge flow and there is a dynamic, multi-path, knowledge network which reaches people inside and outside the organization (Akgün et al., 2003, p. 858). A socio-cognitive perspective on strategic processes then also compels us to recognize that it is not only the key decision makers that influence other organisational members, but that they themselves are influenced by them, simply through everyday interaction.

Taken together, unlike the purely cognitive perspective (which is mostly influenced by the 'computer model' of the mind and stresses the interaction between cognitive processes) the theoretical framework outlined here hence suggests that:

- **Various mental orientations** may exist in organizations (Allard-Poesi, 1998, p. 406). Usually, in studies conducted from a cognitive perspective it is e.g. assumed that there is one 'dominant logic' prevailing in the organisation, or the mental maps of the CEO are taken as representative of the mental map of the entire organisation (cf. 2.4). Cognition in organisations or collective strategic orientations, however, is not equal to the aggregate of individual cognitions. The interaction among individuals may lead to higher (or lower) levels of knowledge creation, as is the case in group problem solving where interactions among individuals may lead to either synergism or groupthink phenomena (Lant, 2002, p. 356).

- Seen over time, collective cognitive representations are of an **evolutionary nature**. I.e., these knowledge structures are continuously changing, especially when minority beliefs are expressed consistently at the public level and when a negotiation process occurs between these deviants and the majority (Allard-Poesi, 1998, p. 406).
- In line with the above, (shared) cognitions should then not be examined as a phenomenon in themselves but as always in the making (Moscovici, 1988, p. 219). Some of their elements are more stable than others – elements which are called 'core' elements – due to their cognitive centrality, as opposed to 'peripheral' ones which are more related to specific actions or issues and are unstable (cf. e.g. Lyles & Schwenk, 1992). Orientations which are intrinsically linked to interactions in a social group are continuously changing. In this construction process the degree of change may be more or less pronounced, according to the degree of inconsistency between the practices and beliefs of the group members (Allard-Poesi, 1998, p. 408), and to the influence of subgroups or individuals whose knowledge structures are different, who predispose of another status, or exercise special power (cf. also Chapter 5).
- Strategists develop **different forms** of strategy schemata. Specifically, this depends not only on the orientations previously held by actors, but also on their involvement in the task, on the group's participative mode adopted during the (decision) process, the consistency of the viewpoints expressed by members, the way conflict is solved (control, rejection, avoidance or negotiation), and on the norms induced by their tasks and by their social and cultural context (Fiol & Lyles, 1985, p. 804). The dimensions will result in various forms of socio-cognitive conflict, leading to different kinds of influence processes and consequently to different forms for the collective knowledge structures (cf. Chapter 5).

With these arguments, the SCP thus also explicitly directs attention to the different **forums** in the strategy context in which strategic activities take place. As has been discussed in 3.4.2, the nature of these different activities clearly varies according to whether it is about taking decisions, formulating plans, or informal get-together-events among a firm's top management team, etc. In line with this, also the kinds of social interactions occurring between the respective participants vary, influenced by both the specific context in which they take place, as well as the actors that are present. Accordingly, the cognitive effects or changes will be different.

What then are the **implications** of adopting a socio-cognitive perspective to strategic processes? At the general level, it becomes visible that the overall extent of cognitive convergence, its speed and particular form depend on the kind of strategic processes in an organisation. Therefore it is important to carefully consider the dimensions of the process(es) and their respective values (cf. 3.4). This gives insights into who are the actors involved, how formalized or institutionalized are the processes, how 'open minded' and adaptable is the organisation, etc.

More specifically, it is essential to differentiate between the different strategy forums and activities. With this view on the 'lower' level then, in analogy to the dimensions of the overall strategic process, the respective characteristics of those 'micro' dimensions can be examined. By thus sensitizing managers to the importance of the 'correct' design of such activities and forums, this understanding may support the management in **forming an adequate group** of organisational members participating in generating, discussing, combining, and deciding on strategic ideas and issues. In addition, also the wider context, including tools and methods, must be carefully regarded.

Overall, the SCP emphasizes that strategic processes are a socially constructed, multidimensional and multifaceted concept. As seen, different theories point to different parts of the process. Taking this into account, the SCP is therefore based on different theories and like this tries to incorporate values, contexts, and power, and to capture the dynamic nature of the process to adapt to the environment and change the environment in return. The SCP is particularly valuable since it not only applies the information-processing concept to social stimuli, but also draws attention to the social context in which people do their thinking, judgment, and sensemaking (Akgün et al., 2003, p. 843). This social context in turn affects the cognitive processes (Schwarz, 1995, p. 362 ff.). In this sense, the SCP goes beyond both the structural approach (which emphasizes organizational routines and cultures) and the cognitive approach (which emphasizes individual cognitive and learning processes) (Hayes & Allinson, 1998, p. 848 ff.). By incorporating social and cognitive perspectives, the SCP combines different views on the overall strategy process as well as cognitive paradigms that so far have been often treated as competing theories (i.e., cognitivism versus situated cognition, individual cognitive psychology versus models of socially shared cognition or cognition at the group level). Already Bandura's (1986) sociocognitive theory indicated that human behaviour is best understood by *reciprocal systems of causality* of behaviours, environmental factors, personal characteristics, and cognition (Bandura, 1986). In line with this, the SCP emphasizes the

interactive cycle of individuals' behaviours and actions, outlining how the cognitive responses of individuals are influenced by interaction with others, how individual cognitive processes are mediated *in* and *by* these social interactions, and how organizational norms and routines affect the cognitions and behaviours of individuals. By recognizing, different from the cognitive perspective, the **bi-directionality** of these influence processes (i.e. dialectics) (Akgün et al., 2003, p. 843), the approach can thus be used as a valuable basis for gaining a more comprehensive and accurate picture of strategic processes overall, as well as a better sensitivity and guidance to examine and understand what is going on inside the little 'elements', e.g. strategic decision making processes, that constitute this ongoing process.

Regarding the first, overall, **research question** it can now be said that:

- (Strategic) knowledge structures (can) never get completely shared or parallelized. Collective knowledge may exist as highly shared 'strategy' schemata among key actors, it may exist as unevenly distributed knowledge among participants, and it may be shared or gain equivalent meanings through heedful interrelating (cf. e.g. Weick & Roberts, 1993). Apart from but also related to the possibility of different *forms* of collective strategy schemata, there are also different emergence processes (Allard-Poesi, 1998, p. 407) as well as different relationships with the individual level of cognition, depending in particular on the participative mode or the relationships between key actors.
- Direct social interactions *and* 'non-social' interactions in the same context contribute to the parallelisation of knowledge structures. I.e., shared strategic knowledge and orientations can and do develop in different settings in the organization and through different means. Regarding the 'non-social' occasions, especially institutionalized formal rules, handbooks, and other storage mediums for organisational knowledge (cf. 4.4) play a role. Social processes that matter are both formal and informal interactions where actors are in direct contact with each other (either face-to-face or via electronic communications).
- Finally, due to the eminence and crucial importance of **politics** and **power** in strategic processes, even if the majority shares a common orientation or knowledge structures, this does not necessarily mean that it is also their will or their behaviours which finally impact on the real important strategic activities carried out by the organisation. The transition from strategies as *strategic orientations* to strategies as real *manoeuvres* or visible *action structures* is not straightforward and is influenced to a large extent exactly by such power and political issues. Researching these issues in more detail would consequently be another interesting endeavour.

Now, it has been shown that the form and the extent of shared strategic orientations depend critically on the socio-cognitive dynamics occurring during (group) interactions. As argued before, the socio-cognitive perspective thus sensitizes the researcher to consider more specifically the different forums in which strategic activities take place. Here then, a look at all the possible existing occasions for such interactions would clearly be beyond the scope of a singular project. Instead, however, in the following a move is now made away from the rather general level regarded so far, to picking out exactly one such specific micro setting for strategic activity, i.e. strategic decision making, in order to examine the specific socio-cognitive processes occurring in this particular context.

4.6 Towards examining the socio-cognitive processes in decision making teams

The outline and discussion of the socio-cognitive perspective on strategic processes so far has shown that, apart from generally sharing the same broader (organisational) context, social interactions play a crucial role in contributing to the development of shared strategic orientations among key organisational actors. In this context, such interactions do not merely occur 'on the fly' and unsystematically, but specifically concrete group or team settings constitute important forums in which strategic activities take place and strategic issues are dealt with. Here then, strategic decision making is one specific and important forum among these (cf. 3.4.1.3). Apart from (possibly) leading to concrete formulated plans or decision outcomes, collective decision making processes also provide an important occasion for discussion, sharing strategic ideas and knowledge, and thus for contributing to sharedness in cognitive structures among the participants involved.

In line with this, the work's **second major research question** specifically focuses on the *nature* of social interactions in strategic decision making groups and on the *role* these interactions have for the (non-) development and change of shared knowledge structures. To investigate this, a move is now made from regarding more generally the overall strategic process(es) to the 'micro' level, i.e. into concrete groups. With this specific focus, the aim is to finally derive and to discuss an integrated model of strategic decision making from a socio-cognitive perspective (i.e. a model of interaction processes in one specific social context in the organisation). In line with what has been outlined at different points in the preceding sections, this socio-cognitive view on strategic interactions to be presented will then incorporate concepts from both situated cognition and information-processing theory (cf. 4.3 and 2.4.3.1).

For developing this socio-cognitive view now, on the group level of analysis the cognitive dimension alone[80] will first be briefly dealt with, i.e. information processing and 'social' cognition in (small) groups. Then, in the next chapter, the second crucial component of such a socio-cognitive view, namely the *social* dimension, is regarded in depth, i.e. social interactions in groups. Following from this, in Synthesis 2, an integrated model of small group decision making is presented and discussed. This model will bring together all the different issues and aspects touched on at various parts of the work. Finally, an own exploratory study of simulated strategy teams is conducted. With this, certain selected theoretical arguments advanced that far are investigated and are deepened through findings from the empirical reality.

4.7 Collective information processing

Drawing on the above, apart from the fact that a focus on a specific forum is in line with the sensitivity warranted by adopting a SCP on strategic processes to differentiate between strategic activities, types of social interaction and contexts, another compelling reason for this concrete focus is related to the recognition of the 'difficult' nature of the research object in question itself: Already at the level of individuals, cognitive processes and structures are by their very definition phenomena which are hard to capture because they cannot be directly observed. While at the general, more abstract level, especially sociology has provided some insights through theoretical explanations for the existence and emergence of collective representations (cf. 4.4), the present research context (and 'clientele') clearly calls for more concrete and 'tangible' insights and approaches to capture this issue. Even though the examination of cognitive structures, and especially of cognitive processes, is difficult, attempts have been made and results provided by researchers investigating shared cognitions or mental models in the context of concrete group problem solving or decision making teams (cf. e.g. Cannon-Bowers, Salas, & Converse, 1993; Mathieu, Goodwin, Heffner, Salas, & Cannon-Bowers, 2000; Mohammed, Klimoski, & Rentsch, 2000).

Here then, although the extension from individual to group cognition is not straightforward and is highly influenced by contextual factors, it has nevertheless been argued that the given understanding of individual cognition can be used as a basis for understanding cognition at the group level. Specifically, Larson & Christensen (1993) for example noted that everything known about individual cognition is inferred from observations of behaviour, so cognition is

---

[80] Clearly, the social dimension and factors cannot really be separated from collective cognitions and information processing in groups. The separation between the two dimensions is hence only made for didactic reasons.

at best an "explanatory fiction". They suggested expanding the fiction to help account for group-level processes (Larson & Christensen, 1993, p. 7).

In this context now, the term **"social cognition"** shall be introduced, which has not been used in the present work so far. This omission was done on purpose because, especially in the management literature, there is a lot of confusing use of the term. Admittedly, at first sight it might seem as if it was exactly "social cognition" that it is all about here. In traditional psychology, however, the term actually denotes something different: I.e., cognition is construed in strictly non-social terms; it is something that happens and exists inside the individual. As such, the subfield of "social cognition" therefore shares both the perspective and many basic assumptions and methods of the large field of cognitive psychology (cf. 4.2). Social cognition thus denotes the study of individual cognitions with a social *content*, i.e. 'about'. What is needed here, however, is cognition beyond the individual and in a social context. In line with this, Larson & Christensen (1993) were among the first to explicitly suggest that it seems feasible that there is another potentially useful meaning that can be ascribed to the term social cognition (cf. Larson & Christensen, 1993, p. 6 ff.). According to these authors, when considering group-level intellective phenomena, such as group problem solving and decision making, it is evident that much of the information processing that contributes to the resultant noetic product has a **distinctively social flavour**. In a **group meeting**, for example, problem-relevant information that is initially held by only one group member can have little impact on the solution-finding process unless that information is introduced into the group discussion. Introducing uniquely held pieces of problem-relevant information into a group discussion is by its very nature a social act. Moreover, it is a social act that is functionally equivalent to the process of memory retrieval at the individual level of analysis. Thus, just as recall is an element of individual cognition that can be essential for individual problem solving, introducing problem-relevant information into a group discussion is an element of 'social' cognition that can be essential for group problem solving.

Following this reasoning, a new or other meaning for the term social cognition has been proposed: I.e., it is suggested that the term 'social cognition' can be usefully applied at the group level of analysis to refer to those social processes like e.g. introducing information into a group discussion that relate to the **acquisition, storage, transmission, manipulation** and **use** of information for the purpose of creating a group-level intellective product. In this context, social cognition then "is not merely cognition '*about*', it is cognition '*by*', with the word 'social' referring to the way in which cognition is accomplished" (Larson & Christensen, 1993, p. 6). At the group level of analysis, cognition *is* a social phenomenon. In fact, this definition of social cognition is consistent with an emerging trend in the small group and interpersonal relations literature to view intragroup **communication** as a form of information processing (e.g. von Cranach, Ochsenbein, & Valach, 1986; Wegner, 1987).

Following Larson & Christensen's arguments, the term social cognition in its meaning as cognition 'by' shall therefore be adopted for the purpose of the present research interests. Also in line with the above arguments, an individual-level model of information processing (cf. 2.4.3.1) will be used as the basis for the own model of the socio-cognitive dynamics occurring in strategic decision making groups. However, even though there are some compelling reasons for adopting such an approach, the authors themselves point to several **caveats** associated with this use of the term 'social cognition' that still have to be noted here (cf. Larson & Christensen, 1993, pp. 6-7). In this regard, *firstly*, it is important not to confuse individual-level and group-level cognitive events. Individual and social cognition are clearly different things. To recall a piece of information from memory is obviously not the same as mentioning that item in a group discussion, despite the fact that these two events serve essentially the same function, albeit at different levels of analysis. *Secondly*, it is not suggested that social cognition is in any way a substitute for, or can take place in the absence of, individual cognition. Quite on the contrary, social cognition depends upon and is supported by individual cognition. *Thirdly*, although the analysis of group problem solving is then guided by an examination of problem solving at the individual level, there is no reason to suppose that every cognitive function used in individual problem solving necessarily has a group-level counterpart. Individual problem solving serves only as an informal model for what may occur in groups. Suggestions are made by way of analogy. *Finally*, all information processing in groups occurs in specific contexts, and by their nature, groups are context sensitive and **context situated** (Levine, Resnick, & Higgins, 1993, p. 586 f.). When performing a cognitive task, groups process information that is available, which also exists in a context. Since the cognitive and group processes involved in information processing are thus generally particular to that specific context, understanding the entire information processing in groups requires an analysis of the respective contexts or at least sensitivity to them (Cronin & Weingart, 2007, p. 770). In line with this, although some degree of social cognition occurs in virtually every kind of group problem-solving or discussion situation, different types of situations call for different types of socio-cognitive activity. The demand for social cognition may consequently vary greatly from one context to the next. When e.g. the available problem-relevant information or knowledge is not openly manifest to the group, a portion of the group's time will necessarily be spent in trying to uncover that information. Or, even though it is held by some group members, it may not be equally distributed among them as a function of either special expertise or unique past experiences. This may for example be the case in an interdisciplinary programme evaluation team where each member has a background in a different academic field or in a multinational firm where top managers from different internationally located units come together. Here then, part of the process is to discover what the various group members know that is relevant to the problem at hand (Derry, DuRussel, & O'Donnell, 1998, p. 33).

Drawing on the above, overall, applying individual level information processing concepts to groups seems clearly useful. Nevertheless, especially in light of the latter arguments pointing to the importance of the context, it is clear that cognitivistic approaches are not sufficient in the present research context.[81] Therefore, in the final model, information processing theories shall be integrated with insights from the situated cognition perspective. In this respect, so far the latter approach has been discussed in the context of explaining cognition at the level of individuals. In line with its basic premises (cf. 4.3), however, situativity theory recognizes that also groups clearly function within broader contexts. Bringing the two together in an analysis of group decision making (from a socio-cognitive perspective) is hence believed to be a powerful approach.

Overall now, although an explicit focus on the cognitive dimension had been attempted in this section, the outlines here have clearly shown that information processing at the group level is essentially socio-cognitive, i.e. the cognitive dimension cannot be discussed without the social. Communication is at the core of shared cognition because shared cognition in groups requires communication among people (Roloff & Van Swol, 2007, p. 172), whereas individual cognition has no such requirement. Having seen the crucial importance of social factors, the following chapter will now provide a detailed outline of factors impacting group interaction processes, (potential) temporal phases and patterns within these, evidence from group learning, as well as forms and functions of social interaction in this setting.

---

[81] A similar conclusion was drawn in the discussion of the general level of strategic processes (cf. 4.5).

5 Social interaction processes in (small) groups

In the preceding chapter it was shown that information processing and learning, i.e. cognitive changes, have to be regarded as situated and that especially at the group level the development of shared knowledge structures is essentially linked to social interactions and communication. Despite this recognition, however, the 'black box' of actual group processes is in fact seldom really investigated and "social interactions" are usually left formulated in such a broad way. The question then is what social interaction processes really are, what do they entail, and how can they be described in a more detailed way? In this regard, what is of particular interest here is the social interactions among strategic actors in the context of dealing collectively with a concrete decision or discussion task. Accordingly, in the following the social dimension is now examined in detail, i.e. the factors and conditions necessary for effective knowledge sharing and information processing, process phases, possible types and patterns of social interaction, their functions, etc.

At an earlier point in the work it was already said that there are in fact few empirical publications on strategy making groups in the literature, especially not on their 'inside', i.e. the real processes and dynamics occurring.[82] Useful insights, however, can be drawn and then transferred to the present context from other areas, i.e. specifically that of small group research. This then provides an opportunity to attempt to build a bridge between two rarely connected areas of research, i.e. the small groups area and the strategic decision making area (Milliken & Vollrath, 1991, p. 1231). Theory and research on small group processes may not only yield some valuable insights into understanding how freely interacting groups can be expected to behave in the decision context but they may also suggest some mechanisms for **designing** and **composing groups** to encourage them to share knowledge and information more effectively, and thus to handle their strategy tasks more efficiently.

At this point it is important to clarify that small group research is actually a vast field in itself. In this context, many different types of groups and tasks can be distinguished and examined.[83] Also, even if only considering *task-oriented* groups, there still is a wide array of different tasks that can and have to be carefully distinguished. As a consequence, in drawing on such insights and trying to apply them here, it is thus imperative to first clarify the specific type of

---

[82] In recent times, however, thanks to the efforts of the so-called 'micro' or 'strategy-as-practice' researchers (cf. 3.2.6), empirical findings from the organisational and strategic reality are now slowly starting to emerge.
[83] To classify and systematize these diverse kinds of groups and task-types, different typologies have been proposed in the literature (e.g. Ardelt-Gattinger & Gattinger, 1998, p. 2 ff.; McGrath, 1984, p. 41ff. and 53 ff.; Zysno, 1998, p. 10 ff.).

group and task dealt with. As discussed in Chapter 3, also among groups involved in strategic processes there are different kinds that can be classified as different types of groups and that consequently also have different task structures. The focus here, however, shall be specifically on knowledge and information processing and social interactions in **strategic decision making teams**. In this regard, besides being characterized as formal, interacting, face-to-face groups, they also fit largely into McGrath's (1984) category of "debate & decide" groups. Regarding their specific **task**, as outlined in more detail in Chapters 2 and 3, strategic decisions (and also formal strategy debates) are usually characterized as being complex, unstructured and often highly 'political'. The starting point in such groups, and hence the reality dealt with here, then is (often) the following:

A complex and new decision problem exists for which so far there is no well-proven solution, but instead partially diverging and partially converging interests have to be taken into account. Also, potentially high conflict potential is at stake. A project group is formed for discussing and deciding the task at hand.[84] This kind of group is put together according to certain problem specific criteria. The group members then each come to the group meeting(s) with different partial solutions and different goal representations. Their task is multifaceted: Firstly, complex problem solving, integration and distribution performances are demanded of them. In addition, they often also have to coordinate the implementation of their decision(s). Consequently, group members are under a lot of **pressure**: Vis-à-vis their organization they as a group are responsible for the group's performance or results. As individuals they have to account for their own contributions to the group task vis-à-vis the rest of the group. At the same time, however, they also have to be able to legitimatize the group decision in front of their respective work or relational (departmental/ functional) context. This makes not only high cognitive but also social demands on the group members. To illuminate this situation, the socio-cognitive perspective thus seems exactly what is needed here.

5.1 *A general framework for the study of groups*

The specific focus here concerns the dynamics, i.e. the interaction and communication patterns, in strategy groups as they debate and process strategic information. Any such 'black box', however, is clearly always embedded within a specific context or environment, and so the behaviours and interactions occurring are closely connected with other aspects like the structural characteristics of the group, the strategic context, or the concrete content of the

---

[84] The recognition here is that strategic decision making is not only or not necessarily accomplished by the TMT (cf. Chapter 3).

issue (cf. 3.4.1). For looking at such groups and finally arriving at a comprehensive socio-cognitive model of strategic decision making processes, a first step thus is to outline a general conceptual framework for the study of (small) groups that provides a larger picture of the entire problem.

In line with the complexity and broadness of the overall research field, there are many different perspectives from which groups can be viewed and from which researchers have been engaged in studying them (cf. Poole & Hollingshead, 2004). As a result, also a number of different conceptual frameworks can today be found in the literature. One of the earliest and most widely cited models (or 'maps'), laying out systematically the various parts of the research problem, was proposed by McGrath (1984), a highly-regarded social psychologist well known for his significant contributions to the field (see Figure 13 for an adoption of the original model). The model signifies and is based on the core assumptions of the most dominant and traditional perspective in small group research, i.e. the **functional perspective**.[85] Specifically, in this perspective groups are regarded as *goal-oriented*; behaviour and performance are assumed to vary in quality and quantity can be evaluated; interaction processes have utility and can be regulated; and internal and external factors are said to influence group behaviour and performance via interaction (Hollingshead et al., 2004, p. 21 ff.).

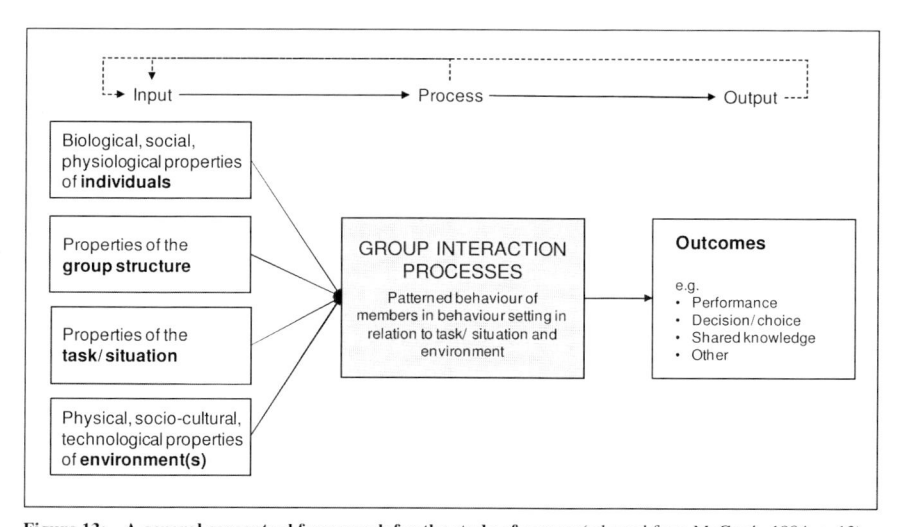

Figure 13: A general conceptual framework for the study of groups (adopted from McGrath, 1984, p. 13)

---

[85] In line with the present interests and the research context, this functional view is judged as the most suitable perspective here. For an excellent collection and discussion of other perspectives on the topic, however, see Poole & Hollingshead (2004).

In line with the above, proponents of this perspective agree that the central feature, the "essence", of a group lies in the interaction of its members, i.e. the *behaving together*, in some recognized relation to one another. **Group interaction processes** is consequently the centrepiece of the model (McGrath, 1984, p. 12). However, not only is the output or outcomes from any such processes determined by the nature of the interactions taking place within the group, but the process itself is clearly influenced by a number of factors that shape that group process. These major classes of **inputs** (cf. Figure 13) set the conditions under which group interaction takes place. Moreover, the effects of these four sets of properties, singly and in combination, are forces that shape the group interaction process. The group interaction process itself is both the result of these shaping forces and the source of some additional forces. While interaction is greatly affected by those sets of 'input' variables, it is also patterned in part by forces internal (or indigenous) to the interaction process itself. Finally, the interaction process and its results represent sources (forces) that potentially lead to changes in those input conditions. These sets of 'outputs' of group interaction processes are thus parallel to the input classes and, in fact, (may) represent changes in those input variables (McGrath, 1984).

Overall, the model is a quite general framework whose strength lies in its ability to predict and to explain task-oriented group performance as influenced by static **inputs** and **processes**. Even though it thus incorporates neither cognitive issues explicitly nor a more detailed differentiation of the possible interactions, it nevertheless serves as a good and valuable basis for outlining an overall picture of the situation at hand.

5.2 Process research on group decision making

The issue of interest here has been termed "decision making" and the focus is explicitly on examining the dynamics in this particular context. What is important to note, however, is that group decision making is here understood as an ongoing social process; not only as the final point in a decision-making process. In line with this, the concrete encounter(s) between the participants can also be regarded as formal discussions on the specific issue at hand that finally lead to some result or to a non-decision (Beck & Fisch, 2000, p. 184). The terms *group decision making* and *group discussion* will therefore be largely used interchangeably in the following.

Now, as evidenced by the above framework, group researchers clearly recognize the central role that interaction processes play as mediators between inputs and group outputs. Nevertheless, like the majority of group research generally, also investigations dealing specifically with decision making or problem-solving tasks in fact rarely use true process analysis approaches. The social interaction phenomena underlying e.g. minority influence, groupthink, or the social information processing in groups thus usually remain in the black box of input-output designs (Beck & Fisch, 2000, p. 196).

Different from this and to fill this void, the central interest in the present context concerns what is occurring 'inside' the decision making process. It is assumed that the processes whereby group members share knowledge and information contribute to or mediate the development of shared cognitive structures (to varying degrees) among the involved participants.

In the strategy field there is in fact quite a large area that is specifically devoted to research on strategic decision making (cf. 0). As mentioned above already, however, most of these efforts still treat the process itself as a kind of 'black box'. This is certainly also largely due to the fact that it is very difficult to really gain access to such groups or sites since strategy is a very sensitive topic area. In-depth studies on the true dynamics occurring e.g. in strategic discussions, planning or decision committees, are thus still quite rare. In those few cases where strategy researchers have made steps forward and attempted to incorporate process variables into their designs (e.g. Knight et al., 1999), they nevertheless have done so by focusing on or picking out merely a few variables (e.g. interpersonal conflict, agreement-seeking), and by staying on with the 'remote' quantitative approach of using large-scale questionnaires. As the framework above has clearly shown, however, these aspects only represent a very small piece of the entire complex picture.

While the difficult access to the strategy field thus makes it hard to really do in-depth research and examine more than merely a few process variables by means of incorporating them into large-scale quantitative questionnaires, strategy researchers may gain promising insights through other means, namely by becoming more alert to other adjunct research fields and academic areas (including their respective methods). In this regard, especially a set of **works from social and organisational psychologists and communication theorists** is particularly valuable (e.g. Bales, 1950a; Bales, Cohen, & Williamson, 1982; Beck & Fisch, 2000; Boos, 1996, 1998; Boos, Scharpf, & Fisch, 1991; Poole, 1981, 1983; Poole & Roth, 1989a, 1989b). Insights from these have so far almost never been integrated into the strategy context, which is certainly a huge deficiency. Whereas organizational and social psychologists deal with many different types of groups and tasks, among these a special interest in fact concerns complex and ill-structured tasks and heterogeneous group members. Exactly this is clearly the kind of task and context strategists often are faced with in decision making situations. In addition, although also not strictly from true observations in board rooms or strategy discussions, the literature on **group learning** seems useful as well. Therefore, in the following, such findings and arguments as regards important process variables and conditions (for successful knowledge sharing and growth), phases, and interaction and communication patterns, shall be outlined to illuminate more on the dynamics and the processes that might be occurring and contributing to a convergence of knowledge structures in strategic decision making. From all this, finally the own socio-cognitive model that is to be presented will integrate these insights and discuss them with regard to the concrete research context at hand.

5.2.1 Factors in group interaction processes and conditions for successful cooperation, knowledge sharing and growth

In line with the high importance that teams and groups assume today in all kinds of different work environments and organizational settings, there exists a significant amount of research that is concerned with examining the factors that affect group interaction processes, and with this determining the **conditions** for successful team cooperation, performance and accomplishment of collective efforts. Even though almost no insights have been published yet regarding real life interactions or participation in corporate boardrooms or in critical strategy meetings, interesting results can be found in a closely related field of inquiry, i.e. research into collaboration in innovation projects or new product development teams (e.g. Akgün, Lynn, & Yılmaz, 2006; Koners & Goffin, 2007; Madhavan & Grover, 1998; Scholl, 2004).

In this context, a first crucial issue is the prevalence of divergent motivations, and especially of **role or loyalty conflicts** that are often reported from teams who are composed of individuals from different areas of functional expertise, hierarchical position, age or tenure, or, as often the case in strategic contexts, competing departments (marketing, finance, logistics, etc.). In such cases, individual members are on the one hand supposed to work task-oriented on the creation of a certain concept or concrete suggestions. On the other hand, however, they have often been committed by their respective superior or department and are being exploited by these. Strategies to solve such conflicts might involve indifference, increasing non-attendance, or hidden interferences (Scholl, 2004, p. 106).

On the part of **team leaders** (or higher ranked members), individual persons often do not work towards achieving the most intensive, open and productive cooperation and discussion, but are rather interested in enforcing their own goals whatever it may take. Such behaviours may extend from ignoring others' opinions, smoothing conflicts merely superficially and manipulating information, to off-pressing divergent views (e.g. Amason, Thompson, Hochwarter, & Harrison, 1995; Putnam, 1986). In such cases then the final decision or discussion outcome is unlikely to truly reflect the collective knowledge and views on the issue at hand. In addition, one might also expect that rather little cognitive convergence has occurred since the team members have neither had the opportunity nor the will to share all that they know. Also, individual internal cognitive 'barriers' might have been erected due to the perceived dominance and uncooperative behaviour of (a) certain group member(s) (Pelled et al., 1999).

Furthermore, another crucial aspect determining the productiveness or efficiency of task-oriented work groups is related to the extent that such teams succeed in increasing both individuals' as well as the group's collective knowledge base. Even though concise measurements of **knowledge growth** or developments are truly difficult to achieve, there are a number of factors that have been shown to be valuable indicators for the quality and potential of productive communication in discussion groups. Among these, **group size** is an important variable. In this context, an increase in the number of discussants and people involved in a decision certainly also implies a wider range of ideas, expertise and knowledge. A growth in knowledge stock from the existent potential of knowledge can, however, only result if through communication and discussion the existing knowledge and information is exchanged, applied and evaluated. Here then, a number of communication and organizational problems arise that may lead to process losses, which in turn limit the realization of the group's knowledge potential. The actual increase in knowledge through discussion therefore results from the difference between the knowledge potential and the process losses (Scholl, 2004, p. 116). It first increases with the number of participants, reaches, however, soon a climax, and decreases again with a further increase in the number of people involved. Consequently, the knowledge potential does not increase linearly but according to a flattening curve. Groups may thus be too small because the optimal knowledge potential is not reached or too large because process losses become too high (Scholl, 2004, p. 116).

The specific curve of the knowledge potential also depends on the **diversity** in knowledge among the participants. The more diverse the experiences and knowledge of the participants, the steeper is the curve of the knowledge potential. Also this increase, however, is not linear due to the fact that even with quite diverse functional backgrounds there are always certain overlaps in the existing knowledge, such that each additional person can add less and less problem relevant knowledge. In addition, also here process losses have to be taken into account. I.e., the more heterogeneous the experiences and insights of the participants, the more difficult it is for them to communicate successfully and to learn from each other (cf. e.g. Maznevski, 1994). They may not only be experts in very different fields (e.g. marketing versus accounting or engineers versus business graduates), but they also speak quite different 'languages' and are often even distinct in their general thinking. Consequently, the participants have to be willing to reflect critically upon grim beliefs and things taken for granted, possibly to even give those up and to structure their knowledge anew (Scholl, 2004, p. 118). Such (cognitive) restructuration is very difficult to achieve for people, necessitates usually longer time periods, and is most likely to be found in crisis situations where the usual knowledge clearly failed (cf. 0). Due to this, as detailed by Festinger (1954) in his theory of social comparison, people tend to interchange cognitively and communicate predominantly with those others that have similar views as themselves. If opinions or conceptions diverge too strongly, disagreements result, and communication is ended rather quickly or even fails. In line with this, research has in fact shown that it truly seems particularly problematic for participants to learn from those who, due to their different experiences and insights, would have to offer the most (e.g. Lau & Murnighan, 1998; Mohammed & Angell, 2004).

The cognitive aspect, i.e. the most intensive exchange as possible of knowledge contents, information and opinions, is not the only factor determining the productiveness of a discussion. Another important role is ascribed to the **mutual sympathy** of the participants and their **willingness to cooperate** and engage in a goal oriented discussion. Also here relevant empirical evidence exists that supports the close relations between the three variables of cognitive, affective and conative consensus (e.g. Amason, 1996; De Dreu & Nijstad, 2008; Ilgen, Hollenbeck, Johnson, & Jundt, 2005; Quigley, Tesluk, Locke, & Bartol, 2007).

Furthermore and as partially already hinted at in the context of outlining the role of team leaders, the **exercise of power und influence** constitutes another important dimension influencing the processes and outcomes of group discussions and decision making. The explicit distinction made between these two terms is related to the thesis that while the exercise of power interferes knowledge growth in cooperative work, ('sensitive') influence attempts may further it. The imposition of power often leads to more pronounced information pathologies and less personal knowledge increases (Scholl, 2004, p. 134). As a consequence it impacts negatively on team performance and with this also on the degree to which a convergence of knowledge structures can be expected to occur at the group level.

Since **power** and **influence** are therefore some of the most critical factors to be taken into account in the present context, a final note shall be made regarding some of the conditions that have to prevail or that may further an actor's ability to apply such means in the first place. Among these, researchers have delineated 'resources' such as hierarchical position, functional competence and capabilities, information from outside the organization, acknowledgement or support, impressive personality, mobilization of additional persons, or organisational affiliation (cf. e.g. Finkelstein, 1992; Lovaglia, Mannix, Samuelson, Sell, & Wilson, 2004; Scholl, 2004, p. 128 f.).

Finally, related to the power issue and detailing the above, **status differences** among group members are another crucial factor affecting interaction and performance. In this regard, not only do high-status members participate more and are therefore often more influential than low-status members, but member roles and status are also important because they serve a kind of 'weighting' function (Gibson, 2001, p. 126). For example, information and experiences contributed to group interactions by individuals with higher status (e.g. a leader or a facilitator) may be weighted more heavily than information contributed by other individuals, thus biasing cognitions in the direction determined by the member with the highest status (e.g. Bandura, 1997; Bartunek, 1984; Bougon et al., 1977). Here then, evidence suggests that discussions and results are in fact often dominated by the inputs of (a) high status member(s) (e.g. Earley, 1999; Walsh et al., 1988). In support of this and specifically from the strategy context, Walsh et al. (1988) were among the first to differentiate between and to capture potential collective beliefs in groups (a linear combination of the members' individual schemata prior to interaction) and 'negotiated collective beliefs' (computed by weighting the members' schemata according to the level of participation in the group discussion). Their results indicated that the negotiated beliefs were indeed better predictors of performance than the unweighted beliefs (Walsh et al., 1988, p. 202 ff.).

Taken together and to conclude from this section, although the list of factors and conditions discussed here may possibly be even extended, it has nevertheless been shown that there are truly many issues that should be considered and be kept in mind when looking at group processes and trying to examine knowledge sharing and the (potential) convergence of knowledge structures.

5.2.2 Phases and temporal patterns in group processes

Apart from the influential factors and conditions for successful interactions discussed above, another crucial issue that has been given a lot of research attention in the past is the question of whether groups, confronted with a project (e.g. a decision to make or a problem to solve), follow a particular sequence of phases of task fulfilment, or whether certain sequential patterns may be detected in the interactions. Here then, as regards specifically these more macro *process levels* of group task performance, historically, the study of how structure and process are related in group interaction began with Bales' work on task groups (Bales, 1950a). The effort to examine process issues focused on ideas that groups talk in patterns, that these patterns are stable over time, and that groups go through phases in their history of working on a task together (Bales & Strodtbeck, 1951). Bales tried to tie behaviour of individual actors to dynamics of interaction and emergent structures. Initial findings of Bales and his colleagues have been subject to intense efforts to replicate results and to extend theoretical explanations. As a result, theories of how social structures emerge, how actors come to occupy particular positions in group social structures, and how structures are communicated from actor to actor have resulted from this research program (Shelly, 1997, p. 355).

Also based on these early insights, over time several normative or "fixed sequence" models of problem solving have been proposed. The best known of these, however, still is Bales and Strodtbeck's (1951) three-phase sequence of **orientation, evaluation,** and **control**. While this *phase movement hypothesis* has been particularly stimulating for researchers interested in communication processes (e.g. Poole, 1981; Poole & Roth, 1989b), at the same time it has been increasingly questioned by a number of researchers who argue that in problem solving, even if phases can be distinguished, there is a recycling of different phases, especially for difficult and complex issues (cf. e.g. Hirokawa, 1982; McGrath, 1991). In this context, Hirokawa (1983) tested a sequence model of problem solving phases and did neither find the theoretically proposed sequence, nor any other specific sequence as being superior for group productivity. Based on these results he proposed a **task-contingent model** which posits that there is not a single fixed sequence of phases that leads to high performance, but rather that groups do show certain phases contingent upon task requirements, but not necessarily in a fixed order (Hirokawa, 1983, p. 60 ff.).

Even more complex results challenging the original unitary model have been arrived at by Poole and colleagues (Poole, 1981, 1983; Poole & Roth, 1989a, 1989b). They distinguished between *task content, task process,* and *relational activity*. For task content they observed that as the group progresses on the task, different phases recycle several times. However, also here no support was found for a single best phase sequence. Instead, how many phases can be distinguished and how often a phase is recycled, is the result of an interaction between task process activities, relational activities, and task content activities. For example, Poole and Roth observed that the **level of conflict** combined with the **power structure** of the group predicts the amount of solution searching activity that will occur (Poole & Roth, 1989a, 1989b).

Moreover, failures to find single sequences of decision making phases have also been reported from research in organizational psychology. Instead, iterative processes and recurrent cycles of different sets of phases seem to be the prevalent case (e.g. Mintzberg et al., 1976, p. 263 ff.), influenced by problem type and problem complexity (e.g. Nutt, 1984, p. 415 ff.).

Taken together, although certain phases and periods in the history of interaction in particular groups may often be discerned and any group's task process is in fact intrinsically patterned, groups nevertheless do not follow a unitary pattern of interaction. Instead, the structure of the group's task seems to be flexible, and it is influenced by the state of the entire coordination network, i.e. members, tasks, tools and their interrelations (McGrath & Tschan, 2004, p. 61). In line with this, what is important therefore is to look at the dynamics of interaction and to understand these dynamics as both initiation and receipt of activity. Specifically, explaining dynamic, emergent patterns of initiation and receipt of activity in interaction is important to understand how social structures emerge from and are maintained by interaction; i.e. it is both from sequences of interaction, and repeated patterns that emerge for actors in these sequences or cycles, that social structures are reified and realized for actors (Shelly, 1997, p. 336). Here then, as has been hinted at before, these social structures and factors will in turn also affect individuals' cognitive structures and processes.

5.2.3 Evidence from processes of group learning

As discussed in previous parts of the present work (cf. Chapter 4), from the cognitive perspective, at both individual and organisational levels changes and developments in knowledge – in particular changes in knowledge structures or schemas – are often also referred to as "learning". In line with this, another field of research from which interesting and valuable insights may be gained for answering the present research question is the literature on group learning. In this regard, whereas the particular focus here will be on the different kinds of social factors and conditions that impact on learning in particular group settings, the essential role of groups as carriers of different kinds of knowledge and context for broader organisational learning has been emphasized before already (cf. 4.4). Hence, in the final section here, some outlines will be provided that clarify more specifically the relationship between group learning and organisational learning. By thus clearly classifying the own research within the overall literature also the ground is prepared for the subsequent development and discussion of the own socio-cognitive model on group decision making in strategic processes.

Now, due to the high importance groups are accredited with as the "micro-underpinnings" of organisational learning, researchers interested in the latter consequently often also conduct research at the more confined group level. In line with this, while primarily well known for their work on understanding organizational learning, the extensive research efforts done by Argote and her colleagues provide crucial insights also into the specific processes of learning at the **group level** (cf. e.g. Argote, 1999, pp. 99-141; Argote & Ophir, 2002, pp. 181-207). Here then, several processes have been outlined that have to occur in order for groups to learn, or, in the language of the present context, for "cognitive change(s) to occur". I.e., broadly speaking, group learning is said to involve the processes through which members **share, generate, evaluate**, and **combine** knowledge. In the following now, each of these process phases shall be discussed in detail, thereby focussing especially on the variety of social factors impacting at the different stages. Before doing so, however, it is important to note that although these processes emphasize different aspects of group learning and help to organize relevant empirical findings, there is of course considerable overlap and feedback among all of these. Also, some processes may occur very explicitly, while others may be more implicit. Further, factors that affect one process may affect others. Factors that affect e.g. whether an individual is likely to share knowledge (may) also affect the 'weight' the knowledge receives once it is communicated (Argote, 1999, p. 104). At this point then, the close connection and hence inseparability between the social and the cognitive dimensions is clearly obvious again.

5.2.3.1 Sharing knowledge

Apart from other influences that derive more generally from participation and work in the same organisational context, it is the sharing of information and knowledge which is an essential part in the process of parallelisation in cognitive structures. Looking closely at the factors affecting knowledge sharing in groups thus clearly is of particular importance in the present research context.

In this regard, in 1985 Stasser and Titus published the first paper that examined collective information sharing in groups (Stasser & Titus, 1985). This study and the information sampling model the authors proposed initiated further research designed to better understand how group members share information during discussion, and how such information pooling affects group decisions. The discussion bias revealed by this research shows that (decision-making) groups tend to discuss shared information that is commonly known by all members more than unshared information that is known by a single member (cf. e.g. Stasser, 1999).

Moreover, this line of research suggests several **conditions** under which information will be shared in a group discussion. Summarizing these findings, information is most likely to be shared when: Group members are not overloaded with information, diversity of views exists in the group (i.e. the percentage of "shared" information is low), some group members are recognized for having special expertise, leaders are present in the group, groups are small in size, tasks are seen as having some answers that are better than others, group members are given experience or training with the task, and group meetings last long enough to get past the initial tendency to focus on information members hold in common (Argote, 1999, p. 109 f.).

5.2.3.2 Generating new knowledge

In addition to acquiring knowledge by sharing information and knowledge that members already possess, groups also acquire knowledge by generating new or 'emergent' knowledge. Such knowledge, which no individual group member possessed before the group meeting, can develop through group discussion and interaction (Argote, 1999, p. 114). Regarding the conditions that increase the likelihood that new or emergent knowledge will be generated, like with the sharing of information also here group compositional aspects are essential. Having individuals with different views in a group often leads to conflict that can create new knowledge. For example, **conflict** may stimulate divergent thinking (i.e. the process of considering an issue from multiple perspectives) and, coupled with an absence of **pressure** to conform, this conflict may then lead to the creation of new knowledge (Levine et al., 1993, p. 596 f.). Despite these positive effects, however, both these aspects, i.e. conflict and pressure to act, may clearly also impact negatively on the group processes. Concerning the former, research has shown that conflict is in fact a two-edged sword. Here then, not only is the specific strength of prevailing conflicts important to consider, but also its *type*. I.e., whereas a certain degree of task conflict may have favourable effects on cognitive task performance, emotional conflict against that is most often clearly detrimental (e.g. Pelled et al., 1999). Moreover, as regards pressure to act, especially in the strategy context, this is a crucial factor as in many cases there is in fact high pressure (time wise and from superiors or other actors). Under these conditions, the entire process of acquiring and pooling information is likely to be much quicker and 'dirtier'. Both more superficial and fewer direct exchanges then clearly feature in the extent to which new knowledge can be generated.

Finally, apart from these factors, new knowledge can also be created by providing group members with **experience working together** (e.g. in the strategy context if the same managers work together more often or come together in different or repeated meetings).

Besides, groups can acquire and generate new knowledge by 'importing' it from outside the group.

5.2.3.3 Evaluating knowledge

Once information has been shared or new information generated, groups must evaluate the information they have acquired. In order to evaluate hypotheses and other information, groups need to determine whether the information provided by a member is accurate or appropriate, and whether it should figure in their final output. This involves both implicit and explicit judgements of the expertise, status and role of the individual offering the information, as well as political considerations of the implications of accepting it. In this context, research on **perceptions of expertise** and on **minority influence** offers valuable insights that are relevant for understanding how groups evaluate the contributions of their members (cf. Argote, 1999, p. 118 ff.).

Factors that affect whether an individual is likely to volunteer information also affect whether the information is likely to be accepted and acted upon. Expertise can provide validation of information. Stewart and Stasser (1992; 1995), for example, found that group members were more likely to accept and remember information contributed by a recognized expert than by someone not perceived as having expertise.

With experience working together groups learn who the experts are in various areas. Here then, as argued before, especially in the strategic decision making or planning context, it can be expected that the respective group members often do not work together for the first time but have interacted at other occasions before such that a certain amount of **'meta-knowledge'** (Wegner, 1987; Wegner et al., 1991) already exists. Also, because high-level strategic problems do not fall neatly into one functional area but rather require the input from many different ones, strategic planning committees might often be composed of members with different functional expertise. Being aware of the respective expertise then is crucial in the context of evaluating the information contributed by the different group members.

Furthermore, apart from predisposing of recognized expertise, individuals are also likely to persuade the group to accept their point of view when they take a consistent – but not rigid – stance, when they are perceived as not having a personal stake in the group's decision (i.e. are perceived to be concerned primarily with the group's welfare rather than with own personal interests), and when their position is supported by another group member. Referring back to 5.2.1, all these issues are then in fact in line with the outlines provided above in the context of discussing the more general factors impacting group interaction processes.

5.2.3.4 Combining knowledge

Having acquired information and determined (either implicitly or explicitly) the weight it receives, group members finally have to combine the various bits of information into a collective product (Argote, 1999, p. 122). Here then, several additional lines of research are relevant for understanding how groups accomplish this; i.e. descriptive work on *social decision schemes*, *models of participation* in decisions, and normative models of *persuasive argumentation* (cf. e.g. Isenberg, 1986; Laughlin & Earley, 1982; Madsen, 1978; Vinokur & Burstein, 1974).

Regarding the first of these research streams, i.e. so called **social combinations views** to group decision making, studies conducted from this approach demonstrate all of the assumptions of the functional perspective (cf. 5.1) (Hollingshead et al., 2004, pp. 21-62). Besides being used for predicting or describing how groups combine their individual preferences into a single group response for a given type of task, the approach can also be applied for prescribing the best way to do that. In this context, social combination models formalize the processes by which a group maps a distribution of member preferences (e.g. the number of team members who believe that their firm should enter a strategic alliance with another major competitor in its market and those who opt against it before group discussion) into a collective group decision (the 'go' or 'no-go' decision). A 'social decision scheme' then is a rule or procedure that converts individual preferences into a group product (Davis, 1982); it thus describes the social processes by which a group makes a decision. These processes can be explicit or implicit. Laughlin and Hollingshead (1995, p. 95) postulated five ways that group members can resolve disagreement to reach consensus on a collective group response: Voting, turn taking, demonstration, random selection, and generation of a new alternative. One major finding discovered by researchers using the social combination approach is that groups rarely consider alternatives that are not advocated by at least one member prior to the group discussion. Another is that group processes vary depending on the nature of the task (cf. e.g. Davis, 1982; Laughlin, 1980). As mentioned before, the type of task thus is a critical factor that affects the decision scheme groups employ. Whereas "truth-wins" or "truth-supported-wins" models best predict the probability that the group will select the correct answer for intellective tasks, the tasks managers are faced with in strategic discussions correspond more to what is termed *'judgemental tasks'*. These are problems or decisions that involve evaluative, behavioural, or aesthetic judgments for which there is no demonstrably correct solution. Since here the group objective is to achieve consensus, majority or plurality models best predict the probability of the group choice for judgmental tasks (Argote, 1999, p. 123).

Apart from such insights provided by researchers taking a social combination view to the study of group tasks performance, aspects of work on **leadership** and **participation** are also relevant for understanding the social decision schemes used in naturalistic groups. In this context, Vroom & Yetton (1973), for example, have proposed a model of decision making which postulates that there is a continuum of decision making styles ranging from autocratic, in which a manager makes the decision him or herself, to highly participative, in which the group makes the decision. Depending on the type of style or approach taken to strategic discussions and decisions in a particular situation, also the opportunities for the exchange of diverse views and the sharing of knowledge among strategic actors will vary and with this clearly also the degree to which a convergence of knowledge structures can be expected to result from the interactions.

The third contribution to be considered in relation to questions concerning how groups finally combine different kinds of information and knowledge into a collective product comes from **persuasive arguments theory** (as well as work on **social influence**) (cf. e.g. Laughlin & Earley, 1982; Madsen, 1978; Zuber, Crott, & Werner, 1992). According to this theory, the greatest choice shifts found after group discussion occur when: (1) the preponderance of arguments in the "population" of arguments favours one alternative, and (2) the probability that a given individual group member possesses the arguments is low. Group discussion exposes individuals to new arguments. When there are many more arguments in favour of one alternative than the others, individuals' preferences shift to that alternative during group discussion (Stasser & Titus, 1987). Here then, even though caution is needed not to equal overt choice preferences with individuals' more deeply held cognitive preferences, the different influencing factors outlined (may) nevertheless also constitute important indicators for the degree or the likelihood of cognitive convergence.

Overall, as a final note in the context of discussing works from the social combinations view, it needs to be emphasized that despite their important contributions to group decision making, the majority of these studies are still today laboratory studies where groups (often students) are convened for the purpose of forming a judgment or making a decision. The social decision schemes used by these groups may be more explicit and perhaps more collective than one finds in ongoing groups in organized settings (Argote, 1999, p. 125). As the evidence from research on innovation teams or other live project groups shows (cf. 5.2.1), in such natural situations a number of other influence processes are potentially involved, or leaders may be present who do not even consult with group members. Above all, and of particular relevance in strategic contexts, **political factors** have been shown to be a critical influence on how knowledge is combined (Pfeffer, 1981).

5.2.3.5 Potential impediments to group learning

So far, in the above sections the focus has been on the different factors that can be regarded as *contributors* to knowledge exchange throughout the different stages of the group's learning process. While group settings thus generally offer high potential for value-added activities and increases in both individual and collective knowledge, there are clearly also limits to group learning. One important issue often discussed in this context is the **groupthink phenomenon**. Groupthink is a collective striving for unanimity that supersedes group members' efforts for thorough information processing (Janis, 1972). Because groupthink promotes quick compromises and avoidance of disagreements in group decision making, this consensus-seeking tendency leads to an incomplete survey of alternative courses of action, poor information search, selective bias in processing information, and failure to evaluate alternatives realistically (Hollingshead et al., 2004, p. 29). As a consequence, it may block the learning processes that generally occur in groups as members gain experience working together. Groupthink has been shown to take place when the group is highly cohesive, is insulated from other influences outside the group boundary, and is in highly stressful situations (e.g. hostile or extremely dynamic competitive environment, time constraints, etc.).

Related to this, failures of truly reflective discussion may also occur if teams are too busy or are accustomed to routine (cf. e.g. Gersick & Hackman, 1990). In addition, even if there is intensive group discussion, considerable research shows that such discussions are often ineffective due to their vulnerability to **process failures** such as ignoring relevant information not already shared by group members (cf. e.g. Brodbeck, Kerschreiter, Mojzisch, & Schulz-Hardt, 2007; Thompson, Levine, & Messick, 1999) or inappropriate deference to authorities (Janis, 1972).

Moreover, another, in fact one of the most intensively researched and still equivocal issues in the entire area, is the question concerning the effects that **diversity** in group composition has on group processes and performance. Here, despite the substantial amount of works on the topic (cf. e.g. Baringa, 2007; Dahlin, Weingart, & Hinds, 2005; Kauer, Waldeck, & Schäffer, 2007; Pelled, 1996; Pelled et al., 1999; Simons et al., 1999; Thomas, 1999; Watson, Kumar, & Michaelsen, 1993), findings and thus conclusions continue to diverge greatly. In this regard, in the context of group learning and growth in collective knowledge stocks the benefits of diversity in functional areas or members' backgrounds for acquiring new knowledge have been emphasized. Diverse groups are more likely to share "unshared" information and to generate new knowledge as a result of their interaction. Since diversity means more different views it also implies potentially more differentiated solutions or complex knowledge structures. Diversity causes group members to rethink their positions and to create new approaches and alternatives that accommodate different views. Due to this, it then is particularly beneficial for the creation of new knowledge. Too much diversity, however, can impair the generation of new knowledge if there is not at least some overlap or base of common understanding (e.g. Knight et al., 1999; Mohammed & Ringseis, 2001; Olson, Bao, & Parayitam, 2007).

In light of these findings and controversies, Dahlin, Weingart & Hinds (2005) conducted a study that was specifically aimed at contributing to a better understanding of the effects of team diversity in the context of knowledge work. The results of this study show that teams who need to make complex links between unique information categories (e.g. top management teams) might in fact suffer when diversity in expertise is high. When nationality diversity, however, is moderate to high, this may be beneficial. Thus, while dispersal of information among different experts in the group might interfere with a team's ability to integrate the information, national differences seem to add richness of insight that cross-cuts these divisions. With this, the study finally suggests that diversity has a complex relationship with information use, undoubtedly as a consequence of team processes (Dahlin et al., 2005, p. 1120). Taken together, given the persistence of disparate findings and examples about the concrete effects of member heterogeneity, no general conclusions or advices can and should be given as regards the optimal composition of groups for a specific task at hand. At least a partial reconciliation of the prevailing controversies, however, may nevertheless be achieved by carefully considering the particular dimension of heterogeneity focused on, the performance measure used, the nature of the task, and the time span of the study (Argote, 1999, p. 112).

Finally, apart from the specific phenomenon of groupthink and diversity considerations, another potential impediment to group learning is '**psychological safety**' (Edmondson, 1999). Psychological safety, which is characterized by a willingness to confront one another and openness to experimentation, has been shown as one predictor of group members' sharing intention to change their repertoire of behaviours. In cases or contexts where group members believe that they are at risk if they speak openly, the different potential process failures outlined previously, are then likely to be exacerbated by such a lack of psychological safety. In this regard, as emphasized by concrete data from Edmondson (2002), it is specifically the role of **power** and people's fears of offending those who have power, which inhibit collective reflection processes (Edmondson, 2002, p. 140).

5.2.3.6 The relationship between group learning and organisational learning

Now, despite the potential negative effects that may derive from the social and psychological factors at work during group encounters, the above outlines have underlined the importance of such group settings as essential forums in which people openly share their individual knowledge and together create new 'products'. Whereas the specific focus in the present chapter is primarily on social issues in such confined group contexts, it must still be clearly recognized that the interactions occurring in these groups are always situated in a wider organisational context and each individual participant is also a member of other social and work groups, functional departments, and at times even organisational units. Consequently, besides the immediate effects these interaction processes have on the group itself and its concrete output(s), the changes and developments in states of knowledge and mental frames that occur in this micro-context finally also constitute an essential underpinning for general learning throughout the wider organisation (cf. 4.4). Despite this close link, however, group learning must clearly not be equated with organisational learning. Instead, in order for the knowledge 'carried' by the group and its members to also contribute to sharedness among a wider clientele and to cause lasting effects, certain **conditions** have to be fulfilled. In this regard, an important condition is that the course and the results of the communication processes that took place among the group's participants are made accessible and transparent to all or at least a number of other organisational members. Besides 'simply' spreading the knowledge through direct communication with others, true transparency presupposes material storage places for knowledge stocks and symbolic values, such that collective reflection processes can take place on these (Probst & Büchel, 1994, p. 21 f.). Prior to this stage, however, an essential determinant for whether any such transmission outside of the particular group occurs in the first place can in fact be seen in the depth or extent to which cognitive changes and developments have actually occurred during the group's exchanges. If the agreement reached was e.g. rather superficial or the group did not have the time to truly reflect on the issues at hand, nothing really new may have been learned that could be spread or stored within the wider organisation. Besides the requirements for further communication and transparency, a final condition is that the collective negotiation processes become truly integrated and institutionalized in the entire system. If this happens the knowledge created in groups and carried by their members is turned into replicable and outlasting organisational knowledge (Klimecki et al., 1994, pp. 66-68).

Taken together, since groups may be considered as particular kinds of an organisation's different local knowledge bases (Pautzke, 1989, p. 80 ff.), the learning that takes place in them hence constitutes an important element of the overall organisational learning process. Nevertheless, even though at its very basis organisational learning relies on the people and groups as agency for the transferral of meanings, associations, and worldviews (Hedberg, 1981), not all learning among these also necessarily leads to developments in the organisational knowledge base. In addition, even if some changes occur, a further distinction needs to be made between whether such developments constitute lower- or higher-level organisational learning. Whereas the desired consequence of the former is a particular behavioural outcome or immediate effect on a concrete activity, the latter aims at adjusting overall rules and norms. The associations that result from this higher-level learning then have long term effects and impacts on the organisation as a whole (Fiol & Lyles, 1985, p. 808). In analogy to this distinction in the general organisational learning literature, it is exactly such more deeply rooted developments of strategy-related frames of reference (Shrivastava & Schneider, 1984), interpretive schemes (Bartunek, 1984), or new cognitive frameworks within which to make strategic decisions, which are of focal interest to illuminate on how strategies as shared strategic orientations among an organisation's key actors emerge.

5.2.4 Forms and functions of social interaction

So far now, the discussion has focused on issues concerning the rather '*macro*' level of group interactions (i.e. general factors and conditions for successful cooperation and knowledge exchange, phases in group problem solving, as well as clarifying the relationship between learning in groups and organisational learning). In doing so, any detailed differentiation of the specific kinds of interactive behaviours or forms of communication going on at the different points or phases of the processes has been foregone. The central role that successful **communication** among group members plays e.g. for determining whether or not knowledge and information are shared, has nevertheless been pointed out repeatedly. Drawing on this, in order to now finally have a closer look specifically at the different forms or structures of such series of interactive behaviours or communication, i.e. a group's *communication pattern*, and their particular **functions**, a *micro-view* on the interaction process is adopted in the following. In this context, a number of approaches for analysing interactions in small groups have been developed over time. Common to all of these is the basic assumption that there are certain situation invariant structures which exist independently of specific situative conditions. The earliest research examining the verbal behaviours in groups was conducted by Robert F. Bales

(1951), which resulted in his widely known "Interaction Process Analysis" (IPA). Specifically, the IPA is an observation method for examining the social and emotional behaviour of individuals in small groups, their problem solving attempts, roles and status structures, and the change of these over time. As one of its central features, Bale's approach is based on the assertion that, in principle, all interactive behaviour can be regarded as having a *task component* and an *interpersonal component*. Here then, generally, this can be regarded as a fruitful approach to better understand interactions and communication patterns in small groups. Still, a major limitation of this work, however, is the fact that Bale's conclusions derive primarily from investigations involving lab groups and self-help or training groups. As a consequence, the applicability or suitability of Bale's original IPA to other contexts such as interactions in work groups or decision making teams in real world organisations is clearly limited. In recognition of this, different 'modern' forms of interaction analysis strategies have been proposed. Among these, one approach that is particularly suited in the present research context has emerged from the work of a group of German researchers around Dieter Beck, Rudolf Fisch, Margarete Boos, a.o. Overall, these researchers still continue the Balesian tradition. At the same time, however, they extend the traditional IPA focus to make their approach and methods more suitable for the analysis of social interactions in clearly task-oriented groups and cases where intensive discussions play a major role, i.e. conferences or the like. In this context then, another process dimension has been found to be important, namely *procedural* interactions. Following from this, analytically *at the behavioural level,* interactions in work groups can thus be differentiated into three kinds of action types that each have a different functional meaning for the interaction process: Taskwork (task-oriented), group orientation (procedural), and socio-emotional (regulation) forms of interaction (cf. e.g. Fisch, 1994, 1998; Stempfle, 2004). The **task-oriented aspects** refer to rational, reflexive, and argumentative interaction, e.g. analysis, questioning, giving information, or giving opinions. As such they contribute to an increase in knowledge and to a high quality decision. The **procedural aspects** are concerned mostly with the formal aspects of the organization of a group decision process. Regarding the third dimension, within the **social-emotional aspects**, a distinction is made between social-emotional *positive* forms such as friendly, person-oriented, supporting, and warm interactions; and social-emotional *negative* forms such as negative evaluations of persons, personal attacks, or emotional outbursts. Finally, in line with enabling the differentiation of three focuses of action, this functional consideration then also allows for distinguishing between different types of information exchanged in the decision-making process.

Like this, the relative weight of task relevant, procedural, and social-emotional information can be determined (Beck & Fisch, 2000, p. 184).

5.3 Synthesis 2: A socio-cognitive model of strategic decision making processes

Now, considering all the above together, the interaction and hence inseparability of the social and the cognitive dimensions has been underscored repeatedly (cf. particularly Synthesis 1 in 4.5). To finally integrate the various *social* and *cognitive* insights and pieces discussed, an own socio-cognitive model of strategic decision making processes is to be presented in the following. Underlying the development and the particular purposes of this model is the conception of what a "model" is that was originally suggested by Herbert Stachowiak (1973) in his general models theory (GMT). According to the author the term is characterized by three features: Firstly, a model is always an *image* of something, a representation of some natural or artificial originals, which can in turn be images themselves. Secondly, a model does not capture all attributes of the original but only those that appear relevant to the developer or the user of the model; it is hence characterized by the principle of *reduction*. And finally, it is the developer who *pragmatically* decides to institute a model for some original, guided by questions *for whom*, *why*, and with which *purposes*.

In line with these outlines now, the own model presented in Figure 14 clearly represents merely an *abstraction* of the reality of strategic decision making processes. Certain attributes have been consciously neglected in order to emphasize those features which appear to be most central in light of the present research context. Here then, the overall purpose of the model is to make accessible the complex reality of group decision making and to represent a view on these kinds of processes that integrates explicitly ideas from **situated cognition** and **information processing theory**. With this, a synthesis of all the different insights outlined in the preceding parts of this work is achieved. Both researchers and practitioners are enabled to gain a better understanding of the socio-cognitive dynamics in strategic decision making processes and of the essential elements involved and the relations between these. The model and its different aspects will now be described below.

5 – Social interaction processes in (small) groups 163

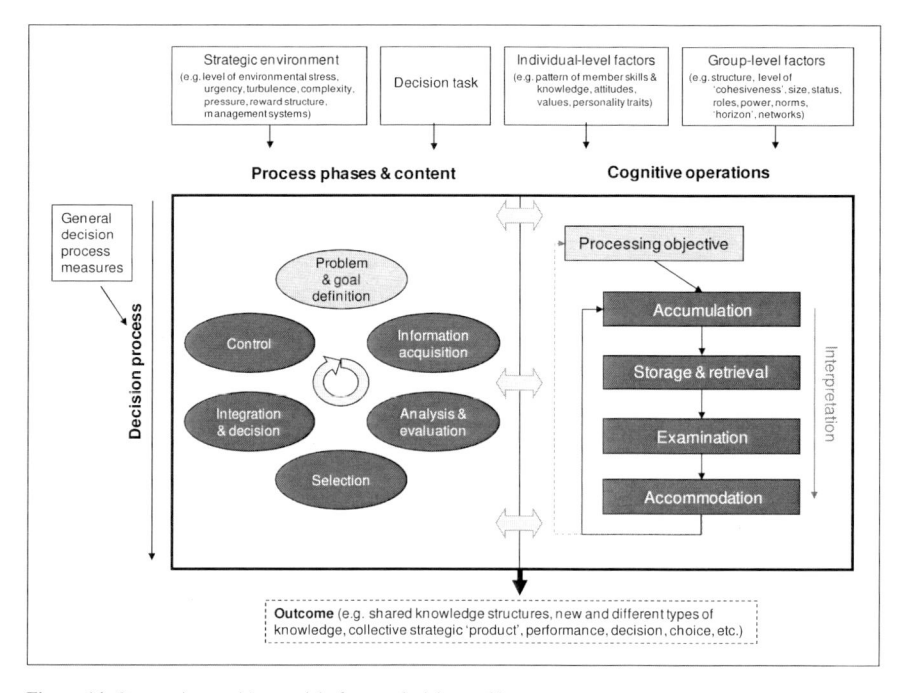

Figure 14: Own socio-cognitive model of group decision making

As stated above, one of the most distinguishing features of the socio-cognitive view on strategic decision making processes is that the approach integrates the situated cognition perspective with concepts from information processing theory. In line with this, the model essentially consists of three major parts, i.e. the group of **context** factors, the overall **process** itself, as well as a specification of the different kinds of **outcomes** (cf. 5.3.1.8) from these processes.

Concerning the first of these, most of the 'peripheral' elements, which surround the model's centrepiece, have already been outlined in other parts of this work and need therefore not be described in detail here again.[86] Nevertheless, before focussing on the specific cognitive and social *processes* occurring during the group's interactions, it must still be reemphasized that the entire decision process is deeply embedded within a **context** and is influenced by different factors there from. In this regard, one first crucial aspect of the model hence concerns the general *strategic environment* the whole process is situated in. Factors summarized in this category are e.g. the level of environmental stress, urgency or turbulence, the overall com-

---

[86] I.e., both individual-level and group-level factors have been the subject of the first part of the present chapter. Discussions concerning the importance of considering the specific strategic context, the type of issue or decision task, as well as general decision process measures, were provided most intensively in Chapter 3.

plexity of the strategic situation, the pressures on the group deriving there from, as well as the existence and characteristics of the specific management systems installed. Apart from, but at the same time closely related to this general strategic frame, is the specific *issue* or *decision task* at hand. This in turn largely determines who exactly the involved *individual actors* in the discussion processes will be, and consequently what the patterns of member skills and knowledge are, the prevailing personality traits, attitudes and values of the participants. Interlinked with these issues is finally the specific *group context* in which the interactions take place. Influential factors here are e.g. the size of the group, its level of cohesiveness, the importance of power and status differences, as well as the group's overall "horizon" (i.e., will the individual members have to interact in similar situations again in the future, are they dependent on each other in some other ways, or is all this not the case?).

Building now on what largely constitutes the context(s) for the ensuing discussions, before finally describing in detail the individual elements of the **process part** of the model, the general idea and reasoning underlying the model's centrepiece shall be sketched first:

By its very definition and purposes, the model explicitly takes into account both the social and the cognitive dimensions of group decision making processes. The process part of the model thus includes two chambers. I.e., on the left side, based on a synthesis from relevant research on the more *overt* processes in group discussions (cf. e.g. Bales & Strodtbeck, 1951; Gersick, 1988; Gibson, 2001; Nutt, 1984; Stempfle & Badke-Schaub, 2002; Tuckman & Jensen, 1977), the different process phases and their contents are outlined. Here then, however, while the labelling of these phases follows earlier approaches in this area, rather than depicting these in a strictly linear manner as is commonly done, the own model clearly recognizes the oftentimes cyclical nature of decision making (cf. 5.2.2), in which a reversion to previous activities, a recurrence or even an absence of individual phases is possible.

Regarding the cognitive dimension, the suggestion made previously (cf. 4.7) is taken up, namely that individual information processing can be taken as a useful baseline to look at the phenomenon at the group level.[87] The right-side chamber of the model hence draws on the basic cognitive processes outlined in models of individual information processing (cf. 2.4.3.1) and adjusts them to represent the different cognitive operations at the group level. Here, since

---

[87] While the interest here is explicitly in groups, it may nevertheless be noticed that a similar stance concerning the transferability of ideas from individual information processing theories to 'higher' levels is generally found in the organisational learning literature, albeit clearly at a more abstract level. In this regard, Huber (1991, p. 88 ff.), for example, describes organisational learning processes as information processing processes that lead to changes in the range of an organisation's potential behaviours. Organisational learning then involves essentially four phases of information processing, i.e. acquisition, distribution, interpretation, and storage of information.

the entire group interactions clearly extend over some time, it is also recognized that interpretation activities occur throughout the entire process and thus impact on all the different stages.

Despite these differences in terms of the respective focus on more overt (social) activities on the left side versus concealed cognitive activities on the right side, as mentioned above, these two chambers are nevertheless seen as intrinsically linked. This constant interaction between social and cognitive factors is visualized by the arrows permeating the vertical line in the middle. For didactic reasons now, since it is concepts from individual information processing theory that are taken as the very basis of the overall synthesis here, the categories of the cognitive dimension shall serve as the respective headings in the following detailed outlines. Under each of these, however, the different aspects identified as regards the more overt process dimension on the left side will be integrated. Like this, the intrinsic linkage between the two is demonstrated even more clearly.

5.3.1 Towards an integrated view on strategic decision making processes

Having clarified the broader context and conditions, as well as the overall reasoning underlying the specific design of the model, the focus now goes concretely to describing the sequence of the discussion process itself.

Here then, as a start, an interdepartmental (possibly also interdisciplinary and/ or intercultural) management team may be imagined, which has been assembled to accomplish a generally stated task, such as "Develop a strategic concept for the market launch of a new car model in Eastern Europe". As teamwork begins, each constituent brings to the meeting activity a network of ideas representing the individual's prior knowledge that is relevant to the group's task. Each individual's network represents thought patterns and knowledge characteristic of the disciplines, departments, cultures and "communities" to which that member belongs. Because individuals have some common backgrounds (including their broader institutional context) each individual network overlaps to some degree with ideas of other members. This is the group's task-relevant *shared knowledge*. In addition, each individual possesses task-relevant *private knowledge* that is not known by other members and that may or may not be shared with them (Derry et al., 1997, p. 33). In line with this, the different strategic actors also each predispose of idiosyncratic strategy schemata, views and opinions regarding the strategic reality. All this constitutes the 'input' to the decision process. As the process ensues, members of the group then share some of their ideas, beliefs and values about the task, and they process ideas shared by others. Apart from other, better measurable or observable outcomes, shared strategic orientations or knowledge structures can finally be considered as a potential result of the overall interactions. The specific steps (phases) towards arriving at such outcomes are the following:

5.3.1.1 Processing objective

In the classical information processing models the emphasis is on steps that follow the perception of some environmental stimuli (cf. Figure 3 in 2.4.3.1). In recognition of the fact that such stimuli arise from somewhere external to the perceiver, also in the present model the overall processing objective is hence slightly offset from the ensuing internal cognitive processes.

In a similar vein, the starting point of all group problem solving or discussion is the initial **identification** and **definition** of the problem(s) to be tackled. Here then, in the present context the basic assumption is that there *is* some kind of issue that requires attention, because it is exactly for this reason that the group came together in the first place. Even though a problem or overarching objective for the discussions might thus already have been identified by some organisational participant(s), this, however, neither has to mean that also all members of the specific group are truly aware of the problem nor that they define it in the same way. Whereas individual level problem identification is the result of basic perceptual and judgmental processes, group-level problem identification hence clearly requires more than just individual cognition. It also requires social interactions in terms of group members communicating their perception that a problem exists (cf. e.g. Gorse & Emmitt, 2007; Roloff & Van Swol, 2007).

Drawing on the above, the importance of considering and differentiating the particular type of group and the context in which the interactions are observed becomes clearly obvious in discussing this initial phase. Specifically, in experimental studies that have used laboratory groups, often no discussion occurs concerning what exactly the problem at hand is or the strategies to use to solve it are. The reason for this absence or rather short length of this phase may be attributed to the fact that in such settings it is usually already thanks to the experimenter's efforts that the nature of the problem has been made quite clear (Larson & Christensen, 1993, p. 9 f.).

Compared to such artificially constructed situations, in the strategic reality of interest here, the situation might be quite different. On the one hand, due to the dynamic and complex nature of competitive environments, there are continuously a large number of issues that would require attention and solving. A crucial step then often is to firstly identify the most pressing of these problems.[88] On the other hand, these strategic issues, once generally identified, are by their very definition in the majority of cases still highly complex and ill-structured. In line with this, even though, as mentioned at the outset, with the specific focus here on decision making processes it is assumed that at least the overall topic and goals have been determined and are quite clear prior to the group encounter, strategy meetings with less explicitly defined discussion directions and unsure outcomes are not uncommon. As a consequence, exactly such searches for and attempts to more concretely define the problem(s) at hand may often already constitute the central issue of the entire strategy meeting. In line with this, the importance of such kinds of **agenda building** processes and the **issue selling** activities associated with these is clearly recognized and documented in the strategic management literature (cf. e.g. Dutton et al., 2001; Kauer et al., 2007; Kirsch, 1994, p. 125 ff., 1996, p. 145 ff.; Tepper, 2004).

Moreover, apart from recognizing that especially in the strategy context group discussion may often serve as the very medium through which problems are identified and openly communicated in the first place, in all cases, there then still often exist considerable differences as regards how exactly the problems are perceived on the part of the individual actors involved. This within-group variability in problem conceptualization is likely to arise as a function of differencing background experiences among group members, which may result in different **framing** (e.g. Sillince & Mueller, 2007; Tindale, Sheffely, & Scott, 1993). In the present context specifically the often different functional responsibilities or affinities and roles play an important role.

The existence of multiple-problem conceptualizations is a uniquely group-level phenomenon that has both advantages and disadvantages for the group. On the one hand, different conceptualizations may make it more difficult for the group to coordinate its (subsequent) information gathering and problem solving activities (Larson & Christensen, 1993, p. 10). Also **conflicts** among participants are more likely to arise already at this early stage, which in turn may possibly cause additional **process losses**. On the other hand, however, given that the group is aware of its heterogeneity or has even been consciously set up in this constitution to reap the potential benefits of diversity, members may then also ask one another expressively to share their individual conceptions of the problem. Like this discrepancies may be surfaced already

---

[88] Issues concerning how managers identify problems in the first place and how they make sense of these have already for long been of great interest to management and organisation scholars. Since most of these works, however, are largely concerned with the individual level and not the group context of interest in the present outlines, a thorough discussion of these shall be forgone here (cf. e.g. Kiesler & Sproull, 1982; Weick, 1995).

early in the process, which may (in turn) prevent misunderstandings and conflict at the later, potentially more critical, phases.

Considered altogether now, actions taken by group members that alert one another to certain kinds of problems, and discussions that shape the way in which those problems are conceptualized and which (possibly) lead to resolving differences in perceptions, can thus be generally considered as essential aspects for the development of shared knowledge structures.

5.3.1.2 Accumulation

Up to this point now, the group's activities and interactions have not yet been targeted directly at working on the concrete issue or sharing knowledge and information necessary for solving the task at hand; this process only starts once the group has clarified its concrete direction. Once this identification and conceptualization of a (strategic) problem has been accomplished, groups are then usually faced with the task of acquiring additional problem-relevant information before they can come up with a workable solution, e.g. a specific strategic concept. Even though currently very little is known about how groups assess their information needs, it is clear that groups too, just like individuals, have to deal with the reality of limited resources (cf. 2.4.2). Besides the cognitive limitations virtually all humans are faced with, especially in the strategy context the often quickly changing environmental and competitive conditions in today's global markets pose particularly pressing problems that make **time** an important factor and often scarce resource (e.g. Eisenhardt, 1989b; Grant, 2003; Haleblian & Finkelstein, 1993). Also, by their very definition strategic problems differ from other more operational issues since they are usually poorly-structured and highly complex. In these cases then, as argued before already, the overall problem solving process is likely to be more nearly **cyclic** than linear, with teams revisiting the information acquisition stage again and again until enough of the right types of information is obtained to permit a solution to be found (cf. e.g. Mintzberg et al., 1976, p. 263 ff.; Silver, Cohen, & Rainwater, 1988, p. 169 ff.).

Here then, as regards the acquisition of such information, this can in fact be accomplished through different *means*. For example, the overall information requirements may be broken down into smaller work packages, which are separated within the group. Even though individual participants may then work on and acquire certain information and knowledge partially on their own for some time, still at this stage elements of 'social cognition' already play a role (Larson & Christensen, 1993, p. 14). I.e., informally discussing what kinds of information are needed to solve a given problem, jointly deciding which member should devote how much of

5 – Social interaction processes in (small) groups

his/ her time and energy to obtaining it, and lending assistance and backing one another up as that information is actually being gathered, all obviously include a social component.

Concerning more concretely the *sources* from which the group or its different members may acquire problem relevant information, here again elements from the overall strategic context may be noticed, especially the existence and characteristics of the particular information and communication systems installed in the wider organisation. These primarily computer-based systems assist strategic actors both in their daily individual work and even more importantly in their collaborative efforts (for an overview of strategic information and communication systems cf. e.g. Bamberger & Wrona, 2004, pp. 243-262). Apart from general intra- and internet-based systems, examples of such sources for valuable strategic information and knowledge include central data-warehouses (e.g. Gluchowski, Gabriel, & Dittmar, 2008, p. 117 ff.; Wall, 1999, p. 295 ff.), executive information systems (e.g. Swiontek, 1997, p. 55 ff.), or expert systems (e.g. Wall, 1999, p. 308 ff.).

Moreover, irrespective of whether certain pieces of information have now been gathered by individual group members alone, the collection of information was 'outsourced' to non-group members, or it was jointly achieved by multiple participants, the knowledge thus accumulated then finally needs to be shared among all the actors involved. I.e., in order to have a chance to become (potentially) integrated in the final group concept and to contribute to more deeply rooted cognitive changes or developments, the different pieces of information and knowledge have to be actively and explicitly introduced into the overall discussion process. Here, regarding the specific processes by which this sharing can happen, it has been argued that it is crucial that the group takes time to raise questions and to reflect on what happens as members work (e.g. Edmondson, 2002, p. 130 ff.) (cf. also 5.2.3.1).

Drawing on the latter, activities related to sharing then also shape two other important cognitive operations: knowledge storage and retrieval. Even though 'originally' at the individual level both these processes are in fact predominantly cognitive in nature, at the group level, however, it will be seen that they are particularly strongly impacted by social factors.

5.3.1.3 Storage

The high importance that the storage and organisation of information has in theories of human memory has already been outlined in Chapter 4. A comparable situation exists at the group level of analysis. What is of concern here, however, is the way information is **distributed** across individuals (e.g. Baba, Gluesing, Ratner, & Wagner, 2004; Brodbeck et al., 2007; Salomon, 1993). In this regard, besides the pattern of communication permitted among group members, also the way in which information is distributed within the group can affect its problem solving performance – even when free and open communication is permitted (e.g. Shaw, 1964, 1978). Here then, as discussed before, one crucial aspect generally is whether the information is initially shared or unshared (cf. 5.2.3). In addition, irrespective of the concrete sharing behaviour during the meeting itself, even when information is acquired by a single group member, and thus is initially unshared, there are a variety of ways in which it can be converted to shared information already **prior to** a formal group discussion (Larson & Christensen, 1993, p. 15). While in artificial, i.e. experimental situations this may not play such an important role, in the organisational reality this 'history' or 'extended' view clearly is an important aspect to be taken into account. For example, the person who collected the information or 'possesses' the knowledge could **informally convey** his or her findings to one or more other members before the group as a whole meets. Social networks thus are important; and especially in large, possibly globally operating organisations the frequency with which the team members or key actors in question interact outside of concrete decision making forums in their daily routines is clearly of interest.

Moreover, besides opportunities for disseminating information and knowledge through such informal encounters and exchanges, another possibility for openly 'storing' relevant information outside the individual actor's own memory is that the person might **prepare a document** reporting the information and circulate it to the rest of the group. A variant of the latter is to enter the information into a **central repository** like a database to which all group members have access. In addition, also a concrete **agenda** can inform everyone in the group about which members hold what general types of problem relevant information (Larson & Christensen, 1993, p. 15 f.). Regarded generally, here then the above mentioned importance and value of the different **information** and **communication systems** available for the strategic actors are apparent again (cf. 5.3.1.2).

Furthermore, another aspect often stressed in the literature dealing specifically with group-level 'storage' is the importance of **meta-knowledge**. Meta-knowledge refers to information that provides clues about the types of problem relevant information that particular members are likely to have. While such knowledge does not bear directly on the problem or issue at hand, this pool of information can nevertheless be crucial for effective problem-solving or discussion since it gives members indirect access to problem-relevant information that they themselves do not possess. In line with this, research on **transactive memory** has found that groups can communicate more efficiently about the distribution of knowledge when members share a mental model about each other's areas of expertise (e.g. Wegner, 1987; Wegner et al.,

1991). The distribution of meta-knowledge then is increased to the extent that members are aware of the formal roles, areas of expertise, and information gathering activities of other members. Such awareness may often come about in a rather haphazard fashion, e.g. as a by-product of conversations held for other purposes (Larson & Christensen, 1993, p. 16 f.).

In the present strategic decision making context then, members are likely to know at least a minimum about the other people in their team. I.e., even if the participants do not know each other too well personally before their meeting, they usually are aware of who the others are because function, departmental affiliation or hierarchical position are normally the primary criteria for why exactly these managers are brought together to work on an issue in the first place. Often, specifically in cases where the overall strategic process and decision making are predominantly top-down oriented, it is also the same high ranked top managers who come together to decide on strategic issues in their organisation. Consequently, in the majority of strategic decision making situations a considerable amount of such meta-knowledge can be assumed to exist. However, in cases where there are more diverse and changing actors, e.g. middle managers, external stakeholders or consultants, involved in the strategic processes, more variance and hence less meta-knowledge is to be expected. Following from the latter point, apart from but related to the crucial importance that the **frequency** with which the team comes together in this particular composition thus has for the development of meta-knowledge among the participants, this frequency of encounters then clearly also impacts on the specific social interactions taking place in the group (e.g. whether the roles are already fixed, a climate of sympathy or antipathy prevails, trusting relationships have been established, etc.).

Overall, these various actions taken by group members – informally sharing information prior to a formal discussion, entering it into openly accessible databases, setting up an agenda or creating meta-knowledge about the existence of that information – can all be considered as important contributors to the development of shared knowledge structures. Also, recognizing these actions (along with the others discussed above) highlights the fact that decision processes are certainly not 'closed' in themselves but that they have a 'before' and an 'after'. Many critical aspects of groups occur outside of, and well before, discussions held for the purpose of finding a problem solution (cf. McGrath, 1991, p. 147 ff.; and also Section 0). Hence, what this shows again is that even though social interactions within a concrete strategy forum are clearly important, the overall situated nature of cognitions always has to be taken into account, too.

Coming back to a particular decision making group and its specific members, as outlined, the information and knowledge they need can generally be 'stored' in many different places. However, what then is important in all cases is that the knowledge and information disseminated and accessed gets truly stored in the memory of the individual participants. Only through this, cognitive changes can also persist over time. Here, with individual-level learning it is known that **elaborative processing** improves memory or storage through the enhancement of retrieval cues (Anderson, 2005, p. 193 f.). *Elaboration* refers to a process by which subjects create additional ways of recalling information. In the context of group interactions, the discussions in the group can serve as a form of elaboration or practice. Through elaboration, the learning becomes stronger, and it is stored with multiple group members. Also **time** and a group's **external environment** affect (group) storage – through practice (i.e., reinforcement of the learning through rehearsal) (Wilson, Goodman, & Cronin, 2007, p. 1049).

5.3.1.4 Retrieval

Apart from proper storage, in order to be processed further in the decision process, information and knowledge must be successfully retrieved. In this regard, factors concerning the individual level, i.e. affecting the memory of the individual as well as how he or she generally uses information when making decisions, will influence whether or not specific pieces of information come to light (again) in the discussion (Larson & Christensen, 1993, p. 19). Beyond these intra-individual factors, however, it is in this context then that the importance of the **social dimension** is most pronounced. While the argument has been throughout that also at the individual level cognitive issues cannot be properly discussed without considering the broader environment or social context, this interlinkage is even more obvious in a group setting. I.e., whether or not information gets introduced into a group discussion, has the potential to be stored and thus to be later further processed, depends heavily on a variety of **social factors**. In this respect, one generally important aspect here is (again) the creation or existence of **meta-knowledge** (cf. 5.3.1.3). Apart from helping group members to understand how information is distributed in the group, it also helps them to anticipate the communicative styles, interests, beliefs or problems that are likely to arise. Besides, especially in ongoing groups also group **norms** can be regarded as beneficial (e.g. Jehn, 1997). In other cases, the presence of a 'sensitive' but knowledgeable **leader** fulfilling an integrative function can affect retrieval positively (e.g. Kauer et al., 2007).

Apart from such positive effects, however, **social processes** in groups may also interfere with effective retrieval (e.g. Finlay, Hitch, & Meudell, 2000). For example, the combination of

status differences and evaluation apprehension may combine to cause low-status group members to withhold knowledge or cues for retrieving collective learning (Wilson et al., 2007, p. 1051). Overall, given the importance of social issues such as **status, familiarity, leadership style,** and **group faultlines** (cf. 5.2.1), it is hence clearly necessary to understand how exactly these (can) affect the outcomes.

5.3.1.5 Examination

The preceding sections have outlined the different means through which knowledge can be acquired, the importance of storage in memory, as well as the different factors impacting successful retrieval in group situations. Once an item of information has now been introduced into a discussion (through retrieving what has been acquired and stored before), everyone in the group finally has direct access to it. It can consequently be examined and scrutinized by all participants for its implications, and it can become integrated with other pieces of information or knowledge for formulating a solution to the problem at hand. Also here then, as with other phases of collective problem solving, much of what goes on during group discussion actually takes place and exists within individual groups members, i.e. is individual-level cognition (Larson & Christensen, 1993, p. 22). Apart from this, however, joint evaluations and analyses clearly play an important role, particularly because it is exactly here that the elaboration of ideas mentioned before is most pronounced. Concrete evidence from the strategy context supports this assertion. Conducting an in-depth and longitudinal analysis of the development of strategic ideas, Schwarz & Nandhakumar (2002) for example found that by sharing their knowledge during the debates, especially during the middle parts of the overall process, involved strategic actors contributed to further elaboration of the ideas. The patterns of interaction and the process of strategic synthesis thus offer possibilities for organizational members to influence existing strategic ideas by elaborating or abandoning the ideas or even generating new ones.

5.3.1.6 Accommodation

Following the examination and evaluation of ideas, the final steps towards a decision or joint strategy concept include the selection and integration of the information and knowledge accumulated and introduced into the discussion before. In the strategy context, "strategic synthesis" is a term that may be used in this context (cf. e.g. Schwarz & Nandhakumar, 2002). Here then, as by now there clearly is a plurality of ideas, information, knowledge and opinions regarding the issue at hand, the crucial question concerns which of these really make their way into the final group concept, as well as what the participants actually 'accommodate' into their individual cognitive structures. In this regard, while sharing mental models does not mean having the same opinion, a basis for persuasion in the group, however, is the degree of sharedness of cognition between members, either in the discussion of information or opinions. The more a member's opinion or information is shared with others, the more likely the person's view is going to predominate. Sharedness lays the groundwork from which a group can converge to a common view. In fact, even when members are in the minority opinion in a group, research shows that they can heavily influence the group's decision if they have other forms of shared cognition in the group like shared information or a shared belief system (Roloff & Van Swol, 2007, p. 173 f.). Further important is the ability to demonstrate the correctness or soundness of the solution or information. Also, ideas or alternatives that are consistent with prior assumptions or representations are easier to defend and hence more likely to end up as the group's collective choice (Tindale et al., 1993, p. 482 f.). Thus, positively seen, shared information, shared preferences, and shared belief systems play a crucial role in group decision making and are powerful glue drawing a group toward consensus. On the other hand, however, implied in all this are also the dangers that may result from too much overlap or conformity, namely 'stale' thinking or the perpetuation of one 'dominant logic' which may in fact no longer be 'appropriate' in the current strategic environment (Bettis & Prahalad, 1995). Moreover and partially related to this, even though roles, status or politics clearly play a role throughout the entire decision making process, research suggests that it is particularly at these final and most crucial stages where strategic synthesis is most influenced by power and politics keeping out, adjusting or adding new ideas until the final strategy plan is established (Schwarz & Nandhakumar, 2002, p. 78). As a consequence, despite prior thorough acquisition and evaluation of potentially large amounts of strategically relevant information and knowledge, all these efforts might possibly finally be overridden by the imposition of the opinion or concept of a single or a few powerful actors.

Overall, following from these insights, clearly different socio-cognitive processes and phenomena have to be recognized in decision making groups, reaching from conformity, over normalizations to polarization (Allard-Poesi, 1998, p. 403 f.). Considering the development of shared strategic orientations, there are thus both different emergence processes as well as related to this different forms of strategy schemata in the group. Still, even though the particular extent to which a concrete convergence will finally have happened will hence vary, at least a minimum of the impressions gained during the social interactions and discussions will have become cognitively accommodated in the individuals' minds (cf. Chapter 4). This accommodation then finally clearly also impacts on both any future needs or desires to accumulate new or additional information, as well as on the overall processing objective the group sees itself faced with. For example, having analysed and integrated all the information accumulated, the group may realize the necessity to investigate new or some specific issues in more depth, or it may even rethink the entire problem conceptualization agreed upon at the outset of the interactions. Exactly these feedback loops then are also recognized explicitly in the above model (cf. Figure 14).

Irrespective of any such cognitive accommodations and integration processes, however, a different situation has finally to be recognized as regards the group's concrete decision or strategy concept. I.e., although the interactions might have been quite intensive and fruitful, especially in the strategic reality meetings or decision making episodes often end without any concrete or final decisions taken (cf. e.g. Jarzabkowski & Seidl, 2008; Jarzabkowski & Sillince, 2007; Tepper, 2004). Exactly this then underscores again the cautions voiced before of carefully distinguishing between strategies as *ex ante mental orientations* or deeply held beliefs and knowledge, and overt behaviour and observable *manoeuvres* or *action structures* (cf. 2.2). Specifically, cognitions and knowledge clearly do underlie people's behaviour and shape it to large extents. Nevertheless, this link is not strictly deterministic. Instead, in line with the socio-cognitive perspective advanced here, a variety of contextual, primarily social factors interfere and may often prevent consensus. Inversely, even if an overt agreement is achieved at the end of the decision process, this does not necessarily mean that it is also truly accommodated cognitively, i.e. agreed upon internally or mentally shared by all the participants involved. Recognizable links between the different levels and areas do exist, but the transition is not straightforward.

5.3.1.7 Interim summary and specifics of the model's "centrepiece"

Now, before advancing to the final part of the model, i.e. a discussion of the *outcomes* of group decision making, an interim summary and evaluation of the model's centrepiece shall follow.

In line with the overall aim of presenting a socio-cognitive view on group decision making processes which integrates explicitly the situated cognition perspective (cf. 4.3) with concepts from information processing theory (cf. 2.4.3.1), the above outlines have clearly shown the usefulness of applying ideas from individual cognition to the group level. Nevertheless, a few crucial cautions regarding these outlines have to be recognized:

Firstly, although the different cognitive operations have been dealt with largely separately for the sake of clarity, it must be reemphasized that, in practice, these processes are of course **intertwined**. Even though any model always merely represents a simplified image of the actual complex reality, the one here nevertheless highlights the interactions among these processes by incorporating explicitly certain feedback loops and reciprocal effects between the different cognitive operations as well as process stages. In this regard, one general and particularly important principle about collective cognitive change is that sharing and jointly examining information and knowledge affects the robustness of the group learning through storage and retrieval (Wilson et al., 2007, p. 1052).

Moreover, concepts from individual information processing serve as the basis of the model. Nevertheless, the two levels, i.e. individual and group, must still by no means be equated (cf. 4.7). Instead, certain **unique group aspects** have to be recognized. Among these, one of the uniquely "group" aspects of cognitive change is that the processes of sharing, storage, and retrieval alter not only the individuals' and the group's knowledge, but they also affect such social issues as the group's norms, member roles, the internal group climate, or extent of political behaviour. Another aspect here is that the retrieval process can also serve as a sharing mechanism. In individual learning, retrieval is a largely nonverbal, cognitive process (cf. Chapter 4). In groups, however, as has been seen, retrieval often requires verbal interaction.

Finally, in line with the latter argument and as already discussed in 5.2.3, the literature on group learning provides interesting insights that are clearly of value in the present research context. However, at this point it is crucial to keep in mind that at its core the specific focus here concerns the strategy schemata and cognitive changes of the individual strategic actors involved in the processes. Hence, even though the (potential) outcome is a parallelization in these orientations across the different actors, at its very basis these changes still primarily occur at the **individual cognitive level**. Here then, in line with the constant reference to the situated cognition perspective throughout the present work, it is exactly such concepts as social learning (Bandura, 1977) and situated learning (Lave & Wenger, 1991) which have been widely shown to be useful for examining and explaining individual cognitive change in social situations.

In a similar vein as cautioning against a levels fallacy between individual and group cognition, in the present research context also clarity about the difference between "team mental models" and shared or overlapping "strategy schemata" is of importance. The former refers explicitly to something that exists within a specific team and pertains particularly to the concrete task at hand (cf. e.g. Klimoski & Mohammed, 1994; Mohammed & Dumville, 2001;

Mohammed et al., 2000). Even though the discussion here is about group decision making on a strategic issue, all the outlines above have clearly shown that this kind of interaction merely constitutes one small element or 'episode' within the overall strategy process (cf. Chapter 3 and also e.g. Hendry & Seidl, 2003, p. 175 ff.; Kirsch, 1991, p. 131 ff.). Consequently, it is actors' more general, encompassing and enduring strategy schemata or strategic knowledge structures which are of interest here. These are affected in and by concrete group interactions, but they are neither entirely bound to this context nor are they merely influenced or shaped there.

Taken together and in line with the assertions of the socio-cognitive perspective, social interactions taking place during group discussion can now be summarized as generally serving three distinct functions (cf. Sniezek & Henry, 1990, p. 67 ff.). First, such interactions help to **bring** problem-relevant **information to light**, whereby through sharing information and knowledge ideas are further differentiated, elaborated, or abandoned. Second, they serve as a means of **influencing** the **individual-level cognitive processes** that take place within each group member. I.e., by highlighting certain items of information, drawing attention to faulty logic, presenting arguments in support of particular conclusions, etc., group members can affect one another's perceptions, judgements and opinions (Stasser & Davis, 1981), which in turn initiates cognitive changes and may lead to shared strategic orientations. Finally, social interaction also serves as the vehicle by which group members' perceptions, judgments and opinions are **combined** in order to generate a single group solution. Particularly when there is no easily demonstrated or objectively verifiable correct answer to a problem, like in the present case, discussion may fail to produce a uniform set of perceptions, judgements and opinions within the group. As a consequence, different members may prefer rather different solution alternatives. If a single group solution is to be put forth, however, some way must be found to overcome these differences. Coalitions may thus be sought and compromises pursued in order to achieve at least **overt** consensus (e.g. Komorita & Kravitz, 1983; Putnam, 1986). Here then, as argued above, a distinction has to be made between open, but merely superficial, agreement, and truly deep cognitive acceptance. The model developed recognizes exactly this possible variety in 'outcomes'. A brief discussion of these is now presented in the following section.

5.3.1.8 Outcomes and "products" of group interaction processes

In line with the preceding arguments, it is overall important to note that the outcome of the entire decision process must neither (necessarily) be any particular action or behaviour, nor even a concrete and tangible "product" such as a written down strategic concept. Instead, the *immediate* outcome is first of all new or improved knowledge, representing at the same time "a change in the group's repertoire of *potential* behaviour" (Wilson et al., 2007, p. 1043).

Apart from this and besides having outlined mechanisms whereby knowledge is shared and integrated, a more differentiated look at the different kinds of other "products" groups (may) produce shall complement the discussion of the socio-cognitive model described so far. Here then, a specific and useful framework for discussing the different routes knowledge takes in becoming a product in and through group interactions has been proposed by Smith (1994). This framework identifies three classes of information or knowledge produced by groups: Tangible, ephemeral, and intangible (cf. Smith, 1994, p. 20 ff.; and Derry et al., 1997, pp. 31-33, for a similar discussion). Regarding the first, basically two different forms of **tangible knowledge** are distinguished, one of which is the *target products* (e.g. strategy papers, team reports, corporate presentations) that provide evidence of goal attainment. On the way to the production of these target documents, groups typically produce *instrumental products* (e.g. graphs, data matrices, preliminary drawings or slides) that provide input to their thinking and problem solving. These are, however, not intended to stand alone as target products.

Another important type of information in the present research context then is the **ephemeral product**. Ephemeral products are transitory representations, such as temporary whiteboard sketches or lists on a flip chart that are produced as by-products of meetings. Ephemeral products support knowledge negotiation among group members and are typically discarded after use. Even though they thus exist only briefly, other products might finally incorporate ideas developed with them (Derry et al., 1998, p. 32).

The third kind of knowledge produced during group interaction and distinguished by Smith (1994) is **intangible knowledge**, which includes both private and shared knowledge. This kind of knowledge then corresponds largely to the contents that make up managerial knowledge structures and thus constitute (parts of) the actors' respective strategy schemata. In line with the various outlines in different sections of this work, some of this, to large extents tacit, strategic knowledge remains private (owned by one individual), while other is shared among the participants (in the sense of overlapping or converging knowledge structures).

Finally, apart from outlining and specifying these different classes of information or knowledge produced by groups, Smith (1994) further proposed that group processes should

5 – Social interaction processes in (small) groups   179

be modelled by developing a vocabulary for describing how information is transformed from one state to another and by identifying typical sequences of information transformations, or "conversational phrases". From this point of view, **negotiation** (as the term is understood in the situated-cognition literature) is seen as an important transformational form made up of phases for passing intangible (private and shared) thoughts through an ephemeral form (such as conversation) in which they are combined and transformed into shared mental models on strategy (Derry et al., 1997, p. 33).

In sum, it has been seen that there are or can be quite different outcomes or "products" as a result of group discussion processes. Still, in the literature and in the majority of studies in the area, the primary concern is with "performance". This, however, is merely one kind of possible aspect that may be examined or measured. In addition, and even more importantly, any kind of end-performance must then clearly also be regarded and evaluated in relation to the processes occurring during the group interactions. Only rarely, however, are such considerations included so far.

5.3.2 General meaning and implications of the socio-cognitive perspective on group (decision making) processes

In the following section, the model presented above shall now be evaluated in its general meaning and value, and the implications of adopting a socio-cognitive perspective on group (decision making) processes will be discussed.

As outlined, the model can and is primarily meant to apply to a specific and confined group problem solving session. Still, it can also be regarded more widely and thus be applied to represent and illuminate decision processes more generally. In this regard, the model is in fact in line with certain other quite general and abstract models that have been suggested earlier (e.g. Corner, Kinicki, & Keats, 1994; Daft & Weick, 1984). Despite this broad similarity, however, the present model is much more detailed than any of the existing ones. Specifically, by differentiating a larger number and more clearly the different phases of the process, a better guidance is achieved that enables paying particular attention to what needs to be considered at the individual points of the process. Also, the interaction between the cognitive and the social dimensions is incorporated and made explicit. In addition, besides being applicable to strategic decision making contexts, the model may also be used to examine and describe other group processes resulting from task-oriented interactions. In these cases then some of the phases might not exist or be of little importance, e.g. when all the information is on the table and must not be acquired first, or when the problem has been clearly defined and phrased already.

Regarding the second central research question in the overall work, i.e. **"What is the *nature* of social interactions in strategic decision making groups and what is the *role* of these interactions for the (non-) development and change of shared knowledge structures?"**, it has been shown that social interactions are absolutely essential, and that there is a plurality of different types of social influences and factors that impact individual and group information processing and cognition. As discussed in 4.2, however, truly deep and lasting cognitive changes happen only slowly such that the question regarding shared or parallelized strategic orientations is finally a very complex issue. This is both the case looking at the overall strategic process(es) (cf. Synthesis 1 in 4.5), but even more so in such confined settings as concrete decision making processes.

In line with this, another important issue to note is that although in or through social interactions in decision making processes a convergence of strategic orientations may occur, even if such shared orientations exist, this only implies *potential* behaviour and thus does neither necessarily have to translate directly into a consensual "product" like a decision nor even into visible actions. The reasons for this potential non-translation are clearly related to the way the final agreement, if there is one, was actually reached. As discussed before, the final agreement of a decision group may for example result from interactions dominated by highly formal relationships between participants who were not particularly committed to the decision process. Or it may be the product of an informal participative mode between truly involved group members, which has produced conflicts and negotiation processes. As a consequence, depending on its actual emergence process, a final consensus may or may not reveal **private agreement** on the part of group members. Here then, if such "private agreement" was really achieved, also deeper and lasting cognitive changes are more likely.

Related to this and going finally beyond the model at hand, exactly this dimension may also have a crucial impact on the future **implementation** of the decision or corporate strategic plan (e.g. Whitney & Smith, 1983), and even on **organizational performance** (e.g. Bourgeois, 1980). Specifically, in line with the distinction made in strategic management between the *making of strategy* and the *implementation* of such plans (cf. 3.2.1), in the present context it thus seems to be particularly fruitful to also specify more concretely what kind of consensus was finally obtained, i.e., is it a superficial compromise response that does not actually represent individual knowledge or beliefs, or is it a thoroughly negotiated and differentiated concept that integrates and is based on a variety of carefully examined knowledge and information?

Taken together and following from all of the above, the **value of the own model** developed and discussed here is that it specifies and details both the conditions, the processes, as well as the (potential) outcomes of social interactions between group members. This perspective thus sheds new light onto the socio-cognitive dynamics involved in a concrete strategic decision making context as well as in strategic processes more generally.

Here then, as a result of these conceptual thoughts and outlines certain **managerial implications** become obvious as well. I.e., in contrast to the arguments of the purely cognitive approach, organisations must not be envisaged in terms of a system of entirely shared ideas and beliefs among their members. Instead, organisations, and thus also groups, imply diversity in meaning and orientations (Allard-Poesi, 1998, p. 408). Far from inhibiting consensus in decision making or discussions, however, such general cognitive and social diversity can still enable shared *strategic* orientations to emerge in so far as the participants involved in the processes openly express and share their divergent viewpoints and knowledge ('strategies for the organisation') (cf. 3.3.2). All this hence implies not only promoting diversity in thinking (individually held knowledge structures), but also encouraging the free expression of opinions and judgements in the organisation as a whole, as well as in specific groups.[89] A variety of ways and possibilities may be imagined for accomplishing this; e.g. by asking for voluntary participation in a task, with the help of self-organized groups, by promoting informal relationships both among managers at the top level as well as across the organisational hierarchy, or by including more lower level managers or other actors in the overall strategic process through participation in strategy workshops, official meetings, or casual interchanges over lunch with the firm's executives.

5.3.3 Towards examining the empirical reality of socio-cognitive dynamics

Whereas so far the majority of outlines and developments achieved in the present work have been of a conceptual and largely theoretical nature, throughout it all explicit links and references have been made to the strategic reality in which the entire research is situated. There, the complexity of both such strategic environments as well as of the specific phe-

---

[89] As we have seen, exactly this *sharing* is a very important aspect, which often happens insufficiently. In these cases then, however, also the knowledge elements existing on the side of the individual actors involved in the process(es) cannot become part of the shared orientation of the key decision makers.

nomenon of interest has been outlined in detail. In line with this, it is by now clear that to study the (non)-development of collective or shared knowledge structures this can only be done longitudinally, 'in situ', and in the context of various types of interactions: I.e., decision making, informal meetings, day-to-day interactions, etc. Consequently, in order to conduct an empirical investigation and examination of the 'reality' of socio-cognitive dynamics, the present perspective clearly promotes an in-depth research approach. Additionally, the socio-cognitive perspective also leads to the adoption of an interactionist perspective on organisations, whereby the organisation is viewed as a continuous collective reconstruction that evolves and develops in interactions (Allard-Poesi, 1998, p. 410). It is interactions and communications in particular that activate cognitive and social dynamics. These in turn allow organisational members and strategic actors to develop individual realities and shared conceptions of these realities (Berger & Luckmann, 1966; Blumer, 1969).

As outlined in detail in 3.4.1.3 and Synthesis 1 in 4.5, there are in fact a plurality of occasions and forums in which communications and interactions among strategic actors may occur in the ongoing strategic process. Due to the considerable difficulty or even impossibility of adequately tracing such 'transient' social cognitions, however, it is finally particularly **small groups** (e.g. decision making groups) which permit an in-depth analysis of these dynamics, and which can thus be regarded as a relevant level of analysis for the empirical study of shared orientations in organisations (Allard-Poesi, 1998, p. 410). As depicted in the above model, attention must here be paid both to the initial conditions (i.e. the situative factors) and to the processes occurring during the group interactions. Did members have very different knowledge structures of the strategic reality before the group work started? Did they commit themselves to the task? What are the norms induced by the task? What kinds of relationships exist between these people? Etc. The specification of these dimensions makes it possible to better interpret the strategy schemata developed and to establish the validity of the results obtained, particularly if different groups are studied and compared.

Moreover, shared strategic orientations have been understood as being always in the making and as occurring in interactions that are themselves also always in the making (cf. Synthesis 1 in 4.5). In this perspective then the study of shared strategy schemata can no longer be limited to the investigation of 'shared' beliefs or other aggregates of individual measurements or "end products". The socio-cognitive perspective demonstrates that "the whole is different from the sum of its parts". The rejection of the individual-social or cognitive-social dichotomy requires considering interactions as the unit of analysis. As shown, particular attention has to be paid to communication, which through the influence processes that it activates, allows something individual to become social. More precisely, the points of agreement and disagreement expressed during group interactions can be seen as a manifestation of the development of a collective representation of the strategic reality. The similarity of group members' representations over time has to be studied, and the beliefs on which participants agreed during group work have to be compared with those appropriated at the individual level (Allard-Poesi, 1998, p. 410).

In sum, a study of shared strategic orientations and knowledge thus clearly requires a multi-level and processual approach. Specifically, the study of the emergence process(es) and of the nature of such cognitive structures requires that the dynamics of the content and the form of the discussions and discourse be investigated further (Allard-Poesi, 1998, p. 411). I.e., do participants anchor their thinking in examples and situations which they have experienced, or in some more abstract elements (e.g. Klimoski & Mohammed, 1994)? Do they deal with one problem after the other or do they think recursively? On what aspects of the issue do they easily come to an agreement? How are conflicts expressed and solved? Do the people avoid divergences or do they negotiate? What are the functions and forms of interaction? So far, not many researchers have investigated these dimensions (for exceptions see e.g. Fiol, 1994; Langfield-Smith, 1992).

Taken together, a socio-cognitive approach to cognition in strategic processes then appears to call for:
- Field observation approaches focusing on small groups as the level of analysis (Allard-Poesi, 1998, p. 412);
- The investigation of both individual knowledge structures and the content and form of their interactions over time, i.e. the socio-cognitive dynamics occurring within the processes;
- And for putting in relation and examining the final "product" or outcomes in light of the surrounding social factors and processes that have been accompanying the interaction process(es).

Exactly this shall be done in an own empirical investigation in the remainder of this work.

6 Empirical study of social interaction processes in decision making groups

6.1 Rationale of the empirical study

So far, in this work a general model of the emergence of shared strategic knowledge structures in strategic processes was outlined and discussed first. In line with the socio-cognitive perspective taken and developed in this context, social interaction processes constitute the centre piece of this framework as they are considered as crucial mediators between the individual and the collective cognitive levels (and hence between 'individual strategies' and 'organisational strategies' as shared strategic orientations) (cf. Chapter 2). Detailing this, the discussion then showed that there are in fact many occasions ('forums') in which such social interactions among key actors (can) take place (cf. Chapter 3), and that consequently there is also a variety of ways and means through which shared strategic knowledge (structures) (can) develop in strategic processes (cf. Chapters 4 and 5). Following from these results and observations, both theoretically as well as empirically, it is hence very difficult, if not impossible, to investigate all the different aspects of the overall phenomenon in one project. The value of the general framework presented in the first part of the present research thus rather lies in its ability to provide an overview of this complex and ongoing process, and in its contribution to answering the first overarching research question here (cf. Synthesis 1 in 4.5). Besides, by including and (already) differentiating in more detail certain specific and important elements in the whole process, the framework also points to different aspects that can or should be examined in more depth. Here then, the second research question in the present work draws exactly on this in that it focuses on the nature of social interactions in strategic decision making groups and on the role of these interactions for the (non-) development and change of shared knowledge structures. In order to answer this question, the preceding chapter first dealt with social interaction processes in (small) groups, which, together with the 'cognitive' insights in Chapter 4, finally led to the development and detailed discussion of an own socio-cognitive model of group decision making processes (cf. 5.3).

In the present chapter now, an own empirical study is presented and discussed that aims at investigating in more detail the overall processes occurring in collective decision making. The reason for choosing to do more in-depth research in exactly this kind of 'forum' was already outlined before, namely that decision making is in fact one of the core activities of strategists in strategic processes (cf. Chapter 3). Group discussions and decision making processes are hence of central importance if one wants to better understand how strategies come about and how shared (strategic) knowledge structures develop among an organisation's key actors.

Drawing on the above, in the real strategy world such decisions and meetings are clearly very sensitive issues. The lack of more in-depth research and insights into social interactions and decision making in these contexts is thus not only due to the general difficulty of truly conducting *process* research, but also due to the difficulty of being allowed access to do research in these specific settings. Nevertheless, to still be able to contribute to more knowledge and insights in this area, a creative research approach had to be developed. Specifically, since not much is yet known on this specific issue, the approach is clearly exploratory and hence adopts a qualitative methodology (cf. Section 6.3 for details on this). In line with this, the choice was made for a **free simulation** of such a group decision situation in which ad hoc groups have to solve a concrete and complex strategic issue.

As a research methodology, (free) simulations have been employed increasingly in recent years, and are today considered as valuable approaches not only in research on small groups generally, but also specifically in investigations on (strategic) decision making (cf. e.g. Kilduff, Angelmar, & Mehra, 2000; Nees, 1983; Sagie, Elizur, & Koslowsky, 1995; Song, Calantone, & di Benedetto, 2002; Wolfe & Jackson, 1987). Besides, also in organisational research more generally, simulations and experimental designs are increasingly popular since also in those contexts similar situations as those found in strategic management exist that involve complex, political, controversial and high stake issues. In line with the definition of strategic processes in this work, which recognizes that strategic issues are not necessarily confined to the 'executive suite', the latter hence again supports the choice of method taken here.

Coherent with the general focus of the present work on socio-cognitive dynamics, the **overall interest** in the present context then is to look at the entire interaction processes occurring in decision making forums. In these collective contexts, the social and the cognitive processes taking place unfold through communication, i.e. problem solving/ decision making (with its cognitive dimension) and communication processes are intrinsically linked. The analysis of communication in terms of the task-related contents thus constitutes the primary access to research into the socio-cognitive dynamics in the context of group decision making. Besides, however, also the group's process management and the relationships between the team members are important. In line with this, the present investigation is first of all oriented at a rough structuring commonly found in the literature, i.e. the investigation and analysis of the interaction data is differentiated into three levels (cf. 5.2.4): The *task-oriented* level (i.e. specific content level), the meta-communicative level concerning the *regulation/ organization* of the interaction process, and the *socio-emotional* level. These levels will then be detailed further in the context of a *functional conception* of task-oriented group interaction. The functions correspond to the demands imposed on groups in the context of the specific type of task at hand, i.e. debating and deciding a complex strategic issue.

The **concrete aim** of the empirical study finally is to contribute to a true **process view** on social interactions in strategic decision making teams and to illuminate more thoroughly on the first part of the overall work's second research question, i.e. the *nature* **of social interactions** in this specific group context. In line with this, the focus is specifically set on investigating which kinds of interactions occur (and to what relative extent) on the three functional levels of content, process and relationships, how the group processes develop over time, and what the individual behavioural patterns are. In addition, through a more detailed analysis and a 'tracing' of the "individual strategies" and the "group strategies" it shall be seen in how far knowledge is shared and what actually the **factors and conditions** are **that contribute to** this **sharing**. While it is recognized that truly deep and lasting cognitive changes occur mostly only slowly and that cognitions are by their very nature impossible to actually 'observe' (cf. 4.2), from these data links shall nevertheless be established to the underlying thought processes and **indications** are to be derived concerning the degree to which **cognitive developments** occurred at both the individual and the respective group levels. The insights are also to be discussed in relation to the socio-cognitive model developed in the preceding chapter.

To these ends, the chapter is now organized as follows: First, a brief section outlines again the most important aspects found in the literature so far on group decision making and on the specific task at hand. From this, the detailed research questions in the empirical study are derived. The outline of the concrete methodological approach in terms data collection (including first simulation approaches generally and then the own design, participants, and realisation of the simulation) is then followed by a description of the specific approaches and methods for analysis used. Specifically, the group discussions are investigated with regard to a number of different variables that each captures different aspects of the group interaction. Group-related and person-related analyses are conducted, whereby for the former an additional distinction is made between variables whose values characterize the interaction as a whole, and variables whose values are examined over the *course* of the session. Specific methods of analysis are employed for these different aspects, respectively. Before then presenting and discussing the results, an outline of criteria for assessing the quality of the whole present empirical research is made. Finally, an overall evaluation of the study and implications from the empirical findings are discussed.

6.2 A multi-level and multi-functional process analysis

6.2.1 Group decision making on complex tasks[90]

The situation in which the current study is created is quite commonly found in the context of strategic processes in real world organisations: Managers/ strategists, who are often representatives of different departments (functional or even geographical units), come ad hoc together, for example in the context of an ongoing project, to exchange opinions and information, and thus to contribute to the solving of a current issue. In a sociological sense, these managers do not constitute a 'group' but an 'aggregate', which is determined by the task at hand and which thus also derives its structural characteristics there from. This can for example be different functional responsibilities and hierarchical graduations among the team members. Following the tradition of small group research (cf. Chapter 5), however, such an aggregate will here be subsumed under the term "group".

Furthermore, a widely-used definition of 'group' in laboratory studies is the following: "Any number of persons engaged in a single face-to-face meeting or a series of meetings in which each member receives some impression of the other as distinct person even though it was only to recall that the other was present" (Bales, 1950a, p. 33). A listing or discussion of the variety of existing definitions of 'group' shall be forgone here. Regarded broadly, the type of group subject to the current study can be classified under the above cited definition by Bales. However, this definition is still largely empty and does not yet give a detailed description of the specific type of group focused on here. Therefore, two additional defining characteristics[91] shall be outlined briefly below. Since they are necessary for pointing to the ecological validity of the underlying group concept, and with this to the potential for generalization of the findings derived from this research (Boos, 1996, p. 13), they will be taken up again in Section 6.6 in the context of "Quality criteria".

---

[90] A differentiated and detailed discussion of (strategic) decision making (processes) was already presented in Chapter 3, and in Chapter 5 the same was done as regards the area of small group research. The outline here shall therefore be restricted to taking up some of the most essential findings from the existing literatures, which are directly applicable and thus relevant for the specific empirical investigation at hand.

[91] These two criteria have been adapted and modified from Boos (1996, p. 14 ff.).

1. *Sense of identity* and role behaviour in ad hoc groups

Generally, groups that have been created for research or training purposes are more than merely a swift encounter or a brief conversation, and therefore more than what Luhmann (1984) calls a "simple social system" and Goffman (1961) an "encounter". Presumably, however, the participants will never meet again in this specific constellation and the time horizon over which they have to work and cooperate with each other is thus only fairly short. Since ad hoc groups cease to exist when the members depart from each other, the ability for latency that is required for the development of an identity with a system is consequently not given in these cases (Boos, 1996). However, a sense of identity can also be endowed by the extent of the externally given *pressure to act* that the group is exposed to. In the present research context, the groups are given an authentic task that strategists in their everyday work are often faced with and that they have to work on within a given time frame. In accomplishing their task, the groups know that they have to present and defend their final concept in front of a jury that evaluates each concept in comparison with those presented by the other groups that have worked on the same task at the same time. As findings from research on intergroup behaviour suggest (cf. e.g. Tajfel, 1982) already the salience of another social category different from the own may suffice to have an enduring influence on peoples' social identity and possibly their behaviour. Taken together from these conditions, a certain pressure to act and necessity to conform to rules induced by the simulation in terms of taking up and 'living' their assigned roles can thus be assumed here. The participants act according to rules that are defined by this interaction frame and which are determined through common or similar educational socialisation. In line with this, group is here conceived of as an analytical category in the sense of "specific context of actions" (Neidhardt, 1979, p. 641).

2. The *task* as a generative mechanism for the formation of interaction patterns

In the context of the research design used in the present study, the groups have only a limited life span of approximately two hours, and thus no opportunity to produce stable interaction structures. The task given to the groups, as well as the instructional guidelines concerning the role the team members are supposed to adopt in the meeting (and the procedural approach to the preparation and execution of the session) merely constitute a "generative mechanism" for the course of the group interaction (Poole, 1983). It is assumed that the participants will display interaction processes as a result of the task-specific demands and structural specification, which will follow certain characteristic patterns and regularities.

The specific type of group task used is characterized as "debating and deciding" a complex strategic issue. According to their classification into the circumplex of McGrath (cf. also 5.1) tasks of the type "debate and decide" require activities from groups that he calls "generate" and "choose" activities (McGrath, 1984, p. 80 ff.). This means, the task structure cannot be described objectively and there is not a single correct solution. Concerning the issue of complexity, a problem is said to be complex when 1) many different knowledge fragments are necessary for its solution and 2) when different contexts underlie these fragments which lead to different views of the overall problem (Kirsch, 1998, pp. 141-143). The contexts can be of functional, hierarchical, or personal nature. Further characteristics laid out in research on problem solving for when to consider a problem as complex are the following: Many different influences and factors have to be considered; these factors are in a close but often unclear relation to each other; they reciprocally influence or change each other, or are even substituted for by other factors; and in addition, the goals to be attained are imprecise and multifaceted (Dörner, Kreuzig, Reither, & Stäudel, 1983, p. 19 ff.). In cases where groups are faced with such a kind of task, they are thus put into a situation that is not only cognitively but also socially highly demanding. An active process of problem structuring is required and a creative search for solutions on which the group can agree. The result can then often be called a "negotiated decision". All this is quite commonly found in the strategic reality of organizations (cf. e.g. Walsh & Fahey, 1986; Walsh et al., 1988).

From these outlines now, the importance of paying attention to process issues (especially regarding the social interactions and communications as well as the relations among the actors involved) seems clear. Nevertheless, as has been outlined in previous chapters, any real 'diving' into management teams or groups is still largely forgone in strategy research. Instead, decision making, TMT performance, or the effectiveness of strategic decisions are usually investigated by conducting large-scale studies, administering quantitative questionnaires, using proxies for cognitions, or taking individual level data/ answers and merely aggregating these post hoc to represent the 'group' (Wrona & Breuer, 2009, p. 83).

A similar picture of empirical research remote from *process* emerges when looking into the literature on small group research. Here, the performance of groups subject to task specific or group structural conditions is often investigated by experimentally creating the variables of interest and then making the groups interact under these conditions. Only ex post the researcher then tries to investigate the result in its conditional variability as closely as possible. What happens *in between*, however, i.e. the process through which the result materializes, is only rarely analysed systematically. This omission is particularly critical since the effectiveness of a group effort or a decision, especially in the context of complex tasks, is clearly highly dependent on the process of its very development. For example, the extent to which a given problem has been penetrated, the degree of differentiation to which it was dealt with, to which different perspectives were considered and heterogeneous solution suggestions were integrated, all play a role in determining the value of the collective solution, the extent to which the group members can truly identify with their 'product', or the degree to which real, i.e. lasting, cognitive changes have occurred among the participants. Therefore, instead of trying to investigate the effectiveness of collective work only substantially, criteria for procedural rationality (Simon, 1978) should be developed, i.e. such criteria that account for the group process as a dynamic phenomenon and not simply as a 'black box' in an input-output-relation. Especially in the face of an unspecific starting position with unclear or yet undefined goals, the rationality of a decision clearly depends on the process of argumentation, whose development can be said to be ill-defined, dynamic and sequential (e.g. Fisher, 1970, p. 52 ff.). In light of the identified gaps in existing empirical research, the present study therefore explicitly aims at contributing to a process-oriented investigation of group performance and cognitive change in collective decision making. For this, a *multi-functional* and *multi-level analysis* of the interaction processes shall be conducted. The following section now outlines in detail the specific interests and derives the concrete questions guiding the present investigation.

6.2.2 Interests and specific questions in the empirical investigation

In line with the overall aim of the empirical study, which is to contribute to a truly *process view* on social interactions in strategic decision making groups (cf. 6.1), there are a number of different detailed questions that are to guide the own investigation. These are specified in the present section.

Generally, different approaches exist in the literature for looking at group process issues and for conceptualizing how the structure and the overall process of the collective efforts for accomplishing a group task may be patterned (cf. Poole & Hollingshead, 2004). The present empirical investigation sets out by following the modern version of the Balesian tradition of research into interaction processes (cf. 5.2.4). Works in this tradition are based on the assumption that individual interacts ("components") can be classified according to the *function* they have for the accomplishment of the task at hand. In line with this, first insights into social interaction processes shall be gained by asking:

➢ Which kinds of social interaction processes occur in decision making groups on the levels of *content*, *process* and *relationships*; and what is the relative importance of these different functional areas?

This question shall be investigated both at the group level (6.7.1), as well as subsequently at the individual level for each group member (6.7.5).

Apart from the rather broad distinction between these three functional areas of social interaction, a specific interest in the context of the overall work concerns the cognitive level, and specifically the link between the social and cognitive dimensions. Even though the different cognitive processes that are said to take place primarily during problem solving, i.e. *generative*, *exploratory*, *comparative*, and *selective* (cf. 0 and particularly the discussion of the own model in 5.3), are not directly observable, they may nevertheless become "visible" for the observer in form of the *ideas* or *suggestions* that are being discussed and developed by the groups during their interactions. Therefore, in a second step the focus shall be put on the *content-related* aspects of the communications, first in their entirety (6.7.2), and subsequently especially as regards the *suggestions* and their 'fate' (6.7.3):

➢ What is the nature of the spectrum of solutions that the groups develop?
  - How many ideas or suggestions are generated and how do these develop further?
  - Which of these are accepted and become part of the final decision/ concept?
➢ Are there differences between the groups in terms of the quantity and quality of their respective spectrum of solutions?

With this focus on the concrete suggestions voiced during the discussion for solving the strategic issue at hand, insights can be gained into the extent to which the given problem was penetrated, the degree of differentiation to which it was dealt with, to which different perspectives were considered and heterogeneous solution suggestions were integrated. These findings also provide indications for the complexity or depth of cognitive operations, and the degree of cognitive changes or convergence concerning the issue at hand that has occurred over the course of the discussion.

Moreover, in line with the overall aim of contributing to a process view of group decision making and of empirically "evaluating" the socio-cognitive model developed for this context in the preceding chapter, a further interest then concerns the investigation of what was discussed in 5.2.2 under the so-called *phase theories*. Some authors, like e.g. Bales & Strodtbeck

(1951) have proposed models for describing problem solving processes which postulate a rather strict temporal phase ordering in interpersonal processes (extending from *orientation*, over *evaluation*, to *control*). In line with the mixed empirical support such linear models have received over the years, other researchers nowadays assume an alternation of phases whereby phases in which action possibilities are generated and further ramified take turns with phases in which such alternatives are narrowed down again (e.g. Dörner, 1999; Hirokawa, 1983; McGrath, 1991; Poole, 1981, 1983; Poole & Roth, 1989a, 1989b; Ward, Smith, & Finke, 1999). In order to capture the dynamics characterizing the particular interaction processes at hand and to link these empirical insights with the own theoretical model proposed in 5.3, the following questions shall be investigated (6.7.3):

➢ How does the group interaction develop **over time**?
➢ Are there concrete **phases** that can be distinguished (e.g. orientation, goal definition, action OR exploratory, generative, comparative, selection (integration) processes)? If yes, do they occur in a linear fashion or rather in a cyclical way?

Having investigated and compared the overall group processes over time and especially the development of ideas and suggestions within all groups, explanations for potentially divergent processes across the groups have to be sought. Generally, differences in terms of the specific task-oriented content and procedural characteristics in group discussion processes are often related to external influences (cf. the own socio-cognitive model developed in 5.3). Here, however, since the instructions and conditions in the simulation are held constant for all groups, factors internal to the groups themselves need to be scrutinized. In this respect, in addition to content-oriented problem solving, a central requirement for problem handling is *group organisation*. Here, the group has to unfold a minimum level of activity in the area of process management (moderation and structuring of the group process) and interface management (definition and assignment of sub tasks, establishment of a group structure and ongoing coordination between group members or sub groups) (Stempfle & Badke-Schaub, 2002, p. 60). Also important, and a necessary prerequisite in any group efforts, is the existence of at least a minimum level of cooperation willingness between each other. There thus is a necessity in groups to arrange the relationships between their members and the overall 'climate' in such a way as to allow for collective work on the problem (6.7.4).

➢ How is the prevailing 'climate' in the groups? I.e., is there a more cooperative or a rather competitive and hostile atmosphere?

> How is the overall process organized? Or is there any concrete organization and structure at all that can be discerned?

Examining these questions is important since both issues are assumed to impact on the specific contents generated and dealt with during the interactions as well as on the 'success' of individual suggestions and the quality of the overall decision outcome.

With the questions so far, the focus has then been largely on examining the decision processes at the level of the group and on making comparisons *between* the groups. In order to understand, however, why a certain climate and process organization prevail inside the individual groups, and why certain contents and issues develop, one has to look at the individual team members since it is their behaviours which together account for the concrete interaction pattern a particular group displays. To this end, the following questions shall be investigated (6.7.5):

> Do the members within each different group display different behavioural patterns?
> What kinds of interaction patterns are characteristic for the individual group members? E.g.:
> - Does someone argue particularly strongly social-emotionally? The other maybe more task-oriented?
> - Do some members behave more cooperatively (or competitively) towards the others in the group?
> - Is there someone who dominates the entire interaction process? Are others (therefore) maybe prevented from saying or contributing anything?
> - Is there someone that takes particular care of looking after a good process management?

By answering these questions individual interaction profiles shall be created. These findings may then possibly give hints to explain the respective success of individual solutions, be related to the overall level of group 'productivity' and thus the quality of the final concept, as well as to the extent of information sharing and knowledge exchange.

Now, prior to moving on in the following to a description of the specific methodological approach taken in the present empirical study, the here outlined concrete questions for guiding this investigation are again summarized concisely in Table 7. In addition, in order to allow for a better navigation through the results presented later (cf. 6.7), also the reference sections, in which the respective data analyses and discussions concerning the individual focus areas can be found, are included in this table.

Table 7: Overview of specific questions in the empirical investigation

Questions	cf.
➢ Which *kinds of social interaction processes* occur in decision making groups on the levels of content, process and relationships; and what is the *relative importance* of these different functional areas?	6.7.1
➢ How are the different values of the detailed *content-related* aspects of the communications linked to the *underlying cognitive thought operations* in the groups?	6.7.2
➢ What is the nature of *the spectrum of solutions* that the groups develop? ➢ How does the group interaction develop *over time*?	6.7.3
➢ How is the prevailing 'climate' in the groups? ➢ How is the overall process organized?	6.7.4
➢ Do the members within each different group display different *behavioural patterns*? ➢ What kinds of interaction patterns are characteristic for the individual group members?	6.7.5

6.3 Methodological approach

Before describing concretely the collection of the data in the present study, first, the overall methodological approach taken here shall be outlined. In this regard, as mentioned already at the outset of the present chapter, since not much is yet known on the specific issues of interest, the investigation is clearly exploratory and hence adopts a qualitative methodology. In order to substantiate this choice, the present section first outlines some of the general characteristics of qualitative empirical research and indications for it, as well as the role of theories and prior knowledge in this kind of research. To further underline the appropriateness of this methodological approach for the present study, its advantages will finally be stressed in light of the own research interests and in comparison to quantitative means.

Generally, the label "qualitative research" is a generic term for a range of different research approaches. Broadly summarized, three theoretical positions can be distinguished here, i.e. the traditions of symbolic interactionism and phenomenology,[92] ethnomethodology and

---

[92] **Symbolic interactionism** and **phenomenology** tend to pursue subjective meanings and individual sense attribution. It is the view of the subject that is in the foreground. Fields of application include e.g. biographical research and the analysis of everyday knowledge. This perspective traces its roots to the works of the early American pragmatists James, Dewey, Peirce and Mead. Today it is most often associated with Blumer (1969).

constructivism,[93] and structuralist or psychoanalytical positions[94] (Flick, Kardorff, & Steinke, 2004b, p. 5). These differ in their theoretical assumptions, their understanding of their respective object of study, and consequently also in the specific goals and methods they apply.[95] Despite all this heterogeneity, however, there are still certain **basic assumptions** and **features** that are common to all of them (Flick et al., 2004b, p. 6):

In this regard, starting with an initial, generic definition, qualitative research can be described as "a situated activity that locates the observer in the world. It consists of a set of interpretive, material practices that make the world visible" (Denzin & Lincoln, 2005, p. 3). In line with this, a first crucial characteristic of qualitative research then is the nature of the specific scientific interest: I.e., qualitative methods are often used when the object of study is new or under-researched, and the aim thus is to describe, understand, and comprehend the research area that is being *explored*. Concerning the nature of the phenomena explored with qualitative approaches, it is especially issues involving social processes and social structures that are in the focus here. As these kinds of sociological phenomena are usually very complex, large scale studies with standardized questionnaires and statistical tests would clearly not be appropriate to capture them in their entirety. Instead, compared to quantitative studies, the number of cases researched is mostly fairly small. These few cases, however, can and are then examined in-depth (Wrona, 2005, p. 5 ff.). In line with this, qualitative research claims to describe life-worlds 'from the inside out', from the point of view of the people who participate. By doing so it seeks to contribute to a better understanding of social realities and to draw attention to processes, meaning patterns and structural features (Flick et al., 2004b, p. 3).

Regarding the concrete collection and analysis of data, qualitative research is generally characterised by the fact that there is no single method but a spectrum of methods belonging to different approaches (Flick, 2002a, p. 226 f.). Although the particular choice of method will hence depend on the specific research questions and the research tradition, a general fea-

---

[93] **Ethnomethodology** and **constructivism** are interested in everyday routine and the construction of social reality. The goal is to describe the processes involved in the construction of existing everyday, institutional or 'simply' social situations and social order. Areas of application are for example the analysis of life-worlds and organizations, evaluation research or cultural studies. Important representatives of these traditions are e.g. Schütz (1962), Berger & Luckmann (1966), Gergen (1985, 1999), Glaserfeld (1995) for constructivist ideas, and Garfinkel (1967) for ethnomethodology.

[94] **Structuralist** or **psychoanalytical** positions proceed from an assumption of latent social configurations and of unconscious psychic structures and mechanisms. Characteristic of this perspective is the largely hermeneutic reconstruction of 'action and meaning-generating deep structures' that is executed according to psychoanalytic or objective-hermeneutic ideas. Family research, generation research and gender research are typical fields of application here. Some fundamental works have been written e.g. by Reichenbach (1938), Dilthey (1968), Gadamer (1975).

[95] For readers interested in details on the respective traditions, good and concise overviews are for example provided in Flick et al. (2004) and Denzin & Lincoln (2005), which also include numerous references to further readings and to the original literatures.

ture is that qualitative data collection, analytical and interpretive procedures are bound to a considerable extent to the notion of contextuality. Besides, during all phases of the process, interpretation and sensemaking play a crucial role. Specifically, non-standardized data is collected, e.g. in the form of open interviews, field protocols, or other documents like diaries, etc. (Denzin & Lincoln, 2005, p. 25 f.). Here then, data collection is characterized, above all, by the principle of openness (Hoffmann-Riem, 1980), which allows for being more 'involved' than other research strategies that work with large quantities and strictly standardized methods and normative concepts (Wilson, 1970). Depending on the specific method or approach employed, the analysis can then be described as interpretive, hermeneutical or category/ theory building. Finally, in line with being characterized as open, the entire qualitative research process proceeds in a circular manner, rather than following any strictly pre-structured way of procedure (Flick, 2002b, p. 73).

Drawing on the above, an *indication* for qualitative research can then clearly be seen in the specific research problem at hand: I.e., generally, qualitative approaches are said to be indicated when the aim is to derive **precise** and **'thick' descriptions** of social realities (e.g. Eisenhardt, 1989a; Geertz, 1973). While in the quantitative methodology it is about testing and verification ('context of justification'), here the researcher is in the **'context of discovery'** (Popper, 2002). In line with this, as the specific research is new, previous knowledge is clearly limited, and no real theories exist that could be applied in this case. Whereas the ex-ante development of hypotheses is hence harshly rejected, it is nevertheless important that the researcher discloses his prior knowledge.[96] In this regard, although the aim and thus 'outcome' of qualitative research is to develop propositions, hypotheses or theories, existing theories and prior knowledge still play a role also in this methodology. They can be seen as sensitizing constructs, enable a better focus, (may) give a heuristic framework, and with all this can finally have a function for leading to scientific discovery (e.g. Kelle, 1998; Strauss & Corbin, 1996).

Following from these outlines now, it is clear that there are numerous reasons for having chosen such an interpretive stance over that of a positivistic methodology and quantitative methods for the present research purposes. First of all, one of the primary starting points of

---

[96] In line with the variety of different approaches that are generally subsumed under the label "qualitative research", there are in fact different views regarding the importance and the role of existing theoretical knowledge for qualitative projects. Whereas for qualitative content analysis theoretical concepts are for example explicitly incorporated in the research, adherents of other qualitative traditions advance more radical positions that may even clearly reject the recourse to any prior knowledge as this is regarded as limiting the ability to really make new discoveries (for example in Grounded Theory according to Glaser's (1978) original ideas).

the entire work was in fact the observation that even though quantitative approaches clearly still dominate research on group decision making, their achievements so far must be regarded quite critically. Due to their very nature, the quantitative studies conducted in the present research area have stayed much too remote and superficial, and have hence left a number of gaps behind. In trying to contribute to closing these 'white spots', the explicit interest here is in those under-researched 'true' *process* issues. Here then, not only is there merely little so far on this topic, but to really investigate social interactions in specific decision making contexts (or in strategic processes generally), one has to truly 'immerge' in them. Exactly this is only possible with qualitative methods. With these approaches the researcher is closer to the subject(s) and research object, which also allows for 'thick' and contextualized descriptions of the phenomena at hand.

Drawing on this, in line with these own concrete interests, the specific qualitative perspective taken in the present work hence corresponds broadly to the ethnomethodological and constructivist tradition. Their goal is to describe the processes involved in the construction of existing (everyday, institutional or simply 'social') situations, millieux (e.g. Hildenbrand, 1983) and social order. To do so, the data tend to be collected in focus groups, by ethnographic methods or (participant) observation, and they are evaluated by means of discourse or conversation analysis (cf. for an overview and references to further reading Bergmann, 2004, pp. 72-80; Flick, 2004, pp. 88-94). The specific approaches to data collection and analysis adopted in the present research then also correspond largely with this perspective (cf. 6.4 and 6.5).

Of course, instead of taking a constructivist stance and conducting a qualitative multi-functional and multi-level analysis, another approach for investigating social interactions occurring in the context of strategic decision making processes could have been to merely administer a *questionnaire* to a large number of relevant people, asking them to think back to their last decision process on a strategic issue in a team context and to answer a few questions.[97] Here then, such an approach would obviously not only have been quite remote from the actual processes with no chance of looking really 'inside' them, but a number of other problems that would have occurred are easily imaginable (e.g. problem of participant recall; truthfulness or honesty; isolation from group and task context; etc.).

Moreover, also the concrete objects of interest *inside* the overall interactions, i.e. cognitive structures and cognitive processes, are by their very definition hardly visible and can hence

---

[97] For example: How many suggestions have you made during the last discussion process? How did you behave towards your fellow team members? How was the ‚climate' in the group? How much was your own opinion taken into account? How much did you learn during the interactions? Etc.

not really be described objectively. Since knowledge is thus conceived of here as subjective (cf. 4.1), it clearly also calls for qualitative and interpretive approaches to investigate it.

Finally, regarding the overall **goal** of the present research, in line with the qualitative stance taken, the aim is to work towards finally being able to derive propositions, and not to test any existing theories or ex ante hypotheses. Nevertheless, as has been seen in the preceding chapters, theory and prior knowledge still play an important role. Specifically, to illuminate on the specific research area, insights from different fields have been brought together and have been discussed in the context of the present research situation. In addition, as will be seen, this existing knowledge also played an important focusing and sensitizing role for the development of the own coding scheme used in the analyses of the data collected (cf. 6.5.2.1).

6.4 Data collection

Actual strategy meetings or official conferences, in which members of an organization's TMT or other important strategists come together in order to discuss and decide on crucial and sensitive strategic issues, usually do not allow access for direct scientific observation. In such cases, however, where due to the sensitivity or non-disclosure of the true research sight entering the field is not possible, laboratory experimentation, e.g. in the form of standard experiments or simulations, provide valuable alternatives for researchers to still be able to gain information and insights on the phenomena of interest, which are hardly accessible otherwise (cf. e.g. Kilduff et al., 2000; Nees, 1983; Song et al., 2002). In line with this, before describing in detail the specific *free simulation* design developed for the present research, the following section first provides some more general outlines concerning the characteristics and reasoning underlying simulation approaches to data collection.

6.4.1 Simulations

As a specific research strategy simulations are generally subsumed under the label "laboratory experimentation". This includes a diversity of quite different approaches to data collection, ranging from standard laboratory experiments over experimental simulations, to the here adopted so-called "free simulation" technique (cf. e.g. Fromkin & Streufert, 1983, p. 215 ff.). What all of these have in common is the fact that instead of waiting for the conditions of interest to occur, the experimenter or researcher *creates* a situation and *manipulates* events within this situation (Weick, 1965, p. 198). Apart from this unifying characteristic, however, simulations must be clearly distinguished from experiments. Specifically, standard laboratory experiments take place in highly controlled environments and participants are randomly assigned to concrete experimental groups. The focus of the investigation tends to be on the concrete stimulus characteristics that are contained in the limited number of some clearly defined independent variables. With these characteristics such 'traditional' experiments then allow to identify cause-effect relationships and with this to *test* hypotheses or theories (for more details on 'classical' experiments cf. e.g. Bortz & Döring, 2006, p. 54 ff. and the literature referenced there).

In contrast to collecting data in such confined, highly artificial settings and subjecting them to statistical analyses, simulation is generally defined as the exercise of a *flexible* "imitation of processes and outcomes for the purpose of clarifying or explaining the underlying mechanisms involved" (Abelson, 1968, p. 275). Simulation techniques usually exhibit a much greater complexity and expose participants to a number of "real-world-like" events (Fromkin & Streufert, 1983, p. 420). Experimenters who use this research method may hence be said to be creating field research in the laboratory. In line with this, in order to ascertain the usefulness of a simulation and the scientific value of the resulting findings it is therefore of utmost importance to outline the involved issues or the scenario and the conditions in the 'lab'-session as close to the reality of interest as possible. At the same time, however, it is important to recognize that the objective is not to duplicate reality in vitro but to create and observe a system that complies with the same behavioural pattern. With these aims in mind, simulations thus generally offer an avenue to economically complement field studies and to deal with a non-forthcoming research context without reducing the essentials of the situation studied (Nees, 1983, p. 176).

Given this overall context and underlying reasoning, there are a number of different examples for how and when organizational researchers have used simulation approaches for collecting empirical data. These vary from relatively simple forms of role-playing experiments (e.g. Jones, Linder, Kiesler, Zanna, & Brehm, 1968) and experimental simulations (e.g. Sagie et al., 1995) to more or less free simulations (e.g. Chanin & Shapiro, 1985; Wolfe & Jackson, 1987) and partially or all computerized simulations (e.g. Abrahamson & Rosenkopf, 1997; Lant & Mezias, 1990). Of these, the two most common and distinctive types of simulations are experimental simulations and free simulations. Here then, concerning the former, *experimental simulations* in fact exhibit considerable similarities to the above sketched standard experiments as they still constitute a design in which all events (over time) are predetermined by the researcher and where the number of independent variables is strictly limited (Fromkin & Streufert, 1983, p. 425). The defining characteristic of the *free simulation* technique against that is that events which occur during the simulation are shaped to large extents by the behaviour of the participants themselves during the experiments. Subjects are free to modify the inputs to themselves by their own behaviour. A free simulation then is a research method where participants are placed in a complex environment which represents the criterion environment as much as possible, and where they are generally free to behave within the boundaries of established rules and the interaction of simulation parameters, participants' own past behaviour, and the past behaviour of others with whom they are interacting. Through their actions the participants attempt to cope with (change) environmental characteristics or the behaviour of others. Finally, the ongoing events are determined by the interactions between experimenter-determined parameters and the relatively free behaviour of all participating groups (Fromkin & Streufert, 1983, p. 423). With all this, in contrast to standard experiments and also to experimental simulations, which are both often criticised for their strong artificiality (Weick, 1967, p. 10), the particular advantages of such free simulations are seen in their much higher relationship to criterion settings and the true involvement of the participants. This consequently reduces experimental artefacts and increases the generalizability of the resulting findings.

Following from these outlines now, in line with the fact that there are clearly different kinds of simulations, this overall approach has to be seen more as a categorical label for delineating the type of "setting" in which a particular investigation is conducted. In this context then, depending on the concrete research interests at hand, data may be collected by means of a diversity of different *methods*, including both quantitative and qualitative methods. According to the specific research objectives and the methodological approach adopted, generally, with simulation studies contributions can thus be made to *testing* hypotheses or theory as well as to *building* theory (Fromkin & Streufert, 1983, p. 424).

Drawing on the above outlines, with its specific characteristics, the free simulation technique adopted in the present context then clearly provides a valuable setting for conducting exploratory research and for following a qualitative methodological approach (cf. 6.3). In line with this, although only partial inferences can be drawn from such free simulations due to the limited amount of control exerted over their course and the usually high number of involved variables, the particular value of the technique lies in the contributions the resulting findings can make to *contexts of discovery* (Popper, 2002). Coherent with this, apart from the general need to ensure the realism of any simulation, to judge the quality of the overall research, it is hence criteria for evaluating qualitative research against which these kinds of studies finally have to be compared. To satisfy this requirement for the present research, a separate discussion of such quality criteria is included in 6.6. This section is integrated subsequent to the now following detailed description of the own free simulation of a complex strategic decision task and to the methods for data analysis used (cf. 6.5).

6.4.2 Free simulation of a complex strategic decision task

In line with the above outlined importance of ensuring a high level of realism of the free simulation, in the present study a situation was created in which participants were assigned to work together in groups on a specific real-world case of a company whose management was just faced with the necessity to deal with a complex strategic decision issue. The study was situated in the context of a post-graduate business course on strategic management. As part of course requirements, the students had already prior to the day of the actual simulation worked intensively with the case and had delivered individual reports with strategic recommendations for the company in question. Like this it was ensured that all were knowledgeable of the over-all case and that each also had his/ her own 'strategy' for the company in mind.

A note on business case studies

Working with business case studies is a common and popular teaching method in business and management courses. For instructors it allows training as well as evaluating their students' ability to apply the theoretical knowledge they have learned. At the same time, real cases are often much more appealing for students than 'dry' book concepts and theories. Irrespective of the topic area they tackle specifically (e.g. marketing, finance, strategy, etc.) they are usually all based on real world examples of concrete companies or industry sectors. Like this, in case discussions students are introduced to the reality of decision making – including incomplete information, time constraints, and conflicting goals – giving them first-hand experience in analyzing business situations. Case studies "stimulate students' thinking, challenge their capabilities, and prepare them for future managerial decision making" (Harvard Business School, 2009). As such, on the "content"-dimension, they provide a good approximation for real world management situations and can thus be regarded as valid material for the research simulation here.

Regarding the "context"-dimension, working with case studies, individually or in groups, is a task that is not entirely novel or unusual for the students as they engage in such activities repeatedly over the course of their studies. The students can thus be expected to know broadly how to approach and how to organize such a meeting in order to be productive and accomplish the respective task. This kind of pre-knowledge concerning structural and procedural aspects is important in terms of the simulation's 'real-world-check' since also managers are clearly used to come together and to interact in these kinds of situations. In addition, a certain pressure to act, like managers are faced with in reality, had to be present as well. This was induced by making the outcome of their collective efforts part of course credit in terms of a presentation and defence of their concepts, which the students knew they had to perform later on in front of the entire class.

For investigating the actual group interactions then, students were purposefully[98] assigned to teams to work out collectively as 'managers' a concept for the future strategic behaviour of the case company. Like in the strategic reality, also here each 'strategist' already had an own 'strategy' in his/ her mind prior to the discussions. The assumption for, and consequently the aim of, team work generally then is that by putting people together they will be able to utilize and integrate the individuals' different knowledge, expertise, and perspectives to arrive at the best solution possible.

6.4.3 Concrete scenario

In order to enable an impression of the strategic context the participants were put in, a short description of the concrete real-world business case shall be given here:[99]

The case study is entitled **"Robert Mondavi & the Wine Industry"**. As already implied in this title, the case company (of which the participants were to image being high-ranked managers) is the ***Robert Mondavi Winery*** based in Oakville, **California**. When the company was founded in 1966 by Robert Mondavi, the son of Italian immigrants, it was the first major winery built in Napa Valley since the era of Prohibition. Having started with the goal of producing wines that would rival the best wines of Europe, over the course of the next thirty-five years Robert Mondavi managed to create one of the world's finest and most innovative winemakers. The company also enjoyed considerable financial success. In 2001 Robert finally stepped down as chairman of the board of the company, handing the position over to his son Michael.

The case then is based in **February 2002**, where Michael Mondavi and the winery's new CEO look back on the past two quarters and assess the **challenges** facing the company. Among the number of challenges that can be discerned, a first one concerns the general faltering of the economy over the past six month, due to which also the firm's own sales have

---

[98] Cf. 6.4.5 for details on the research participants and on the group composition.
[99] Due to copyright restrictions, the entire material cannot be provided here. Any enquiries for copies of the original case, however, may be addressed directly to Harvard Business School Publishing (http://hbsp.harvard.edu). The official case reference is: ***9-302-102*** (Rev.: May 3, 2002).

softened. Apart from this, imports from Australia pose a substantial and persistent threat as they have been growing roughly 30% per year since 1995. In addition, many rival wineries have merged, and large alcoholic beverage companies are making an aggressive push into the premium wine business. Mondavi against that still remains an independent company on the US market in 2002.

Important **characteristics of the company** can be summarized as follows:
- family-owned with a long tradition in the wine business;
- reputation as a leading innovator in the industry (especially as regards production technology);
- strong commitment to contribute to the creation of a true wine culture among the American consumers (wine is regarded as "liquid art", the company acts as 'wine educator' for fine wines);
- the company markets several different product lines whereby high quality is stressed throughout;
- despite considerable diversity in the brands offered, there is merely one single sales force that is responsible for supporting all of the company's brands;
- currently, the winery is strongly dependent on the US markets in terms of revenues.

Besides information on the company itself, the case study further provides a detailed description of the situation in the **global wine industry** in 2002, in terms of both wine **production** and wine **consumption**. Here, specific emphasis is put on outlining the different historical traditions, and hence 'wine cultures', in the "Old World" (i.e., European markets) and in the "New World" (i.e., especially Australia, the US, South America, South Africa). Due to this, also the practices and attitudes towards producing wine as well as consuming it differ significantly around the world.

Finally, a discussion is provided on the three different types of concrete **competitors** Mondavi faces. These include 1. rival firms focused on making premium wines, 2. large volume producers moving aggressively into the premium wine business, and 3. global alcoholic beverage companies that are acquiring wineries to complement their beer and distilled spirits businesses.

In light of all this information, the **overall question** in the case then concerns **how to strengthen the firm's competitive position** with adequate strategic plans for the future.

Following from these outlines, the Mondavi-case clearly represents a complex, highly important, and potentially conflict-laden strategic situation, where there is no obviously given or single one correct solution/ strategy to be 'discovered'. In line with this, the case study is hence clearly suited for the present research purposes.

6.4.4 Realisation of the simulation

The objective of the session is to have the 'managers' bring their different individual strategies together into a collective decision. In the present study the participants did not know prior to the actual simulation that they would have to come together to work out a group concept for the case company. This information was withheld deliberately in order to prevent that the students would get together before the session and share their knowledge and individual views, or already discuss possible joint solutions. In reality such informal or 'offline' social exchanges in other occasions ('forums') can of course be assumed to be an important part of the entire process of cognitive convergence between an organization's members (cf. 5.3). For the purpose of the present investigation, however, it was important to hide this information in order to be able to really observe the groups in sharing and integrating their different perspectives and knowledge in the simulation setting, and to see how in this formal decision making context social interaction processes evolve.

Upon arrival in class the students were introduced to what was awaiting them during that day's lecture time. Overall, six groups á four participants were formed. Only three of the groups, however, were part of the present study.[100] While the others were brought to another room and taken care of by the course instructor, the experimenter stayed with the chosen research participants and gave them a detailed debriefing concerning the specific objectives and conditions of the study, and their particular role and task in it. After all twelve students had agreed to participate and to be videotaped during their interactions the three groups were led individually to different rooms. The set up in each room was identical: They were prepared like normal meeting rooms with tables and chairs, a whiteboard and a flipchart. Normal white paper as well as overhead slides and pens were provided. One research assistant was present in each room during the course of the entire process to take care of the videotaping and to hand each participant a sheet with the detailed instructions for their task upon arrival. Apart from that, the assistants were instructed not to interfere with the interactions. The written instructions (cf. 6.4.6) contained all necessary information such that no one needed or requested any further clarifications. From then on the groups were left to themselves and were completely free in how to organize the process and solve the task during the given time frame of

---

[100] The restriction to three groups was due to resource constraints in terms of the limited availability of video equipment.

approximately 90 minutes. During that time the experimenter checked silently from time to time on whether everything was running smoothly. In none of the groups any problems or disturbances occurred during the investigation. Once the groups gave a signal that they had finished, each team member was given an additional questionnaire, which asked them for their individual ratings concerning the quality of the process, the result of their discussion, degree of satisfaction with the group session, extent of conflicts, agreement-seeking behaviours, their perceptions of the other participants, perception of own learning, etc. (see Appendix). The underlying rationale for having them answer these questions was to also gain insights into the group members' own perceptions and feelings concerning the interaction process. Having this kind of participant perspective in addition to that of the researcher herself clearly enhances the validity of the overall findings and interpretations (cf. 6.6 on "Quality criteria" – specifically *communicative validation*).

6.4.5 Research participants

The twelve participants in the study are all students enrolled in a post-graduate management course at a leading European business school. An important prerequisite for being admitted to the overall programme of study is to already hold a graduate degree (diploma, master's degree or equivalent), which may be in any kind of subject or discipline, i.e. ranging from the natural sciences, engineering, over arts and literature, political sciences, psychology, to business or management studies. Apart from their diverse disciplinary backgrounds, the students are also characterized by their national and cultural diversity. While the majority has European roots, the present sample also included one participant from the Americas. At the time of the study, the students had already completed one semester of their one year programme at another one of the several internationally located institutions belonging to the business school.

Despite their lack of extensive managerial experience, the participants nevertheless fulfil many of the criteria desired for the present simulation. Specifically, in the strategic reality of interest here, TMTs, strategy teams or task forces often consist of or are explicitly composed to include members that are from diverse functional, disciplinary, and in multinational organizations often also cultural backgrounds (cf. Chapter 5). Like this different kinds of knowledge, ideas and perspectives are brought into the discussion and decision process, which offer the potential to arrive at more differentiated and varied strategy outcomes. Apart from this kind of cognitive diversity to be assumed as concerns the specific issue at hand, like real world managers, the participants in the present investigation also clearly have a lot of overlapping cognitions. I.e., in line with their common organisational 'socialisation' within the school, these pertain to the more general knowledge of the routines, processes and behaviours necessary to successfully 'move' through a post-graduate institution.[101] In addition, an *overarching common objective*, like that of performing one's job well, exists in terms of the students' intent to do well in their studies so as to be able to find a good job afterwards. Following these outlines, the rationale underlying the concrete choice of participants for the three experimental groups thus was to compose the teams of members with possibly diverse disciplinary and cultural backgrounds. Care was also taken to prevent any gender from dominating within a particular group. In addition, in order to prevent that pre-existing 'coalitions' between students would cause an unwanted bias in the interactions, it was attempted to put students into one group who had preferably spent their first semester at different locations.[102] Table 8 gives an anonymized overview of the compositional characteristics of the participants in the three research groups.

Table 8: Overview of compositional characteristics of research participants

Group #	Gender	Nationality	Field of prior studies	Name code given
1	f	German/ Polish	Marketing/ Mngmt	M
1	f	French	Lang/ Litt	R
1	m	Spanish	Engineer	Y
1	m	Italian	Architecture	N
2	f	American	Psychology	A
2	m	German	Economics	D
2	m	British	Economics	Ja
2	f	French/ German	Mngmt/ Busin	Ju
3	m	French	Political Science	G
3	f	German	European Studies	S
3	m	French	Engineer	M
3	f	German	European Studies	H

6.4.6 Instructions to the participants

As outlined above, a general introduction and explanation of the overall research project was given verbally to the students prior to assigning them to their concrete teams. Upon arrival in

---

[101] Emphasizing again the fact that there already is a considerable degree of cognitive overlap in terms of the rather broad knowledge concerning general processes, functions, rules and routines in the organisation, is important to justify the explicit focus on the sharing of knowledge and convergence of cognitions concerning the specific strategic issue or environment at hand, rather than dealing with all kinds of cognitive structures or processes theoretically possible (cf. Chapter 4).

[102] In the present study specific care was taken to minimize the effects of group *faultlines* or sub-group development (Chatman & Flynn, 2001; Edmondson, 1999; Jehn, Northcraft, & Neale, 1999; Lau & Murnighan, 1998). In the strategic reality exactly this pre-existence of coalitions or the development of these during the processes themselves clearly constitutes an important factor. Inducing such kinds of different conditions in a real experimental set up and investigating their effects on the interaction processes would hence be an interesting area for further research (cf. 7.3).

their respective meeting rooms, each participant then received an identical[103] sheet of paper which contained the detailed written instructions concerning the context they were to imagine being in, their specific task, and the concrete role they were to adopt during the decision process. These instructions read as follows:[104]

Instructions:

Prior to starting the group work, here are some important instructions concerning the procedure of the session and your concrete task and role into which you are supposed to put yourself for the discussion:

For the following team work you are to **imagine being a high-rank manager at Mondavi.**

In light of the substantive changes in the market environment that Mondavi is facing, and which you already know from the case study, the company's board has composed a strategy team. **You are one of the members of this group.** The team has been given the task to work out collectively a concept for strengthening Mondavi's strategic position in the global wine industry. Prior to the meeting, each member has prepared individually for the group meeting. In your case, this preparation was accomplished through the individual reading of the case study and the written assignment in which you had to answer certain questions. Each of you already worked out a recommendation regarding Mondavi's strategic options in this context. The assumption is that this "strategy" reflects your own perspective on the situation and that you regard it as the best way for 'your' company, i.e. for Mondavi.

You now come together with three other managers from your company who also each have their own "strategy" in mind. The objective of your meeting is that during the course of the group interactions you **exchange and discuss your respective perspectives**, and like that finally **work out a collective concept** and agree on strategic options, which you then present to Mondavi's board of directors (here: the entire class).

Each of you is expected to **bring in his/ her own position and ideas** into the group discussion. Like in reality one can assume that these will initially be partially contrary and that everyone is convinced by their own position and knowledge. It is not about the speed of your agreement but about **your discussion and interactions**. This shall enable you to illuminate **the issue from all sides** and to take into account as many different aspects as possible in order to thus be able to finally come to the best possible strategic decision(s) for your company.

There is a time frame of **one hour** for your meeting. Try to respect this frame since also in the real everyday business life time is a scarce resource.

You'll find the concrete task below here as well as written on the whiteboard in this room.
We wish you good luck with your meeting and are curious how Mondavi will position itself in the future!

---

[103] The original intention had been to vary the instructions given to the respective participants. This, however, was found to be not feasible in the present qualitative study since any effects that might have been induced by varying e.g. the different roles of the individual team members would have been hardly traceable to whether they were really due to the different instructions. For this, a larger sample and an investigation with a real controlled experimental set up would be needed.

[104] Verbatim translation of the original German version of the instruction sheet.

> **Topic of your strategy meeting:**
>
> ➤ „Which strategic direction should Mondavi embark on in the future?"
>
> > For answering this question different decisions have to be taken and different aspects are to be worked out with regard to:
>
> - **Products** (e.g. high-end versus low-end, wide product range versus focus?)
> - **(geographic) Markets** (e.g. focus on the US market versus global presence?)
> - **Sourcing** (e.g. own vineyards versus outsourcing/ make or buy of 'raw materials'?)
> - **Marketing/ distribution channels** (e.g. supermarkets, speciality stores, direct sales?)

6.4.7 Data preparation

As mentioned before, the group interactions were all videotaped whereby a digital format was used. Afterwards, the material was then prepared in such a way as to allow the videos to be played and analysed with specific software that is particularly developed for the analysis of video-taped interaction data. The concrete programmes used here are *Elan* and *Videograph*.

In addition to the videos, verbatim transcriptions of the discussions were made by a specialist for this kind of work. In these, besides transcribing the concrete spoken contents, notes were also included regarding important non-verbal behaviours (e.g., loud laughter, or periods where the participants did not talk but resort back to reading in their material). Finally, the time in the videos was specified in regular intervals, which allowed working closely with the videos when analysing the transcripts.

6.5 Data analysis

The specific questions to be answered in the present investigation were outlined in detail in 6.2.2. In line with the various interests underlying these questions and the fact that they refer to partially different levels (group and individual) and functions of the interaction process, the analysis of the data clearly necessitates multiple methods and approaches. It was consequently done in different steps. Also, as characteristic for qualitative research projects generally, the overall approach adopted here started quite openly. I.e., before truly performing any concrete analyses or interpretations, a considerable amount of time was spent 'merely' looking at the video material collected in order to get a feeling for the data and for what could be expected from it. In addition, over the course of the first concrete analyses more ideas emerged concerning interesting facets in the material to look at. Having started 'only' with the rather broad aim of conducting a functional analysis of the social interaction processes in strategic decision making teams, the original research questions became formulated in more detail and additional ones were added.

Despite its overall openness and circularity, the research process, including data analysis, clearly did not start with an 'empty mind'. Instead, it was guided by the different insights and existing theoretical approaches, specifically the functional perspective, found in the literature concerning the area of interest here. These have largely already been discussed in the preceding chapters (cf. especially Chapter 5).

In the following, a description of the different approaches and methods employed to analyse the data collected in the simulations is now provided. This will be done by dividing the entire analysis into several parts, i.e. for the different question blocks the different methodical procedures will be outlined respectively.

6.5.1 Functional content analysis of small group interactions

Not only is the overall field of small group research rather vast, but even narrowing the focus to looking at the specific processes occurring between 'input' and 'output' leaves the researcher with a huge array of possible research questions and aspects to look at *inside* such processes. In line with this, the analysis of social interactions in small group processes can and is being done from different perspectives (cf. e.g. Poole & Hollingshead, 2004), and depending on the concrete interests at hand also the respective methods employed vary accordingly.

In light of the overall research interests in the present work, the functional perspective was chosen as the general ordering framework for analysing the types of events or interacts captured in the data collected. As outlined in 5.2.4, Bale's IPA and subsequently his SYMLOG system constituted the first concrete methods to enable systematic analyses of social interactions in groups. In the tradition of the functional perspective, over time a number of category systems have been developed (e.g. Bales, 1950b; Bales et al., 1982; Boos et al., 1991; Stempfle & Badke-Schaub, 2002). Common to all of these is the distinction they make between behaviours of different functional meaning for the group process. In line with this, in focusing (primarily) on the analysis of the verbal content during the interactions, the coding schemes differentiate group interactions into *task-oriented*, *social emotional* and, in newer category systems that are oriented specifically towards analysing more formal conference settings, also into *process-oriented* activities. Such an approach generally does not exclude the possibility to investigate group interactions in larger scale studies, e.g. within strictly controlled experimental designs with varying the conditions for the different groups.[105] The core approach to the analysis of the data nevertheless remains *content analysis*. Exactly this then also constitutes the starting point in the present analysis of the empirical material. However, simply adopting and applying an existing category system is deemed inadequate here considering the specific research interests at hand. Instead, the existing systems were taken as an initial clue for the own *qualitative* content analysis that was performed on the data collected. From this, an own category system is finally developed which then forms the basis for the other further analyses.

6.5.2 Qualitative content analysis

Qualitative content analysis was chosen as the method for analysing the empirical data at hand. Before describing in the following section the exact procedure for deriving the own coding scheme employed here, a note shall be included on certain general characteristics and advantages of this particular kind of method in order to outline its suitability for the present data analysis.

In line with its derivation from the communication sciences and its original application on material from the mass media in particular (Krippendorff, 1980), the goal of content analysis generally is the systematic examination of communicative material. In contrast to traditional quantitative content analysis, however, in modern qualitative content analysis it is no longer only the content of the verbal material that is targeted but both formal aspects and latent meaning content can be objects of study (Mayring, 2004, p. 266). Important is to understand the material to be analysed as embedded in its *context of communication* (Gerbner, Holsti, Krippendorff, Paisley, & Stone, 1969), i.e. who is the transmitter, subject, socio-cultural background, recipients, target group, etc. The basic idea of a qualitative content analysis then consists of maintaining the systematic nature of content analysis for the various stages of qualitative analysis, without undertaking over-hasty quantifications. I.e., even though the material (usually, though not exclusively, written text) is finally allocated to content analytical categories, the whole coding process itself is in fact an act of *interpretation* (Mayring, 2007, p. 7).

The particular systematic nature characterising content analysis manifests itself in three major aspects: Firstly, in its *rule-governedness*, i.e. it proceeds from pre-formulated procedural

---

[105] In the present case the instructions given and conditions of the set up were held constant across all groups. The crucial advantage of this then is that any potential differences to be observed between the groups can really be related to differences in the internal group dynamics.

models (cf. e.g. Figure 15). Secondly, in its *theory-dependency*: A good content analysis is based on specific theoretical principles, i.e. it follows theoretically underpinned questions and coding rules. And finally, the procedure is described as *gradual* in terms of breaking down the text into single units of analysis, and oriented to a system of categories (cf. Krippendorff, 1980). With all this, qualitative content analysis thus does not seek to shut itself off from quantitative analytical procedures, but rather attempts to incorporate them into the analytical process in a justified way (Mayring, 2004, p. 267).

Apart from these general features, specific techniques exist that each allow for slightly different approaches to how exactly conduct a qualitative content analysis. In light of the present research interests, of the four techniques distinguished by Mayring (i.e. summarizing content analysis, inductive category formation, explicating content analysis, structuring content analysis), the one he labels *inductive category formation* is the concrete procedural method followed here. In this, categories are developed gradually from the material. The flow chart in Figure 15 details this procedure:

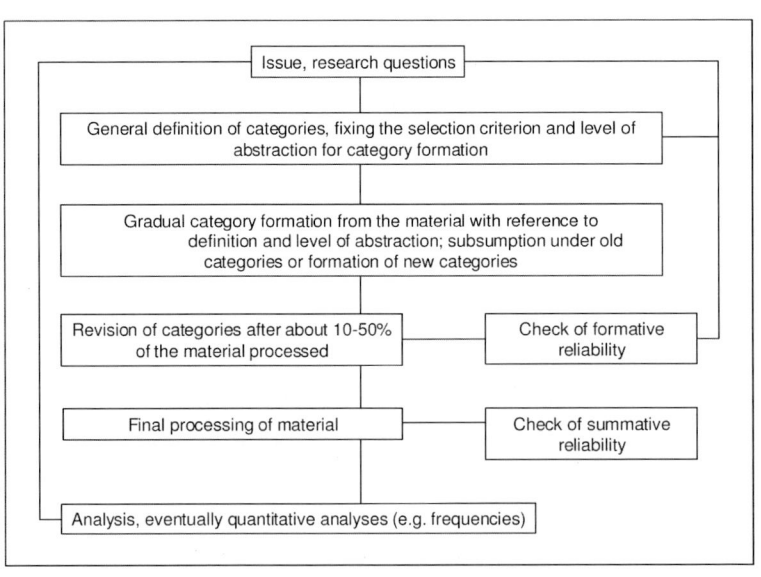

```
┌─────────────────────────────────────────────────────────────────┐
│                    Issue, research questions                     │
├─────────────────────────────────────────────────────────────────┤
│  General definition of categories, fixing the selection          │
│  criterion and level of abstraction for category formation       │
├─────────────────────────────────────────────────────────────────┤
│  Gradual category formation from the material with reference     │
│  to definition and level of abstraction; subsumption under old   │
│  categories or formation of new categories                       │
├──────────────────────────────────┬──────────────────────────────┤
│  Revision of categories after    │    Check of formative        │
│  about 10-50% of the material    │    reliability               │
│  processed                       │                              │
├──────────────────────────────────┼──────────────────────────────┤
│  Final processing of material    │    Check of summative        │
│                                  │    reliability               │
├──────────────────────────────────┴──────────────────────────────┤
│  Analysis, eventually quantitative analyses (e.g. frequencies)   │
└─────────────────────────────────────────────────────────────────┘
```

Figure 15: Flow-chart of procedures for qualitative content analysis with the example of inductive category formation (Mayring, 2004, p. 268)

As implied in the above chart, and of particular importance in the present context, is that although there normally is a system of pre-determined categories at the centre of the analysis (as with quantitative content analysis), this system is revised in the course of the analysis by means of feedback loops and is adapted flexibly to the material. The following section now details how exactly this was accomplished in the present case.

6.5.2.1 Towards the final category system

Above, the theory-dependency of qualitative content analysis has been outlined. In line with this, the starting point for developing the final coding scheme here is derived from the functional perspective which conceptually distinguishes three different functional areas of social interaction (cf. Beck & Fisch, 2000; Fisch, 1994, 1998). At a low level of abstraction the relative importance of each of the different 'dimensions' can be determined with this. Considering the overarching question of determining what kinds of social interactions *generally* take place in the strategy groups the system therefore is useful. However, even though existing approaches like that of Fisch, Beck, Bales and others thus prove valuable as a first initial guidance, in line with following the steps of inductive category development outlined in Figure 15, the more detailed coding units at the higher level of abstraction were then determined gradually. The whole category system was thus fine-tuned and adjusted according to the specific research interests during several iterations of going through the material. (During this, the individual categories were also checked again and again). The detailed procedure for accomplishing this was the following:

Pre-work – Orientation on the basis of the video material

Before really 'immerging' in detail in the material, orientation was first achieved on the basis of looking through the video material several times. Like this a feeling was gained for what was actually going on during the interactions and for how the group processes looked like overall. In this context, as mentioned above, use was made of two particular software programmes specifically developed for conducting video analyses (i.e. *Elan* and *Videograph*). Among a variety of other useful functions, the programmes allow the viewer to put tags on the running films, to name and save these, and like that to be able to easily retrieve critical or interesting sequences. In addition, besides this annotating function, with Videograph the user can also create and save his own coding system next to the video viewer, do 'live' coding while watching the videos, and finally also import those data into Excel or SPSS in order to conduct further statistical analyses. Figure 16 gives an impression of how the video analysis looked like.[106]

---

[106] A good overview and detailed information on ELAN and Videograph as well as on other software programmes for the quantification and analysis of video data in the social sciences is e.g. provided on the

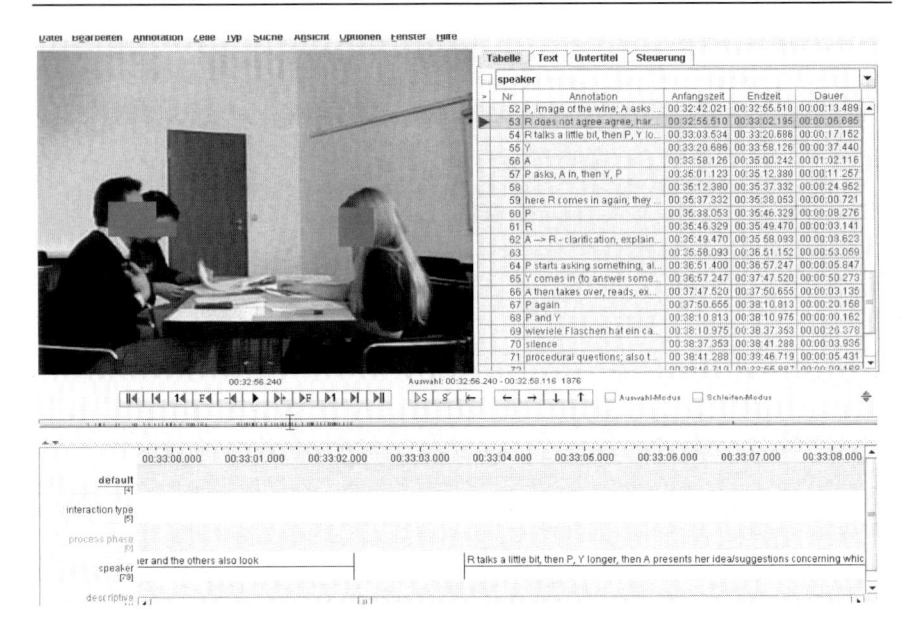

Figure 16: Exemplary screenshot of the video analysis with *ELAN*

Looking at the videos also enabled an impression of the general level of activity of the individual members in the different groups, the respective group climates, the overall process lengths, as well as of whether the participants actually seemed to have been biased or disturbed by the presence of a video camera. All of this was essential and turned out as an indispensible support during the later work with the transcripts. Specifically, despite the numerous advantages of the verbatim written transcripts and the fact that these included even additional aspects (e.g. loud laughter or particularly irritated facial expressions), visual material clearly still allows gaining deeper insights and impressions of the whole interaction processes. Nevertheless, the overall aim in the present analysis was to focus on the verbal contributions during the discussion. The nonverbal aspects or impressions were later thus merely used to facilitate the interpretation of the other findings where necessary.

Coding the interactions – Working with the transcripts

In a second step, following numerous readings of the transcripts, the actual coding of the interactions was then done on the written texts. To code interactions, the literature generally suggests two rules according to which such interactions can be divided: Event-oriented ac-

---

website of Michael Glüer at the Free University of Berlin, Department of School and Education Research (http://www.ewi-psy.fu-berlin.de).

cording to the method of act-to-act coding (*event sampling*), or time-oriented (*time sampling*) (e.g. per minute). A combination of both is also possible such that, for example, per minute one contribution that is important for the process can be coded (Boos, 1996, p. 63).

The minute-rule is usually used in field observations, especially during meetings that last several hours. Like this the observer still has enough capacity to follow the sessions' events as a participant himself. In the present case, however, act-to-act coding was used. This kind of coding procedure is usually indicated and superior to the time sampling when video-taped material of the session exists, in very lively phases of a meeting in which a lot and different things happen within a short time, or when a reconstruction of the process is necessary or desired, e.g. in order to determine the process forms of specific meeting types (Fisch, 1998, p. 196 f.). With this coding rule all contributions that are regarded as important (i.e. having a 'function') for the discussion processes are assigned to one category. Depending also on the specific code assigned (cf. below) one coded unit may comprise a single sentence, a thought, a self-contained statement, or a thematic reference. The unit has to be classifiable into one exclusive category. Often, a participant's contribution contains multiple aspects, i.e. it may be related to different thematic ideas or contain both an own opinion as well as a question to the group. The different aspects are consequently then assigned to different categories. When there is a speaker change, always a new coding is started. Overall, with this coding most of the text in the transcripts was finally assigned to the appropriate categories. In addition, like done initially in the videos, special codes were put that served as tags for marking certain critical or important points in the discussion. These are not part of the category system and do not count into the initial analysis here, but they were facilitators and hence crucial in later steps of the data analysis. In addition to all this, where necessary, also notes were made.

6.5.2.2 The specific coding system

The particular coding system that served as the basis for the development of the own scheme is the so called "conference coding" originally developed by Fisch (1994).[107] In this original coding scheme the three functional areas of social interaction comprise of 15 categories altogether (see Table 9).

Table 9: The categories of the "conference coding" according to Fisch (1994)

Function	Category
content	statement, analysis
	opinion
	information
	explanation
	solution suggestion
directing	question with statement
	question for information
	question concerning the process
	process aspect, suggestion concerning the process
socio-emotional	positive evaluation of persons or actions
	negative evaluation of persons or actions
	approval of matters
	rejection of matters
	positive feelings
	negative feelings

The general distinction into three levels is retained here. Regarding the lower level of abstraction, however, working closely with the empirical material at hand clearly revealed the necessity to undertake a number of considerable adjustments and changes. (Even though the situation for which this conference coding system was developed is quite similar to the present

---

[107] This particular system was taken as the basis here because, different from other systems, there are numerous and repeated references for its scientific quality. In this regard, distinguishing between a task-related and a socio-emotional area of social interaction is a well-established and approved practice in psychology. This functional distinction is for example also the basis of Bales' interaction process analysis (IPA) (Bales, 1950a, 1950b). Since IPA and SYMLOG were specifically developed for the analysis of discussions in self-analytical, leaderless ad hoc groups they are less suited for more structured, task-oriented considerations in the context of official meetings (Fisch, 1998, p. 196). Conference coding then explicitly references IPA, takes up some of its categories, but also modifies some of them and adds others. Concerning the particular categories of the system, they are based on a theory-driven systematic ordering that was obtained through a large body of data from field observations. Thanks especially to the higher degree of differentiation as concerns content-oriented contributions and process-steering they can thus be seen as valid concepts for capturing essential aspects of task-related interactions in group discussions. With this, according to its author (Fisch, 1994, p. 4) the reach of conference coding then ranges over meetings or conferences in which it is about mutual information exchange about a certain issue, about debating and deciding a concrete task or problem, or about enforcing an idea or decision that has already been made by another committee. The system also yielded differentiated and meaningful results for the analysis of interactions in other small groups (up to five persons) who had to deal with tasks characterized as "debate & decide" (Boos, 1996, p. 68).

research context). The specific own coding system that was thus finally developed and is used for the present data analysis is presented in Table 10. To further the reader's understanding and to ensure inter-subject comprehensibility, Table 11 presents detailed descriptions and examples from the empirical data for the individual codes.

Table 10: Own coding system

Function	Category	Code
content-oriented	information, report	I
	analysis, statement, conclusion	AF
	opinion, evaluation	M
	explanation, continuation of an idea/ thought	E
	suggestion, idea, solution proposal - new	Vn
	suggestion, idea, solution proposal - advances, adjusts, resorts to previous	Ve
	question for information	IF
	question for evaluation, opinion, etc.	WF
	explicit content-related steering	Li
	control in terms of summarizing a decision, consensus, etc.	Ke
	control in terms of facts/ checking the state of affairs	Kf
process-directing	explicit process-related steering	Lv
	information, statement, suggestion concerning the process	VG
	question etc. concerning the process	VF
relationship-oriented	consent (with contents), support, understands	Z
	jokes, shows satisfaction, etc.	"+"
	asks for help, etc.	FH
	gives help, shows solidarity	GH
	hesitance, uncertainty, scepticism	US
	rejection, disagreement, etc.	A
	asserts himself, shows antagonism, tension	"-"

Table 11: Detailed descriptions and empirical examples for the individual codes

Code	Description	Example from the data[108]
I	The contribution has a largely informative character.	- „It costs 7-10... Dollars." - „Opus One is not a product, it is a Joint Venture with Baron Rothschild."
AF	The discussion is about issues or facts that are based on observations, analyses of experiences, thoughts, and rational analyses or similar with a deductive character. Decisive for coding AF is the reflexive component. AF sometimes contains implicit evaluations and has to be differentiated from evaluations like Z, A, "+", "-"; those categories require that the evaluation is truly explicit and the main object of the contribution. A distinction from information (I) is possible because "I" has a purely informative character in the sense of "I do not judge, I report".	- „It could be difficult if they do not make any acquisition or partnership!" - „Mondavi wants to go on growing. This means they will always have problems with capacity; they can't produce as much as they would like to." - „The thing is, if we focus on premium wines abroad, it is a good idea to have our own vineyards because then you can control the quality. But it is also much more expensive."
M	It is obvious that the participant contributes a subjectively coloured opinion, often introduced with "I think...", "In my opinion...". The consideration of an issue that was before coded as "I" or "AF" also falls into this category.	- „That's the only thing that we don't do. But actually I like the product line we have. I don't think it is bad." - „Actually I think Asia is very interesting. I like Asia." - „Actually, me personally, I don't like this, ..."
E	Explanations or continuations can follow both "I" and often also "AF" as they complement I- or AF-contributions. Essential is their illustrating, explanatory or expanding character of a previous contribution.	- „... because of two reasons: For the low segment: You don't buy this via the internet, you buy it in the supermarket." - „... because there are already a lot of customers that are not yet used to drink wine; and if one would be the first, this would be quite a nice potential for Mondavi."
Vn	A new suggestion, idea or solution proposal is introduced. To be coded as Vn it has to be clearly identifiable as being related to the completion of the task at hand and be something that could in this form 'end up' in the final strategic concept.	- „Another is to go together with a brewery or a large supplier who offers also other things apart from wine, and ... to extend their product portfolio." - „as a first step they should also go to countries ... expand to the new world, Argentina, Chile etc., but not to sell there but at first only to increase their capacities."

---

[108] Verbatim translation of the original German quotes from the transcripts.

6 – Empirical study of social interaction processes in decision making groups 219

Ve	Like for Vn, also here the contribution must be clearly related to the completion of the task at hand and have the potential to 'end up' in this form in the final strategic concept. Different from Vn, however, is that the suggestion, idea, or proposal does not represent an entirely new area or aspect but it rather advances, adjusts or resorts to previous suggestions. For example, a contribution coded "Vn" has previously introduced "international expansion" as a (strategic) suggestion. The contribution coded as Ve then takes up or develops this idea either in more detail (e.g. focus on China and India in Asia) or possibly in combination with another previously made suggestion (e.g. sell low-end products in Asia and high-end products in the US). Ve can draw on a speaker's own initial suggestion or on that of another group member.	-„I would say Europe as a side focus and as backup for marketing, backup for branding. Or as support for branding. That you take in Europe, that somehow in Europe our name is not associated with Europe, but somehow when we go to other markets, i.e. to America or so, that there somehow this thought of Europe is associated with our brand." -„And what... don't remember who said that, but I think it was you, that depending on what..., on what we focus... if we focus on premium wines then it should not be in supermarkets."
IF	The enquirer requires information or wants to know something. It is about facts, knowledge, opinions, etc. If another group member responds to this a thematic sequence starts, which may then for example be coded as AF, I, or M.	-„And how many products do we have at the moment? 16?" -„But for example in Asia, are there winemakers at all?" -„But where do you sell wine most likely in the US?"
WF	It is not about requesting pure information, but rather about asking for the others' opinion, evaluation, etc. of something the enquirer just talked about himself.	-„And group branding or something like that. Does that make sense?" -„Yes... let's think about it...Extension of the portfolio by means of local adaptations. Something like that?"
Li	These are contributions which really have an impact on the outcome/ direction of the process as regards the discussion/ decision content. The *explicitness* is essential for a contribution to be coded "Li". I.e., the speaker may direct the interaction towards discussing a specific topic, or he may make the decision to do or call something in a particular way that he determines. It is thus about directing towards or determining concrete contents.	-„Yes, we call it partnership. With future buy out." -„Let's start with short run." -„and then...the only thing we are still lacking ... marketing and distribution..."
Ke	Control is an important aspect in task-related interactions on the way to a final consensual solution. Ke is coded when the speaker with his contribution summarizes a decision the group has developed or when he paraphrases a consensus that has emerged over the course of the preceding content-related interactions. This kind of contribution or code then often also represents a kind of critical or turning point as it may mark the end of a specific thematic sequence or phase in the process.	-„So we keep our premium products ... for ... to build our marketing, our image. ... Here we all agree already. ..." -„Ok, now we have made the decision. We focus on Super Premium, this 7-10 Dollar, yes, with potential even higher; on Premium and Woodbridge, i.e. on the mass market..."

Kf	Whereas Ke is coded when control is exerted in terms of summarizing or bringing to the point a decision, Kf signifies control activities aimed at verifying or checking 'facts'. This may be in terms of going back to the material at hand, or in terms of clearly emphasizing the state of affairs the group is currently at. Kf contributions must not necessarily initiate or mark a critical point but they are quite likely to do so.	-„It is written right away here in the first text that Mondavi has problems with its sales since half a year, that the numbers are declining. " -„[Shows R something in the case material] That is the development for example. It doubles..." -„Ok. Now we all know each others positions."
Lv	Like for "Li" codings, the *explicitness* of the steering is important, in this case concerning the group's course of action. Here the broader context is important to consider, too. I.e., a contribution coded as Lv has to have an impact on the course of action; the group will really proceed accordingly. Nonverbal aspects like the slightly assertive tone allow the distinction from more 'cooperative' suggestions for the process which are coded as "VG".	-„Yes. It's optimal like this. ... But someone else could now already do the second one." -„Yes. Yes. We will do this in the very end. First we do the sourcing here."
VG	The contribution has either a largely informative character concerning process aspects or it may include a suggestion or statement concerning how to proceed. VG is thus coded when contributions are related to the further actions in the decision making process.	-„We actually only have to present it on Thursday." -„We should discuss which strategies we have suggested in our work."
VF	The question concerns the course of action in the discussion. The enquirer usually wants to coordinate with the others concerning the process and asks for their opinion regarding e.g. his own process suggestions or suggests alternative ways for how to proceed.	-„How much time do we have?" -„Do you want to write?" -„Or... Should we try somehow to make a concept again?"
Z	A suggestion, an idea, a thought, a statement meet with approval, support or understanding. Any further more detailed explanations for the agreement are then usually coded as "E".	-„Yes, I am with you, too." -„Yes, that is certainly a good point." -„I did the same kind of subdivision. Hmhm. Exactly. Hmhm."
"+"	"+" codes are most clearly indicators for a positive group climate. They are assigned to concrete verbal contributions like jokes, as well as to nonverbal acts or behaviours that clearly express emotions like satisfaction, cheerfulness or laughter.	-„That sounds real cool. Australianischen." -„That is so nice, managers always use the same words several times: „We expand and grow." -„Yes. [to the others:] Let's produce beer. [Laughter] I think beer is..."
FH	Acts which indicate or express a lack of knowledge or ability sufficient to support action. The speaker asks (explicitly) for help, assistance, clarification, etc. For example, he did not understand in terms of content, does not know how to proceed, or wants to reassure that he did sth. correctly.	-„What means „to keep up with so./ sth."?" -„Or what do we want to write here now? ... can you... can you repeat this please? Such that you can dictate it to me?"

6 – Empirical study of social interaction processes in decision making groups   221

GH	Acts of solidarity and affection can be initial, but usually they are responsive to another having asked for help or clarification. If the contribution includes a kind of explanation of any sort, it has to be directly in response to a request or call for explanation from someone else. Otherwise "E" is coded instead of "GH".	-„ [Turned to R, showing her something in the case material]" -„Grow-ing-a-re-a [dictates to R who is writing]" -„Well, those people who sell these fruits, why they do this? Because they have too many fruits."
US	The feeling of uncertainty, hesitance or scepticism must be clearly expressed either verbally or nonverbally. It has to be the main issue of the contribution.	-„I am not sure now whether this is a good idea, but, ok." -„Yes ok, wait, now I have to think..."
A	The contribution is explicitly directed at/ responsive to that of another person. It represents a clear rejection or open antagonism against another's opinion (M), the result of an analysis (AF), or a suggestion (V). Often it is then followed by the speaker's own opinion (M) or an explanation (E). Interrupting while someone else is talking also falls into this category ('uncommunicative behaviour').	-„In my opinion it's not a good idea that you…" -„No, here. Here is growth." -„But there we have no premium segment. That makes no sense. They won't start with the premium segment."
"-"	Any act where a person defends or protects himself or his opinion in a rather ego involved way. The behaviour is a responsive act usually following another's contribution which voiced scepticism or rejection of the present speaker's opinion, result of analysis or suggestion. Asserting one or showing tension is mostly an indicator of a group member's individual uneasiness or peculiar standing in the group.	-„Yes, yes, growth is here. But here is the direct competition that comes from Australia, all the imports." -„Yes, yes, yes, yes, nee, nee I know, I know, I know. I am just saying."

General reasoning underlying the fine-tuned system

While Table 11 contains the detailed descriptions and examples for each of the individual categories, some notes and explanations shall be added concerning the more general reasoning underlying the system.

The most important adjustment concerns the *process directing function* of the social interactions. Control or directing of the process was found to be an important aspect in the discussion processes. Here, however, two different kinds emerged from the data that need to be distinguished. On the one hand, there is steering behaviour concerning the concrete decision or issue *content* dealt with during the meeting. On the other hand, explicit steering may occur concerning the procedure or organisation of the group interactions. Therefore, a category was created on the first dimension where behaviours were coded into which were judged as being explicitly directing in terms of *content* (E.g., D: *"I have written this down for myself: Short run, medium run, long run. If we want to look together at this now."*). The interaction then primarily impacted on the development of the process as regards content. Explicit directing of the concrete course of action or organisational approach against that was coded under the respective category on the process dimension (E.g., H: *"Yes. It's optimal like this. [Louder:] But someone else could now already do the second one."*).

As regards questions raised during the discussions, also here a similar distinction is made in terms of whether the question is concerned with content issues (E.g., S: *„If they buy grapes from someone, why do those people only sell their grapes and don't make wine themselves?"*) or with process issues (E.g., H: *„S, would you like to volunteer to write the things down? [gives the sheets to S] and to copy this here nicely?"*; H: *„Who wants to begin?"*).

Moreover, regarding the first dimension, i.e. content-related interactions, four other categories need to be emphasized particularly: Vn, Ve, Ke and Kf. These are important especially for the further analyses concerning the development and fate of solutions and the look at process phases, respectively. In this regard, the importance of the suggestions (Vs) was already outlined above (6.2.2). Ke and Kf were then added because they are considered important specifically in relation to the socio-cognitive model and its empirical evaluation. In fact, the development of these two categories was truly inductive. I.e., across all groups numerous interactions were found which seemed critical for the interaction processes, but which could not be sensibly subsumed under any of the existing categories. After several iterations of checking the material and rectifying this impression, Ke and Kf were created and judged as useful and informative categories on the content dimension.

Finally, concerning the third dimension, earlier research has shown that problem solving groups communicate comparatively little *explicitly* on this level but that a lot of interactions with socio-emotional function occur rather 'hidden' (Stempfle & Badke-Schaub, 2002, p. 62). Also, certain norms (e.g. dispassion) exist, which demand that task-related factual contributions are in the foreground. Because interest here, however, was also specifically in the 'climate' prevailing in the groups, the tone clearly is important, too. A differentiation was thus undertaken for the area of relationship-oriented interactions that allowed for coding also rather 'small' or nonverbal aspects if these were very explicit in the transcripts (e.g. loud laughter, explicit nodding, etc.). Apart from this specification, however, the categories for accessing interactions with socio-emotional function were still roughly oriented at Bale's original conception (Bales et al., 1982).

Overall, regarding the value of the present system, its hierarchical setup allows analysing information on different levels of abstraction. Like this, on a rough level of analysis, one may for example reveal the respective proportion of the group's communication as regards the area of content and the area of coordination, respectively (cf. particularly 6.7.1 for these respective results). At the same time, questions on a very fine-grained level of abstraction may be answered. For example: How often and in which phases are decisions concerning the course of action taken? Was the social climate more negative/ hostile or was it quite relaxed? Were many suggestions made or did content-oriented interactions consist more of giving opinions or asking questions? Was attention paid to organising the overall course of action? Etc.

Taken together, the development of this category system and the meticulous coding of all the data (transcripts) with these codes thus constitute the first step in the present data analysis. The following analyses, which aim at answering the other question blocks, then take the results of this analysis as a basis for conducting additional in-depth examinations.

Archiving and further processing of the material

Following from the above outlined importance that the here coded data has for the other analyses, a final note shall be made concerning the archiving and further processing of the material. In this respect, thanks to its systematic nature, qualitative content analysis is generally well suited for computer-supported research. Different from quantitative computarized content analysis, however, this is not a matter of automized analysis, but rather of support and documentation of the individual research steps as well as support functions in searching, ordering and preparing for quantitative analyses (Mayring, 2004, p. 269). In line with this, the specific coding in the present study was 'practically' executed in **Maxqda**. The codes were then counted and entered into Excel. Some of these data were finally also processed further to allow for a few statistical tests conducted with SPSS.

6.5.3 'Suggestions' part

Apart from the overall interest in the relative importance of social interactions with different functional orientations, the specific focus in the present context also concerns the link between the social and cognitive dimensions. In the existing category systems, however, no real connection is made to the cognitive level. To get an idea of managers' thought and action strategies in collective decision making situations, i.e. of their cognitive processes and cognitive development, it has been suggested that examining the ideas and issues being generated, evaluated and selected allows gaining insights into such otherwise 'hidden' cognitive processes (cf. 6.2.2). Therefore, a closer look is taken here at the *content-related* aspects in the interactions and thereby especially to doing a fine-grained analysis of the specific suggestions brought into and developed during the discussions (for the respective results cf. 6.7.2

and particularly 6.7.3). For this, those contents that have been coded as Vn or Ve in the initial analysis are subjected to further analyses and interpretations by means of different analytical procedures. Examining the nature and development of suggestions within the groups as well as differences between them thus enables an approximation and making of assumptions about cognitive changes and knowledge development. In addition, it also sheds light on certain process characteristics like the degree of argumentative elaboration, interconnectedness, the 'success' of suggestions, as well as the overall temporal development of the group processes. To this end, the following steps were executed:

- First, a look was taken at the Excel sheets from which for each group the respective absolute number of suggestions can be seen. Also from this, the relative number of suggestions made by the different group members can be derived. These data allowed for gaining a first indication for the degree of issue elaboration within each group as well as for a rough comparison across the three cases.
- In a second step, a more detailed look was taken at the specific nature of the suggestions. For this, the sections coded as such were extracted from the transcripts and entered into another Excel sheet so as to allow looking at their concrete contents. In this context, the suggestions were also classified according to the particular content category they referred to primarily (cf. 6.4.6). Like this, more insights could be gained into the groups' respective degree of issue elaboration and especially the interconnectedness of their argumentation.
- Besides categorizing them according to the specific content they dealt with, the documentation of the suggestions was also done by noting their order and the points in time they had occurred at during the process. By looking at the results from this perspective, valuable insights could be gained regarding the *temporal development* of the overall group processes. For this then, also the Ke codes were taken into account as well as the 'tags' mentioned previously, which had been set during the analysis to mark certain critical or important points in the discussion. The steps were executed in order to find out the following: Are there *phases* in the group process that can be clearly delineated from each other on the basis of differences in communication behaviour and issues dealt with? Are there temporal sequences that occur in a similar way in all three groups? And if such sequences exist, is it possible to discern generalisable patterns in the temporal development of collective problem solving across the different groups? The insights gained from these specific analyses are of particular importance for discussing and evaluating the own socio-cognitive model developed in 5.3.

- Finally, in order to investigate the 'fate' of the different suggestions during the processes and to also determine the 'success' of individual team members in pushing through their ideas, in a last step the final concepts were regarded as well as the original statements each of the participants had handed in prior to the actual group interactions. These were set in relation to the insights derived from the previous analyses of the suggestions introduced and developed over the course of the discussions.

6.5.4 Behavioural analysis – Process management and team climate

Having determined differences in the degree of issue elaboration, interconnected argumentation, varying 'fates' of individual solutions as well as overall temporal developments in the group interactions, the question then arises *why* these differences may exist. To obtain information about potential influencing *factors* and *conditions*, the two other functional dimensions of social interactions are deemed crucial, i.e. the organisation of the process and the relationships and 'climate' prevailing in the groups. Here then, one method for the multi-level observation of groups that aims specifically at the analysis of the socio-emotional exchanges and the group internal behavioural constellations is the SYMLOG system, which was developed by Bales, Cohen and Williamson (1979/82). Generally, this method is attributed a number of merits and it has been employed in different research settings. In the present research context, however, SYMLOG is judged as only limitedly suitable. Therefore, instead, the own coding system is used because thanks to its high level of abstraction for all three dimensions the scheme allows for a more detailed look at both the groups' behaviours regarding organisational issues as well as the respective 'climate' and relationships prevailing in them. In addition, in contrast to the authors of the original SYMLOG, in the present case also the videos are available. Whereas their system is valuable for use in cases where the research situation necessitates 'online' coding and an analysis 'on the fly', in the present context there is rich data and hence more opportunities for much more fine-grained and in-depth analyses.

The specific steps that were executed here were then similar to those in the context of the focus on the content-oriented interactions: I.e., the 'behavioural' analysis was first conducted on the *group level* where initial clues were derived from the counts of the codes. Whereas regarding the groups' process management these quantified data basically sufficed, for examining the respective team atmospheres in more depth, careful and repeated looks at the original video material supplemented the analyses (cf. 6.7.4 for the results concerning group process management and group 'climate'). In addition, the results obtained from the **questionnaire** administered to each of the group members at the end of the simulation were also taken into account here. In this regard, although interviewing the different team members individually would clearly have contributed even more in-depth insights, the questionnaires still added valuable data concerning the participants' own perceptions and feelings of the overall interaction process, its results, and especially their fellow team members. The researcher's interpretations and perceptions are clearly only one 'lens' through which to look at the whole process, and the participants that were themselves part of the interactions may possibly perceive the entire situation quite differently than an outsider. Consequently, since the insights from the answers to the questionnaire hence helped to verify the researcher's own interpretations of the relations and the atmosphere in the group, they can thus also be regarded as one important quality measure for the data and conclusions at hand.

In the final part of the analyses the focus was then moved away from the predominantly group level to look specifically at the individuals *within* the groups (cf. 6.7.5 for the respective results). Here, in order to derive certain selected **member profiles**, the codes of the primary analysis served as the basis again, supplemented, however, by the impressions gained from having repeatedly studied the videos. Specific questions of interest in this context for example were: How much did the individual participate overall in the respective group? How much on which dimension, i.e. did he/ she contribute more in terms of steering the process or in terms of content-related interactions? Was he/ she particularly aggressive or rather cooperative and helpful? Etc.

Taken together, with all these procedures for conducting 'behavioural' analyses, light could be shed onto why the different groups varied in terms of their overall performance (factors and conditions), and also why *within* the groups suggestions of specific group members came through more often than others.

6.6 Quality criteria

Generally, any study's conceptualizations, measurement processes, and interpretations should be judged as carefully made, systematically addressed, and representative of the study's intended underlying construct (or idea or theory) (Lee, 1999, p. 146). Therefore, it is imperative that some discussion of the results of these checks be included in any research report. In line with this, before presenting the concrete findings of the data analyses in the following sections, a note and evaluation regarding the quality of the overall empirical research process have to be included.

In this regard, ascertaining the scientific value of a project's empirical evidence is of course generally important for any scientific research. For quantitative research, however, there are 'clear' criteria for doing so (cf. e.g. Bortz & Döring, 2002, p. 192 ff.). In qualitative research like the present exploratory investigation conducted in the context of a free simulation setting, evaluation against that is more peculiar and hence critiques are often voiced against this kind of research. Due to the comparatively low formalizability or standardizability and the oftentimes intentional focus on individual cases, the 'traditional' criteria, i.e. *objectivity, reliability* and *validity*, from experimental-statistical, hypothesis-testing research and from psychometrics are clearly difficult in qualitative research. As a consequence, generally, there are then three positions among qualitative researchers concerning this issue: I.e., quantitative criteria for qualitative research, independent criteria of qualitative research, and postmodern rejection of criteria (Brühl & Buch, 2006, p. 8).

The most extreme of these positions is the latter which is advanced by proponents of radical constructivism. The argument here is that due to the ambivalent and highly subjective character of qualitative research, there can be no quality criteria whatsoever (cf. e.g. Richardson, 1994, p. 517 f.; Shotter, 1990, p. 69). In line with regarding reality as socially constructed, both the perceptions of research problems as well as all individual observations are necessarily idiosyncratic. Intersubjective reconstruction is hence impossible and qualitative research is consistently considered as constructed research (Steinke, 1999, p. 50). The problem with this position then is clearly obvious as it risks that qualitative research becomes arbitrary and random. Lacking any possibilities for comparing and evaluating the quality of results, severe consequences thus result for further recognition of qualitative research beyond its own narrow scientific community (Steinke, 2004, p. 185).

In contrast to this rejection of any quality criteria, another position is to evaluate qualitative research by means of *transferring* the 'traditional' quantitative criteria to qualitative research. The conception underlying this position is that all research can and must generally be evaluated by some "unity-criteria". Even though these criteria are mostly advocated by researchers that represent a strongly positivistic position, there are also some avowed qualitative scholars that still argue for keeping them (cf. e.g. Lincoln & Guba, 1985; Wrona, 2006). According to the latter, due to the crucial differences between the two types of research, a direct transfer of the quantitative criteria to qualitative research meets with considerable problems. Instead of rejecting them, however, it is suggested to *reinterpret* the quantitative criteria in terms of their original intentions in order to then confer these intentions to the qualitative research process (Steinke, 1999, p. 44). By doing so, the 'quantitative' names of the criteria are retained, which shall also contribute to improving communication between qualitative and quantitative researchers (Brühl & Buch, 2006, p. 36). Here, however, despite acknowledging this potentially 'camp-bridging' value of the approach, at the same time it needs to be recognized that often in these cases the content of the criteria then is fundamentally changed compared to the conventional quantitative conception. In light of this, even though there are in fact many incentives to formulate evaluation criteria coming out of the debate about quantitative criteria (Steinke, 1999, p. 131 ff.), if these same terms then have differing definitions, a retention of the original names and a mere *reinterpretation* might finally lead to only more confusion and misunderstandings among researchers from the two sides. A simple *transfer* of the quantitative criteria against that would be even more critical since these criteria were developed for completely different methods and the basic assumptions of the corresponding methodologies and epistemological theories are hardly compatible with qualitative research. Expecting that the latter can or should conform to the criteria of quantitative research would hence be truly injustified (Steinke, 2004, p. 186).

Following from the above now, in recognition of the fundamental differences between quantitative and qualitative research enquiries and therefore the cautions voiced against transferring or reinterpreting quantitative criteria for evaluating the quality of qualitative research, in the present work the position is taken that independent criteria for qualitative research are needed which have their own profile and which take account of the specific nature of qualitative research. In this regard then, different authors have suggested different 'exclusively' qualitative criteria so that there are in fact a variety of suggestions existing in the literature by now (cf. e.g. Bortz & Döring, 2002, pp. 326-329; Mayring, 2002, pp. 144-148, 2007, pp. 109-115; Steinke, 2004, pp. 184-190). Whereas each of these approaches has its merits, the present investigation finally broadly adopts the stance of Steinke (2004) who suggests the following core criteria for the evaluation of qualitative research: *Inter-subject comprehensibility, indication of the research process, empirical foundation, limitation, coherence, relevance, reflected subjectivity*. With these, Steinke defines a catalogue of criteria according to which qualitative research may be oriented and she outlines procedures for checking them. At the same time, however, the author emphasizes that these "criteria and the checking procedures need to be specified, modified, and if necessary, supplemented by other criteria, in a way that is *specific to the investigation*, that is, according to the research question, the issue and the method being used" (Steinke, 2004, p. 186). In line with this, for evaluating the quality of the present qualitative research project now, the core criteria shall be taken up here and it is discussed how they have been met in the specific research context at hand.

6.6.1 Inter-subject comprehensibility

Due to the limited standardizability of procedures in qualitative research, an identical replication of an investigation is impossible. For qualitative studies, unlike quantitative research, the requirement of inter-subject verification can thus not be applied. What is appropriate, however, and can be considered as one of the most essential quality criteria, is the requirement to produce an inter-subjective *comprehensibility* of the research process on the basis of which an evaluation of results can take place. Among the different ways to assure and check this kind of comprehensibility, **documentation of the research process** is regarded as the principal technique. Here then, in line with the fact that the literature suggests that there are clearly a variety of different elements that can and should be documented, all this has been done in the preceding sections (i.e., disclosure of prior understanding and knowledge in terms of existing theory and literature in the field; collection method and context; data preparation; methods of analysis). Together, with all this, the external public is enabled to follow the investigation step by step, take account of its unique dynamics, and readers can even assess the study and evaluate it in light of their own criteria, instead of predetermined or already applied ones. Documentation can thus be regarded as *the* principal criterion or precondition for the testing of (the) other criteria (Steinke, 2004, p. 187).

Apart from the here provided neat documentation of the overall research process, another way to ensure comprehensibility is the **use of codified procedures**. Even though by its very nature qualitative research is difficult to standardize, it still seeks to find rule-governed strategies and codification of research techniques, which means explanation and systematic analysis of the process with the aim of a logical formulation of methods (cf. e.g. Barton & Lazarsfeld, 1955; Bohnsack, 1999). In this regard, qualitative content analysis, the primary method of analysis used in the present context (cf. 6.5.2), not only constitutes one such codified procedure, but thanks to its systematic nature and clearly outlined procedural steps (cf. e.g. the flow-chart in Figure 15), it is regarded as a particularly good approach for achieving a high degree of objectivation of the research process (cf. Mayring, 2007, p. 12).[109]

6.6.2 Indication of the research process

A second aspect that can be taken as a criterion as to whether its requirement has been met by the qualitative research design is *appropriateness* to the research issue. Here, however, with

---

[109] In line with this, Mayring (2007) even suggests certain own criteria specific for content analysis, which hence are further indicators of the quality of the method (Mayring, 2007, pp. 111-115). In the present context the **stability** of the coding system was ensured by going through it in several iterations and thereby checking it again and again. *Construct validity* can be seen as ensured since the system was largely deduced from existing theory and other 'established' systems.

the criterion of indication it is not only the appropriateness of the methods of data collection and evaluation that is being judged, but that of the entire research process. Specific questions thus address the indication of the qualitative procedure generally, the choice of method(s) of data collection and of data analysis respectively, transcription rules, sampling strategy, as well as individual methodological decisions in the context of the whole investigation (Steinke, 2004, p. 188 f.).

In the present study then, as has been argued before already, the exploratory nature of the overall research and the concrete research interests clearly suggest a qualitative approach. Concerning the choice for using a simulated strategic decision context for data collection, numerous arguments can be found in the literature and have been referenced here, which have either already shown or which point to the (potential) (value) such a (still 'innovative') approach has for illuminating on the issues of interest in a dynamic and otherwise rather 'closed' research context (cf. 6.1). Finally, also the concrete research design then clearly fits the overall approach and can be regarded as appropriate considered in light of the resources available here (i.e., time, size of the project team, financial means, a.o.).

6.6.3 Empirical foundation

Different to quantitative research, hypotheses or theories are generally the outcome or goal of the qualitative research process (Wrona, 2005, p. 19). Nevertheless, qualitative research is of course not entirely without theories but theoretical assumptions and existing literature play an important role as sensitizing lenses, guides, etc. (cf. e.g. Kelle & Kluge, 1999, p. 16 ff.). Whereas such theoretical concepts are then used and included to varying degrees depending on the specific qualitative approach followed in a particular study, the *formation* of hypotheses or theories in qualitative research, however, has to have an empirical foundation in any case. I.e., it should be grounded in the data (Glaser & Strauss, 1967). By developing theories close to the data (e.g. the informant's subjective views and modes of action) and on the basis of systematic data analysis, new discoveries are made possible, and the researcher's prior theoretical assumptions can be questioned or modified (Steinke, 2004, p. 189).

To test the required empirical foundation, several suitable ways can be suggested. Irrespective of whether the research aim is truly verifying or falsifying a theory with the data, or, like in the present study, firstly the development of propositions (e.g. as regards group composition and instructions, conditions for a good team 'climate', appropriate process moderation, etc.), a guarantee of empirical foundation is generally seen in the use of *codified methods*. In line with this, the structured and rule-guided content analytical procedures followed here thus bear testimony to fulfilling this criterion. Also, sufficient textual evidence for the propositions derived can be claimed due to the fact that all the coding and the development of the coding system was done very close to the material.

Moreover, another important point that is generally often mentioned as a quality criterion and that can be subsumed here in the context of demonstrating empirical grounding is *communicative validation* (Steinke, 2004, p. 189). The idea here is to relate the theory developed in the research process back to the study's participants by presenting the findings to the informants and discussing them together. In qualitative research "subjects" are not merely suppliers of data, but thinking persons, like the researcher himself. In line with this, from the dialogue with them, the researcher can gain important arguments for the relevance of the results, especially concerning a validation of the reconstructions of subjective meanings. The subjects' recognition of themselves in the results of the analyses can thus be seen as an important argument for the validity of the findings and conclusions (cf. e.g. Kvale, 1995; Scheele & Groeben, 1988).

However, communicative validation is not in all cases appropriate, for example if the generated theory is beyond the informants' ability to agree (Steinke, 2004, p. 189). Therefore, in light of the specific research interests at hand here, extensive feedback discussions on the entirety of the findings and conclusions with the research participants would have been neither sensible nor feasible (they also can't actually 'see' their own cognitions!). Nevertheless, subsequent to the group discussions, each of the team members was handed a questionnaire which asked them to give their personal ratings concerning different aspects related to the discussion process, its outcomes, the other group members as well as the overall climate in the team. Like this participants' own feelings and perceptions, especially concerning roles and the atmosphere during the interaction processes, could be assessed, which clearly facilitated and enriched the analysis and interpretation of the respective data.

6.6.4 Limitation

Concerning the criterion of *limitation*, this refers to the idea of generalizability, or "external validity" as it would be called in the quantitative vocabulary. In the sense of 'testing the limits' this criterion thus serves the purpose of determining and testing the area of application of a theory or hypotheses developed during the research process (Steinke, 2004, p. 189). Here then, generally, due to the central problem in qualitative research of the missing replicability of research situations that derives from basic methodological assumptions, the idea of external validity is basically not readily compatible with qualitative research (Wrona, 2006, p. 203).

Also, an important *goal* of qualitative research in the first place is in fact to specify concrete action situations, such that broad generalizations are not necessarily aimed at from a qualitative research perspective. Nevertheless, even though findings from qualitative research, by definition, usually have a strongly situative character, it still needs to be clear for what the theory and findings have informative value and explanatory power. In this respect, definitions of the specific type of task (i.e. "debate & decide" type) and group (small-sized ad hoc groups dealing with an intellectual task) under investigation here have already been outlined at the outset of the present chapter. In addition, in the context of presenting the general characteristics of free simulations as a setting for collecting empirical data, the advantages of this kind laboratory research over other standard experiments or experimental simulations were mentioned (cf. 6.4.1). Even though by their very nature simulations are always more remote from any reality observed in actual field research, the relationship to criterion settings is still said to be appreciably high in such freely simulated settings and the participants usually experience intense levels of involvement and identification with the task(s) (Fromkin & Streufert, 1983, p. 421). Having ensured the best possible degree of realism of the strategic scenario used and of the issues of interest, i.e. particularly the conditions for informed task-oriented social interactions, experimental artefacts are consequently reduced and the potential for generalizing the present findings is increased.

Despite all this, however, any determination or discussion in how far the propositions derived from studying such kinds of groups in a simulated research setting are truly applicable in the real strategy world and in how far the insights might even be extended beyond this sort of 'forum', finally clearly needs to be done in light of the concrete results derived from the present analyses. Therefore, in the following now, the findings from the analyses of the data collected are presented. Subsequent to this, in the final discussion and evaluation of the overall empirical study, the issue of limitation as well as the question concerning the relevance of the study for the strategic reality (the other core quality criteria suggested by Steinke), will be reflected upon (6.8). The concrete contributions, in particular in terms of the value added with the empirical findings to existing conceptual and methodological knowledge in the field, as well as suggestions for further research efforts are finally outlined in Chapter 7 where a final summary of the work's overall goals and research questions is presented.

6.7 Results and discussion

In line with the above outline of the concrete questions of interest here, the communication data were analysed in such a way as to enable a presentation and discussion of the results both at the *macro* ('rough') level of analysis of action areas as well as on the more detailed *micro* level regarding each individual dimension and its different categories. In addition, a further differentiation can be made between looking at the respective results on the *group level* and on the level of the *individuals* constituting each of the three discussion groups. The presentation of the results will proceed accordingly:

In the following Sections 6.7.1 to 6.7.4 the results of the analyses for the *group level* will be outlined, thereby progressing from macro to micro considerations. Each of the three groups represents one case. Hence, in each section the different cases are first described and considered individually, followed by cross-case comparisons. Subsequent to this, in Section 6.7.5 profiles of the individual group members are created and the resulting insights are related back to the respective group level results. Like this, a better understanding of the observed cross-case variety, each group's idiosyncratic interaction patterns, and its respective decision results is achieved.

6.7.1 Group level communication at the macro level of action areas

Starting with a look at group communication at the macro level of action areas gives first insights into the social interaction processes that occur in decision making groups on the levels of *content*, *process* and *relationships*. Like this, also the relative importance of these different functional areas can be assessed. Table 12 represents the results of this analysis.

Table 12: Relative importance of the three functional areas of social interaction according to groups

	Group 1	Group 2	Group 3
Content-oriented	64,9%	62,0%	62,7%
Process-directing	8,5%	12,5%	11,8%
Relationship-oriented	26,6 %	25,5%	25,5%
# of codings made	680	545	603
Length of the discussion process (in ca. min.)	90	63	73

Before considering the figures concerning the three levels of action areas in the table above, a first note regards the *length* of the discussion processes. Despite the same rough time frame that was given to all groups, the discussions still varied to considerable extents. As the amount of codings per case consequently varied, too, in order to allow for cross-case comparisons, the results are displayed in terms of the percentages of the overall number of codings made in the respective groups.

Looking now at the *functional areas* of social interaction, a first result of the present analysis is that **content-oriented** contributions clearly make up the major share in the discussions, i.e. the percentages range from 62,0% to 64,9%. The second largest share consists of **relationship-oriented** interactions, where the range is from 25,5% to 26,6%. Thus, in the present study in all three cases about one quarter of the communications was coded as socio-emotional and with this as having primarily a function for the relationships among the team members. Compared to other studies conducted in similar contexts, this share is in fact considerably larger (e.g. Stempfle & Badke-Schaub, 2002). The present finding, however, can be explained by the specific analytical procedures and the coding scheme employed. Specifically, in line with others' as well as the own observation that generally in group interactions relationship-oriented comments are often 'concealed' in content-related communication (Stempfle & Badke-Schaub, 2002, p. 64), particular attention was paid to including this aspect in the analysis. Here then, even though as outlined above, basically only explicit and verbal statements or interactions were coded into one of the categories on this dimension, thanks to the very fine-grained nature of the transcripts and the additional availability of the original video material, a much more detailed and attentive analysis was possible, which finally enabled a more accurate picture of the actual amount of interactions on this more subtle socio-emotional level.

Finally, the smallest share among the three action foci is taken by interactions with a **process-directing** function, i.e. only around 10% of the interactions occurred on the procedural dimension. Here, considering the groups' task at hand, this finding actually seems reasonable since the participants can be expected to know quite well how to proceed in such contexts.[110] As the overall type of discussion task and group situation as such are thus not too novel or complicated for the individuals, in these cases activities in the area of process management (moderation and structuring of the group process) and interface management (definition and assignment of sub tasks, establishment of a group structure and ongoing coordination between group members or sub groups) can be assumed to (have to) occur only limitedly. Nevertheless, despite their smaller overall share, the groups' internal organisation and concrete procedure still constitute important aspects in the decision making process. Especially when set in relation to the final 'outcome' of the process, i.e. here the collective strategic concept, how structured the groups proceeded, whether or not a designated leader or a process moderator

---

[110] I.e., students know how to accomplish this kind of group work. A similar situation exists in the strategic reality where managers are clearly used to interacting in official meetings and hence know about the basic characteristics and fundamental rules of behaviour in these contexts.

were present, etc., are clearly influential elements. These issues will therefore be dealt with in more detail in 6.7.4 where the results regarding the individual 'process' codes are discussed.

Overall now, considering the values of the individual levels of action foci, the three groups all display a very similar pattern. In light of the fact that they were all dealing with the same kind of task, this macro-observation seems reasonable. Also in this context, since the task is defined as an intellective and complex task, content-oriented interactions are clearly in the majority here. These findings then are roughly in line with what other studies have found in similar contexts (cf. e.g. Beck & Fisch, 2000; Boos, 1998; Scharpf, 1988). In addition to this, also the general consistency of the overall functional distributions across the three individually coded groups here underlines the appropriateness and stability of the own coding scheme developed and used in the present analyses.

Apart from the general unity in terms of the overall interaction patterns, however, a slight difference must be noticed and emphasized here as regards the process dimension. Even though the difference between 8,5%, 12,5% and 11,8% does not suffice to also make this finding statistically significant, compared to Group 2 and Group 3, Group 1 with its 8,5% still interacts appreciably less on this dimension. Here then, what becomes clear at this point is that even though the quantified data presented so far are 'nice' as a start, to see whether any such differences are really relevant, and if so, to understand in how far, a deeper look at the entire interaction process is needed. The quantitative macro data thus allow for a first impression and give hints as to where to dig deeper or pay particular attention to in subsequent in-depth considerations. Clearly, such closer considerations are then not only important for the procedural dimension but for the other two functional areas as well (i.e., the relationship-oriented dimension e.g. constitutes of both positive and negative elements which need to be differentiated in detail). Drawing on this, in light of the central research questions in the overall work and the specific interests at hand here, the primary interest first of all concerns the content-oriented interactions. Hence, before presenting the micro level results for the procedural and the socio-emotional levels later on, the following two sections focus on the group results at the micro level of the content dimension.

6.7.2 Group level results at the micro level of the content dimension

Table 13: Detailed results for the content-oriented dimension – all groups

Coding category	Code	relative proportion per code across all individual codes	relative proportion per code on the content dimension	relative proportion per code across all individual codes	relative proportion per code on the content dimension	relative proportion per code across all individual codes	relative proportion per code on the content dimension
		Group 1		Group 2		Group 3	
information, report	I	4,7%	7,3%	4,8%	7,7%	6,1%	9,8%
analysis, statement, conclusion	AF	12,2%	18,8%	9,4%	15,1%	8,3%	13,2%
opinion, evaluation	M	8,7%	13,4%	5,9%	9,5%	4,0%	6,3%
explanation, continuation of an idea/ thought	E	10,1%	15,6%	8,4%	13,6%	5,6%	9,0%
suggestion, idea, solution proposal - new	Vn	2,2%	3,4%	4,0%	6,5%	5,0%	7,9%
suggestion, idea, solution proposal - advances, adjusts, resorts to previous	Ve	6,5%	10,0%	8,6%	13,9%	10,1%	16,1%
question for information	IF	4,1%	6,3%	1,8%	3,0%	3,5%	5,6%
question for evaluation, opinion, etc.	WF	5,1%	7,9%	6,2%	10,1%	5,3%	8,5%
explicit content-related steering	Li	2,2%	3,4%	2,2%	3,6%	2,8%	4,5%
control in terms of summarizing a decision, consensus, etc.	Ke	4,7%	7,3%	9,5%	15,4%	8,5%	13,5%
control in terms of facts/ checking the state of affairs	Kf	4,3%	6,6%	1,1%	1,8%	3,5%	5,6%
		64,9%	100%	62,0%	100%	62,7%	100%

As has been seen above already, generally, in all groups content-related interactions make up the largest overall part. In the present section now, first the relative proportions of the individual codes in the content dimension will be considered for each group individually, followed by cross-case comparisons. These insights are finally considered in relation to the *underlying cognitive thought operations*.

6.7.2.1 Group 1

As can be seen from the figures in Table 13, in Group 1 the codes with the largest relative proportions on the content dimension are AF (18,8%), E (15,6%), and M (13,4%). In this group, analyses, explanations and opinions thus constitute the most frequent content-oriented interactions. Also across all individual codes these are in fact the most frequent. Besides, adding up Vn and Ve, new and advancing suggestions or solution proposals also make up a considerable share (13,4%). Taken together, a similar percentage (i.e. 14,2%) is constituted by questions for information (IF) or for evaluation or opinions (WF).

6.7.2.2 Group 2

A slightly different picture emerges from the results of Group 2. Here, the most frequent individual category is Ke (15,4%), i.e. control in terms of summarizing a decision, consensus, etc. Analyses (AF: 15,1%) and explanations (E: 13,6%) are also high. Considered individually already, "advancing suggestions" (Ve: 13,9%) make up a considerable share in this group. Taken together with Vn, however, suggestions constitute in fact the largest type of content-oriented interactions here. Also across all individual codes, with 12,6% Vn and Ve together are upfront. Questions for information or opinion have a share of 13% on the content dimension. Remarkable in this group is finally that while control in terms of summarizing a decision, consensus, etc. is very high, control in terms of checking facts or the state of affairs is very low (Kf: 1,8%).

6.7.2.3 Group 3

In Group 3, new suggestions, ideas or solution proposals constitute the most frequent type of content-oriented interaction (Vn: 16,1%). Together with "advancing suggestions" the two even make up almost one quarter of all interactions on this dimension (Vn+Ve: 24%). Apart from these, control in terms of summarizing a decision or consensus (Ke) and analyses (AF) also score high with 13,5% and 13,2%, respectively. Similar as in Group 1 and Group 2, questions (IF+WF) make up 14,1%. Important in this group is finally also the 'neutral' sharing of information or reporting behaviour (I: 9,8%).

6.7.2.4 Cross-case analyses and considerations

Whereas looking at the three groups individually is already interesting, more intriguing and revealing insights can be gained when comparing the results between the groups.

Regarding **commonalities**, a first similarity can be observed in terms of the fact that in all groups and to similar extents analytical and evaluative activities are among the most important interactions on the content dimension. Also the amount of questions is almost constant (i.e. around 13% in each group). Generally then, these findings seem reasonable since all of the groups were dealing with the same kind of task, which, by its very nature as an 'intellective' task, clearly calls for analytical, evaluative and explanatory activities. In addition, and also making up a considerable share in all groups, suggestions or solution proposals are of course important in this context. Here then, in line with the outlines in Chapter 5, the importance of carefully considering the specific task groups deal with when investigating their interactions becomes clear again. I.e., in other group situations and confronted with a different kind of task (e.g. a creativity task such as brainstorming, or building group cognitive/ causal maps), the scores on the content-oriented dimension as well as on the other two dimensions might have been quite different.

Moreover, another result that is similar across all three groups is the small proportion of explicit content-related steering (Li: 3,4%; 3,6%; 4,5%). Even though in comparison with other types of content-oriented interactions this kind of activity occurred only rarely here, it still becomes interesting and important when considering which group member(s) actually exert(s) this explicit steering behaviour, i.e. in the context of looking at the individual member profile in Section 6.7.5.

Besides these commonalities and to large extents similar interactive patterns (which can be regarded as induced by the type of task), there are nevertheless two **differences** that become already obvious by merely looking at the quantified contents of the discussions presented so far; these concern the respective relative proportions of suggestions made (V)[111] and the amount of controlling behaviour in terms of summarizing a decision or a consensus (Ke). Here, the results of Group 1 differ quite considerably from those of the other two groups; the numbers suggest that appreciably less suggestions are brought into the discussion process overall and that much less controlling behaviour was exerted in Group 1 than in Group 2 and Group 3. To investigate whether these differences are in fact also statistically significant, further t-tests and a one-way ANOVA were conducted.[112] The results of these tests are presented in Figure 17 and Figure 18, and in Table 14 and Table 15.

---

[111] In the following Vn and Ve will be added up for the respective groups and will be discussed together as 'V'.
[112] These kinds of analyses require information on group *means*. Therefore, the means were computed for each group from the individuals' overall relative proportions of V (Vn+Ve) and Ke, respectively.

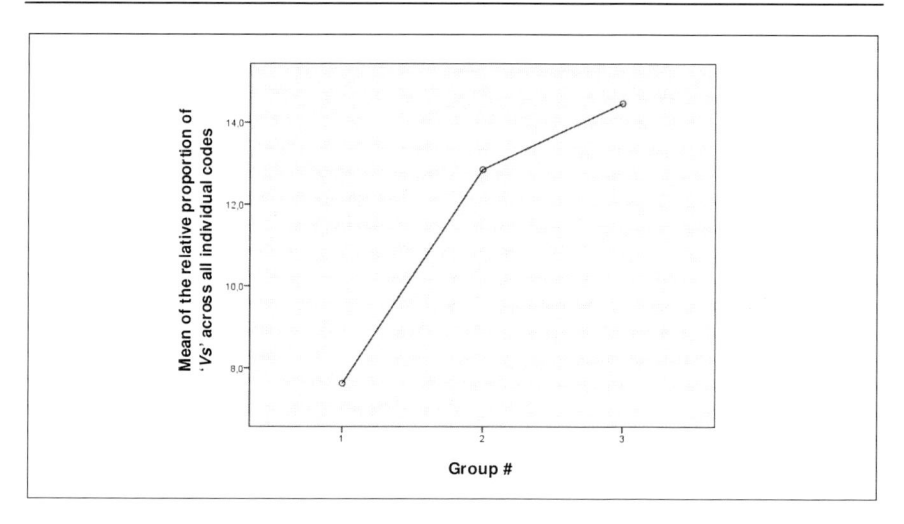

6 – Empirical study of social interaction processes in decision making groups 239

Figure 17: Between-group comparison of the means of the relative proportion of '*Vs*' across all individual codes

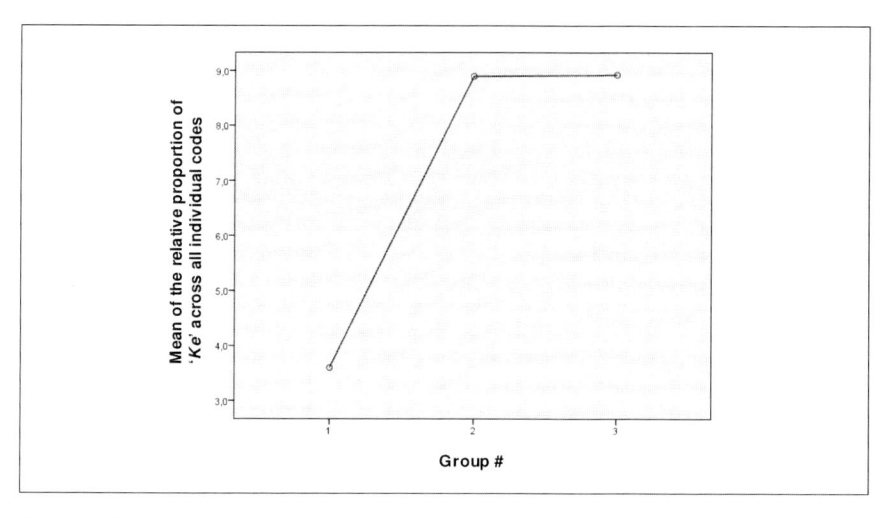

Figure 18: Between-group comparison of the means of the relative proportion of '*Ke*' across all individual codes

Already by looking at Figure 17 and Figure 18, the differences between the groups are clearly obvious. This visual difference is substantiated with the results of the two tests.

Table 14: One-way ANOVA - '*V*' and '*Ke*'

		sum of squares	df	F	significance
relative proportion of '*Vs*' across all individual codes	between groups within groups total	102.485 154.985 257.470	2 9 11	2.976	.102
relative proportion of '*Ke*' across all individual codes	between groups within groups total	75.262 83.968 159.229	2 9 11	4.033	.056

Table 15: t-test statistics – '*V*' and '*Ke*'

	Group #	mean	df	F	significance (two-tailored)
relative proportion of '*Vs*' across all individual codes	1 2	7.625 12.850	6	.452	.097
relative proportion of '*Vs*' across all individual codes	1 3	7.625 14.475	6	.364	.055
relative proportion of '*Vs*' across all individual codes	2 3	12.850 14.475	6	.003	.634
relative proportion of '*Ke*' across all individual codes	1 2	3.600 8.900	6	.000	.056
relative proportion of '*Ke*' across all individual codes	1 3	3.600 8.925	6	.147	.045
relative proportion of '*Ke*' across all individual codes	2 3	8.900 8.925	6	.088	.991

The ANOVA shows that the difference between the three groups in the extent to which suggestions (Vn+Ve) were brought into the discussion process is marginally significant at the 10% level.[113] As regards the decision controlling behaviour (Ke), the group level difference is even marginally significant at the 5% level.[114] The results of the t-tests between the individual cases, respectively, confirm the observation that Group 1 differs significantly from Group 2 and Group 3. The mean comparison between the latter two groups against that yields no significant results.

Taking into account again the results presented in Table 13, whereas Group 1 thus exerts particularly little content-oriented controlling behaviour (Ke), compared to the other two groups it has instead a higher score as regards giving subjective opinions or evaluations (M: 13,4%

---

[113] The choice for a particular significance level lies at the discretion of the researcher and is usually made with regard to the specific research context and questions at hand. In cases where the consequences of wrongly rececting the null-hypothesis or of wrongly accepting its countpart are very severe (like e.g. in medical research), it is common to apply very strict criteria and to test at a significance level of 1% (0.01). Other popular significance levels, however, are 5% (0.05) and 10% (0.1). Especially in innovative, exploratory research that aims at generating new impulses for the scientific communitiy, significance levels of 10% are regarded as justified and not uncommon (cf. e.g. Bortz, 2005, p. 114 and p. 123).

[114] Even though these significances are not too high certain tendencies can still be seen. These might be more pronounced with larger samples.

vs. 9,5% and 6,3%). Considering these figures, since less efforts were hence undertaken in Group 1 as concerns controlling, explicitly summarizing, or putting together/ deciding on what has been exchanged in the discussion, a first hint can be derived that suggests more subjective and less rational interactions and behaviour in this group compared to the others. To substantiate this impression, further qualitative analyses were conducted which are presented in later sections.

As regards the **suggestions**, even though with 10% "advancing suggestions" (Ve) still have a considerable share in Group 1, taken together with "new suggestions" and then compared to Group 2 and Group 3, the significantly lower proportion is striking. Here then, since in light of the overall research interests in the present work it is exactly this aspect which is of utmost importance, a closer look at the concrete contents of the suggestions is taken below.

Before, however, in the final part of this section, the *observed* details of the content-oriented dimension shall be set into relation to the *underlying* cognitive processes occurring in the groups. In this context, as outlined in Chapter 4 and in the own socio-cognitive model in 5.3, even though they are clearly not directly observable, psychological research suggests that in decision-making contexts the primary thought operations involve *generative*, *exploratory*, *comparative*, and *selective* processes. These correspond largely with the phases outlined in the own socio-cognitive model in 5.3 (i.e. *generative* → accumulation; *exploratory*, *comparative* → examination; *selective* → accommodation).

Considered in light of the present analyses and codings, making or advancing suggestions (V) can then be seen as an indicator for *generative* processes; analyses, giving opinions and evaluations (AF, M, E) imply *exploratory* and *comparative* processes; and summarizing a decision or a consensus (Ke) points to *selective* processes. Here then, as has been shown, Group 2 and Group 3 both score high regarding the V code, which suggests a large amount of generative processes. Whereas AF, M, and E are strong in all three groups, from the different kinds of cognitive operations it is especially in Group 1 where exploratory and comparative processes dominate over generative and selection process. Finally, as outlined above, Ke is particularly strong in Group 2 and Group 3; hence also selection processes are of high importance in these groups.

Overall, in the content-oriented area of interactions, analytical and evaluative activities as well as the introduction of suggestions or solution proposals and the control thereof constitute the most frequent action foci. In terms of the **underlying thought operations** this finally means that clearly all of the outlined kinds of cognitive processes take place in any of the groups. In Group 2 and Group 3, however, generative and selective processes are stronger than in Group 1. Still, in the former two groups exploratory and comparative processes nevertheless also occur in similarly considerable amounts as in Group 1, whereas in the latter group it is exactly primarily these two kinds of cognitive operations which predominate over other processes.

In the following now, a deeper look is taken at the results concerning particularly the suggestions and their 'fate'.

6.7.3 Results concerning the 'suggestions'

As has been argued before (cf. 6.2.2), the specific and detailed focus on the 'suggestions' during the discussions is closely in line with the work's overall interest in the socio-cognitive dynamics occurring in decision making processes. I.e., even though the different cognitive processes taking place during problem solving and the (potential) development or change of (shared) strategic orientations are not directly observable, looking at the ideas or suggestions that are being shared and discussed during the interactions nevertheless provides important indicators and insights into those dynamics. The present section therefore focuses specifically on the **nature of the spectrum of solutions** that the groups developed. For each of the three cases the presentation and discussion of the respective results will be the following:

First, the overall number of suggestions is given, including a separation between 'new' and 'advancing' suggestions. These then constitute the 'pool' for the subsequent in-depth analyses to be presented. In this regard, in line with the concrete task (cf. 6.4.6), which already involved a rough pre-structuring of the complex strategic decision situation into different (choice) components, by examining in depth each of the coded suggestions they could further be individually characterized in terms of the respective **category** they pertain to. Here, besides the four strategic content areas of *product*, *market*, *sourcing* and *distribution/ marketing*, a fifth *mixed* category was added inductively since a suggestion must clearly not always fall neatly into one of the original topic areas. Exactly the latter then also provide clues for the groups' degree of **interconnectedness** and **complexity** in cognitive and argumentative processes, i.e. when e.g. product and market, marketing and market, or issues beyond the explicitly given categories constitute the essence of the suggestions. Generally, by following this analytical approach, insights are gained into the extent to which the problem was actually **penetrated** and into the degree of **differentiation** to which it was dealt with. In addition, differentiating and tracing in detail the individual suggestions and their development over the course of the discussion and with respect to *when* in the process they occurred, also allows for making first important links to the **temporal development** or phaseal structure of the group processes (cf. 5.3.2).

In line with the previous then, it can thus be reemphasized here that due to the fact that complex issues like the present strategy task clearly consist of multiple aspects, merely considering the overall number of suggestions made or the final outcome alone would clearly not be sufficient. In a third step, the essences of the groups' final concepts are therefore presented and considered by relating them to the results derived from the prior analyses of the suggestions made *over the course* of the entire process. Like this, insights are gained regarding the **'fate' of individual suggestions**, i.e. which of them are accepted and become part of the final concept. In addition, in this context also the degree to which **heterogeneous solution suggestions** are integrated as well as the **'success' of the different group members** in terms of pushing their own views through can be assessed.[115]

From all this then, in the final parts of this results section for each individual group, reflections about the **complexity or depth of cognitive operations**, and the **degree of** (potential) **cognitive changes** or **convergences** concerning the issue at hand that have occurred over the course of the discussion are outlined. In this context, recourse is also made to the individual statements each team member had worked out and handed in prior to the actual simulation.[116] These statements are valuable in so far as they provide information about the participants' strategic concepts, which they had in mind for the case company before entering the group discussions. As such they can be regarded as 'proxies' for the individuals' original concealed cognitive structures and orientations.

Having presented the results of all three cases, a comparative discussion finally closes this results section.

6.7.3.1 Group 1

Whereas in the previous Section 6.7.2 the respective proportion of the suggestions within the content-oriented dimension was outlined, in the focus here are the individual suggestions themselves. In this regard, over the course of the entire discussion, in Group 1 15 'new' suggestions were made and 44 suggestions were coded as taking up or extending previous ones. Overall, there are thus 59 suggestions to be considered here (cf. Table 13 and also Table 16).

---

[115] This issue is considered in further depth in 6.7.5 where 'profiles' of the individual group members are developed.
[116] These original documents are available from the author upon request.

Table 16: Numerical overview of the suggestions in Group 1

Strategic content category	new suggestion (Vn)	advancing suggestion (Ve)	sum
	15	44	59
product	4	27	31
market	3	4	7
sourcing	2	7	9
distribution/ marketing	3	2	5
mixed	3	4	7

Concerning the distribution of the individual suggestions across the different strategic content categories, the respective results are displayed in Table 16. Here then, even though the number of *new* suggestions does not vary greatly between the different categories, the *overall* majority of suggestions clearly concerns product issues. To investigate these results in more depth, the transcripts were revisited and a closer look was there taken at the concrete content of the sections coded as such. In addition, also the respective broader discussion context and the part of the process (in terms of the approximate time) the suggestions are made in are considered. Since this contextual consideration of all the suggestions is clearly imperative for the analysis, merely presenting the coded sections alone here would hence not further the reader's understanding. Therefore, Table 17 presents an *information overview* of the suggestions in Group 1 that includes the specific code (Vn or Ve), the participant who introduced the suggestion, the strategic content category it was assigned to, and the approximate time of the process it occurred in.[117]

Table 17: Information overview of suggestions in Group 1

Code	Participant	Strategic content category	time (approx.)
Vn	N	product	8:00
Vn	N	market	8:30
Vn	N	product	8:45
Vn	Y	product	10:18
Ve	N	product	13:20
Ve	Y	product	15:00
Ve	Y	product	15:30
Vn	N	mixed	21:40
Ve	N	sourcing	23:05
Vn	M	sourcing	23:35
Ve	Y	sourcing	23:50
Ve	N	product	24:25
Ve	N	mixed	25:00

---

[117] The interested reader who wishes to consult the respective parts in the full transcripts may receive these upon request from the author.

Vn	N	distribution/ marketing	29:40
Ve	N	distribution/ marketing	30:00
Ve	N	product	33:00
Ve	M	product	34:30
Ve	M	product	35:00
Ve	Y	product	35:10
Ve	R	product	35:40
Ve	N	product	39:00
Ve	N	product	39:20
Vn	M	distribution/ marketing	40:05
Ve	Y	product	41:00
Vn	M	sourcing	43:00
Ve	M	sourcing	43:00
Ve	R	product	49:00
Ve	M	product	49:10
Ve	Y	product	49:15
Ve	Y	product	52:40
Ve	M	product	53:20
Vn	N	product	56:00
Ve	N	product	56:15
Ve	M	product	56:25
Ve	M	product	56:50
Ve	M	product	57:10
Ve	N	product	57:40
Ve	N	product	58:20
Ve	M	product	59:15
Ve	M	mixed	60:30
Ve	N	sourcing	61:35
Ve	M	sourcing	61:40
Ve	M	mixed	61:50
Ve	M	market	62:05
Ve	M	mixed	64:00
Vn	Y	market	66:00
Vn	Y	market	66:10
Ve	Y	market	68:20
Vn	N	mixed	68:30
Ve	N	sourcing	70:40
Vn	N	mixed	72:00
Ve	M	distribution/ marketing	72:00
Vn	Y	distribution/ marketing	72:20
Ve	N	product	73:15
Ve	N	product	74:45
Ve	M	product	74:55
Ve	N	market	80:00
Ve	M	market	83:00
Ve	N	sourcing	85:20

As a result of these in-depth considerations of the data, it becomes obvious that the group discusses the product issue quite controversially. Whereas the sheer number of advancing suggestions in the *product* category could also mean deeper and more differentiated considerations and real developments of once introduced suggestions, in the present case there are in fact a lot of repetitions. For example, the initial 'new' suggestion concerning the mass market is taken up and discussed repeatedly without actually adding any more details or extending this idea. A similar picture is observed as regards the suggestion to focus on a particular product segment (i.e. 'Super Premium'). Only towards the end of the discussion process the suggestions become more concrete and are finally accepted. Up to this point, however, a lot is repetitive. Regarding the product issue, the group thus talks kind of in circles. As regards the issues of *market* and *distribution/ marketing*, the similar small amount of new and advancing suggestions in those two categories indicates that both are not discussed in depth. This impression is substantiated by looking into the transcripts. For both issues a very short period of time is allocated to discussing them which occurs basically only during the late part of the overall interaction. Concerning the question of *sourcing*, a phase early in the process can be discerned in which the issue is on top of the agenda. The topic is taken up and developed further later on before finally a decision is made.

Drawing on the above, regarding more specifically the **temporal development** of the group discussion, seen over the course of the interactions, the first and also dominant issue throughout is the product. Whereas sourcing ideas are discussed repeatedly in between, considerations concerning where (market) and how exactly to sell the product (distribution/ marketing) occur merely briefly towards the very end of the process. In line with this, in this group there are in fact no real phases to be discerned. The participants almost 'jump' directly into the discussion without displaying any orientation or acquisition phase. Coherent with the fact that they talk repeatedly about the product issue, also over the course of the process no real pattern emerges. Merely towards the end after having realized the need to come to a conclusion, a phase can be seen in which a selection and integration of the issues takes place.

Overall, regarding the spectrum of solutions, Group 1 can in fact be described as quite undifferentiated. Their suggestions are also neither very complex nor interlinked as evidenced by the large amount of (repetitive) product considerations and the rather small number of suggestions that are 'mixed' or go beyond the concrete content levels stated explicitly in the task itself. Also, since the group focuses primarily on discussing questions regarding the product, they clearly do not truly penetrate the overall complex strategic issue. Instead, they rather beat around the bush without introducing and developing many concrete suggestions. All this is then also reflected in the group's final concept (cf. Table 18).

Table 18: Final strategic concept of Group 1

Content
focus on the mass market in terms of product
keep premium products (i.e. luxury) for the image/ brand name
luxury wines in the US
new markets for those wines, i.e. China, India, Japan; not EU except for Germany (and UK)
sourcing in cost efficient regions (Australia) and vertical integration of winemakers and distribution
reduce costs while keeping prices constant – increase margins
differentiation and segmentation of the sales force according to (product) categories

Table 18 displays the essence of the final strategic concept of Group 1.[118] As can be seen, elements relating to all of the specific strategic content categories as well as some 'mixed' decisions are represented. This, however, can clearly be attributed to the concrete task that was given to the participants, which explicitly required them to consider and answer those different content dimensions. Nevertheless, as is known from the results above, the issues of distribution and market were in fact only touched on briefly towards the end of the interactions and were thus not really considered in depth. Transferring this observation to the strategic reality, such superficial considerations could then clearly lead to decisions which later on show to be suboptimal or even wrong. At this point then, also the necessity to examine the process itself through which such decisions or concepts come about is clear again since only like that one is able to know *that* and *in how far* content-wise different emphases and thorough analyses occurred during the discussions. Exactly this knowledge, however, is important in order to be able to judge whether the outcome of a group meeting is truly justified and well-grounded. Taking into account the overall length of the discussion and thus the time the group spent on its task (i.e. 90 minutes here), overall, the concept of Group 1 is finally quite ‚thin' with only a few detailed aspects (cf. the discussion of the results of Group 2 and Group 3 below).

Concerning the **'fate' of individual suggestions**, a first striking result is that regarding the product issue, it is in fact N's very first suggestions introduced right in the beginning of the discussion which are finally taken up in the group's end concept. In terms of sourcing, over

---
[118] Copies of all groups' original documents are available from the author upon request.

the course of the discussion it is primarily N and M who make suggestions on this topic. Also here the final decision to pursue vertical integration was voiced by N already in the very beginning. For the market question it is basically the suggestions brought in by Y which are integrated without lots of controversy around them. Considered in their entirety, overall, the majority of suggestions come from N and it is also his original ideas which largely characterize the final group concept. N is hence the most 'successful' with his suggestions. Apart from the rather low heterogeneity of individual solutions voiced in the discussion, from those introduced there is also a large number which are neither accepted nor rejected explicitly, but which are merely not decided upon at all.

Taken together now, as argued above already, from these results it can be suggested that the **complexity and depth** of cognitive operations in Group 1 is not too high as they do not manage to become truly concrete, beat around the bush, and, overall, do not generate many 'innovative' suggestions (cf. Section 6.7.2).

In terms of the question regarding **cognitive changes** or a **(potential) convergence** in (strategic) knowledge structures among the participants, there are, however, two sides. I.e., on the one hand, the controversial and long discussions about the product issue in fact suggest positive effects since by considering an issue repeatedly and from different sides the chance for a convergence and actual cognitive 'acceptance', and thus lasting cognitive changes, is clearly much higher (cf. 4.2 and 5.3). Also, looking at the individual statements in fact shows that before the meeting R for example suggested that Mondavi focuses on the premium wines. In the end of the discussion process, however, R agrees with the suggestion to focus on wines for the mass market. Consequently, the discussion process and the group interactions made R change her position. Whether or not R is truly and lastingly convinced, however, still remains another question of course.

Drawing on the latter argument, here then on the other hand, the dominance of N and M throughout the whole discussion might prevent exactly this. I.e., Y and R did not have the chance to really introduce their knowledge or defend their positions. Especially R might therefore finally only have agreed superficially to the end concept without actually having mentally accommodated any of the contents discussed and decided on by the others. These issues shall be examined in more detail in the context of the 'climate' discussion and the individual member profiles.

6.7.3.2 Group 2

In Group 2, over the entire course of their interactions 22 new suggestions were made and 47 sections were coded as representing suggestions that take up or extend previous ones. In this group, the sample for the subsequent analyses thus consists of 69 suggestions overall.

Table 19: Numerical overview of the suggestions in Group 2

Strategic content category	new suggestion (Vn)	advancing suggestion (Ve)	sum
	22	47	69
product	3	3	6
market	4	10	14
sourcing	2	5	7
distribution/ marketing	9	18	27
mixed	4	11	15

Table 19 displays the distribution of the individual suggestions across the different categories in Group 2. The first obvious result here is the comparatively high amount of suggestions dealing with distribution/ marketing issues (both new and advancing). Market and mixed issues and product and sourcing ideas each are contained in about an equal number of suggestions, respectively. Table 20 provides some more information on the suggestions in this group.

Table 20: Suggestion information Group 2

Code	Participant	Strategic content category	time (approx.)
Vn	A	product	7:25
Vn	A	distribution/ marketing	7:30
Vn	A	distribution/ marketing	7:35
Vn	A	mixed	8:00
Vn	Ju	distribution/ marketing	9:00
Vn	Ju	market	9:30
Vn	Ju	mixed	10:00
Vn	Ja	market	11:25
Vn	Ja	distribution/ marketing	11:35
Vn	D	distribution/ marketing	12:30
Vn	D	sourcing	14:00
Vn	D	mixed	14:20
Vn	D	mixed	14:40
Vn	D	market	15:14
Vn	Ju	product	17:00
Ve	Ju	mixed	18:00
Vn	Ju	distribution/ marketing	19:15
Ve	Ja	product	20:10

Ve	D	mixed	20:40
Ve	Ju	market	21:50
Ve	Ju	market	22:05
Ve	Ju	market	22:15
Ve	D	market	22:55
Ve	A	market	23:45
Ve	D	market	23:50
Ve	D	mixed	24:05
Ve	D	mixed	24:40
Ve	Ju	sourcing	25:20
Vn	Ja	market	27:10
Ve	D	market	27:30
Ve	A	mixed	29:15
Ve	D	sourcing	29:55
Ve	Ju	sourcing	30:30
Ve	D	sourcing	31:15
Ve	Ju	mixed	33:05
Ve	A	product	33:10
Ve	A	market	33:40
Ve	Ja	market	34:35
Ve	Ju	market	34:45
Vn	Ju	distribution/ marketing	35:50
Ve	Ju	sourcing	37:10
Ve	A	mixed	37:40
Ve	Ja	distribution/ marketing	38:00
Ve	Ja	distribution/ marketing	38:15
Ve	Ju	distribution/ marketing	38:25
Ve	Ju	distribution/ marketing	38:45
Vn	Ju	distribution/ marketing	39:15
Ve	Ju	distribution/ marketing	39:20
Ve	Ja	distribution/ marketing	40:10
Ve	Ju	distribution/ marketing	40:55
Ve	Ja	distribution/ marketing	41:50
Ve	Ja	distribution/ marketing	42:10
Ve	Ju	distribution/ marketing	42:25
Ve	D	distribution/ marketing	42:30
Ve	Ju	distribution/ marketing	42:40
Ve	D	mixed	47:20
Ve	Ju	product	49:10
Ve	Ju	mixed	50:57
Ve	D	distribution/ marketing	51:55
Ve	Ju	distribution/ marketing	52:40
Vn	D	product	54:45
Ve	Ja	distribution/ marketing	56:40
Ve	Ju	distribution/ marketing	56:45
Ve	D	mixed	58:55
Vn	D	sourcing	58:20
Ve	D	mixed	60:00

6 – Empirical study of social interaction processes in decision making groups   251

Ve	A	distribution/ marketing	60:25
Ve	D	distribution/ marketing	60:30
Vn	D	distribution/ marketing	61:35

Considering in detail the contents of the different suggestions outlined in the above table, the largely balanced picture already indicated by the mere counts of the different categories is also reflected in the qualitative analyses. Specifically, even though ideas concerning marketing and sales clearly present the largest share, overall, across all categories the suggestions can be described as quite diverse and differentiated. Rather than merely repeating the same ideas advanced previously (due to controversies about them), the participants often truly take up their own or others' ideas and develop these further and in more detail. In line with what was already indicated in the previous section with the relatively large proportion of suggestions in the content dimension, Group 2 thus really advances a qualitatively valuable spectrum of solutions. Here then, the considerable amount of suggestions falling into the mixed category (especially product-market combination) also evidences the noticeable degree of interconnectedness in the group's discussion.

Concerning the question of whether or not it is possible to discern certain **phases** in the group process, here already the mere look at the contents of the participants' suggestions in temporal order allows anticipating a quite structured and patterned procedure. Examining the data in more detail substantiates this impression. In fact, the entire discussion process of Group 2 can be described as truly structured and organized from the beginning on. As a result, it is even possible to identify different critical moments in the process which mark end or starting points for what might be seen as concrete phases. Here then, largely in line with the literature and the own model developed in 5.3, the group sets out with an *acquisition phase* in which each of the participants first shares his or her ideas concerning the issue at hand with the rest of the group. In this phase then, the suggestions concern all the different issues (cf. roughly till about minute 19 in Table 20[119]). Following this, as all of the 'material' is on the table and the task is clear, the group proceeds in a very structured way by dealing with each of the different elements required by the given task one after another. Compared to the rather short acquisition phase, this overall *examination* and *evaluation phase* is clearly longer, and may in fact again be subdivided according to the specific issue the group deals with during the respective parts

---

[119] In all the three rooms used for the simulation the respective research assistants turned on the videorecording already prior to when the participants actually started their interactions on the given task. Due to this, the recording had already been on for about 5 to 7 minutes in the different cases. The transcription, however, only started at the beginning of the actual group interactions. In line with this, it is the absolute times of the video running that were recorded in the transcripts and which are also used in the presentation of the results here.

(i.e., first product, then market, followed by sourcing, and finally distribution/ sales issues). Here then, *integrative* sub-phases can be discerned for the different issues, respectively.

Overall, the nature of this group's discussion process supports the observation made previously and advanced in the own model that group (decision making) processes can truly be seen as consisting of different phases. Despite this general structuring into different phases, however, as argued in the literature as well as recognized in the own model, such phases, their respective length and concrete sequence still are by no means deterministic or uniform across all groups or situations (cf. Group 1 and Group 3). In addition, and as evidenced in the present case, even though a rough overall pattern may be discerned, there nevertheless clearly also is a recycling and recurrence to other activities or phases at different points of the process. I.e., acquisition or orientation activities for example occur also during later parts of the process where the majority of interactions are already oriented towards evaluating or integrating information or ideas. Inversely, if like in the present case the task itself consists of distinctive elements and these may be dealt with one after another, integrative or selection activities concerning particular issues may already be observed early on in the process.

Table 21: Final strategic concept of Group 2

Content
produce and sell only wine
high (Premium and higher)
brand consolidation
local adaptations to the portfolio
global presence (in the long run)
in EU only JVs/ partnerships
focus on Asia (EU and Russia nothing)
focused sales force for each distribution channel
Popular Premium in supermarkets, Luxury in speciality stores
development of the wine culture, "demystification"
market research
in other markets JVs/ partnerships as a start to gain market knowledge; later own production, outsourcing for the US market (through partnerships)
"backward outsource integration"
quality controls

Regarding the final strategy concept of Group 2 now (cf. Table 21), the very structured and thorough procedure is finally also reflected herein as it includes a number of different elements that relate to the individual content levels.

Considered in relation to the variety of individual suggestions advanced over the course of the discussion, the concept truly contains a number of differentiated ideas brought into the discussion by different group members. However, despite this seemingly openness and equality in terms of who was able to introduce and develop suggestions during the course of the interaction, examining the final concept in more detail and considering it in relation to the individual positions the participants voiced in their introductory round as well as by looking at the individual statements they developed before the group meeting, a strong overlap with the original ideas and structure of D's "strategy" is obvious. In this group then it was clearly D who was the most successful with his overall suggestions and with subtly leading the group to accept his own ideas.

Despite the fact that it is thus to large extents D's ideas and suggestions which characterize the final concept, regarding cognitive changes and a (potential) convergence in cognitive structures between the participants, however, this group nevertheless constitutes a good example for seeing how, over the course of the interactions, its members take up the knowledge from or accommodate their cognitive structures to those of the others. In this regard, at a later point in the process Ja for example suddenly talks naturally about an issue (i.e., the *sales force*) that he had not suggested at the outset of the discussion. Also new associations seem to have been built during the interactions, specifically concerning the issue of the *wine culture*. Here, one of the group members (Ju) introduces the idea and in the end it is truly part of the group's concept. Such incidences may then be seen as indicators for cognitive changes or even convergence.

Apart from these effects, however, there are clearly also indications which support the fact that generally people's cognitive structures are relatively stable and resistant to change (cf. 4.2). Here, D for example stays quite strongly with his own ideas and suggestions over the course of the entire process and introduces again and again what he had already in the very beginning (e.g. arguments related to *branding*). In a similar way also Ju resorts repeatedly to the issue of wine culture which constitutes her own original concept. Still, the others take up this idea and integrate it without controversies into the final concept.

Taken together, concerning the nature of their cognitive operations, Group 2 has been shown to be quite differentiated and to truly penetrate the complex issue. Also, indications for cognitive changes on the part of individual members as well as a certain degree of convergence in knowledge structures seem discernable here.

6.7.3.3 Group 3

Already in the previous section the considerable share, i.e. almost one quarter, that suggestions take in the content-oriented dimension in Group 3 has been emphasized. Specifically now, in this case 30 new suggestions were introduced and 61 were coded as advancing or extending previous ones. With altogether 91 suggestions the present sample for the in-depth analyses is thus remarkably large.

Table 22: Numerical overview of the suggestions in Group 3

Strategic content category	new suggestion (Vn)	advancing suggestion (Ve)	sum
	30	61	91
product	9	16	25
market	3	8	11
sourcing	4	5	9
distribution/ marketing	9	22	31
mixed	5	10	15

Looking at Table 22, the first noticeable result is the clear dominance of product and especially of distribution/ marketing issues among the suggestions. Nevertheless, market and sourcing topics are by no means neglected. In addition, with in sum 15 suggestions also the mixed category has to be noticed here. Table 23 presents more information on these suggestions.

Table 23: Suggestion information Group 3

Code	Participant	Strategic content category	time (approx.)
Vn	G	distribution/ marketing	6:40
Vn	G	product	7:30
Vn	G	market	8:30
Vn	H	mixed	9:30
Vn	H	product	9:35
Vn	H	distribution/ marketing	10:00
Vn	H	distribution/ marketing	10:20
Vn	H	distribution/ marketing	10:30
Vn	H	mixed	11:10
Ve	H	product	9:45
Ve	H	distribution/ marketing	10:40
Ve	H	mixed	11:00
Vn	M	product	13:10
Ve	M	product	14:50
Ve	S	distribution/ marketing	14:55
Vn	M	product	15:05

6 – Empirical study of social interaction processes in decision making groups 255

Vn	M	sourcing	15:35
Vn	M	market	15:40
Vn	S	market	16:30
Vn	S	product	16:50
Ve	S	distribution/ marketing	17:00
Ve	M	product	17:20
Ve	M	product	17:25
Vn	G	product	17:30
Ve	G	product	18:00
Ve	S	product	18:20
Ve	M	mixed	19:00
Vn	H	product	19:40
Ve	H	mixed	19:25
Ve	H	product	19:30
Ve	H	product	20:15
Ve	H	product	20:25
Ve	H	product	20:30
Ve	S	product	20:45
Vn	M	sourcing	21:35
Ve	M	market	22:10
Ve	H	market	22:15
Ve	S	market	22:20
Ve	H	market	22:30
Vn	H	mixed	23:05
Ve	S	market	24:10
Vn	S	mixed	24:20
Ve	H	mixed	24:40
Ve	H	mixed	24:50
Ve	H	mixed	26:00
Ve	H	market	26:40
Ve	M	market	27:20
Ve	M	market	27:30
Vn	M	distribution/ marketing	28:45
Vn	G	distribution/ marketing	29:15
Ve	G	distribution/ marketing	29:45
Ve	G	distribution/ marketing	30:00
Vn	S	distribution/ marketing	30:10
Ve	H	distribution/ marketing	30:40
Ve	H	distribution/ marketing	31:15
Ve	M	mixed	31:55
Ve	M	distribution/ marketing	32:45
Ve	M	distribution/ marketing	33:05
Ve	M	distribution/ marketing	33:30
Vn	H	distribution/ marketing	33:35
Ve	G	distribution/ marketing	34:05
Vn	M	sourcing	35:00
Ve	S	sourcing	35:20
Vn	M	product	35:35

Ve	M	product	35:45
Ve	H	sourcing	36:15
Ve	M	sourcing	36:20
Vn	H	sourcing	37:00
Ve	M	product	43:25
Ve	H	mixed	47:00
Ve	G	sourcing	47:10
Ve	M	sourcing	50:00
Vn	M	product	51:20
Ve	M	product	51:25
Ve	M	product	51:30
Ve	M	product	51:40
Ve	H	distribution/ marketing	51:50
Vn	H	distribution/ marketing	53:00
Vn	S	mixed	54:20
Ve	S	mixed	55:00
Ve	H	distribution/ marketing	58:00
Ve	H	distribution/ marketing	58:50
Ve	H	distribution/ marketing	59:30
Ve	S	distribution/ marketing	59:50
Ve	H	distribution/ marketing	60:00
Ve	S	mixed	60:10
Ve	H	distribution/ marketing	68:25
Ve	H	distribution/ marketing	69:10
Ve	H	distribution/ marketing	69:15
Ve	M	distribution/ marketing	69:20
Ve	H	distribution/ marketing	70:25

The large amount of suggestions involving distribution/ marketing issues was already mentioned above. In this regard, in the present case the suggestions falling into this broad category can in fact be again subdivided into ideas concerning the sales force and the concrete places where or channels through which to sell the products, as well as specific advertisement considerations. In line with this, the discussion on these issues occurs basically in two blocks, i.e. once in the middle of the overall process, and then again at the very end where a number of the previous ideas are detailed or extended even more. Together, all this suggests a quite differentiated approach that also involves a noticeable portion of creativity (e.g. in terms of the suggestions concerning *restaurant partnerships*). Further indicators for the group's complexity and penetration into the overall issue can then also be found in the context of the suggestions falling into the other categories. A considerable 'block' in the beginning for example deals with product issues. Here, apart from the concrete product segment to be targeted itself, also the *quality* aspect is developed. The latter represents in fact a more overarching topic that goes beyond the four concrete levels at hand. The group thus also thinks about the general positioning and standing of the case company. The noticeable amount of suggestions combining market and product considerations further underlines the many connections the participants make throughout their discussion and hence the thorough penetration of the complex issue they achieve. Overall then, not only quantitatively but also qualitatively Group 3 develops a large and differentiated spectrum of solutions. The task is well thought through and involves a lot of concrete and 'innovative' content. In addition and even more importantly, over the course of the process all group members are able to bring in their respective ideas and views, and even though overall some of them contribute more (i.e., H and M), in most of the cases they nevertheless relate nicely to each other instead of merely following their own concepts. Remarkable is finally that even towards the end new suggestions are still brought in at several points.

Considering the above, certain hints regarding the **temporal development** or the structuring of the overall group process have already been made. Specifically now, in a similar way as was found in Group 2, also here the group proceeds in a quite structured and 'conscious' way towards solving the problem at hand. They check off the different issues one after another. In line with this, apart from the rough idea one can get from looking at the information on the suggestions provided in the above table, a detailed examination of the transcript as well as of the original video then truly allows to discern certain phases in the group process. In this regard, similar as in Group 2, also here the team members first share their different views and strategies by taking turns during an initial *acquisition phase*. Following this, they proceed towards *examining* and *developing* the ideas further. As can also be seen from the above table, here they proceed largely by following the pre-structured content requirements of the given task. Having noticed the progression of the time available, a phase involving *integrative activities* is initiated (after about minute 40). This basically ends at minute 55 (*"Now we have the most important things."*). In light of this statement, however, what is particularly interesting here is that the discussion then still ensues for another 20 minutes and that during this period even further ideas and suggestions are developed, especially regarding the area of marketing.

Taken together, also in Group 3 an overall process pattern can thus be discerned that is largely in line with the own model and arguments in the existing literature. Still, similar general cautions and confinements apply as have been outlined in the above section in the context of discussing the results of Group 2. In this regard, what can be seen quite nicely from the present case data is the fact that instead of having one single linear process, the interaction actually involves a number of different smaller circles or sub-phases in which the group displays elements of generative, exploratory, and integrative, as well as control activities. Hence, different from the assertions of the strict phase models, neither are generative activities clearly confined to the early parts of such processes nor does controlling behaviour only occur in the very end. Instead, as evidenced in the present case, generative processes and controlling behaviour, as well as also exploration, (can) in fact occur throughout the entire process.

Table 24 now presents the aggregated final concept of Group 3.

Table 24: Final strategic concept of Group 3

Content
strategy 'organic growth'
positioning against the beer producers
ensure the quality
marketing in the direction of high quality wines
keep Woodbridge (as Popular Premium brand)
Woodbridge more intensively to Asia
premium-wines more intensively in the US market
export to Asia, possibly to Latin America
intensified use of own grapes for high quality wines (acquisition of new land)
intensified acquisition of grapes for the normal wine qualities
restructuring of the sales force (regional sales force with employees specialized on products/ product categories)
strengthen the image by means of more marketing – massive TV advertising
supermarkets (lower wines)
wholesalers
restaurants

In line with the high degree of differentiation and interconnectedness the group already displayed during the discussion process itself, also the result above reflects the complexity of their interactions. Specifically, apart from the four concrete questions, also overarching strategic ideas are included, such as the one regarding the general corporate strategy and the differentiation in terms of where exactly to sell which product.

Considered in relation to the plurality of individual suggestions introduced and developed over the course of the entire process, i.e. examining their 'fate', and relating this also to their respective 'authors', the largely balanced picture and open communication culture mentioned above is also reflected here. I.e., it is clearly not one particular group member who finally pushed his or her views/ concept through and who could thus be called 'most successful'.

Instead, even though certain concrete ideas (e.g. the restaurant issue) can clearly be attributed to a specific person and to what he or she had in mind (i.e., in the original concept) before the meeting or during its initial phases, overall, the final strategy proposal here really represents a group concept that was developed by all of the team members together.

Finally, concerning the degree of cognitive changes or (potential) convergence, all the above outlines in fact suggest that in this group all team members actually truly support the final decision as they have been actively involved in shaping it. Also, since each of them was able to bring in his or her respective ideas and extensive discussion on these took place throughout the process, enough material and time for reflections on these were available. These factors then certainly enhance the likelihood that lasting cognitive changes as well as a convergence among the participants have occurred.

Drawing on the latter, before finally examining in more detail exactly such factors or conditions that may foster or prevent groups from working together successfully, sharing their knowledge and producing consensual outcomes that are also truly mentally internalized, in the following section a comparative and more general discussion of the present section is presented first.

6.7.3.4 General and comparative discussion

Even though all three groups were confronted with exactly the same task and the same group situation and environment, the fact *that* certain differences exist between the cases became clear already through the quantitative counts of the overall codes at the rough level, as well as the details of the individual dimensions (cf. Sections 6.7.1 and 6.7.2). The in-depth considerations concerning primarily the coded suggestions now made these divergences even more obvious. Specifically, the focus on the ideas and solution proposals was shown to be a truly valuable approach since, in light of the work's overarching research questions, it allows to gain insights into the groups' development and thus to also make statements about the respective socio-cognitive dynamics occurring in them. Here then, especially for examining and understanding the latter, merely considering the outcome or final concepts is hence clearly not enough. This is even more so if the aim is to later go even further and to see what happens outside the concrete meetings at other points and different occasions during the overall strategic process.

Considering now the results of the different groups presented here and comparing them, although judging performance or qualitative outcomes is clearly always difficult and in large parts subjective, the above outlines nevertheless allow to argue that, generally, better results are achieved when more individual and diverse elements and ideas are discussed and carefully developed during the discussions, and are finally allowed to become part of the group's concept. Not only is the respective outcome more thought through and thus 'solid', but by allowing all group members to contribute their ideas to the discussion, it is also more likely that each one truly identifies with the collective decision and hence that lasting cognitive changes have occurred on the part of the individuals. Where there is one very dominant person, overall, fewer pieces of (diverse) information and knowledge are being shared and evaluated. If this participant then also manages to push through exactly his or her own ideas, others may feel passed over, are not really convinced, and may consequently have agreed merely superficially due to time constraints or fears of oppression. Especially later in the overall process, e.g. in repeated meetings or when the decision or the concept is to be defended in front of other people or carried to other (group) contexts, problems are then likely to arise due to this.

Detailing the above, the results have shown that it is in Group 3 where clearly the most suggestions are made, especially in comparison to Group 1. Even though also in Group 2 the overall number of suggestions is clearly higher than in Group 1, seen in light of the success and fate of individual suggestions and also looking at the individual statements, in the latter the final concept is strongly imprinted by the 'original' ideas of one particular person. Even though also in Group 3 the respective amount of suggestions contributed during the process itself differs notably between the members, the specific development and final integration of ideas here can be described as more 'democratic', balanced and reflected. In sharp contrast to both these cases, Group 1 basically focused on or circled around one specific issue, i.e. the product, and finally had only little time left to deal in detail with the other issues on the agenda. As a consequence, their final concept can be regarded as the least differentiated, reflected and deep. The solution of Group 2 against that is clearly differentiated, thought through and quite complex. Still, as argued before, it actually represents mostly the ideas and structure that one of the participants had had already before the entire interaction. The most integrated and truly 'group concept' thus is the one of Group 3, which is not only differentiated but has elements from all members as well as commonly developed ideas in it. It is in this case then where real and lasting cognitive changes on the sides of all group members, and hence a convergence in knowledge structures, can most likely be assumed.

Apart from considering and comparing the outcome of the processes in terms of the concrete concepts and the cognitive implications, the second major aspect investigated in the present section concerned the **temporal development** of the overall group processes, where the relation was made back to the own model developed in Section 5.3 and to the general **phase discussion** (5.2.2) in group process research. In this context, taking and tracing the coded suggestions as a first clue and going on from there again deeper back into the material, allowed deriving valuable results for this. Specifically, as has been shown, in both Group 2 and Group 3 the phases outlined in the model could in fact broadly be seen in the present empirical reality. Considering Group 1, however, apart from their final rather short *integration* activities, in this case it was hardly possible to discern any other concrete process phases. Instead, the group seemed rather unorganized without having properly established orientation or direction. Whereas this particular group might be seen as an extreme case, these findings nevertheless underscore the assertion that overall it is not possible to propose any uniform model(s) of group interaction processes. A model like the own developed for the (strategic) decision making context here is valuable though for giving a general impression. At the same time, however, it needs to be recognized that in reality such processes are neither absolutely linear nor do they consist of clearly separate phases. Instead, during the whole process different phases and activities iterate, recycle and overlap such that in the end it is several smaller circles that may be discerned in which decisions concerning different aspects of the complex problem at hand are taken, respectively.

In line with this, even though as argued in the literature certain concrete phases can thus in fact be distinguished in group decision making/ the interactions, the observations here have also shown that overall such processes are truly of an *evolutionary nature*. I.e., in all three cases, and particularly visible in Group 3, one could see how the ideas and suggestions developed over time during the interactions and the discussion, and how finally it was all integrated and put down. Here then, apart from the importance of considering the concrete task and situation the group is confronted with, such processes are clearly also always impacted and shaped to considerable extents by the individual participants and their particular characteristics and behaviours. As a consequence, due to the prevailing different socio-cognitive dynamics both the (written) outcomes as well as the respective cognitive implications will vary.

Finally, in light of the results presented here, particularly those regarding the temporal development of the group processes, another specific observation is that such issues can really only be examined well with truly qualitative approaches.[120] The quantified data have been shown as valuable for a start and for giving a rough picture of the cases and the people's be-

---

[120] A similar call for more qualitative, in-depth enquiries is also voiced by Elsbach et. al (2005) who examined situated cognitions more generally in organisations rather than in concrete group settings.

haviours. However, as soon as considerations about concrete contents are needed and one really wants to understand how exactly a certain result or concept came about and to evaluate its quality, one has to resort to the entire discussion material, regard it in-depth again, and pay attention to a complexity of influencing and interacting factors.

In line with the above, whereas certain factors have already been touched on that (seemed) to have varied between the present groups, in order to be able to explain in more detail why the differences described so far came about, in the following a more detailed look is now taken at the micro level results for *group process organisation* and *team 'climate'*. From this, insights are finally to be derived and outlines to be made about certain **factors and conditions** that might contribute to or prevent good 'results' in such cases.

6.7.4 Micro level results for group process management and team 'climate'

A consideration of the results in the content-related dimension was already provided in Section 6.7.2, followed by more detailed insights concerning the nature of the groups' spectrum of solutions and the overall temporal development of the different interaction processes (Section 6.7.3). In order to better understand and explain these results and the differential quality of the final concepts seen so far, below the results of the *process-directing* and the *relationship-oriented* dimensions are presented and discussed, respectively. In a similar way as in the context of looking in detail at the content-related interactions, the respective counts of the codes serve as a starting point here from which the discussion proceeds into more details by considering the material in more depth again, i.e. the transcripts, as well as especially for the relationship-oriented dimension also the video material.

6.7.4.1 Group process management

Wide agreement exists in the relevant literature on (small) groups (cf. Chapter 5) concerning the importance of group organisation and process management issues. In line with this, especially in conference settings and situations similar to the present research context, functional considerations of group processes today explicitly include a *process-directing* dimension (cf. 5.2.4). Although by their very definition, in task oriented groups content-related interactions are in the majority, organisational issues clearly matter too and may in fact be regarded as one explanatory factor for the groups' overall performance and differences therein. In this regard, as has been seen above, already a look at the rough level suggests that there are differences

6 – Empirical study of social interaction processes in decision making groups   263

between the three groups here. Table 25 outlines the details of the results of the process-directing dimension for the three cases.

Table 25: Detailed results for the process-directing dimension – all groups

Coding category	Code	relative proportion per code across all individual codes	relative proportion per code on the content dimension	relative proportion per code across all individual codes	relative proportion per code on the content dimension	relative proportion per code across all individual codes	relative proportion per code on the content dimension
		Group 1		Group 2		Group 3	
explicit process-related steering	Lv	2,4%	27,6%	3,1%	25,0%	3,5%	29,6%
information, statement, suggestion concerning the process	VG	4,4%	51,7%	7,5%	60,3%	5,0%	42,3%
question etc. concerning the process	VF	1,8%	20,7%	1,8%	14,7%	3,3%	28,2%
		8,5%	100%	12,5%	100%	11,8%	100%

Even though the differences across groups outlined in the above table cannot be said to be statistically significant, as mentioned already in 6.7.1, Group 1 nevertheless displays notably less process-directing interactions than the other two groups. To investigate whether these scores truly mean something and if so what exactly, the codes here then serve as kinds of tags that mark the respective parts in the discussions, which are to be considered in more detail. One interest in this context concerns the question *when* in the overall process such process management activities occurred. In this regard, looking at the respective incidences, the analyses then clearly support the impression advanced previously that Group 1 was in fact rather unorganized and proceeded without actually giving a lot of thoughts towards managing the process well. Specifically, apart from a brief process-related comment right in the beginning of the discussion (N: „We should discuss which strategies we have suggested in our work." – 7:25), and even though N later actually recognizes that they are getting slightly lost (N: „But we are losing our way here now a little." – 28:06), no further considerations concerning group or process organisation occur until the discussion is already long under way. Only after almost minute 40 Y asks the others how much time they have left and initiates with this a short sequence wherein the group thinks about organising its discussion for the first time. Overall, however, the vast majority of the process-related interactions occur only after minute 75 where the group realizes that it still has to integrate its arguments and put them down in written form. Since time is running out by then, the team needs to rush in order to still accomplish all aspects of its task in the end. Taken together, the results of Group 1 here thus show that the team did not really manage its time, got lost in controversies about a particular detail, and hence finally also took the longest to fulfil the task requirements. The lack of an explicitly communicated plan for how to proceed can then also be related to the low quality of its overall results.

Even though also in Group 2 and Group 3 process-directing interactions take only a small share of the overall discussion, the in-depth considerations here display a quite different picture compared to that in Group 1. Specifically, in both groups right at the beginning there is a short but crucial sequence in which the respective groups orient themselves and make sure that the task requirements and the overall approach how to solve it are clear to all members:

> Group 2 – D: „*First of all, understanding... Does anyone have problems of understanding the task? No, ne? It's all clear?*" (6:17)

In addition, both teams begin their discussion with a phase in which they first take turns in order to allow everyone to openly share his or her own position on the issue at hand with the rest of the team:

> Group 2 – D: „*Should we take a round and everyone says what he has done himself?*" (6:48)

> Group 3 – H: „*Should we somehow go around such that each one first says his position?*" (5:45)

Following this introductory or 'orientation' phase, both teams then proceed in a quite organized and structured way and have an explicit eye on the time available already from early on:

> Group 3 – H: „*Should we maybe write it down right away, the ideas?*" (6:00)

> Group 2 – D: „*We have to look a little at the time, ne....*" (ca. 19:00)

> Group 2 – D: „*Five minutes for each, and then we have five minutes left for the review.*" (26:54)

> Group 2 – D: „*Suggestion, if we tick off the points now...*" (40:00)

Finally, apart from these few, but crucial, process-related comments at the very beginning and after about half of the time, the remaining majority of process-steering behaviour then occurs in the final phase of the discussion processes in which the teams integrate and write down what they have decided till then. Here then, this observation is in fact largely similar across all three groups.

Taken together, these results and the empirical evidence now support the assertion made earlier that the comparatively 'thin' result of Group 1 is closely related to its failure to establish any consent or invest at least a short moment into considerations concerning the structure of their overall interaction process. As Group 2 and Group 3 were much more systematic and controlled, they finally also achieved better strategic concepts.

Clearly, the kind of task dealt with here and especially the group work situation were not really novel for the participants (like meetings are of course also a common activity for strategists), such that the general way how to behave was obviously known. Nevertheless, the results still show that at least a minimum of proper process management or group organisation and initial orientation, particularly in terms of determining and having an eye on the overall agenda and on the given time frame, are always needed. Otherwise there is the danger of loosing or never attaining direction, getting lost in focussing on a specific detail and hence forgetting the overall picture, which may then finally result in bad or at least suboptimal outcomes. In addition and related to the previous, also an explicit, but **'sensitive', process steering** seems beneficial as evidenced here particularly in Group 3. There, H managed the process well in that she clearly directed the others, especially in the integration phase, but not in a way that would be perceived as dominating but merely by taking care that the process runs smoothly and that in the end all is well integrated and written down.

6.7.4.2 Group 'climate'

Apart from ensuring a certain degree of process organisation, another crucial factor to be considered in the context of investigating collective discussion processes and their outcomes is what may be termed group 'climate'. Since it is the individual group members and their behaviours which determine or 'create' the prevailing atmosphere in a group meeting, the overall climate is clearly strongly influenced by the specific characteristics of the participating individuals. However, before considering in more detail the *within-group* results in terms of distinctive member profiles in the next section, in the present section the focus first remains on the group level and on a comparative discussion of the relationship-oriented results across the three cases. Table 26 shows the respective details of the analysis.

Table 26: Detailed results for the relationship-oriented dimension – all groups

Coding category	Code	relative proportion per code across all individual codes	relative proportion per code on the content dimension	relative proportion per code across all individual codes	relative proportion per code on the content dimension	relative proportion per code across all individual codes	relative proportion per code on the content dimension
		Group 1		Group 2		Group 3	
consent (with contents), support, understands	Z	8,8%	33,1%	12,3%	48,2%	9,0%	35,1%
jokes, shows satisfaction, etc.	"+"	3,8%	14,4%	5,1%	20,1%	8,0%	31,2%
asks for help, etc.	FH	1,9%	7,2%	3,3%	12,9%	3,0%	11,7%
gives help, shows solidarity	GH	2,5%	9,4%	2,8%	10,8%	1,7%	6,5%
hesitance, uncertainty, scepticism	US	2,4%	8,8%	1,1%	4,3%	1,0%	3,9%
rejection, disagreement, etc.	A	5,0%	18,8%	0,7%	2,9%	2,3%	9,1%
asserts himself, shows antagonism, tension	"-"	2,2%	8,3%	0,2%	0,7%	0,7%	2,6%
		26,6%	100%	**25,5%**	100%	**25,5%**	100%

A common and 'natural' distinction regarding relationship-oriented interactions is clearly that between *positive* and *negative* socio-emotions. In line with what is also found in most other category systems (cf. e.g. Bales et al., 1982; Fisch, 1994, 1998), the individual codes in the present scheme thus reflect exactly this, too. Specifically, Z, "+", FH and GH denote interactions among the team members that have primarily a positive function or effect on their mutual relationships, or that indicate a trusting and cooperative atmosphere (FH and GH). A, "-", and also US against that point to tensions, disagreements, or even antagonism among the group members.

Looking now at the figures presented in the above table, a first obvious result here is that in all three groups the majority of interactions with a socio-emotional function are clearly positive. This result, however, is not too surprising. Not only is it necessary to keep in mind the special context of the present simulation, but also in other similar 'real' situations, certain norms of politeness clearly exist such that one might expect that in most cases (at least at the surface) positive interactions are in the majority.[121] Indicators for a negative or antagonistic atmosphere against that are usually much more difficult to find as they are often only very subtle. Also, already one explicitly aggressive or assertive statement may in fact invoke an atmosphere or a feeling between members that will then overshadow the entire ensuring discussion with a negative tone.

---

[121] In how far this is true, however, or whether in the strategic reality there are occasions, 'forums', or tasks in which the atmosphere is openly hostile, would be an interesting question for future research (cf. 7.3).

Drawing on the above, looking at the results here, a clear difference between the groups can be observed regarding the shares of the three codes in the negative section of the socio-emotional dimension. By making up in aggregated form almost 10% of the overall coded interactions of Group 1, the 'climate' in this group seems clearly a lot more negative compared to that in Group 2 and Group 3. Here then, even though across all codes on the three dimensions the individual proportions make up only a small share, respectively, it is then exactly those codes which are interesting and important to investigate in more detail. Since, as argued before, it is especially the tone or other nonverbal elements that are essential to consider here too, the videos served again as important material at this point. Some quotes from the discussion in Group 1 are presented below that represent examples of rejecting and assertive behaviour in this case:

(„A") – R: „*In my opinion it's not a good idea that you ...*" (48:00)

(„-„) – M: „*Yes, yes, growth is here. But here is the direct competition that comes from Australia, all the imports.*" (74:04)

Besides such statements *per se*, what is particularly important here is of course the context in which they occur and especially the reaction such behaviours invoke. E.g.:

(„A") – N: „*No, this [shows something] sector is increasing. This here.*"

(„-„) – M: „*... it is premium...it is eight to seventeen.*" (55:33)

Even though not perfectly well displayable with merely a short written excerpt from the transcript, it is nevertheless clear that here an antagonistic behaviour provoked an even more negative, i.e. assertive, reaction.

Apart from these concrete quotes, a variety of other incidences were found in Group 1 that indicate disagreements, ignorance, or passive rejection. I.e., particularly disrupting another while he/ she is talking or starting one's own contribution with *"yes, but... "*, are clearly examples of such behaviour.

Compared to the results and insights from Group 1, the overall atmospheres in Group 2 and Group 3 were much more positive and cooperative.

In this regard, especially in Group 2 the figures as well as the in-depth considerations of the videos clearly indicate a very positive climate here. However, in light of the previously discussed fact that in this group the final concept was to large extents similar to the original ideas one of the team members had had before the discussion already, it may be argued that the 'climate' here was in fact *too* harmonious. Whereas too much controversy or assertive behaviour may prevent good results, in order for group work to really augment the performance any of the individuals would have been able to display alone, at least a certain amount of questioning and challenging the diverse ideas seems warranted. Otherwise, not only could the dominant member have worked on the issue alone, but there is also the danger of groupthink (Janis, 1972) or myopia of learning (Levinthal & March, 1993).

In Group 3 then, even though also here the overall climate was clearly friendly, exactly such small incidences of disagreement or tension were observed. Considering, however, like above in Group 1, the context and especially the reaction towards such disagreeing behaviour, a different picture emerges:

> H: „*But there we have no premium segment. That makes no sense. They won't start with the premium segment.*"
> S: „*Na, ok, but then Woodbridge...*"
> M: „*Good.*" (24:17)

As this exemplary sequence shows, while there is first a rejection, this, however, is afterwards accepted and another team member even approves, too. As such the comment was finally rather constructive rather than that it induced a hostile atmosphere. Done in moderation disagreements may hence actually be beneficial since certain criticisms and reflections are clearly necessary and will finally benefit the group's work. In this context, considering the insights from Group 3, it may also be suggested that once a good and trusting relationship and recognition of one another's expertise has been established, criticisms and partial rejections will not actually 'hurt' the overall atmosphere or relationships in the group, but instead they are rather constructive. In line with this, as evidenced by the data from Group 3, in the end of the process there was in fact even a lot of joking and signs of satisfaction. This shows that even though there were some disagreements and controversies during the course of the discussion, in the end there is collective consent. Considered in light of the fact that the final result presented by Group 3 was already before judged as the most differentiated, complex and true 'group product' (cf. 6.7.3), it finally seems that exactly this mix between friendly and in parts critical behaviour is an important condition for good group performance.

6.7.5 Within-group results: Individual member profiles

So far now, the focus in all of the preceding results sections has been on the aggregate level and on comparisons *between* the three groups. Nevertheless, already in this context at different points the behaviour and certain characteristics of individual members *within* the respective groups have been touched on. What this shows is that even when conducting analyses at the group level, these can or should never be done in complete isolation from the individual members since it is them together who account for the concrete interaction pattern a particular group displays. Drawing on this, in order to now understand better *why* the specific 'climates' and process patterns that have been observed prevail, and why certain contents and issues develop, this results section finally focuses specifically on the *within-group* results. By creating individual interaction profiles, the findings may give hints to explain the respective **success of individual solutions**, be related to the overall level of **group 'productivity'** and thus the quality of the final concept, as well as to the **extent of information sharing**, knowledge exchange, etc.

Since some of the overall questions of interest here (cf. 6.2.2) have already been seen or at least hinted at above, the particular interest now concerns: 1. the overall participation rate of a team member, 2. on which dimension he/ she was most active, 3. whether explicit steering was executed (both content- and process-related – Li and Lv), and 4. whether his/ her socio-emotional behaviour was more positive or rather negative towards the others. To derive such characteristic interaction profiles for the individual members, the quantified data are examined both on the macro level for the respective participant and on the micro level. The overall procedure will be strictly group by group, i.e. within case analyses. Only in the final section a note is made on some general and overarching implications and conclusions from the here presented findings.

6.7.5.1 Group 1

Table 27 presents the detailed results for each member of Group 1.

Table 27: Individual member details Group 1

Code	# codings	member N per person across all dimensions	member N person's share of 100% of the group for the respective code	# codings	member M per person across all dimensions	member M person's share of 100% of the group for the respective code	# codings	member Y per person across all dimensions	member Y person's share of 100% of the group for the respective code	# codings	member R per person across all dimensions	member R person's share of 100% of the group for the respective code
I	12	5,0%	§ 37,5%	12	5,2%	37,5%	4	2,7%	12,5%	4	6,4%	12,5%
AF	31	13,0%	37,3%	23	10,0%	27,7%	23	15,4%	27,7%	6	9,6%	7,2%
M	19	8,0%	32,2%	11	4,8%	18,6%	22	14,7%	37,3%	7	11,2%	11,9%
E	31	13,0%	44,9%	20	8,7%	29,0%	16	10,7%	23,2%	2	3,2%	2,9%
Vn	8	3,4%	53,3%	3	1,3%	20,0%	4	2,7%	26,7%	0	0,0%	0,0%
Ve	17	7,1%	38,6%	17	7,4%	38,6%	8	5,4%	18,2%	2	3,2%	4,5%
IF	9	3,8%	32,1%	9	3,9%	32,1%	8	5,4%	28,6%	2	3,2%	7,1%
WF	7	2,9%	20,0%	19	8,3%	54,3%	8	5,4%	22,9%	1	1,6%	2,9%
Li	5	2,1%	33,3%	8	3,5%	53,3%	1	0,7%	6,7%	1	1,6%	6,7%
Ke	14	5,9%	43,8%	15	6,5%	46,9%	3	2,0%	9,4%	0	0,0%	0,0%
Kf	§§ 6,75	2,8%	23,3%	10,75	4,7%	37,1%	9,75	6,5%	33,6%	1,75	2,8%	6,0%
	** 36,2%	* 67,1%		33,5%	64,3%		24,2%	71,5%		6,1%	42,6%	
Lv	4	1,9%	25,0%	9	3,9%	56,3%	1	0,7%	6,3%	2	3,2%	12,5%
VG	14	6,5%	46,7%	9	3,9%	30,0%	4	2,7%	13,3%	3	4,8%	10,0%
VF	1	0,5%	8,3%	6	2,6%	50,0%	1	0,7%	8,3%	4	6,4%	33,3%
	** 19	* 8%		41,4%	10,4%		10,3%	4,0%		15,5%	14,3%	
	** 32,8%											
Z	22	9,5%	36,7%	24	10,4%	40,0%	8	5,4%	13,3%	6	9,6%	10,0%
plus	§§ 16,5	7,1%	63,5%	7	3,0%	26,9%	1,5	1,0%	5,8%	1	1,6%	3,8%
FH	0	0,0%	0,0%	3	1,3%	23,1%	2	1,3%	15,4%	8	12,7%	61,5%
GH	7	3,0%	41,2%	7	3,0%	41,2%	2	1,3%	11,8%	1	1,6%	5,9%
US	1	0,4%	6,3%	3	1,3%	18,8%	10	6,7%	62,5%	2	3,2%	12,5%
A	9	3,9%	26,5%	9	3,9%	26,5%	8	5,4%	23,5%	8	12,7%	23,5%
minus	4	1,7%	26,7%	5	2,2%	33,3%	5	3,4%	33,3%	1	1,6%	6,7%
	* 32,9%	* 25%		32,0%	25,2%		20,2%	24,5%		14,9%	43,0%	
total	*** 35,0%	100%		33,8%	100%		21,9%	100%		9,2%	100%	

* represents the person's own extent to which his/ her overall coded interactions had a content-, process-, and relationship-oriented function, respectively
** represents the person's respective share of the group's overall amount of content-, process- and relationship-oriented interactions, respectively
*** signifies the person's overall participation rate in the group
§ signifies the person's respective share of all the interactions in the group that were given that specific code; the same applies for all the rows below
§§ in a few instances a specific contribution judged as functional for the discussion process could not be attributed to one particular participant alone but several members interacted simultaneously, e.g. when all resorted for a moment back to the case material in order to check the facts (Kf), or in terms of laughing loudly together ("+"). To ensure a correct weighting of this interaction and to avoid biasing the coding, the specific code was then split equally across the involved participants

The above figures show that in Group 1 N was clearly the member with the highest participation rate overall. With 36,2%, 32,8%, and 32,9%, respectively, he has a share of approximately one third on all three functional dimensions. Looking specifically at the content-related interactions, N makes even more than half of the new suggestions during the discussion process (53,3% or 8 out of 15). Where he scores low against that, at least compared to the group's second most active member M, is in terms of *asking questions* and in *explicit steering behaviour* (both content- and process-related). Almost half of the *suggestions concerning process issues* (VG: 46,7%), however, come from him. Regarding N's socio-emotional behaviour, even though he displays a considerable amount of antagonistic (A) and also assertive ("-") behaviour, at the same time he often behaves positively (Z, "+") towards the others in the group; and together with M he is also the one that gives most help to his fellow team members. At the same time, to a similar extent as M, N is 'responsible' for controlling or summarizing decisions or results (Ke: 43,8%).

Looking more specifically at the results of the team's second most active member M, whereas overall she participates only slightly less than N, she is particularly active in terms of displaying explicit steering behaviour (Li: 53,3%; Lv: 56,3%). While the amount of new suggestions she makes is even less than that of Y, she advances as many suggestions as N (Ve: 17 out of 44). Different from N, however, on all three dimensions M asks notably more questions than him.

By far the least active member in Group 1 is R. Especially in terms of content she has a mere share of 6,1% overall on this dimension, contributes no new suggestions, and advances only two ideas. Remarkable with her profile is that despite her overall low participation rate, in terms of antagonistic contributions, in absolute terms R scores similar as the other three group members (i.e. "A": 23,5%). The implication of this (which is in fact substantiated by considering the video material in addition) is that R actually does not agree with the progression and the arguments advanced by the others. Still, due to the dominance and 'strong' characters of especially N and M, she is not able to really get through in this group and hence rather withdraws. This helplessness is then again also reflected in the large amount of help-seeking interactions she displays (FH: 61,5% of the entirety of this kind of interactions in this group).

Y, finally, can be described as the most 'moderate' member in the team. I.e., overall his participation rate is notably lower than that of N and M on all three dimensions. Nevertheless, he still contributes some new suggestions and advances others (# Vn: 4; # Ve: 8). On the content dimension he is the one that argues in the most 'subjective' way as evidenced by the comparatively high share of opinions he voices (M: 37,3%). Considering his socio-emotional behaviour, Y is neither strongly more positive nor negative than the others in the team; only his high degree of uncertain or sceptical interactions is notable here (US: 62,5%). Despite all this, as has been seen in Section 6.7.3.1, the group's final concept in fact incorporates some ideas that can be clearly traced to the suggestions Y made during the discussions.

Overall then, in line with what has been hinted at already in previous sections, the results here underscore the observation that the discussion process in Group 1 was clearly dominated by two specific members, i.e. N and M. Whereas the latter actually exhibited more explicit steering behaviour, the most 'successful' in terms of imprinting the final concept with his own 'original' ideas was clearly N. Here then, considered particularly in light of the findings presented as regards R, the negative effects that one or several dominant persons in a group may have become obvious. Specifically, while during the interactions R basically did not voice any suggestions, looking at her own strategic concept that she had worked out prior to the discussion shows that she actually had certain good and valuable ideas. The dominant and selfish behaviour of both N and M during the interactions, however, then prevented especially her as a rather shy member from contributing ideas that might actually have advanced and enriched the group and its overall performance.

6 – Empirical study of social interaction processes in decision making groups 273

6.7.5.2 Group 2

Table 28: Individual member details Group 2

Code	# codings	per person across all dimensions	person's share of 100% of the group for the respective code	# codings	per person across all dimensions	person's share of 100% of the group for the respective code	# codings	per person across all dimensions	person's share of 100% of the group for the respective code	# codings	per person across all dimensions	person's share of 100% of the group for the respective code
		member D			member Ju			member A			member Ja	
I	12	5,5%	§46,2%	8	5,9%	30,8%	0	0,0%	0,0%	6	5,7%	23,1%
AF	15	6,8%	29,4%	19	14,0%	37,3%	5	5,8%	9,8%	12	11,5%	23,5%
M	12	5,5%	37,5%	9	6,7%	28,1%	8	9,3%	25,0%	3	2,9%	9,4%
E	22	10,0%	47,8%	12	8,9%	26,1%	4	4,7%	8,7%	8	7,6%	17,4%
Vn	8	3,6%	36,4%	7	5,2%	31,8%	4	4,7%	18,2%	3	2,9%	13,6%
Ve	14	6,4%	29,8%	19	14,0%	40,4%	6	7,0%	12,8%	8	7,6%	17,0%
IF	5	2,3%	50,0%	1	0,7%	10,0%	2	2,3%	20,0%	2	1,9%	20,0%
WF	12	5,5%	35,3%	2	1,5%	5,9%	12	14,0%	35,3%	8	7,6%	23,5%
Li	10	4,6%	83,3%	0	0,0%	0,0%	2	2,3%	16,7%	0	0,0%	0,0%
Ke	§§ 27,83	12,7%	53,5%	9,5	7,0%	18,3%	8,83	10,3%	17,0%	5,83	5,6%	11,2%
KI	§§ 3,25	1,5%	54,2%	2,25	1,7%	37,5%	0,25	0,3%	4,2%	0,25	0,2%	4,2%
		41,7%			**26,3%**			**15,4%**			**16,6%**	
Lv	6	2,7%	35,3%	2	1,5%	11,8%	7	8,2%	41,2%	2	1,9%	11,8%
VG	26	11,8%	63,4%	8	5,9%	19,5%	1	1,2%	2,4%	6	5,7%	14,6%
VF	2	0,9%	20,0%	5	3,7%	50,0%	1	1,2%	10,0%	2	1,9%	20,0%
		15,5%			**11,1%**			**10,5%**			**9,6%**	
Z	22	10,0%	32,8%	22	16,3%	32,8%	7	8,2%	10,4%	16	15,3%	23,9%
plus	§§ 10,5	4,8%	37,5%	2,5	1,8%	8,9%	6,5	7,6%	23,2%	8,5	8,1%	30,4%
FH	0	0,0%	0,0%	3	2,2%	16,7%	11	12,9%	61,1%	4	3,8%	22,2%
GH	8	3,6%	53,3%	1	0,7%	6,7%	0	0,0%	0,0%	6	5,7%	40,0%
US	1	0,5%	16,7%	1	0,7%	16,7%	0	0,0%	0,0%	4	3,8%	66,7%
A	2	0,9%	50,0%	2	1,5%	50,0%	0	0,0%	0,0%	0	0,0%	0,0%
minus	1	0,5%	100,0%	0	0,0%	0,0%	0	0,0%	0,0%	0	0,0%	0,0%
		20,3%			**23,3%**			**28,6%**			**36,8%**	
total		**40,3%**	100%		**24,8%**	100%		**15,7%**	100%		**19,2%**	100%

* represents the person's own extent to which his/ her overall coded interactions had a content-, process-, and relationship-oriented function, respectively
** represents the person's respective share of the group's overall amount of content-, process-, and relationship-oriented interactions, respectively
*** signifies the person's overall participation rate in the group
**** signifies the person's respective share of all the interactions in the group that were given that specific code; the same applies for all the rows below
§ in a few instances a specific contribution judged as functional for the discussion process could not be attributed to one particular participant alone but several members interacted simultaneously, e.g. when all resorted for a moment back to the case material in order to 'check the facts' (KI), or in terms of laughing loudly together ('+'). To ensure a correct weighting of this interaction and to avoid biasing the coding, the specific code was then split equally across the involved participants

Table 28 presents the results of the individual members of Group 2. Also here then, as touched on repeatedly already in the previous results discussions for the aggregate level, there is one particular person, namely D, who clearly stands out in this group with a participation rate of over 40% overall. Even though among the three others Ju still participates more than Ja and A, in this group it is still truly all four participants that are involved in the discussion process. Concerning D specifically, whereas his share then is the highest on all three dimensions, it is particularly in the content- and process-related interactions (41,7% and 50%, respectively) where his dominance is most pronounced. Concerning the former, D both contributes the most 'pure' information (I: 46,2%) and makes the most new suggestions (# Vn: 8 out of 22). He also advances ideas but to a lesser extent than Ju (D's # Ve: 14; Ju's # Ve: 19). Very crucial here is the high proportion of explicit content-related steering behaviour D exerts (Li: 83,3%). In addition, he is also responsible for more than half of the control activities in this group (Ke: 53,5%; Kf: 54,2%). As regards the second dimension, D clearly makes the most suggestions concerning the process and, even though less than A, also steers explicitly here (VG: 63,4%; Lv: 35,3%). In terms of D's relationship-oriented behaviour, despite his content-related dominance, he can clearly be regarded as a helpful and 'positive' team member. In fact, since as has been seen in the context of the 'climate' discussion above, in this group there is basically no truly antagonistic or assertive behaviour by anyone, the respective scores on the negative side can thus be neglected for all individual members here. Regarding D's overall 'success' then, even though his aggregate share of suggestions introduced or developed in the process is slightly lower than that of Ju, the group's final concept nevertheless looks basically like the one he had worked out alone already prior to the meeting. The dominant position D took during the course of the interactions, especially in terms of explicit steering as well as controlling behaviour, seems to explain these results.

With an overall share of about one quarter of the interactions, Ju is the second most active person in Group 2. Whereas, as mentioned above, she makes the highest number of advancing suggestions, very different from D Ju exhibits basically no explicit content-related steering behaviour and also only very little so on the process dimension. Instead, compared to her team members, she is rather 'analytical' (AF: 37,3%) and takes care of controlling facts (Kf: 37,5%).

With merely 15,7% overall, A is the one with the lowest participation rate in the group. Even though she was thus quite silent, the large share of explicit process-oriented steering behaviour she exhibited (especially during the integration phase towards the end of the process) nevertheless implies that she was still a respected and important member of the team.

Apart from his less explicit steering-oriented behaviour, Ja can finally be ascribed a similar role as A in this group. Like her, he also contributed and brought through less suggestions and ideas than Ju and especially as D. Socio-emotionally, besides the higher degree of sceptical or uncertain interactions, he basically displayed a similarly positive and cooperative behaviour towards the others as each of the other four group members did as well.

Taken together then, the results here underscore the positive and 'consensual' discussion process evidenced before. Even though D clearly dominated in all respects, his kind of dominance was actually rather subtle or at least not perceived in a bad way by the other team members (cf. also 6.7.6 where the results of the questionnaire administered to the participants are discussed). Instead, by emphasizing and arguing strongly content-related rather than socio-emotionally (negative), D actually succeeded in managing the overall process in a way that allowed the group to proceed with structure and organisation. From the beginning on the other group members showed respect for him and hence largely followed his way and accepted his suggestions.

6.7.5.3 Group 3

Table 29: Individual member details Group 3

Code	# codings	per person across all dimensions	person's share of 100% of the group for the respective code	# codings	per person across all dimensions	person's share of 100% of the group for the respective code	# codings	per person across all dimensions	person's share of 100% of the group for the respective code	# codings	per person across all dimensions	person's share of 100% of the group for the respective code
	member G			**member S**			**member M**			**member H**		
I	8	7.7%	§21.6%	3	2.7%	8.1%	12	8.7%	32.4%	14	5.6%	37.8%
AF	8	7.7%	16.0%	6	5.5%	12.0%	19	13.8%	38.0%	17	6.7%	34.0%
M	2	1.9%	8.3%	7	6.4%	29.2%	2	1.5%	8.3%	13	5.2%	54.2%
E	11	10.6%	32.4%	5	4.6%	14.7%	10	7.3%	29.4%	9	3.6%	26.5%
Vn	4	3.8%	13.3%	5	4.6%	16.7%	9	6.6%	30.0%	11	4.4%	36.7%
Ve	5	4.8%	8.2%	10	9.2%	16.4%	19	13.8%	31.1%	27	10.7%	44.3%
IF	1	1.0%	4.8%	7	6.4%	33.3%	6	4.4%	28.6%	7	2.8%	33.3%
WF	1	1.0%	3.1%	7	6.4%	21.9%	3	2.2%	9.4%	21	8.3%	65.6%
Li	2	1.9%	11.8%	2	1.8%	11.8%	7	5.1%	41.2%	6	2.4%	35.3%
Ke	7	6.7%	13.7%	12	11.0%	23.5%	16	11.7%	31.4%	16	6.3%	31.4%
Kt	5	4.8%	23.8%	8	7.3%	38.1%	2	1.5%	9.5%	6	2.4%	28.6%
	**14.3%	*51.8%		19.0%	65.9%		27.8%	76.5%		38.9%	58.3%
Lv	4	3.8%	19.0%	4	3.7%	19.0%	4	2.9%	19.0%	9	3.6%	42.9%
VG	7	6.7%	23.3%	8	7.3%	26.7%	1	0.7%	3.3%	14	5.6%	46.7%
VF	1	1.0%	5.0%	2	1.8%	10.0%	0	0.0%	0.0%	17	6.7%	85.0%
	**16.9%	*11.5%		19.7%	12.8%		7.0%	3.6%		56.3%	15.9%
Z	15	14.4%	27.8%	7	6.4%	13.0%	13	9.5%	24.1%	19	7.5%	35.2%
plus	§§12.25	11.8%	25.5%	9.25	8.5%	19.3%	4.25	3.1%	8.9%	22.25	8.8%	46.4%
FH	1	1.0%	5.6%	1	0.9%	5.6%	0	0.0%	0.0%	16	6.3%	88.9%
GH	4	3.8%	40.0%	2	1.8%	20.0%	3	2.2%	30.0%	1	0.4%	10.0%
US	1	1.0%	16.7%	1	0.9%	16.7%	1	0.7%	16.7%	3	1.2%	50.0%
A	3	2.9%	21.4%	3	2.7%	21.4%	5	3.6%	35.7%	3	1.2%	21.4%
minus	2	1.9%	50.0%	0	0.0%	0.0%	1	0.7%	25.0%	1	0.4%	25.0%
	*24.8%	*36.7%		15.1%	21.3%		17.7%	19.9%		42.4%	25.9%
total	***17.3%	100%		18.1%	100%		22.8%	100%		41.8%	100%	

* represents the person's own extent to which his/her overall coded interactions had a content-, process-, and relationship-oriented function, respectively
** represents the person's respective share of the group's overall amount of content-, process-, and relationship-oriented interactions, respectively
*** signifies the person's overall participation rate in the group
§ signifies the person's respective share of all the interactions in the group that were given that specific code; the same applies for all the rows below
§§ in a few instances a specific contribution judged as functional for the discussion process could not be attributed to one particular participant alone but several members interacted simultaneously, e.g. when all resorted for a moment back to the case material in order to 'check the facts' (Kf), or in terms of laughing loudly together (*+*). To ensure a correct weighting of this interaction and to avoid biasing the coding, the specific code was then split equally across the involved participants

The above displayed results concerning the interaction patterns of the individual members in Group 3 show that with 41,83% of the overall contributions H is the most active person here. Among the rest, the respective shares are largely balanced with around 20% each. Whereas H thus clearly dominates on all three dimensions, the distance is most pronounced as regards process-oriented interactions (56,3% altogether). Here then, even though at first sight H seems to be truly dominating the overall process, considering the results in more detail actually shows that in this case the dominance is actually not so much in terms of trying to push her own suggestions through or preventing the others from making or advancing ideas. Although overall H still introduces and develops the highest share of suggestions here (Vn: 36,7%; Ve: 44,3%), especially M but also S and G are involved in this respect. Even more importantly, as outlined in the previous discussion on the success of individual solutions and the consideration of the group's final concept, in this case the final outcome can be considered as a true group 'product' that integrates the ideas that all four members developed together during the course of their interactions. In this context then, H's role clearly was that of taking care of organizing and steering the overall process, both explicitly (Lv: 42,9%), but also in terms of asking questions. In this regard, apart from the large share of process-related questions she poses, she also remarkably often asks the others for their opinions and evaluations (WF: 65,6%) as well as for their help (FH: 88,8%). In terms of her socio-emotional behaviour, H clearly interacts mostly in a positive way, and as particularly obvious from the videos, especially towards the end of the process she is the one that displays a large amount of tension releasing and joking behaviour. Even though a few antagonistic or assertive behaviours may also be noticed with her, the 'negative' share is roughly the same across all four team members.

Whereas as mentioned initially, overall the other three members participate to about equal extents, M is the one who besides H is the most active in terms of content-related interactions, especially due to the number of suggestions he makes (# Vn: 9, # Ve: 19) as well as his explicit content-related steering (Li: 41,2%). S and G then can be considered as the 'moderate' team members, whereby S still introduces and develops more suggestions than G (# Vn+Ve S: 15; G: 9). The latter against that displays more relationship-oriented behaviour, especially in terms of giving help.

Overall then, the most crucial insight from this group is that even though H is clearly the most talkative person, she does not 'overrun' the others with her own views but explicitly calls for and encourages their contributions. H may thus be considered a good group leader: She is knowledgeable herself but also seeks the others' input. In addition, she also takes care of a good process management and organisation in the group such that the ideas can be developed cooperatively and also become integrated within the given time frame and with respect to the task at hand.

6.7.5.4 Comparative discussion of the within-group results and implications

Overall now, considering the entirety of insights derived from the within-group analyses, an issue that emerged and was discussed throughout all three cases is that of 'dominance'. Here then, however, it was found that there are clearly different kinds of 'dominant behaviour'. I.e., in Group 1, N and M largely dominated the discussion in a way that can be described as 'ignorant' of others' views, and hence as rather 'selfish'. In Group 2 against that, D's dominance was much more subtle; even though he clearly participated most and also shaped the final concept to large extents, he still allowed the others to contribute, and like that gave them the impression that their views and ideas mattered, too.

Moreover, whereas in both Group 1 and Group 2 the dominance of the respective members referred mostly to content-related interactions, in Group 3 H clearly dominated the interactions in terms of *steering* the concrete *process*. What this observation shows is the importance of looking closely at what exactly the contributions of the respective participants entail and hence what *function* the interactions have for the overall group process.

Furthermore, especially the notable contrast between Group 1 and Group 3 in terms of heterogeneous arguments considered in the discussions points to the importance of also allowing and explicitly encouraging more silent or shy members to participate and contribute their ideas. In Group 1 R was in large parts basically neglected or shut off especially by N's selfish behaviour. In Group 3 against that, in terms of his overall participation rate G was also a rather silent participant (cf. 6.7.6 below for the reasons from his own view). Nevertheless, due to the cooperative behaviour of the others and the positive atmosphere, he was still heard in the group and hence able to contribute to the final concept.

Finally, in all cases, in the end it was still the most 'talkative' person who was most 'successful' in terms of shaping or imprinting the group product with the own knowledge and opinions. However, despite this clear finding, it is here where keeping in mind the specific simulated setting is most important. Specifically, in this study actually no true **power** differences existed or were induced, and the participants had (at least at the outset) all the same **status**. In real business discussions or strategy meetings of this kind against that the situation is likely to be different in this regard (cf. Chapters 3 and 5). There, even though a particular member may be the most active one during a discussion, he or she might in fact not have the official status or the power to also enforce the final decision in the end. Nevertheless, in line with the universal 'rules' and regularities in terms of human cognitive functioning (cf. Chapter 4), as regards cognitive implications and effects, the chance of influencing the cognitions of others is still high with many contributions also in this context.

6.7.6 Interaction processes and learning from the participants' views

Finally, in line with the qualitative approach adopted in this study, so far all the results and discussions thereof have reflected the interpretations of the researcher herself. Whereas a considerable degree of subjectivity is by definition part of any qualitative research project, in the present context an attempt was undertaken to also incorporate the views of the research subjects themselves, and hence to provide for communicative validation in so far as the phenomenon at hand permits to (cf. 6.6). Here then, while truly assessing the participants' actual cognitive structures and processes by asking them is clearly not possible, the questionnaire (cf. Appendix) administered to each of the individual group members after the discussions still allows gaining some valuable additional insights. I.e., regarding the overall interaction processes and the group 'climate', characteristics and behaviours of individual group members as perceived by the participants themselves, as well as subjective perceptions of individual learning or 'cognitive growth' through the discussions.

In this respect, due to the limited number of individual cases, the answers to the questionnaire[122] could clearly not be subjected to statistical tests. Instead, a qualitative analysis was conducted here whereby the individual answers were looked at in detail, compared between the members within the three groups, as well as also finally across the groups. In addition, since the videotaping of the interactions was only terminated after the groups actually left their rooms, material was also available concerning the way the questionnaires were actually filled out in the different groups. This finally also helped to increase the validity of the conclusions drawn from the analysis of the answers provided by the participants.

Before presenting and discussing some of the most important results in this context, a note of caution concerning the analysis and interpretation of these data remains to be included. Specifically, thanks to its careful design the entire simulation here created a decision making situation that allowed to investigate the specific interests at hand in a situation that was as close to reality as possible. As regards participants' own retrospective perceptions and 'truthful' reflections concerning the discussion processes and their fellow team members, however, one clearly has to bear in mind their specific situation as graduates, who care both about their

---

[122] The numerical data of the answers to the questionnaire are available from the author upon request.

overall course grade as well as about not openly degrading another in front of the instructor. As a consequence, a certain mutual 'niceness' bias and overly positive evaluations of the entire interaction processes and of the final result have to be taken into account. Despite this, however, the questionnaire data still yielded some interesting results, which generally supported the findings from the other data analyses and the researcher's own interpretations, but which also gave some additional insights:

Taken together, regarding the impressions gained and results discussed concerning the nature of the overall interaction processes and specifically the 'climate' in the respective groups, these were also reflected in the questionnaires. Specifically, the harmonious and cooperative atmosphere observed in **Group 2** was clearly mirrored by the very consensual and throughout positive answering behaviour of all four team members in this group. All described the team atmosphere as very good and dynamic, and stated that it was neither difficult to arrive at a joint solution nor to voice one's own (even if dissenting) opinion. In line with this, in an almost identical way all members described the respective others as strongly supportive, helpful and sympathetic, and did not perceive any hindrances caused by anyone. Also concurrent with the previous results and conclusions, the notably more active and imprinting behaviour of D was actually not perceived as such, at least not negatively. In line with this, also no one really seemed to have realized that the final concept in fact was largely determined by D's ideas. However, even though, overall, little differentiation was made in terms of characterizing the other team members, D was then still seen as particularly knowledgeable and influential by the other three participants.

Considering the results from **Group 1**, whereas also here the overall group process and climate were consistently judged as good by the members, the more competitive and less 'symbiotic' atmosphere seen before was also reflected in the way the questionnaires were actually filled out. I.e., in comparison to Group 2, the participants really filled out the questionnaires seriously and without joking or cross-checking their answers with the others. In addition, even though real negative descriptions of the others were nowhere made, in this group the participants nevertheless differentiated notably between the individual members in their respective characterisations of them. Apart from the results concerning the perceived influential nature and role of N and M that concur with the author's own outlines above, quite surprising is the finding that the perceptions regarding the role of Y and R, respectively, varied among the different team members. I.e., while R is perceived by N as truly too silent, not influential and rather submissive, R herself as well as M actually conceived of Y as the person in the group that contributed the least to the discussion. This finding then underlines the importance of clearly differentiating and disclosing the perspective that certain data represents and was analysed from.

Regarding **Group 3**, even the way the members answered the questionnaires indicates and hence supports the more differentiated and thoughtful approach attributed to this group. Specifically, not only did also here the team members differentiate between their fellows in terms of their respective characteristics and behaviours during the discussion, but three of the four participants even took the opportunity to provide additional comments on the questionnaire where requested. Thanks to this, the reason for G's rather low overall participation rate is clear, namely because of his language difficulties as he himself states. Besides, in line with the above findings and results, M and especially H are perceived by the others as particularly knowledgeable and influential. Regarding the members' own evaluation of their final concept in terms of the overlap with their own original strategic ideas, it is here where this overlap is consistently by all members perceived as only moderate in comparison to the other groups where this clearly varied between the dominant and the more silent members. Exactly this then shows again that in Group 3 the final concept truly corresponds to a group 'product' that was developed collectively over the course of the interactions.

Finally, a last note shall be made regarding the issue of cognitive developments or changes. Here, in fact similar across all groups, none of the participants stated that contributions by other team members would have initiated any great increases in knowledge or radical changes in terms of their view on the strategic situation they had been faced with. In this regard, the rather limited time the teams had for their interactions and in-depth exchanges clearly explains these perceptions. On the one hand, this finding supports the assertion that in most cases truly deep and lasting cognitive changes or developments occur only slowly (cf. 4.2). On the other hand, however, the peculiar nature of cognitions and hence the difficulty of assessing them appropriately is also underlined again. Here then, the often employed simple large-scale questionnaires remote from any process or context information thus seem even more questionable in light of the entirety of findings derived from the present empirical study.

6.8 Evaluation and general implications of the empirical study

From the outset of the present research endeavour, the complex and hence challenging nature of the phenomenon of interest was clear. Both the difficulty (even impossibility) of gaining access to observe social interaction processes in real strategy teams as well as the 'invisible' nature of cognitions hence necessitated an innovative and creative approach that would overcome the limitations of previous research and yield valuable new insights on the issues in question. The variety and richness of findings discussed in the previous sections bear testimony to the fruitfulness of the efforts undertaken. Still, before summarizing the major results and discussing general implications specifically with regard to the strategic reality, certain limitations inherent in the study must be recognized first.

6.8.1 Limitations

Overall, besides the general limitations inherent in any qualitative and hence interpretive research, the most essential limitation of the present study clearly lies in the fact that it was not conducted with a real world strategy team in the context of an organisation's ongoing strategic process, but that instead a free simulation of such a decision making situation was used. Here then, not only was the context 'artificial', but also the subjects were not experienced managers but graduate students. The reasons for having chosen this kind of methodological approach were already outlined elsewhere (cf. 6.3). Also, any empirical method or research approach clearly always has its own limitations and points of critique that may be voiced against it. In the present case then, despite the obvious problems inherent in the approach, other research has demonstrated the value that can still be derived from simulating real world situations (cf. e.g. Boos, 1996; Kilduff, Angelmar, & Mehra, 2000; Lant & Mezias, 1990; Nees, 1983; Wolfe & Jackson, 1987). Also, different from 'classical' experiments and also experimental simulations, which are both often criticised for their particularly strong artificiality, free simulations like the one used here have by their very nature a much higher relationship to criterion settings and the participants usually experience intense levels of involvement (Fromkin & Streufert, 1983, p. 421). In line with this, by having used a real strategy case and ensured adequate conditions for informed task-oriented social interactions among the group members, experimental artefacts were consequently reduced, which in turn increases the potential for generalizing the present findings. In addition, regarding specifically the research subjects themselves, using graduate (or even undergraduate) students as participants is a quite common approach that is used throughout in psychological research where the interest is in the more universal cognitive functioning and behaviours that are said to be largely uniform across all (grown up) human actors (cf. e.g. Braisby, 2005; Eysenck & Keane, 2005; Fiske & Taylor, 1991).

Finally, besides these cautions, another problem to be recognized is the fact that even though a processual approach was successfully adopted here, in reality such decision making activities clearly extend over longer periods of time than the situation created here. In light of the concrete research interests in the present case, however, this 'one shot' approach is still justified since the aim was explicitly to investigate in-depth the specific micro interaction patterns occurring inside the groups and not to follow the ideas and issues beyond this concrete group context or even to their potential implementation. Doing so and regarding longer periods of time, repeated meetings of the same group or of individual actors with others in the organisation in other 'forums', would then be interesting areas for further research (cf. Chapter 6).

6.8.2 Summary and implications for the strategic reality

Taken together, the entirety of empirical results derived from the study conducted here has provided valuable in-depth insights on the social and cognitive processes occurring in decision making groups, and has shown *that* and *in how far* interactions with different functional meaning can be differentiated. In this regard, in line with the concrete type of task at hand, i.e. debating and deciding a complex strategic issue, content-related interactions were clearly in the majority (cf. 6.7.1). Here then, by looking in detail and 'tracing' the individual ideas and suggestions introduced and developed further during the course of the discussions, indications for the groups' respective degrees of argumentative differentiation, complexity, and interconnectedness in cognitive operations were gained. In addition, by further relating these insights to the participants' own 'original' or initial concepts and to the collective end results, assumptions could be made concerning the extent to which cognitive changes occurred on the side of the individuals, as well as where the specific social interactions contributed most to a (potential) convergence or parallelisation of knowledge structures among the actors involved. I.e., particularly in those cases in which the overall issue was discussed in both more breadth and depth, and where at the same time all members were able (or enabled) to contribute their own ideas and to comment on those of others (cf. particularly 6.7.3). In this regard, while the importance of thorough discussions and involvement of all group members is also stressed in the general literature on small group research, the focus there usually merely concerns measuring or evaluating some concrete output or level of performance (e.g. Jehn et al., 1999; Maznevski, 1994; Milliken & Vollrath, 1991). Different from these existing approaches, in the present study the entire process over time was differentiated in detail whereby also explicit links to the underlying cognitive dimension were established. In line with this, the discussion of the observed overall temporal development of the group processes in relation to the own socio-cognitive model of group decision making (cf. 5.3) finally showed that whereas it is in fact possible to discern certain concrete process phases, these occur neither in an entirely linear fashion, nor is there a uniform pattern that would be applicable across all groups.

As already partially seen in this context and substantiated by the further analyses conducted, the observed differences in terms of the groups' final results and their overall temporal development could clearly be related to issues of process management (process-steering function) and to the respective relationships and 'climate' (socio-emotional function) prevailing in the teams (cf. 6.7.4). For this, the role and specific behaviours of individual participants were shown to be essential to consider, too (cf. 6.7.5).

Drawing on the variety of insights on social interaction processes in the teams and the factors and conditions for successful group performance discerned, a number of implications can now be derived that are clearly valuable beyond the concrete context examined here and that thus can be applied to the **strategic reality** in actual organisational decision making teams:

In this regard, a first major (practical) implication concerns the importance of a good **process organisation**, i.e. in terms of first clarifying the overall objectives of the discussion and of subsequently ensuring an adequate procedure towards achieving the goals set. Whereas in the present simulations the task was in fact already quite pre-structured, in the strategic reality exactly this is often not the case. Instead, firstly jointly defining a strategic issue might even be the aim of the entire group encounter. Since already in the groups examined here being aware of 'where to head' was shown to be important in order to not get lost in the complex task, this can be considered as even more crucial in the real world then. Having or setting up an agenda and taking a few moments at the beginning of the discussion to clarify this issue are hence clearly advisable. Besides, during the ensuing discussion process itself, a certain degree of structuredness or continuous awareness of the overall course of the process is crucial in order to ensure a good final result. As evidenced by the groups studied here, having someone in the team who takes care of ensuring exactly this steering and moderation of the process in a manner that is not perceived as dominant or imposing by the others contributes to augmenting the collective performance.

Moreover, apart from the concrete process steering function, but partially related to and already implied by the latter arguments, are the issues of **dominance and leadership**. Whereas a good process moderator is generally beneficial, it becomes problematic if there is someone that clearly dominates the interactions, both in terms of content- and process-related interactions. In this regard, the results from Group 2 have shown that even though thanks largely to D's active involvement the group was actually well organized and presented a good result, its end concept finally represented basically only the ideas of the dominant member D. In those cases then, not only can the extent of growth in knowledge and real identification with the collective product on the side of the different actors be expected to be rather low, but the dominant member could in fact even have done the work alone while the others could have performed other value adding activities for their organisation.

Besides cases in which there is only one very dominant person, also two or more too strong or opposite 'poles' can be considered as a hindrance (cf. Group 1). Here, each of them is first of all concerned with how he can bring through his own position. Even though knowledge and ideas of diverse members can and are actually exchanged then, if no one really accepts the others' views, these elements are also little likely to lead to cognitive changes or a convergence in strategic orientations (cf. Chapter 1 where the conditions for cognitive changes were outlined in detail). In the worst case, not even a 'superficial' consensus is finally attained and the team might terminate its interactions without agreeing on a joint decision or concept for its assigned task.

Developing these ideas even further, although in the present study no actual **power** or **status** differences between the participants existed or were induced by the task, in the reality of strategic decision making exactly this is quite often the case as such teams may be composed of members with diverse functional, hierarchical, or local affiliations, and hence responsibilities. Accordingly, also their respective perceptions of the issues at hand as well as motivations to cooperate or achieve a consensus will clearly vary. Despite the absence of such pronounced differences in the present teams, already here it could be seen that the individual members clearly all had their own 'strategies' for the case company in mind originally. Whereas due to this diversity in (possible) inputs, group work can thus lead to more differentiated and detailed results than any one team member would have been able to achieve alone, for such augmented group performance to really materialize, however, a number of **boundary conditions** need to be ensured which are essentially linked to group **compositional aspects**. In conclusion of the present section and in light of the findings of the entire empirical study, the following may hence be suggested as regards factors to keep in mind in the context of composing teams that are supposed to work collectively on a complex strategic decision task:

Since a good overall process management seems essential, a specific team member might be explicitly assigned the task to act as a **moderator** of the process. In order to prevent others from perceiving this person as too dominant in terms of impacting also on the concrete contents developed, that person might then even refrain from being involved in the content-related interactions and instead concentrate on steering the group's organisation/ procedure. Here then, whereas this role can clearly also be fulfilled by someone internal to the organisation itself, another possibility might be to purposefully seek the advice or help of some external consultants or experts that are specifically trained for doing this kind of job.

Besides, whereas the presence of certain too assertive or oppressive team members is clearly negative, having a **'sensitive' leader** who also encourages the more silent members to contribute their views and ideas, and who is at the same time recognized by these for his expertise, seems what is needed in those cases. In line with this, in order to reap the benefits of diversity in knowledge and experiences, the group must clearly not be too harmonious throughout or have entirely shared orientations. Instead, it is rather important that all **share** the same **overall objective** and display a general cooperative attitude towards the others, while at the same time being also critical and challenging of others' ideas and beliefs as well as of their own.

Exactly this shared objective, or better the absence of it, however, is finally what is frequently observed in the reality of organisations. As a consequence, it also constitutes one of the most crucial reasons why collective activities in these kinds of sensitive and highly important forums often lead to only suboptimal results or even to complete failures. Clearly, these effects vary and are highly dependent on the type of task a group is faced with as well as on such surrounding conditions like the degree of pressure to act or the urgency of the issue. Still, in any case, an important and useful way to remedy these effects is to take particular care of **framing** the task correctly. Specifically, the people involved must not feel threatened (as they would for example if they had to decide on a new cost reduction strategy that would affect their own personal or departmental budgets), or at least not to varying extents. Also, the reasons why a consensual decision is necessary to obtain and the benefits for all of cooperating must be communicated clearly. To obtain the required commitment to the process, certain **incentives** may finally be created that induce both higher and more similar motivations on the side of the individual participants.

Now, having summarized the empirical results and discussed the variety of implications derived there from specifically for the reality of strategic decision making and interactions in organizational groups, these findings will be taken up again and reflected upon in the following Chapter 7, which presents the final summary and conclusions of the overall work. In this context then, apart from considering the value added with the conceptual parts of the research, as regards the empirical study the focus there will be particularly on its contributions in terms of both methodological and conceptual additions to existing knowledge in the field of research on strategic management (cf. 7.2).

7 Final summary and conclusions

7.1 Overall goal and research questions

In line with having developed into a truly multi-paradigm discipline, the present work started from the observation that in order to shed more light on the emergence of organisational strategies as shared strategic orientations and to better understand the strategic management process, it is essentially the *socio-cognitive dynamics* occurring in the context of strategic processes that need to be examined. Here then, even though the cognitive stream on the one hand, and so-called micro approaches on the other, have by now both evolved into prominent perspectives in the discipline of strategic management, respectively, neither of them truly considers the crucial interrelatedness of these two fundamental dimensions. To overcome this deficiency, the overarching goal and subject of the first, conceptual, part of the present work thus was the development of a socio-cognitive perspective on strategic processes, and the discussion of a general framework depicting the emergence of organisational strategies from this view. In this context, the first central research question asked:

- **How (and to what extent) do shared or parallelized strategic knowledge structures (among key decision makers) develop in strategic processes?**

To answer this question and to move towards the own perspective, first a detailed outline and meticulous compiling of the state-of-the-art of the cognitive approach to strategic management was undertaken (Chapter 2). Following this, on the basis of reviewing the existing traditional perspectives and perceptions regarding process issues in strategic management, the own – socio-cognitive – view on the ongoing process was presented. Here, the essential dimensions (i.e., the nature of the basic process, actors involved, activities carried out, strategic content, internal and external context) that need to be considered to characterize different kinds of strategic processes were subtracted and differentiated, followed by a first tentative discussion of the implications that the respective values of these dimensions might have for the parallelization of strategic orientations (Chapter 1).

In order to scientifically substantiate the cognitive side of the own perspective, a detailed consideration of the literature and insights provided by the traditional cognitivist approaches as well as by the newer situativity theories was conducted. Rather than actually being in opposition to each other, as often perceived by non-psychologists like the majority of management scholars, the two approaches were shown to each provide valuable, and in fact complementary, explanations for individual level cognitive phenomena. Here then, especially situated cognition with its focus on the role of the environment, the context, social interaction, culture, and the situation in which actors find themselves, was shown to provide a variety of fresh ideas and concepts whose potential has so far only rarely been recognized by strategy researchers. An outline of different models of socially shared cognition and approaches to collective knowledge in organizations then supplemented the psychological basics of the present work to also account for cognitive issues beyond the individual actor (Chapter 1). In a first synthesis, an integration of the variety of these different insights finally led to the specification of the socio-cognitive perspective on strategic processes (Synthesis 1 in 4.5). In summary, the essentials of this view are the following:

Rather than being in opposition to the purely cognitive approach or to socio-political approaches, the socio-cognitive perspective goes beyond how such approaches would explain the overall process by explicitly recognizing that social, especially political, and cognitive dimensions **interact during the strategic process itself**. In addition, in line with pointing to the **dynamic** and, seen over time, **evolutionary nature** of collective orientations, the socio-cognitive perspective also points to the fact that there are clearly **various strategic orientations** existing in organizations. Usually, in studies conducted from a cognitive perspective it is e.g. assumed that there is one "dominant logic" prevailing in the organisation, or the mental maps of the CEO are taken as representative of the mental map of the entire organisation. However, cognition in organisations or collective strategic orientations is not equal to the aggregate of individual cognitions, but the interaction among individuals may lead to higher (or lower) levels of knowledge creation. In this context then, it is also important to recognize that it is not only the key decision makers that influence other organisational members, but they themselves are influenced by them, simply through everyday interactions. In line with this, and even more importantly, the socio-cognitive perspective then also explicitly directs attention to the **different *forums*** for interactions existing in the strategy context and to the **diverse strategic activities** actors engage in. Since the nature of these different activities clearly varies according to whether it is about taking decisions, formulating plans, or informal get-together-events among a firm's top management team, also the kinds of social interactions occurring between the respective participants vary, influenced by both the specific context in which they take place, as well as by the actors that are present. Accordingly, the cognitive effects or changes will be different. For example, where the overall strategic process or the concrete strategic activity are very formalized and 'planned', a more thorough and conscious gathering and analysis of relevant information is to be expected, which increases the face-value of the information and knowledge itself. In those cases, however, where then the number and the diversity of actors involved in or allowed access to the 'executive strategy suite' is rather limited or is always confined to the same top management team, also more pronounced power struggles and political activities often prevail. This in turn not only limits the potential pool of knowledge and insights available, but the resulting interpersonal struggles are also very likely to decrease the extent to which members actually truly share individually held information and views concerning the concrete strategic issues at hand. If in addition to this also the frequency of such explicit strategy encounters is rather low, even less cognitive developments and convergences in strategic orientations on the side of the involved key actors will occur. Quite a different situation against that is to be found in cases where not only the quantity of opportunities for strategic discussions is higher, but especially where the strategic activities are more democratic, explicitly allow heterogeneous participants from different organisational levels to contribute, and possibly even take place in less formalized forums. With fewer pressures to act immediately or to obey some strictly set rules or hierarchies, the actors will not only have the chance (and the motivation) to share more of their individual knowledge, but also to really listen to the others and with this to possibly truly cognitively accommodate these inputs, and hence to finally converge in orientations.

Regarding the **first overall research question**, it could thus be said that: Firstly, (strategic) knowledge structures (can) never get completely shared or parallelized. Secondly, direct social interactions *and* 'non-social' interactions in the same context contribute to the parallelisation of knowledge structures. As regards the latter, especially institutionalized formal rules, handbooks, and other storage mediums for organisational knowledge play a role. Social processes that matter are both formal and informal interactions where actors are in direct contact with each other. And thirdly, due to the eminence and crucial importance of **politics** and **power** in strategic processes, even if the majority shares a common orientation or knowledge structures, this does not necessarily mean that it is also their will or their behaviours which finally impact on the real important strategic activities carried out by the organisation (cf. 4.5).

Moreover, in light of the findings to that point, which showed that the overall extent of cognitive convergence, its speed and particular form depend on the kind of strategic processes in an organisation (as determined by the values of their different dimensions), and that it is hence also important to carefully differentiate between the different strategy forums and activities, a move was then made away from the rather general level to picking out exactly one such concrete micro setting for strategic activity, i.e. strategic decision making. With the aim of examining the specific socio-cognitive dynamics occurring in this particular context, the work's second research question asked:

- **What is the *nature* of social interactions in *strategic decision making groups* and what is the *role* of these interactions for the (non-) development and change of shared knowledge structures?**

In order to illuminate on this question in terms of both the cognitive and the social dimensions, first, collective information processing was considered whereby the term "social cognition" as cognition 'by' was introduced (4.7). Specifically, in line with the fact that in traditional psychology cognition is considered as something that happens *inside* the individual, "social cognition" thus usually only denotes the study of *individual* cognitions, merely with a social *content*, i.e. 'about'. More recently, however, it has been suggested that the term "social cognition" can also be usefully applied at the *group* level of analysis to refer to those social processes (like e.g. introducing information into a group discussion) that relate to the acquisition, storage, transmission, manipulation and use of information for the purpose of creating a *group-level* intellective product. In this context, social cognition then is not only cognition 'about', but it is cognition 'by', with the word "social" referring to the way in which cognition is accomplished.

Following this excursion to collective information processing, specific insights from the literature on social interaction processes in (small) groups were provided. These included a detailed discussion of factors impacting group interaction processes, (potential) temporal phases and patterns within these, evidence from group learning, as well as forms and functions of social interaction in this setting (Chapter 1).

Based on these outlines, in a second synthesis, an own integrative socio-cognitive model of strategic decision making processes was developed and discussed in detail (Synthesis 2 in 5.3). In line with being built explicitly on ideas from both situated cognition and information processing theory, this model essentially consists of three major and distinctive parts: Firstly, it identifies a variety of crucial context variables and input factors. Secondly, it provides a detailed account of the specific discussion process and contents, as well as of the corresponding cognitive operations. And finally, a range of different potential outcomes from the interactive processes is denominated. Drawing on these elements, in the context of discussing the model, the specific kinds of social interactions occurring between group members were laid out and a number of other social and 'boundary' conditions were exposed that impact on whether or not group members actually share individually held 'old' information, together

7 – Final summary and conclusions

generate 'new' knowledge, jointly examine, evaluate and process the available information, and finally integrate all this into ('overt') group products. As also discussed, however, regarding truly deep and lasting cognitive changes, not only are these by their very nature hard to actually observe, but they also happen only slowly. The question concerning shared or parallelized strategic orientations was hence shown to be a very complex issue, both when looking at the overall strategic process(es), and even more so in such confined settings as concrete decision making processes. In line with this, it was recognized that although in or through social interactions in decision processes a convergence of strategic orientations may occur, even if such shared orientations exist, this only implies *potential* behaviour and thus does neither necessarily have to translate directly into a consensual 'product' like a decision, nor even into visible (strategic) actions. The reasons for this potential 'non-translation' are clearly related to the *way* the final agreement, if there is one, was actually reached. With this then, also the importance of truly 'diving' into such discussion processes was finally made explicit here. I.e., already for really evaluating the end result or group performance that is directly at hand it is considered indispensible to also regard the intermediate processes occurring between group *inputs* and *outputs*. This sensitivity to process issues, however, is then even more crucial in cases where insights are to be derived concerning the specific cognitive and social implications, as well as where considerations regarding later group encounters and assumptions about the potential chance of actually implementing the ideas developed or decisions made are envisaged.

Finally, drawing on all the theoretical insights discussed, in order to substantiate these, as well as to investigate the value of the own socio-cognitive perspective and the model developed, in Chapter 6 an own empirical study was presented that involved ad hoc groups in a simulated decision making situation on a complex strategic issue. With this study, the focus was specifically set on illuminating more thoroughly on the first part of the second research question and investigating the ***nature*** and the ***functions* of social interactions** in this kind of group context. As discussed in detail in the respective chapter, the variety of insights derived from this study is generally in line with the issues and aspects outlined and developed in the preceding parts of the work. Besides, thanks to the creative and innovative research approach adopted, a number of additional insights could be gained that would not have been possible with other more traditional means or methods. Specifically, apart from the truly deep insights into the socio-cognitive dynamics occurring in the context investigated, also a number of concrete and **practical implications for** ensuring the **right boundary conditions, appropriate group composition** and **process design** in the strategic reality were derived. In this regard, whereas in the present simulation the participants had a common objective, one of the major impediments to successful cooperation and exchange of knowledge and information in real strategy teams often is exactly the lack of such a shared overall objective and the prevalence of divergent motivations on the part of the individual participants due to different hierarchical or departmental affiliations. While generally the promotion of diversity in thinking is beneficial for achieving higher performance and better reflected strategic concepts and decisions, if the atmosphere is too laden with conflict or with pressures that affect the individual team members to varying degrees, some of them may withdraw silently or may even openly block the interaction process. In order to prevent such negative effects, prior to the discussion encounter careful thoughts must be given to framing the task in a way that suggests opportunities rather than threats, and to emphasizing the benefits for all that will accrue from cooperating productively. Clearly, differences in status, power and interests are largely unavoidable since they are an inherent part in the context of strategic processes. To still make the most of the given situation, during the meeting itself then, a first important aspect is to ensure a good process organisation. For this, a moderator may be installed who takes care that the group knows where it is heading and roughly how to do so. This person might then even refrain from intervening too much in terms of content-related interactions. Here then, whereas this task may clearly be fulfilled by someone internal to the organisation, it might even be advisable to recruit some external consultant or expert who is specifically trained for performing this kind of activity. Besides, while having someone who dominates the entire task-related interaction is clearly detrimental both for the overall atmosphere in the team as well as for the extent to which a true interchange (and possibly also a convergence in orientations) occurs, having a *sensitive* leader against that seems to do exactly the opposite. This person may predispose of a higher status or have more power. What is important, however, is that he is recognized for his valuable expertise, and that he also explicitly encourages his fellow group members to freely express their opinions and judgements. Like this, not only will they be more likely to accept and trust his inputs, but also the overall variety of ideas and information, and the thoroughness of their examination will finally be much higher. As a consequence of such an increase in both the quantity and the quality of contributions and conclusions, also the chance for truly deep and lasting cognitive changes and convergences is augmented.

Finally, a single meeting or even small sequences of meetings among a concrete group of people clearly constitute merely one element of the overall ongoing strategic process(es). Exactly because of this, besides the concrete and 'tangible' outcomes of a specific decision episode, what might be considered even more important is that the team members have actually cognitively internalized what they have seen and discussed and are convinced of the results. In those cases then the positive effects of the socio-cognitive dynamics in one particular context will be carried on throughout the organisation as the respective individual participants come to interact with other people in other forums. There they spread this knowledge and beliefs, which in turn provides further opportunities for the development of shared strategic orientations, and hence the emergence of organisational strategies.

7.2 Theoretical contributions and value added of the overall work

From the above summary and specific answers to the research questions at hand, it is clear that the added value of the work falls into two categories, i.e. both from the conceptual parts and from the own empirical study noticeable contributions to theory and research in the discipline of strategic management are made:

Contributions from the conceptual parts

Regarding the former, a *first* crucial **conceptual contribution** is provided with the development and specification of the **socio-cognitive perspective** on strategic processes (cf. Chapters 2-4 and particularly 4.5). Specifically, for this, first a meticulous and comprehensive analysis of the existing works and state-of-the-art in the area of cognitive strategy research was done. Besides clearly identifying the current deficiency in terms of adequately taking into account the essential role of social factors, this analysis also led to a useful **ordering schema** for the quite vast and confusing amount of literature in the cognitive strategy field (2.4.4). Specifically, the own scheme suggests that a useful systematization and hence a clearer orientation in the "MOC-landscape" can be achieved by classifying the respective works according to the *level of analysis* (i.e., individual, group, organisation, or industry), the *topic area(s)* dealt with (e.g. strategic processes, strategic decision making, strategic groups), the specific *methods* for data collection and for data analysis used, and *the type of study* conducted (e.g. longitudinal case study, large-scale questionnaire analyses, experimental investigation). What is also revealed by these insights is that while especially for individual level cognitions there already is a plurality of studies and a variety of different research methods, truly valuable and scientifically sound insights into group cognitions are comparatively rare. In particular and even more importantly, in those cases where cognitions at the group level (mostly in TMTs) are investigated, this is often done by either using demographic data (such as e.g. age, tenure, education, function) as proxies for the mental structures and processes of the respective team members, or by means of conducting large scale survey-based studies and quantitative analyses. In none of these cases then the essential role of context specific factors and especially social interactive processes is adequately captured. In the present research against this, with the theoretical framework developed exactly these issues are incorporated explicitly.

Moreover, in line with the work's central interest in the dynamics in strategic processes, an own framework with five **core dimensions** (i.e., nature of the basic process, actors, activities, content, and context) was derived on the basis of a thorough and careful review of the exiting works and theoretical approaches to strategy process research. These dimensions and their respective values provide the basis for characterising and analysing individual strategic processes (3.4.1). Of particular significance here is the differentiation and description of the variety of activities strategic actors perform and of the number of 'forums' in which social interactions (can) take place. While so far the focus in strategy research is still primarily on decision processes, researchers are hence sensitized to recognize that such decision making activities merely constitute one element or 'episode' within the ongoing strategic processes.

Furthermore, as a result of having recognized also the often quite superficial treatment or even misuse of psychological concepts and theories in the management and strategy literature, the present work includes a considerable in-depth account of the psychological basics underlying the different aspects of the phenomenon investigated (Chapter 1). A particular contribution made in this context is the incorporation of ideas from **situated cognition**, which has important implications both for strategy practitioners and researchers. Specifically, while situativity theories are so far primarily found in the area of education and learning research, the importance of the context, especially regarding artefacts and tools as well as situational coactors, is clearly also obvious in organisational settings. Different from the widespread traditional cognitivistic conception that managers do or should apply the same decision rules or cognitive schemata across different situations in order to make rational choices, situated cognition suggests that basic cognitive activities (like e.g. strategic problem recognition or the evaluation of strategic alternatives) are in close interaction with the respective organisational context, i.e. they are influenced by the context and in turn retroact on it. In line with having pointed to the variety of different forums in which key actors interact and the plurality of strategic activities they carry out, taking this centrality of the context serious then also means that the schemata individuals apply and the cognitive processes occurring are not uniform all the time or across all situations. Instead, managers apply context-specific schemata, and also the nature of the social interactions among the participants in a specific strategic context clearly varies according to situational factors. To arrive at meaningful research results, from which also practicable managerial suggestions can be derived, strategy scholars should hence incorporate situational specifics and the social factors at work into their research designs and they are advised to use their knowledge of these issues when interpreting the respective results.

Moreover, in line with the explicit sensitivity to the variety of (potential) contexts in strategic processes warranted by the introduction of the socio-cognitive framework into strategy research, this perspective also underlines that both **social** and **non-social interactions** are important for the (non-) development of shared strategic orientations. Here then, apart from the diverse *micro settings* and their respective socio-cognitive dynamics, the theoretical framework developed further points to the importance of considering the *broader organisational context*: I.e., specifically the *size* of the organisation 'emerges' as a crucial variable that determines not only the number and the nature of opportunities for *direct social interactions* on strategic issues, but which also influences whether it is actually through such interactions or rather by means of *'non-socially'* disseminated knowledge (as is e.g. contained in handbooks, central data bases or knowledge repertoires), that a parallelisation in strategic orientations materializes. In smaller and less hierarchical organisations there are clearly more occasions for informal exchanges and unscheduled joint reflections among members from diverse functional and hierarchical levels. Participants are more familiar with each other as the frequency of interactions with the same people is much higher. Here then, what is exchanged by means of such direct social interchanges can also be expected to impact significantly on the individuals' strategic knowledge, beliefs, values, and most likely also (strategic) actions. In large organisations against that all kinds of different procedures and processes need to be much more formalized and rule-guided in order to successfully manage and handle the complexity inherent in systems of larger scale and scope. In this context then also a lot of the information and knowledge regarding strategic issues is usually documented much more explicitly. Concrete strategy plans and targets exist and the organisation's overall vision and mission are clearly written down somewhere. With fewer opportunities for direct social interactions across functions and organisational levels as well as due to higher fluctuations and overall turnover, this kind of concrete 'impersonal' storage of knowledge and guarantee of open access to it for all relevant actors hence constitutes an essential prerequisite for the development and persistence of shared orientations and finally also concerted strategic actions in more complex organisations.

Another issue exposed with the present research concerns the fact that even though recourse is often made in the existing literature to the essential role of social interactions in the strategy context, what exactly these entail is almost no where differentiated in more detail. To fill this void, an own chapter was dedicated in the present work in which insights on interaction processes and social factors from diverse non-strategy or non-management fields are discussed in light of the research context at hand. It was shown here that even though, due to the difficulty of gaining access to the highly sensitive 'strategy suite', little empirical insights have been provided to date on real strategy teams, valuable insights on these kinds of interactions can nevertheless be gained by drawing on findings from other related fields like e.g. research into collaboration in innovation projects or new product development teams (Chapter 1).

In light of all these contributions, the value of the socio-cognitive perspective developed is clearly multi-faceted: I.e., it integrates and builds on knowledge from different disciplines that so far have only rarely been considered in strategic management. Thanks to this **interdisciplinary approach**, the socio-cognitive framework developed thus provides a more comprehensive overview and hence also a better understanding of the strategic management process and of the emergence of organizational strategies. By differentiating and pointing to a number of elements within this ongoing process it then also serves as a valuable basis for other researchers to examine more specifically those aspects (e.g. specific 'forums' and kinds of strategic activities) that have not been the subject of the present work. With all this, the own socio-cognitive approach to strategic processes developed hence sensitizes to and brings itself "fresh" perspectives into the strategy area, encourages more interdisciplinary openness, and explicitly calls for more cooperation among researchers from diverse but adjacent fields.

Besides having outlined this overall perspective, a *second* noticeable **contribution to theory** in strategic management is made with the own **socio-cognitive model** on group decision making developed in the work's second conceptual part (cf. particularly 5.3). Specifically, in line with building on both *situated cognition* and *information processing theories*, the model specifies first of all the *conditions* and the *processes* of social interactions between group members in a formal discussion context. Regarding the former, i.e. the **conditions**, most obviously *individual level factors* like e.g. the pattern of member skills and knowledge, attitudes, values, and personality traits, constitute a first important "input" to the discussion(s). These in turn largely determine the specific kind of *group context*, i.e. the structure of the group, its level of cohesiveness, the prevalence of specific norms, status and power differences, and their respective importance for the ensuing interactions. Clearly interrelated with both these groups of factors and with the more general *strategic situation* (e.g. level of environmental stress, pressure, reward structure, existence and characteristics of the specific management systems installed), the concrete *issue* or *decision task* then constitutes a third

7 – Final summary and conclusions

condition that may even be regarded as the most essential and distinguishing factor determining who is involved in the first place as well as how exactly the processes will be patterned. Here then, in line with the common distinction found in the strategy literature between different *levels* for which strategies can be formulated (i.e., corporate level strategies, business (unit) level strategies, and functional or departmental level strategies), the specific *type of strategy* dealt with in the process regarded is hence of utmost importance to consider. In cases where the issue at stake concerns adjusting or newly defining the organisation's overall vision or mission statement, the entire process is commonly restricted to a confined group of top level managers or particular TMT members that always come together for deciding on such high-stake issues. More diversity and dynamism in terms of group composition and involvement against that can be expected for other kinds of lower level strategies. Not only the group's structural and internal characteristics and its 'horizon', but also the specific processes occurring during the interactions and the social factors at work will hence clearly vary according to the type of strategic issue tackled. When investigating or describing "strategy genesis" researchers are hence called to clarify more precisely both for themselves and their audience the particular *kind* of strategy phenomenon or "organisational strategy" they refer to. Moreover, regarding specifically the model's centrepiece, i.e. the **processes**, even though it is primarily meant to apply to a 'one-shot' group problem solving session, it can also be regarded more widely and thus be applied to represent and illuminate decision processes more generally, or be used to examine and describe other group processes resulting from task-oriented interactions. In this regard, by differentiating clearly the different phases of the process, a good guidance is achieved that enables paying particular attention to what needs to be considered at the individual points of the process. Also, the interaction between the cognitive and the social dimensions is incorporated and made explicit.

Finally, concerning its third component, i.e. the **outcome(s)**, the model also adds to existing theoretical knowledge in strategy research by showing that there are or can be quite different outcomes or "products" as a result of group discussion processes. So far, in the literature and in the majority of studies in the area, the primary concern is with "performance". This, however, is merely one kind of possible aspect that may be examined or measured. By differentiating the various (potential) outcomes of such discussion processes the model hence emphasizes that the outcome of the entire decision process must neither (necessarily) be any particular action or behaviour, nor even a concrete and tangible "product" such as a written down strategic concept. Instead, the *immediate* outcome is first of all new or improved knowledge, representing at the same time (merely) a change in the group's repertoire of *potential* (strategic) behaviour.

Contributions from the own empirical study

Besides these advancements derived from conceptual thoughts and outlines, the work makes **further contributions** to strategy research with the **empirical study** conducted and adds to exiting knowledge in the field with the insights gained from this (cf. Chapter 1). In this respect, while a deeper look at the processes occurring between *input* and *outcome* in group interactions is often called for, such considerations have only rarely been included in research so far. The empirical study conducted here against that took exactly this kind of **processual approach** and looked deeply into the "black box" of group interaction processes. In this context it also showed that this black box is in fact not as dark as often outlined in the management literature. Instead, a variety of insights exists and has been contributed by scholars in other fields that can, at least in parts, be nicely transferred to illuminate on the strategic management process. In line with this, and to enable the entire in-depth study in the first place, a **creative and innovative research approach** was developed. Although simulations and experimental designs are already quite widely used in other areas and have proven their general suitability to different research problems, the potential of these methods, including specifically also the use of video material, has so far only limitedly been recognized by strategy scholars. In addition to this "import" accomplishment, even though there are still refinements that can be worked out to improve the own method employed, it is generally acknowledged in the wider scientific community that developments in methods, particularly in qualitative methods, take place in the praxis of doing research and in the reflections about these practices (including their economic restrictions) (Bohnsack & Przyborski, 2007, p. 503). The present study thus not only raises at least the very awareness among strategy scholars of the spectrum of means and approaches available in other disciplines and applicable in the own, but thanks to the reconstructive display of the own practical experiences it also contributes more generally to the advancement of (qualitative) research methods.

Finally, apart from these concrete methodological benefits, the insights derived from the empirical study also add to theoretical knowledge with the differentiation made concerning the issues of *dominance* and *leadership* in group interactions and for collective performance. In this regard, whereas having a good process moderator is generally beneficial, any such steering behaviour, however, becomes problematic if there is someone that clearly dominates the interactions, both in terms of content- and process-related interactions. On the one hand this shows that it is the degree or expressiveness of dominant behaviour which matters and thus has to be examined. On the other hand, also the value of carefully distinguishing individual behaviour in terms of the concrete *functional meaning* (i.e., task-oriented, procedural, or socio-emotional) it has for the group interactions is underscored.

In addition to this, another particular contribution, which has so far not been emphasized explicitly, is made to *diversity research*. In this regard, initially, at the very outset of the overall project, the intention had been to focus specifically on the effects that differences in national culture have on the socio-cognitive dynamics occurring in decision making teams. Whereas the setup of the empirical study still fulfils the conditions for investigating this variable (cf. 6.4), already during the observations themselves and even more clearly at the later stages of data analysis it became obvious that no clear and scientifically sound relation could be established between behavioural or mental differences and variances in the participants' respective cultural backgrounds. Instead of wanting to imply with this that culture never matters, these results rather underscore that in the context of experienced management teams, who are entrusted with high-stake and complex tasks, it is no longer the members' national heritage which is at the centre. Although communication barriers due to different levels of language proficiency may clearly hamper the interaction processes, the managers have nevertheless all gone through similarly advanced levels of school and university education. As a result, what seem to matter more in these contexts then are factors like the participants' professional backgrounds, their age and tenure, and perhaps most importantly their respective departmental or hierarchical affiliations. This recognition then has crucial implications specifically for those lines of research that focus on the issue of heterogeneity versus homogeneity in group composition. I.e., to arrive at valuable results concerning the effects this has on team outcomes and performance, researchers must be careful to clearly define and distinguish the particular dimension(s) on which the respective teams are characterized as homogenous or as heterogeneous.

Taken together now from both the conceptual and the empirical parts of the work, with all the insights and findings provided it was shown that it is truly essential to look more closely at the specific social interactions in the ongoing strategy process(es), who the actors involved are, and which concrete context(s) these interactions take place in. Apart from the specific micro or group contexts, also the broader organisational context as well as the strategic environment the organisation is situated in clearly have to be taken into account if meaningful statements are to be derived concerning the particular socio-cognitive dynamics and trajectories through which shared strategic orientations, and hence organisational strategies, materialize in the course of the ongoing strategic processes. Concerning more specifically the *practical* implications, since the immediate results or outcomes of concrete group interactions as well as the potential future developments critically depend on exactly these different factors, having been made aware of them through the present work then lastly also enables the people responsible to better steer and design such processes and groups to finally achieve higher organisational performance.

7.3 Future research directions

Essentially, the overall interest in the present work concerned the way or the extent to which shared strategic orientations (among key decision makers) develop in strategic processes. For this, a socio-cognitive framework depicting the emergence of organisational strategies was discussed. Besides pointing to the central importance of social interactions as mediators between the individual and the collective cognitive levels, the framework and the attendant outlines identified and differentiated a number of different forums, and accordingly also kinds of strategic activities, where such interactions (can) take place. Due to the complexity of the ongoing process and hence impossibility of examining in-depth the variety of socio-cognitive dynamics and their respective implications for convergences in strategic orientations, empirically the focus was set on investigating in-depth the group processes and nature of social interactions in one specific core forum, namely decision making groups. Even though the simulation used here thus allowed gaining insights on merely one small fragment of the entire phenomenon at hand, already in this context the *evolutionary character* of the social and cognitive processes occurring in collective encounters was observed. Due to their complex nature and hence the many different elements any strategic decision consists of, in the organisational reality such decision making processes clearly comprise of more than only one meeting, and rather involve a series of such interactions. Here then, at one time certain aspects of the whole may be discussed and agreed on 'tentatively'. Following this, further information is gathered 'offline' or individually by different members, additional analyses and observations of the market are made, etc. Having evaluated whether or not the initial ideas are actually practicable, further adjustments might be made to the original concept(s). In light of this then, an interesting area for future research would hence be to investigate the development of such ideas as well as of the respective social interaction **patterns over the course of several meetings**. Here then, whereas doing so in a real organisational setting would of course be most revealing, as a start, such a 'tracing' can also be done by using similar means as in the present re-

7 – Final summary and conclusions 301

search, i.e. by designing a free simulation that extents over several discussion meetings and thus to conduct in-depth research in these different settings.

Moreover, in line with having differentiated a number of strategy forums and kinds of strategic activities, further research could investigate managerial interactions in the context of **task requirements other than formal decision making** on a concrete issue. Examples for this might be (strategy) workshops, planning cycles, or even informal get-togethers. In this regard, whereas in the present study content-related interactions were found to be in the majority, in other group contexts procedural aspects or even socio-emotional interactions might be most important. While the former could be imagined to be the case where the type of task is rather unknown, more relationship-oriented activities might be required when the respective team members do not (yet) know each other well, or in cultures (e.g. China, India, etc.) where carefully building relationships is a central first step in any business encounter. Concerning the socio-emotional behaviour, it would then clearly also be interesting and relevant to regard more closely in how far the specific atmospheres, i.e. friendly versus more hostile, vary according to the different kinds of forums, the specific issues at hand, and the particular actors involved.

Furthermore, as has been outlined, especially in the strategy context, issues like **power and politics**, as well as differential motivations to cooperate on the side of the different actors, are important factors to consider. Another research option that could lend itself to a true experimental design would then for example be to vary some of the conditions in the simulation by intentionally inducing different statuses, roles, etc., and like that to investigate how this impacts the respective group dynamics and the extent to which shared orientations result from the processes.

Finally, in line with the importance of the aforementioned power and politics in the strategic reality, an important caution made in the present work concerned the fact that largely due to these kinds of factors, the transition from strategies as shared *strategic orientations* to strategies as real *manoeuvres* or visible *action structures* is not straightforward. Knowing more about what **conditions and influences** might prevent (or further) that an agreed upon group **concept** is also **finally implemented** would be another interesting endeavour. Here then, particularly the role of other actors and stakeholders involved in the overall strategic process seems important and valuable to consider in future research. In this respect, in line with the value hinted at above of including external consultants as facilitators or supporters in concrete meetings or discussions, it would hence also be interesting to investigate more generally the actual role and the impact that particularly **third party people** from external strategy consultancies have on these overall strategic processes.

Appendix

Questionnaire administered to the participants[123]

---

[123] Some of the scales used here were adopted from a questionnaire developed by Krüger (2002) in the context of his research on product innovation teams.

Fragebogen zu sozialen Interaktionsprozessen und Wissensteilung in „Strategieteams"

Liebe MEB-Studentin, lieber MEB-Student,

zunächst einmal möchten wir Ihnen nochmals ganz herzlich für Ihre Bereitschaft danken, an unserem Forschungsprojekt mitzuwirken!
Wie Ihnen bereits vor Beginn Ihrer „Strategiesitzung" mitgeteilt wurde, liegt der Fokus des vorliegenden Forschungsprojekts auf der Betrachtung von sozialen Interaktionsprozessen und der Frage, welche Rolle diese beim Austausch von Wissen in strategischen Entscheidungsprozessen spielen. Zur Unterstützung unserer Untersuchung bitten wir Sie, zum Abschluss nun noch einige Fragen zu Ihrem Diskussionsprozess und zu Ihrer Person zu beantworten. Damit helfen Sie uns, die Analyse des vorliegenden Materials durch Ihre persönlichen Eindrücke vertiefen zu können.
An dieser Stelle möchten wir noch einmal betonen, dass jegliche Ihrer folgenden Angaben streng vertraulich behandelt werden und ausschließlich im Rahmen unseres Forschungsprojektes verwendet werden. Ihre Angaben sind somit völlig unabhängig von der Bewertung Ihrer Gruppenarbeit für den Kurs „European Business Environment & Law".

Zunächst einmal ‚global' betrachtet:

1. Wie war Ihrer Ansicht nach die <u>Stimmung</u> in der Gruppe?

```
        sehr              sehr
        schlecht          gut
        1   2   3   4   5   6
        o---o---o---o---o---o
```

2. Wie würden Sie das <u>Aktivitätsniveau</u> während Ihres gemeinsamen Entscheidungsprozesses insgesamt charakterisieren?

```
        wenig             sehr
        dynamisch         dynamisch
        1   2   3   4   5   6
        o---o---o---o---o---o
```

3. Wie schwierig war es insgesamt gesehen aus Ihrer Sicht, zu einer gemeinsamen Strategie zu kommen?

```
        sehr              sehr
        einfach           schwierig
        1   2   3   4   5   6
        o---o---o---o---o---o
```

4. In welchem Maße spiegelt die Lösung Ihrer Gruppe Ihre individuelle „Strategie" wider, die Sie im Vorfeld im Kopf hatten bzw. in der Hausarbeit vorgeschlagen hatten?

```
        sehr              sehr
        wenig             stark
        1   2   3   4   5   6
        o---o---o---o---o---o
```

Appendix

Strategiefindungsprozesse lösen oft <u>Meinungsverschiedenheiten</u> aus. Bitte beantworten Sie einige Fragen zum <u>Diskussionsprozess</u> und der <u>Entscheidungsfindung</u> bei Ihrer Strategiesitzung:

5. Bei Meinungsverschiedenheiten war die Diskussion oder Entscheidung geprägt von…

	gar nicht sehr oft
	1 2 3 4 5 6
Festhalten am jeweiligen Standpunkt	o---o---o---o---o---o
Rückzug Einzelner	o---o---o---o---o---o
Beachtung aller Meinungen	o---o---o---o---o---o
Harmonisierung der Gegensätze	o---o---o---o---o---o
Kontroverser, intensiver Diskussion	o---o---o---o---o---o
Vorschneller Kompromissbereitschaft	o---o---o---o---o---o
Gegenseitiger Annäherung	o---o---o---o---o---o
Häufigem Hin und Her	o---o---o---o---o---o
Einigungen in der „Mitte"	o---o---o---o---o---o
Neutralität Einzelner	o---o---o---o---o---o

6. Wie schwer war es, in der Gruppe abweichende Meinungen zu äußern?

                         sehr   sehr
                         schwer   leicht
                      1 2 3 4 5 6
                      o---o---o---o---o---o

Warum gab es ggf. Schwierigkeiten?

_____
_____
_____

Ein Teilziel unserer Analyse ist es, neben der Betrachtung der Gruppenebene, auch individuelle Interaktionsprofile zu erstellen. Hierfür sind nicht nur unsere eigenen Beobachtungen wichtig, sondern insbesondere auch die der Beteiligten selbst. Im Folgenden bitten wir Sie deshalb um einige Einschätzungen bezüglich Ihrer jeweiligen drei Teammitglieder. Die hier personalisierten Angaben werden im Rahmen unseres Projektes natürlich vollkommen anonymisiert, so dass eine spätere Identifikation einzelner Personen nicht möglich ist.

7. Wie viel Informationen, Ideen und Anregungen haben Sie von Ihren jeweiligen Teammitgliedern bei dieser Sitzung bekommen?

	sehr wenig						sehr viel
	1	2	3	4	5	6	
Person _____ :	o---o---o---o---o---o						
Person _____ :	o---o---o---o---o---o						
Person _____ :	o---o---o---o---o---o						

8. In welchem Maße ist durch diese Informationen, Ideen und Anregungen Ihr Wissen über Mondavis Position und die strategischen Möglichkeiten des Unternehmens erweitert worden?

	sehr wenig						sehr viel
	1	2	3	4	5	6	
Person _____ :	o---o---o---o---o---o						
Person _____ :	o---o---o---o---o---o						
Person _____ :	o---o---o---o---o---o						

Bei kollektiven Entscheidungsprozessen in Managementteams gibt es eine Vielzahl von wechselseitigen Einflüssen. Ein Teammitglied bzw. die Gruppe insgesamt kann dabei durch andere bei der Verwirklichung seiner/ ihrer Absichten in vielfältiger Weise unterstützt (Fragen 9 & 10) oder behindert werden (Fragen 11 & 12). Es können durchaus dieselben Personen einmal förderlich und ein anderes Mal behindernd erlebt werden.

9. Wie stark war der <u>förderliche</u>, Ihre Absichten <u>unterstützende</u> Einfluss Ihrer jeweiligen Teammitglieder auf Ihre Tätigkeit im Verlauf des Diskussionsprozesses?

	sehr geringer Einfluss						sehr großer Einfluss
	1	2	3	4	5	6	
Person _____ :	o---o---o---o---o---o						
Person _____ :	o---o---o---o---o---o						
Person _____ :	o---o---o---o---o---o						

10. Auf welche Weise wurden Sie bzw. die Gruppe von diesen jeweiligen Teammitgliedern im Verlauf der Diskussion <u>förderlich</u> beeinflusst?

Person ___, ___, ___ förderte und unterstützte mich/ die Gruppe in meinen/ unseren Absichten im Strategiefindungsprozess, weil:

		gar nicht	sehr gering →→→→ sehr stark
...sie über besondere Fachkompetenz und Fertigkeiten verfügte, die mich/ die Gruppe voranbrachten	M.:	o	o-----o-----o-----o-----o-----o
	R.:	o	o-----o-----o-----o-----o-----o
	Y.:	o	o-----o-----o-----o-----o-----o
...ich von ihrer Persönlichkeit beeindruckt war und dadurch hinzulernte	M.:	o	o-----o-----o-----o-----o-----o
	R.:	o	o-----o-----o-----o-----o-----o
	Y.:	o	o-----o-----o-----o-----o-----o
...sie weitere Personen für ihre Ansichten mobilisieren konnte, so dass ich meine erste Fehleinschätzung aufgab	M.:	o	o-----o-----o-----o-----o-----o
	R.:	o	o-----o-----o-----o-----o-----o
	Y.:	o	o-----o-----o-----o-----o-----o

11. Wie stark war der <u>hinderliche,</u> Ihre Absichten <u>ignorierende oder störende</u> Einfluss Ihrer jeweiligen Teammitglieder auf Ihre Tätigkeit im Verlauf des Diskussionsprozesses?
    Bitte denken Sie daran, dass auch hinderliche Einflüsse überall vorkommen können und antworten Sie möglichst offen. Ihre Antworten werden streng vertraulich behandelt und in keinerlei Verbindung mit Ihren Leistungen im Kurs oder bei der Gruppenarbeit gesetzt.

	sehr geringer Einfluss		sehr großer Einfluss
	1 2 3 4 5 6		
Person M.:	o---o---o---o---o---o		
Person R.:	o---o---o---o---o---o		
Person Y.:	o---o---o---o---o---o		

12. Auf welche Weise wurden Sie bzw. die Gruppe von diesen jeweiligen Teammitgliedern im Verlauf der Diskussion <u>hinderlich</u> beeinflusst?

Person ___, ___, ___ behinderte und störte mich/ die Gruppe in meinen/ unseren Absichten im Strategiefindungsprozess, weil:

		gar nicht	sehr gering ────────────▶ sehr stark
…sie über besondere Fachkompetenz und Fertigkeiten verfügte, die mich/ die Gruppe z.B. auf eine falsche Spur brachten	M.:	o	o-----o-----o-----o-----o-----o
	R.:	o	o-----o-----o-----o-----o-----o
	Y.:	o	o-----o-----o-----o-----o-----o
…ich von ihrer Persönlichkeit beeindruckt war und mich dadurch z.B. vom besseren Weg abbringen ließ	M.:	o	o-----o-----o-----o-----o-----o
	R.:	o	o-----o-----o-----o-----o-----o
	Y.:	o	o-----o-----o-----o-----o-----o
…sie weitere Personen für ihre Ansichten mobilisieren konnte, so dass ich mich z.B. wider besseren Wissens anschloss	M.:	o	o-----o-----o-----o-----o-----o
	R.:	o	o-----o-----o-----o-----o-----o
	Y.:	o	o-----o-----o-----o-----o-----o

13. Wie stark haben Sie durch die Zusammenarbeit mit diesen Personen im Verlauf des Strategiefindungsprozesses <u>neue Erfahrungen und Erkenntnisse</u> über die strategische Situation gewonnen?

```
                        sehr                sehr
                        gering              stark
                        1  2  3  4  5  6
Person M.:              o---o---o---o---o---o
Person R.:              o---o---o---o---o---o
Person Y.:              o---o---o---o---o---o
```

14. Schätzen Sie bitte – zunächst global – ein, wie ähnlich oder unähnlich Ihnen Ihre jeweiligen Teammitglieder sind.
Scheuen Sie sich nicht, subjektive, auch unsichere Urteile abzugeben.

Ich halte die Ähnlichkeit für: sehr   sehr
                                      niedrig   hoch
                                      1 2 3 4 5 6
                                      o---o---o---o---o---o

15. Tragen Sie bitte nun für Person ___, ___, ___ jeweils durch Ankreuzen ein, wie viel Sie mit Ihnen in Bezug auf Ausbildung, Ansichten etc. gemeinsam haben?

Ich halte die Ähnlichkeit für: sehr   sehr
                                      niedrig   hoch
                                      1 2 3 4 5 6

Ausbildung, beruflichen Werdegang	Person _____:	o---o---o---o---o---o	nicht bekannt o
	Person _____:	o---o---o---o---o---o	nicht bekannt o
	Person _____:	o---o---o---o---o---o	nicht bekannt o
Kenntnisse in Bezug auf die zu treffende strategische Entscheidung	Person _____:	o---o---o---o---o---o	nicht bekannt o
	Person _____:	o---o---o---o---o---o	nicht bekannt o
	Person _____:	o---o---o---o---o---o	nicht bekannt o
sonstige persönliche Ansichten und Meinungen	Person _____:	o---o---o---o---o---o	nicht bekannt o
	Person _____:	o---o---o---o---o---o	nicht bekannt o
	Person _____:	o---o---o---o---o---o	nicht bekannt o

16. Wie haben sich Ihre jeweiligen Teammitglieder <u>Ihnen gegenüber</u> im Strategiefindungsprozess verhalten?
Tragen Sie bitte jeweils den entsprechenden Wert in Richtung der Seite ab, die nach Ihrer Meinung das Verhalten am ehesten charakterisiert.

                       _: o---o---o---o---o---o
kooperativ   _: o---o---o---o---o---o   unkooperativ
                       _: o---o---o---o---o---o

                       _: o---o---o---o---o---o
dominierend   _: o---o---o---o---o---o   sich unterordnend
                       _: o---o---o---o---o---o

	_:	o---o---o---o---o	
sympathisch	_:	o---o---o---o---o	unsympathisch
	_:	o---o---o---o---o	
	_:	o---o---o---o---o	
die gleichen Ziele	_:	o---o---o---o---o	abweichende Ziele
verfolgend	_:	o---o---o---o---o	verfolgend
	_:	o---o---o---o---o	
herzlich	_:	o---o---o---o---o	kühl
	_:	o---o---o---o---o	
	_:	o---o---o---o---o	
meine Interessen/	_:	o---o---o---o---o	meine Interessen/
Wissen einbeziehend	_:	o---o---o---o---o	Wissen missachtend
	_:	o---o---o---o---o	
angenehm	_:	o---o---o---o---o	unangenehm
	_:	o---o---o---o---o	
	_:	o---o---o---o---o	
hilfreich	_:	o---o---o---o---o	blockierend
	_:	o---o---o---o---o	

17. Wenn Sie nach Beendigung der Strategiesitzung nun ein Fazit ziehen: Halten Sie das gemeinsame strategische Konzept letztlich für eher gelungen oder eher misslungen?

Ich halte das strategische Konzept insgesamt für:

                          misslungen   gelungen
                                    o---o---o---o---o

Erläutern Sie ggf. die Gründe für Ihre obige Einschätzung etwas näher:

_____
_____
_____

18. Hätte Ihrer Meinung nach jemand stärker an der Diskussion beteiligt werden bzw. sich beteiligen sollen?

                                      ja o   nein o

Wenn ja, welche Person(en)? _____

Abschließend noch einige Fragen zu Ihrer Person:

19. Wie vertraut waren Sie mit Ihren jeweiligen Teammitgliedern bereits im Vorfeld Ihrer Gruppenarbeit?

	wenig vertraut					sehr vertraut
	1	2	3	4	5	6
Person _____ :	o---o---o---o---o---o					
Person _____ :	o---o---o---o---o---o					
Person _____ :	o---o---o---o---o---o					

20. Wie oft haben Sie mit Ihren jeweiligen Teammitgliedern bereits im Vorfeld im Rahmen Ihres Studiums bei Gruppenaufgaben zusammengearbeitet?

Person _____ :	Noch nie o	1-2 Mal o	> 2 Mal o
Person _____ :	Noch nie o	1-2 Mal o	> 2 Mal o
Person _____ :	Noch nie o	1-2 Mal o	> 2 Mal o

21. In welcher Fachrichtung bzw. welchem Studiengang haben Sie eine Ausbildung?

   _____

22. Was ist Ihre Nationalität?

   _____

23. Welcher Kultur und/ oder Nation fühlen Sie sich zugehörig? (ggf. Mehrfachnennung möglich)

   _____

24. Wie würden Sie Ihre interkulturelle Kompetenz bzw. Erfahrung einschätzen? <u>In Bezug auf interkulturelle Interaktionen</u>…

	sehr niedrig					sehr hoch
	1	2	3	4	5	6
im privaten Kontext	o---o---o---o---o---o					
im Arbeits-/ Studienkontext	o---o---o---o---o---o					

Vielen herzlichen Dank, und wir freuen uns nun auf die gemeinsame Verkostungsprobe!

Bibliography

Aadne, J. H. (2000). *Social interaction in strategy processes. Applied action research in the Scandinavian media world.* Bamberg: Difo-Druck OHG.

Abelson, R. P. (1968). Simulation of social behavior. In G. Lindzey & E. Aronson (Eds.), *Handbook of social psychology* (2 ed., Vol. 2, pp. 274-356). Reading, Mass.: Addison-Wesley.

Abrahamson, E., & Fairchild, G. (1999). Management fashion. Lifecycles, triggers, and collective learning processes. *Administrative Science Quarterly, 44*(4), 708-740.

Abrahamson, E., & Rosenkopf, L. (1997). Social network effects on the extent of innovation diffusion. A computer simulation. *Organization Science, 8*(3), 289-309.

Abric, J. C. (1984). A theoretical and experimental approach to the study of social representations in a situation of interaction. In R. M. Farr & S. Moscovici (Eds.), *Social representations* (pp. 169-183). Cambridge: Cambridge University Press.

Adams, B. (2004). Public meetings and the democratic process. *Public Administration Review, 64*(1), 43-54.

Akgün, A. E., Lynn, G. S., & Byrne, J. C. (2003). Organizational learning. A socio-cognitive framework. *Human Relations, 56*(7), 839-868.

Akgün, A. E., Lynn, G. S., & Yılmaz, C. (2006). Learning process in new product development teams and effects on product success. A socio-cognitive perspective. *Industrial Marketing Management, 35*(2), 210-224.

Allard-Poesi, F. (1998). Representations and influence processes in groups. Towards a socio-cognitive perspective on cognition in organizations. *Scandinavian Journal of Management, 14*(4), 395-420.

Alvesson, M., & Karreman, D. (2000). Taking the linguistic turn in organizational research. Challenges, responses, consequences. *Journal of Applied Behavioral Science, 36*(2), 136-158.

Amason, A. C. (1996). Distinguishing the effects of functional and dysfunctional conflict on strategic decision making. Resolving a paradox for top management teams. *Academy of Management Journal, 39*(1), 123-148.

Amason, A. C., Thompson, K. R., Hochwarter, W. A., & Harrison, A. W. (1995). Conflict. An important dimension in successful management teams. *Organizational Dynamics, 24*(2), 20-35.

Ambrosini, V., & Bowman, C. (2001). Tacit knowledge. Some suggestions for operationalization. *Journal of Management Studies, 38*(6), 812-829.

Ambrosini, V., & Bowman, C. (2005). Reducing causal ambiguity to facilitate strategic learning. *Management Learning, 36*(4), 493-512.

Andersen, R. C., & Pichert, J. W. (1978). Recall of previously unrecallable information following a shift in perspective. *Journal of Verbal Learning and Behavior, 17*(1), 1-12.

Anderson, J. R. (2005). *Cognitive psychology and its implications* (6 ed.). New York: Worth Publishers.

Anderson, R. C. (1977). The notion of schemata and the educational enterprise. General discussion of the conference. In R. C. Anderson, R. J. Spiro & W. E. Montague (Eds.), *Schooling and the acquisition of knowledge* (pp.?). Hillsdale: Erlbaum.

Anderson, R. C., & Pearson, P. D. (1984). A schema-theoretic view of basic processes in reading comprehension. In P. D. Pearson (Ed.), *Handbook of reading research* (pp. 255-291). New York: Longman.

Andrews, K. R. (1971). *The concept of corporate strategy.* Homewood, IL: Irwin.

Ansoff, H. I. (1965). *Corporate strategy. An analytical approach to business policy for growth and expansion*. New York: McGraw-Hill.
Ansoff, H. I. (1976). *From strategic planning to strategic management*. London et al.: Wiley.
Ansoff, H. I. (1980). Strategic issue management. *Strategic Management Journal, 1*(2), 131-148.
Ardelt-Gattinger, E., & Gattinger, E. (1998). Gruppenarten und Gruppenphasen. In E. Ardelt-Gattinger, H. Lechner & W. Schlögl (Eds.), *Gruppendynamik. Anspruch und Wirklichkeit der Arbeit in Gruppen* (pp. 2-9). Göttingen: Verlag für angewandte Psychologie.
Argote, L. (1999). *Organizational learning. Creating, retaining and transferring knowledge*. Boston, Dordrecht, London: Kluwer Academic Publishers.
Argote, L., & Ophir, R. (2002). Intraorganizational learning. In J. A. Baum (Ed.), *The Blackwell companion to organizations* (pp. 181-207). Oxford: Blackwell.
Argyris, C. (1999). *On organizational learning* (2 ed.). Cambridge: Blackwell.
Argyris, C., & Schön, D. A. (1978). *Organizational learning*. Reading: Addison-Wesley.
Atkinson, R. C., & Shiffrin, R. M. (1968). Human memory. A proposed system and its control processes. In K. Spence & J. Spence (Eds.), *The psychology of learning and motivation. Advances in research and theory*. New York: Academic Press.
Axelrod, R. M. (1976). *The structure of decisions*. Princeton, N.J.: Princeton University Press.
Baba, M., Gluesing, J., Ratner, H., & Wagner, K. H. (2004). The contexts of knowing. Natural history of a globally distributed team. *Journal of Organizational Behavior, 25*(5), 547-587.
Bailey, A., Johnson, G., & Daniels, K. (2000). Validation of a multi-dimensional measure of strategy development processes. *British Journal of Management, 11*(2), 151-163.
Bain, J. S. (1959). *Industrial organization*. New York et al.: Wiley.
Balabanis, G., & Spyropoulou, S. (2007). Matching modes of export strategy development to different environmental conditions. *British Journal of Management, 18*(1), 45-62.
Bales, R. F. (1950a). *Interaction process analysis. A method for the study of small groups*. Cambridge: Addison-Wesley.
Bales, R. F. (1950b). A set of categories for the analysis of small group interaction. *American Sociological Review, 15*(2), 257-263.
Bales, R. F., Cohen, S. P., & Williamson, S. A. (1982). *SYMLOG. Ein System für die mehrstufige Beobachtung von Gruppen*. Stuttgart: Klett-Cotta.
Bales, R. F., & Strodtbeck, F. L. (1951). Phases in group problem-solving. *The Journal of Abnormal and Social Psychology, 46*(4), 485-495.
Balogun, J., Jarzabkowski, P., & Seidl, D. (2007a). Strategizing activity and practice. In V. Ambrosini, M. Jenkins & N. Collier (Eds.), *Advanced strategic management. A multiple perspective approach* (2 ed.). Basingstoke: Palgrave Macmillan.
Balogun, J., Jarzabkowski, P., & Seidl, D. (2007b). Strategizing. The challenges of a practice perspective. *Human Relations, 60*(1, Special Issue).
Bamberger, I., & Wrona, T. (1996a). Der Ressourcenansatz im Rahmen des Strategischen Management. *Wirtschaftswissenschaftliches Studium (WiSt), 25*(8), 386-391.
Bamberger, I., & Wrona, T. (1996b). Der Ressourcenansatz und seine Bedeutung für die strategische Unternehmensführung. *Schmalenbachs Zeitschrift für betriebswirtschaftliche Forschung (zfbf), 48*(2), 130-153.
Bamberger, I., & Wrona, T. (2004). *Strategische Unternehmensführung. Strategien - Systeme - Prozesse*. München: Vahlen.
Bandura, A. (1977). *Social learning theory*. Engelwood Cliffs: Prentice-Hall, Inc.
Bandura, A. (1986). *Social foundations of thought and action. A social cognitive theory*. Englewood Cliffs: Prentice Hall.
Bandura, A. (1997). *Self efficacy. The exercise of control*. New York: Prentice Hall.

Bantel, K. A., & Jackson, S. E. (1989). Top management and innovations in banking. Does the composition of the top team make a difference? *Strategic Management Journal, 10*(Special Issue), 107-124.
Barinaga, E. (2007). 'Cultural diversity' at work. 'National culture' as a discourse organizing an international project group. *Human Relations, 60*(2), 315-340.
Barney, J. B. (1986). Strategic factor markets. Expectations, luck, and business strategy. *Management Science, 32*(10), 1231-1241.
Barney, J. B. (1991). Firm resources and sustained competitive advantage. *Journal of Management, 17*(1), 99-120.
Barr, P. S., & Huff, A. S. (1997). Seeing isn't believing. Understanding diversity in the timing of strategic response. *Journal of Management Studies, 34*(3), 337-370.
Barr, P. S., Stimpert, J. L., & Huff, A. S. (1992). Cognitive change, strategic action, and organizational renewal. *Strategic Management Journal, 13*(Special Issue), 15-36.
Bartlett, F. C. (1932). *Remembering. An experimental and social study.* Cambridge: Cambridge University Press.
Barton, A. H., & Lazarsfeld, P. F. (1955). Some functions of qualitative analysis in social research. In *Frankfurter Beiträge zur Soziologie I* (pp. 321-361). Frankfurt a. M.: Europäische Verlagsanstalt.
Bartunek, J. M. (1984). Changing interpretive schemes and organizational restructuring. The example of a religious order. *Administrative Science Quarterly, 29*(3), 355-373.
Beck, D., & Fisch, R. (2000). Argumentation and emotional processes in group decision-making. Illustration of a multilevel interaction process analysis approach. *Group Processes & Intergroup Relations, 3*(2), 183-201.
Benjamin, B. A., & Podolny, J. M. (1999). Status, quality, and social order in the California wine industry. *Administrative Science Quarterly, 44*(3), 563-589.
Bennett III, R. H. (1998). The importance of tacit knowledge in strategic deliberations and decisions. *Management Decision, 36*(9), 589-597.
Berger, P. L., & Luckmann, T. (1966). *The social construction of reality. A treatise in the sociology of knowledge.* New York: Anchor Books.
Berger, P. L., & Luckmann, T. (1969). *Die gesellschaftliche Konstruktion der Wirklichkeit.* Frankfurt a. M.: Fischer.
Bergmann, J. R. (2004). Ethnomethodology. In U. Flick, E. v. Kardorff & I. Steinke (Eds.), *A companion to qualitative research* (pp. 72-80). London, Thousand Oaks, New Delhi: Sage Publications.
Bettis, R. A., & Prahalad, C. K. (1995). The dominant logic. Retrospective and extension. *Strategic Management Journal, 16*(1), 5-14.
Beyer, J. M. (1981). Ideologies, values and decision making in organizations. In P. C. Nystrom & W. H. Starbuck (Eds.), *Handbook of organizational design* (pp. 166-201). London: Oxford University Press.
Blackler, F. (1993). Knowledge and the theory of organisations. Organisations as activity systems and reframing of management. *Journal of Management Studies, 30*(6), 863-884.
Blackler, F. (1995). Knowledge, knowledge work and organizations. An overview and interpretation. *Organization Studies, 16*(6), 1021-1046.
Blumer, H. (1969). *Symbolic interactionism. Perspective and method.* Berkeley: University of California Press.
Bohnsack, R. (1999). *Rekonstruktive Sozialforschung. Einführung in Methodologie und Praxis.* Opladen: Leske und Budrich.
Bohnsack, R., & Przyborski, A. (2007). Gruppendiskussionsverfahren und Focus Groups. In R. Buber & H. H. Holzmüller (Eds.), *Qualitative Marktforschung. Konzepte - Methoden - Analysen* (pp. 491-506). Wiesbaden: Gabler.

Boos, M. (1996). *Entscheidungsfindung in Gruppen. Eine Prozeßanalyse*. Bern, Göttingen, Toronto, Seattle: Verlag Hans Huber.
Boos, M. (1998). "Einer für alle", "jeder für sich" oder "mit den Augen des anderen". Führung und Zusammenarbeit in Gruppenentscheidungen. In E. Ardelt-Gattinger, H. Lechner & W. Schlögl (Eds.), *Gruppendynamik. Anspruch und Wirklichkeit der Arbeit in Gruppen* (pp. 84-95). Göttingen: Verlag für angewandte Psychologie.
Boos, M., Scharpf, U., & Fisch, R. (1991). Eine Methode zur Analyse von Interaktionsprozessen beim Problemlösen und Entscheiden in Sitzungen. *Zeitschrift für Arbeits- und Organisationspsychologie, 35*(9), 115-121.
Bortz, J. (2005). *Statistik für Human- und Sozialwissenschaftler* (6 ed.). Berlin, Heidelberg: Springer.
Bortz, J., & Döring, N. (2002). *Forschungsmethoden und Evaluation für Human- und Sozialwissenschaftler* (3 ed.). Berlin, Heidelberg: Springer.
Bortz, J., & Döring, N. (2006). *Forschungsmethoden und Evaluation für Human- und Sozialwissenschaftler* (4 ed.). Berlin, Heidelberg: Springer.
Bougon, M. G. (1992). Congregate cognitive maps. A unified dynamic theory of organization and strategy. *Journal of Management Studies, 29*(3), 369-389.
Bougon, M. G., Weick, K. E., & Binkhorst, D. (1977). Cognition in organizations. An analysis of the Utrecht jazz orchestra. *Administrative Science Quarterly, 22*(4), 606-638.
Boulding, K. E. (1956). General systems theory. The skeleton of science. *Management Science, 2*(3), 197-208.
Bourdieu, P. (1977). *Outline of a theory of practice*. Cambridge: Cambridge University Press.
Bourdieu, P. (1984). *Distinction. A social critique of the judgment of taste*. Cambridge: Harvard University Press.
Bourgeois, L. J. (1980). Performance and consensus. *Strategic Management Journal, 1*(3), 227-248.
Bourgeois, L. J., & Eisenhardt, K. M. (1988). Strategic decision processes in high velocity environments. Four cases in the Microcomputer industry. *Management Science, 34*(7), 816-835.
Bower, G. H. (1981). Mood and memory. *American Psychologist, 36*(2), 129-148.
Bower, J. L. (1970). *Managing the resource allocation process. A study of corporate planning and investment*. Boston: Harvard Business School Press.
Bowman, C., & Johnson, G. (1992). Surfacing competitive strategies. *European Management Journal, 10*(2), 210-219.
Bowman, E. H., Singh, H., & Thomas, H. (2002). The domain of strategic management. History and evolution. In A. Pettigrew, H. Thomas & R. Whittington (Eds.), *Handbook of strategy and management* (pp. 31-51). London: Sage Publications.
Bracker, J. (1980). The historical development of the strategic management concept. *Academy of Management Review, 5*(2), 219-224.
Braisby, N. (2005). *Cognitive psychology. A methods companion*. Oxford: Oxford University Press.
Bransford, J. D., & Johnson, M. K. (1972). Contextual prerequisites for understanding. Some investigators of comprehension and recall. *Journal of Verbal Learning and Behavior, 11*(6), 717-726.
Braybrooke, D., & Lindblom, C. E. (1963). *A strategy of decision*. New York: Free Press.
Bredo, E. (1994). Reconstructing educational psychology. Situated cognition and Deweyian pragmatism. *Educational Psychologist, 29*(1), 23-35.
Brewer, W. F., & Nakamura, G. V. (1984). The nature and functions of schemas. In R. S. Wyer & T. K. Srull (Eds.), *Handbook of social cognition* (Vol. 1, pp. 119-160). Hillsdale, NJ: Erlbaum.

Brodbeck, F. C., Kerschreiter, R., Mojzisch, A., & Schulz-Hardt, S. (2007). Group decision making under conditions of distributed knowledge. The information asymmetries model. *Academy of Management Journal, 32*(2), 549-579.
Broich, A. (1994). *Die Genese von Unternehmensstrategien. Zur Neuorientierung der Theoriediskussion*. München: Verlag Barbara Kirsch.
Brown, J. S., & Duguid, P. (1991). Organizational learning and communities-of-practice. Toward a unified view of working, learning, and innovation. *Organization Science, 2*(1), 40-57.
Brown, S. M. (1992). Cognitive mapping and repertory grids for qualitative survey research. Some comparative observations. *Journal of Management Studies, 29*(3), 287-307.
Brühl, R., & Buch, S. (2006). *Einheitliche Gütekriterien in der empirischen Forschung? Objektivität, Reliabilität und Validität in der Diskussion* (No. 20). Berlin: ESCP-EAP Europäische Wirtschaftshochschule Berlin.
Bukszar, E., & Connolly, T. (1988). Hindsight bias and strategic choice. Some problems in learning from experience. *Academy of Management Journal, 31*(3), 628-641.
Burgelman, R. A. (1983). A model of the interaction of strategic behavior, corporate context, and the concept of strategy. *Academy of Management Review, 8*(1), 61-70.
Burgelman, R. A. (1988). Strategy making as a social learning process. The case of internal corporate venturing. *Interfaces, 18*(3), 74-85.
Burrell, G., & Morgan, G. (1979). *Sociological paradigms and organizational analysis. Elements of the sociology of corporate life*. Aldershot, Burlington: Ashgate.
Calori, R., Johnson, G., & Sarnin, P. (1992). French and British top managers' understanding of the structure and the dynamics of their industries. A cognitive analysis and comparison. *British Journal of Management, 3*(2), 61-78.
Calori, R., Johnson, G., & Sarnin, P. (1994). CEO's cognitive maps and the scope of the organization. *Strategic Management Journal, 15*(6), 437-457.
Camerer, C. F. (1991). Does strategy research need game theory? *Strategic Management Journal, 12*(Special Issue 2), 137-152.
Cannon-Bowers, J. A., Salas, E., & Converse, S. (1993). Shared mental models in expert team decision making. In N. J. Castellan, Jr. (Ed.), *Individual and group decision making. Current issues* (pp. 221-246). Hillsdale, NJ: Lawrence Erlbaum Associates Inc.
Cantor, N., & Mischel, W. (1977). Traits as prototypes. Effects on recognition memory. *Journal of Personality and Social Psychology, 35*(1), 38-48.
Chaffee, E. E. (1985). Three models of strategy. *Academy of Management Review, 10*(1), 89-98.
Chakravarthy, B. S., & Doz, Y. (1992). Strategy process research. Focusing on corporate self-renewal. *Strategic Management Journal, 13*(Special Issue 1), 5-14.
Chakravarthy, B. S., & White, R. E. (2002). Strategy process. Forming, implementing and changing strategies. In A. Pettigrew, H. Thomas & R. Whittington (Eds.), *Handbook of strategy and management* (pp. 182-205). London, Thousand Oaks, New Delhi: Sage Publications.
Chandler, A. D. (1962). *Strategy and structure. Chapters in the history of the American industrial enterprise*. Cambridge: MIT Press.
Chandler, A. D. (1990). *Scale and scope. The dynamics of industrial capitalism*. Cambridge (MA), London: Belknap Press.
Chandler, A. D. (1992a). Managerial enterprise and competitive capabilities. *Business History, 34*(1), 11-41.
Chandler, A. D. (1992b). Organizational capabilities and the history of the industrial enterprise. *Journal of Economic Perspectives, 6*(3), 79-100.
Chanin, M. N., & Shapiro, H. J. (1985). Dialectical inquiry in strategic planning. Extending the boundaries. *Academy of Management Review, 10*(4), 663-675.

Chatman, J. A., & Flynn, F. J. (2001). The influence of demographic heterogeneity on the emergence and consequences of cooperative norms in work team. *Academy of Management Journal, 44*(5), 956-974.

Chattopadhyay, P., Glick, W. G., Miller, C. C., & Huber, G. P. (1999). Determinants of executive beliefs. Comparing functional conditioning and social influence. *Strategic Management Journal, 20*(8), 763-789.

Chia, R., & MacKay, B. (2007). Post-processual challenges for the emerging strategy-as-practice perspective. Discovering strategy in the logic of practice. *Human Relations, 60*(1), 217-242.

Clarkson, G. P., & Hodgkinson, G. P. (2005). Introducing Cognizer™. A comprehensive computer package for the elicitation and analysis of cause maps. *Operational Research Methods, 8*(3), 317-341.

Coase, R. (1937). The nature of the firm. *Economia, 4*(16), 386-405.

Codol, J. P. (1974). On the system of representations in a group situation. *European Journal of Social Psychology, 4*(3), 343-365.

Codol, J. P. (1984). On the system of representations in an artificial social situation. In R. M. Farr & S. Moscovici (Eds.), *Social representations* (pp. 239-253). Cambridge: Cambridge University Press.

Cohen, M. D., March, J. C., & Olsen, J. P. (1972). *A garbage can model of organizational choice*. Bridgeport, CT: Wiener.

Cohen, W. M., & Levinthal, D. A. (1990). Absorptive capacity. A new perspective on learning and innovation. *Administrative Science Quarterly, 35*(1), 128-152.

Corner, P. D., Kinicki, A. J., & Keats, B. W. (1994). Integrating organizational and individual information processing perspectives on choice. *Organization Science, 5*(3), 294-308.

Craik, F. I., & Lockhart, R. S. (1972). Levels of processing. A framework for memory research. *Journal of Verbal Thinking and Verbal Behavior, 11*(6), 671-684.

Cronin, M. A., & Weingart, L. R. (2007). Representational gaps, information processing, and conflict in functionally diverse teams. *Academy of Management Review, 32*(3), 761-773.

Cyert, R. M., & March, J. G. (1963). *A behavioral theory of the firm*. Englewood Cliffs, NJ: Prentice-Hall.

Daft, R. L., & Weick, K. E. (1984). Toward a model of organizations as interpretation systems. *Academy of Management Review, 9*(2), 284-295.

Dahlin, K. B., Weingart, L. R., & Hinds, P. J. (2005). Team diversity and information use. *Academy of Management Journal, 48*(6), 1107-1123.

Dalgleish, T. (2004). Cognitive approaches to posttraumatic stress disorder. The evolution of multirepresentational theorizing. *Psychological Bulletin, 130*(2), 228-260.

Daniels, K., Chernatony de, L., & Johnson, G. (1995). Validating a method for mapping managers' mental models of competitive industry structures. *Human Relations, 48*(9), 975-991.

Daniels, K., Johnson, G., & de Chernatony, L. (1994). Differences in managerial cognitions of competition. *British Journal of Management, 5*(Special Issue 1), 21-29.

Daniels, K., Johnson, G., & de Chernatony, L. (2002). Task and institutional influences on managers' mental models of competition. *Organization Studies, 23*(1), 31-62.

Das, T. K., & Teng, B.-S. (1999). Cognitive biases and strategic decision processes. An integrative perspective. *Journal of Management Studies 36*(6), 757-778.

Davis, J. H. (1982). Group decision and social interaction. A theory of social decision schemes. *Psychological Review, 80*(2), 97-125.

Davis, T. R. V., & Luthans, F. (1980). A social learning approach to organizational behavior. *Academy of Management Review, 5*(2), 281-290.

De Dreu, C. K. W., & Nijstad, B. A. (2008). Mental set and creative thought in social conflict. Threat rigidity versus motivated focus. *Journal of Personality and Social Psychology, 95*(3), 648-661.
Denzin, N. K., & Lincoln, Y. S. (Eds.). (2005). *The SAGE handbook of qualitative research* (3 ed.). Thousand Oaks: Sage Publications.
Derry, S. J., DuRussel, L. A., & O'Donnell, A. M. (1998). Individual and distributed cognitions in interdisciplinary teamwork. A developing case study and emerging theory. *Educational Psychology Review, 10*(1), 25-56.
Dess, G. G., Lumpkin, G. T., & Covin, J. G. (1997). Entrepreneurial strategy making and firm performance. Tests of contingency and configurational models. *Strategic Management Journal, 18*(9), 677-695.
Dill, W. R. (1958). Environment as an influence on managerial autonomy. *Administrative Science Quarterly, 2*(4), 409-443.
Dilthey, W. (1968). Die Entstehung der Hermeneutik. In W. Dilthey (Ed.), *Gesammelte Schriften, Volume V: Die geistige Welt. Einleitung in die Philosophie des Lebens. Erste Hälfte. Abhandlungen zur Grundlegung der Geisteswissenschaften.* Stuttgart: B. Teubner Verlagsanstalt.
Dörner, D. (1999). *Bauplan für eine Seele.* Reinbek: Rowohlt.
Dörner, D., Kreuzig, H. W., Reither, F., & Stäudel, T. (1983). *Lohausen. Vom Umgang mit Unbestimmtheit und Komplexität.* Bern: Huber.
Dutton, J. E. (1997). Strategic agenda building in organizations. In Z. Shapira (Ed.), *Organization decision making* (pp. 81-107). Cambridge: Cambridge University Press.
Dutton, J. E., & Ashford, S. J. (1993). Selling issues to top management. *Academy of Management Review, 18*(3), 397-428.
Dutton, J. E., Ashford, S. J., O'Neill, R. M., & Lawrence, K. A. (2001). Moves that matter. Issue selling and organizational change. *Academy of Management Journal, 44*(4), 716-736.
Dutton, J. E., & Dukerich, J. M. (1991). Keeping an eye on the mirror. Image and identity in organizational adaptation. *Academy of Management Journal, 34*(3), 517-554.
Dutton, J. E., & Duncan, R. B. (1987). The creation of momentum for change through the process of strategic issue diagnosis. *Strategic Management Journal, 8*(3), 279-295.
Dutton, J. E., Fahey, L., & Narayanan, V. K. (1983). Towards understanding strategic issue diagnosis. *Strategic Management Journal, 4*(4), 307-323.
Dutton, J. E., & Jackson, S. E. (1987). Categorizing strategic issues. Links to organizational action. *Academy of Management Review, 12*(1), 76-90.
Earley, P. C. (1999). Playing follow the leader. Status-determining traits in relation to collective efficacy across cultures. *Organizational Behavior and Human Decision Processes, 80*(3), 1-21.
Easterby-Smith, M., & Lyles, M. A. (2006). *The Blackwell handbook of organizational learning and knowledge management* (2 ed.). Oxford: Wiley-Blackwell.
Easton, D. (1965). *A systems analysis of political life.* New York et al.: Wiley.
Eden, C. (1992). Strategy development as a social process. *Journal of Management Studies, 29*(6), 799-811.
Eden, C., & Radford, J. (1990). *Tackling strategic problems. The role of group decision support.* Thousand Oaks: Sage Publications.
Eden, C., & Spender, J. C. (1998). *Managerial and organizational cognition. Theory, methods and research.* London: Sage Publications.
Edmondson, A. C. (1999). Psychological safety and learning behavior in work teams. *Administrative Science Quarterly, 44*(2), 350-383.
Edmondson, A. C. (2002). The local and variegated nature of learning in organizations. A group level perspective. *Organization Science, 13*(2), 128-146.

Eisenhardt, K. M. (1989a). Building theories from case study research. *Academy of Management Review, 14*(4), 532-550.
Eisenhardt, K. M. (1989b). Making fast strategic decisions in high-velocity environments. *Academy of Management Journal, 32*(3), 543-576.
Eisenhardt, K. M., & Martin, J. A. (2000). Dynamic capabilities. What are they? *Strategic Management Journal, 21*(10/11), 1105-1121.
Eisenhardt, K. M., & Santos, F. (2002). Knowledge-based view. A new theory of strategy. In A. Pettigrew, H. Thomas & R. Whittington (Eds.), *Handbook of strategy and management* (pp. 139-164).
Eisenhardt, K. M., & Zbaracki, M. (1992). Strategic decision making. *Strategic Management Journal, 13*(1), 17-37.
Elenkov, D. S. (1997). Strategic uncertainty and environmental scanning. The case for institutional influences on scanning behavior. *Strategic Management Journal, 18*(4), 287–302.
Elkjaer, B. (2003). Social learning theory. Learning as participation in social processes. In M. Easterby-Smith & M. A. Lyles (Eds.), *The Blackwell handbook of organizational learning and knowledge management* (pp. 38-53). Oxford: Wiley-Blackwell.
Elsbach, K. D., Barr, P. S., & Hargadon, A. B. (2005). Identifying situated cognition in organizations. *Organization Science, 16*(4), 422-433.
Etzioni, A. (1968). *The active society*. London: Collier-Macmillan.
Eysenck, M. W., & Keane, M. T. (2005). *Cognitive psychology. A student's handbook* (5 ed.). New York: Taylor & Francis Inc.
Fahey, L., & Christensen, H. K. (1986). Evaluating the research on strategy content. *Journal of Management, 12*(2), 167-183.
Festinger, L. (1954). A theory of social comparison processes. *Human Relations, 7*(2), 117-140.
Finkelstein, S. (1992). Power in top management teams. Dimensions, measurement, and validation. *Academy of Management Journal, 35*(3), 505-538.
Finlay, F., Hitch, G. J., & Meudell, P. R. (2000). Mutual inhibition in collaborative recall. Evidence for a retrieval-based account. *Journal of Experimental Psychology: Learning, Memory and Cognition, 26*(6), 1556-1567.
Fiol, C. M. (1994). Consensus, diversity and learning in organizations. *Organization Science, 5*(3), 403-420.
Fiol, C. M. (2002). Intraorganizational cognition and interpretation. In J. A. Baum (Ed.), *The Blackwell companion to organizations* (pp. 119-137). Oxford: Blackwell.
Fiol, C. M., & Huff, A. S. (1992). Maps for managers. Where are we? Where do we go from here? *Journal of Management Studies, 29*(3), 267-285.
Fiol, C. M., & Lyles, M. A. (1985). Organizational learning. *Academy of Management Journal, 10*(4), 803-813.
Fisch, R. (1994). Eine Methode zur Analyse von Interaktionsprozessen beim Problemlösen in Gruppen [A method for the interaction process analysis of group problem-solving]. *Gruppendynamik und Organisationsberatung - Zeitschrift für angewandte Sozialpsychologie, 25*(2), 149-168.
Fisch, R. (1998). Konferenzkodierung. In E. Ardelt-Gattinger, H. Lechner & W. Schlögl (Eds.), *Gruppendynamik. Anspruch und Wirklichkeit der Arbeit in Gruppen* (pp. 194-207). Göttingen: Verlag für angewandte Psychologie.
Fisher, B. A. (1970). The process of decision modification in small discussion groups. *The Journal of Communication, 20*(1), 51-64.
Fiske, S. T., & Linville, P. W. (1980). What does the schema concept buy us? *Personality and Social Psychology Bulletin, 6*(4), 543-557.
Fiske, S. T., & Taylor, S. E. (1991). *Social cognition* (2 ed.). New York: McGraw-Hill.

Flamholtz, E. G. (1996). *Effective management control. Theory and practice.* Boston, London, Dordrecht: Kluwer.
Flick, U. (2002a). *An introduction to qualitative research* (2 ed.). London: Sage Publications.
Flick, U. (2002b). *Qualitative Sozialforschung. Eine Einführung* (6 ed.). Reinbek bei Hamburg: Rowohlt Taschenbuch.
Flick, U. (2004). Constructivism. In U. Flick, E. v. Kardorff & I. Steinke (Eds.), *A companion to qualitative research* (pp. 88-94). London, Thousand Oaks, New Delhi: Sage Publications.
Flick, U., Kardorff, E. v., & Steinke, I. (2004a). *A companion to qualitative research.* London, Thousand Oaks, New Delhi: Sage Publications.
Flick, U., Kardorff, E. v., & Steinke, I. (2004b). What is qualitative research? An introduction to the field. In U. Flick, E. Von Kardorff & I. Steinke (Eds.), *A companion to qualitative research* (pp. 3-11). London, Thousand Oaks, New Delhi: Sage Publications.
Floyd, S. W., & Wooldridge, B. (2000). *Building strategy from the middle. Reconceptualizing strategy process.* Thousand Oaks: Sage Publications.
Fombrun, C., & Shanley, M. (1990). What's in a name? Reputation building and corporate strategy. *Academy of Management Review, 33*(2), 233-258.
Forgas, J. P. (1981). What is social about social cognition. In J. P. Forgas (Ed.), *Social cognition. Perspectives on everyday understanding* (pp. 1-25). London: Academic Press.
Fredrickson, J. W. (1990). Introduction. The need for perspectives. In J. W. Fredrickson (Ed.), *Perspectives on strategic management* (pp. 1-8). New York: Harper Business.
Fromkin, H. L., & Streufert, S. (1983). Laboratory experimentation. In M. D. Dunnette (Ed.), *Handbook of organizational and industrial psychology* (pp. 415-465). New York: Wiley.
Gadamer, H. G. (1975). *Truth and method.* New York: Seabury Press.
Gagné, E. D. (1985). *The cognitive psychology of school learning.* Boston: Little Brown and Company.
Gallen, T. (1997). The cognitive style and strategic decisions of managers. *Management Decision, 35*(7), 541-551.
Garfinkel, H. (1967). *Studies in ethnomethodology.* Englewood Cliffs: Prentice Hall.
Gavetti, G., Levinthal, D. A., & Rivkin, J. W. (2005). Strategy making in novel and complex worlds. The power of analogy. *Strategic Management Journal, 26*(8), 691-712.
Gavetti, G., & Rivkin, J. W. (2007). On the origin of strategy. Action and cognition over time. *Organization Science, 18*(3), 420-439.
Geertz, C. (1973). Thick description. Toward an interpretive theory of cultures. In C. Geertz (Ed.), *The interpretation of cultures* (pp. 3-30). New York: Basic Books.
Gerbner, G., Holsti, O. R., Krippendorff, K., Paisley, W. J., & Stone, P. J. (1969). *The analysis of communication content.* New York: Wiley.
Gergen, K. J. (1985). The social constructionist movement in modern psychology. *American Psychologist, 40*(3), 266-275.
Gergen, K. J. (1999). *An invitation to social construction.* London: Sage Publications.
Gersick, C. J. (1988). Time and transition in work teams. Toward a new model of group development. *Academy of Management Journal, 31*(1), 9-41.
Gersick, C. J. G., & Hackman, J. R. (1990). Habitual routines in task-performing teams. *Organizational Behavior and Human Decision Processes, 47*(1), 65-91.
Gibson, C. B. (2001). From knowledge accumulation to accommodation. Cycles of collective cognition in work groups. *Journal of Organizational Behavior, 22*(2), 121-134.
Giddens, A. (1979). *Central problems in social theory. Action, structure and contraction in social analysis.* Berkeley, Los Angeles: University of California Press.

Giddens, A. (1984). *The constitution of society. Outline of the theory of structuration.* Cambridge: Polity Press.
Ginsberg, A. (1990). Connecting diversification to performance. A sociocognitive approach. *Academy of Management Review, 15*(3), 514-535.
Ginsberg, A. (1994). Minding the competition. From mapping to mastery. *Strategic Management Journal, 15*(Winter Special Issue), 153-174.
Ginsberg, A., & Venkatraman, N. (1992). Investing in new information technology. The role of competitive posture and issue diagnosis. *Strategic Management Journal, 13*(Summer Special Issue), 37-53.
Gioia, D. A. (1986). Symbols, scripts and sensemaking. Creating meaning in the organizational experience. In H. P. Sims & D. A. Gioia (Eds.), *The thinking organization. Dynamics of organizational social cognition* (pp. 49-74). San Francisco: Jossey-Bass.
Gioia, D. A., & Sims, H. P. (1986). Introduction. Social cognition in organizations. In D. A. Gioia & H. P. Sims (Eds.), *The thinking organization. Dynamics of organizational social cognition* (pp. 1-19). San Francisco: Jossey-Bass.
Gioia, D. A., Thomas, J. B., Clark, S. M., & Chittipeddi, K. (1994). Symbolism and strategic change in academia. The dynamics of sensemaking and influence. *Organization Science, 5*(3), 363-383.
Glaser, B. G. (1978). *Theoretical sensitivity. Advances in the methodology of Grounded Theory.* Mill Valley: The Sociology Press.
Glaser, B. G., & Strauss, A. L. (1967). *Discovery of Grounded Theory. Strategies for qualitative research.* Chicago: Aldine Transaction.
Glasersfeld, E. v. (1982). An interpretation of Piaget's constructivism. *Revue Internationale de Philosophie, 36*(4), 612-635.
Glasersfeld, E. v. (1995). *Radical constructivism. A way of knowing and learning.* London: The Falmer Press.
Gluchowski, P., Gabriel, R., & Dittmar, C. (2008). *Management Support Systeme und Business Intelligence. Computergestützte Informationssysteme für Fach- und Führungskräfte* (2 ed.). Berlin u.a.: Springer.
Göbel, E. (2002). *Neue Institutionenökonomik. Konzeption und betriebswirtschaftliche Anwendungen.* Stuttgart: Lucius und Lucius.
Goffman, E. (1961). *Encounters. Two studies in the sociology of interaction.* Indianapolis: Bobbs-Merrill.
Golsorkhi, D. (2006). *La fabrique de la stratégie. Une perspective multidimensionnelle.* Paris: Vuibert.
Golsorkhi, D., Rouleau, L., Seidl, D., & Vaara, E. (2009). *Cambridge handbook of strategy as practice.* Cambridge: CUP.
Gomez, P. (1993). *Wertmanagement. Vernetzte Strategien für Unternehmen im Wandel.* Düsseldorf: Econ.
Gorse, C. A., & Emmitt, S. (2007). Communication behaviour during management and design team meetings. A comparison of group interaction. *Construction Management and Economics, 25*(4), 1197-1213.
Grant, D. (2002). The knowledge-based view of the firm. In N. Bontis & C. W. Choo (Eds.), *The strategic management of intellectual capital and organizational knowledge. A collection of readings* (pp. 133-148). Oxford: Oxford University Press.
Grant, D., Hardy, C., Oswick, C., & Putnam, L. L. (2003). *The SAGE handbook of organizational discourse.* London: Sage Publications.
Grant, R. M. (2003). Strategic planning in a turbulent environment. Evidence from the oil majors. *Strategic Management Journal, 24*(6), 491-517.

Gray, B., Bougon, M. G., & Donnellon, A. (1985). Organizations as constructions and deconstructions of meaning. *Journal of Management, 11*(2), 83-98.
Greeno, J. G. (1998). The situativity of knowing, learning, and research. *American Psychologist, 53*(1), 5-26.
Greve, H. R. (1998). Managerial cognition and the mimetic adoption of market positions. What you see is what you do. *Strategic Management Journal, 19*(10), 967-988.
Guzzo, R. A., & Salas, E. (1995). *Team effectiveness and decision making in organizations*. San Francisco: Jossey-Bass.
Hahn, D., & Hungenberg, H. (2001). *PuK. Wertorientierte Controllingkonzepte. Planung und Kontrolle, Planungs- und Kontrollsysteme, Planungs- und Kontrollrechnung* (6 ed.). Wiesbaden: Gabler.
Hahn, D., & Taylor, B. (2006). *Strategische Unternehmensplanung. Strategische Unternehmensführung. Stand und Entwicklungstendenzen* (9 ed.). Berlin: Springer.
Haleblian, J., & Finkelstein, S. (1993). Top management team size, CEO dominance, and firm performance. The moderating roles of environmental turbulence and discretion. *Academy of Management Journal, 36*(4), 844-863.
Haley, U. C., & Stumpf, S. A. (1989). Cognitive trails in strategic decision making. Linking theories of personalities and cognitions. *Journal of Management Studies, 26*(5), 478-497.
Hambrick, D. C., Cho, T. S., & Chen, M.-J. (1996). The influence of top management team heterogeneity on firms' competitive moves. *Administrative Science Quarterly, 41*(4), 659-684.
Hambrick, D. C., & Mason, P. A. (1984). Upper echelons. The organization as a reflection of its top managers. *Academy of Management Review, 9*(2), 193-206.
Hamel, G., & Prahalad, C. K. (1994). *Competing for the future*. Boston: Harvard Business School Press.
Hannan, M. T., & Freeman, J. (1989). *Organizational ecology*. Cambridge (Mass.), London: Harvard University Press.
Hansen, G. S., & Wernerfelt, B. (1989). Determinants of firm performance. The relative importance of economic and organizational factors. *Strategic Management Journal, 10*(5), 399-411.
Hart, S. L. (1992). An integrated framework of strategy-making processes. *Academy of Management Review, 17*(2), 327-351.
Hart, S. L., & Banbury, C. (1994). How strategy-making processes can make a difference. *Strategic Management Journal, 15*(4), 251-269.
Harvard Business School. (2009). Business case studies. Retrieved February 22nd, 2009, from http://harvardbusinessonline.hbsp.harvard.edu/hbsp/case_studies.jsp?_requestid=1220
Hastie, R. (1981). Schematic principles in human memory. In E. T. Higgins, C. P. Herman & M. P. Zanna (Eds.), *Social cognition. The Ontario symposium* (Vol. 1, pp. 39-88). Hillsdale, NJ: Lawrence Erlbaum Associates.
Hayes, J., & Allinson, C. W. (1998). Cognitive style and the theory and practice of individual and collective learning in organizations. *Human Relations, 51*(7), 847-871.
Hedberg, B. (1981). How organizations learn and unlearn. In P. C. Nystrom & W. H. Starbuck (Eds.), *Handbook of organizational design* (Vol. 1, pp. 3-27). London: Oxford University Press.
Hendry, J., & Seidl, D. (2003). The structure and significance of strategic episodes. Social systems theory and the routine practices of strategic change. *Journal of Management Studies, 40*(1), 175-196.
Hickson, D. J., Butler, R. J., Cray, D., Mallory, G. R., & Wilson, D. C. (1986). *Top decisions. Strategic decision-making in organizations*. Oxford: Blackwell.
Hildenbrand, B. (1983). *Alltag und Krankheit. Ethnographie einer Familie*. Stuttgart: Klett.

Hinsz, V. B., Tindale, R. S., & Vollrath, D. A. (1997). The emerging conceptualization of groups as information processors. *Psychological Bulletin, 121*(1), 43-64.
Hirokawa, R. Y. (1982). Group communication and problem-solving effectiveness I. A critical review of inconsistent findings. *Communication Quarterly, 30*(2), 134-141.
Hirokawa, R. Y. (1983). Group communication and problem-solving effectiveness II. An exploratory investigation of procedural functions. *Western Journal of Speech Communication, 47*(1), 59-74.
Hitt, M. A., Dacin, T. M., Tyler, B. B., & Park, D. (1997). Understanding the differences in Korean and U.S. executives' strategic orientations. *Strategic Management Journal, 18*(2), 159-167.
Hodgkinson, G. P. (2001a). Cognitive processes in strategic management. Some emerging trends and future directions. In N. Anderson, D. S. Ones, H. K. Sinangil & C. Viswesvaran (Eds.), *Handbook of industrial work and organizational psychology* (Vol. 2, pp. 416-440). Thousand Oaks: Sage Publications.
Hodgkinson, G. P. (2001b). The psychology of strategic management. Diversity and cognition revisited. In C. L. Cooper & I. T. Robertson (Eds.), *International review of industrial and organizational psychology* (Vol. 16). Chichester: Wiley.
Hodgkinson, G. P., & Johnson, G. (1994). Exploring the mental models of competitive strategists. The case for a processual approach. *Journal of Management Studies, 31*(4), 525-525.
Hodgkinson, G. P., Maule, A. J., & Brown, N. J. (2004). Causal cognitive mapping in the organizational strategy field. A comparison of alternative elicitation procedures. *Organizational Research Methods, 7*(1), 3-26.
Hodgkinson, G. P., & Sparrow, P. R. (2002). *The competent organization. A psychological analysis of the strategic management process*. Buckingham: Open University Press.
Hodgkinson, G. P., Whittington, R., Johnson, G., & Schwarz, M. (2006). The role of strategy workshops in strategy development processes. Formality, communication, co-ordination and inclusion. *Long Range Planning, 39*(5), 479-496.
Hofer, C. W., & Schendel, D. (1978). *Strategy formulation. Analytical concepts*. St. Paul, MN: West.
Hoffmann-Riem, C. (1980). Die Sozialforschung einer interpretativen Soziologie. Der Datengewinn. *Kölner Zeitschrift für Soziologie und Sozialpsychologie, 32*(2), 339-372.
Hoffmann-Ripken, B. S. (2003). *Innovationsstrategien aus einer kognitionstheoretischen Perspektive*. Köln: Eul.
Hollingshead, A. B., Wittenbaum, G. M., Paulus, P. B., Hirokawa, R. Y., Ancona, D. G., Peterson, R. S., et al. (2004). A look at groups from the functional perspective. In M. S. Poole & A. B. Hollingshead (Eds.), *Theories of small groups. Interdisciplinary perspectives* (pp. 21-62). Thousand Oaks, London, New Delhi: Sage Publications.
Homburg, C. (1998). *Quantitative Betriebswirtschaftslehre. Entscheidungsunterstützung durch Modelle*. Wiesbaden: Gabler.
Huber, G. P. (1991). Organizational learning. The contributing processes and the literatures. *Organization Science, 2*(1), 88-115.
Huff, A. S. (1990). *Mapping strategic thought*. Chichester: Wiley.
Huff, A. S. (2005). Managerial and organizational cognition. Islands of coherence. In K. G. Smith & M. A. Hitt (Eds.), *Great minds in management* (pp. 331-354). Oxford: Oxford University Press.
Huff, A. S., & Reger, R. K. (1987). A review of strategic process research. *Journal of Management 13*(2), 211-236.
Hutzschenreuter, T., & Kleindienst, I. (2006). Strategy-process research. What have we learned and what is still to be explored. *Journal of Management, 32*(5), 673-720.

Iaquinto, A. L., & Friedrickson, J. W. (1997). Top management team agreement about the strategic decision process. A test of some of its determinants and consequences. *Strategic Management Journal 18*(1), 63-75.
Ickes, W., & Gonzalez, R. (1994). "Social" cognition and social cognition. From the subjective to the intersubjective. *Small Group Research, 25*(2), 294-315.
Ilgen, D. R., Hollenbeck, J. R., Johnson, M., & Jundt, D. (2005). Teams in organizations. From input-process-output models to IMOI models. *Annual Review of Psychology, 56*(1), 517-543.
Isabella, L. A. (1990). Evolving interpretations as a change unfolds. How managers construe key organizational events. *Academy of Management Journal, 33*(1), 7-41.
Isenberg, D. J. (1986). Group polarization. A critical review and meta-analysis. *Journal of Personality and Social Psychology, 50*(6), 1141-1151.
Jackson, S. E. (1992). Consequences of group composition for the interpersonal dynamics of strategic issue processing. *Advances in Strategic Management, 8*, 345-382.
Janis, I. L. (1972). *Victims of groupthink*. Boston: Houghton Mifflin Company.
Jarzabkowski, P. (2003). Strategic practices. An activity theory perspective based on continuity and change. *Journal of Management Studies, 40*(1), 23-55.
Jarzabkowski, P. (2004). Strategy as practice. Recursiveness, adaptation and practices-in-use. *Organization Studies, 25*(4), 529-560.
Jarzabkowski, P., Balogun, J., & Seidl, D. (2007). Strategizing. The challenges of a practice perspective. *Human Relations, 60*(1), 5-27.
Jarzabkowski, P., & Seidl, D. (2008). The role of meetings in the social practice of strategy. *Organization Studies, 29*(11), 1391-1426.
Jarzabkowski, P., & Sillince, J. (2007). A rhetoric-in-context approach to building commitment to multiple strategic goals. *Organization Studies, 28*(11), 1639-1665.
Jehn, K. A. (1997). A qualitative analysis of conflict types and dimensions in organizational groups. *Administrative Science Quarterly, 42*(3), 530-557.
Jehn, K. A., Northcraft, G. B., & Neale, M. A. (1999). Why differences make a difference. A field study of diversity, conflict, and performance in workgroups. *Administrative Science Quarterly, 44*(4), 741-763.
Jemison, D. B. (1981). The contributions of administrative behavior to strategic management. *Academy of Management Review, 6*(4), 633-642.
Johnson, D. R., & Hoopes, D. G. (2003). Managerial cognition, sunk costs, and the evolution of industry structure. *Strategic Management Journal, 24*(10), 1057-1068.
Johnson, G. (2008). Ritualizing strategic thinking. The effectiveness of the strategic away day. *Strategic Direction, 24*(1), 3-5.
Johnson, G., Langley, A., Melin, L., & Whittington, R. (2007). *Strategy as practice. Research directions and resources*. Cambridge: Cambridge University Press.
Johnson, G., Melin, L., & Whittington, R. (2003). Micro strategy and strategizing. Towards an activity-based view. *Journal of Management Studies, 40*(1), 3-22.
Johnson, M. (1987). *The body in the mind. The bodily basis of meaning, imagination, and reason*. Chicago: University of Chicago Press.
Jones, R. A., Linder, D. E., Kiesler, C. A., Zanna, M., & Brehm, J. (1968). Internal states or external stimuli. Observers' attitude judgments and the dissonance theory self-persuation controversy. *Journal of Experimental Social Psychology, 4*(3), 247-269.
Kahlbaugh, P. E. (1993). James Mark Baldwin. A bridge between social and cognitive theories of development. *Journal of Theory for Social Behavior, 23*(1), 79-103.
Kahneman, D., Slovic, P., & Tversky, A. (1982). *Judgement under uncertainty. Heuristics and biases*. New York: Cambridge University Press.

Kamens, D. H. (1977). Legitimizing myths and educational organization. The relationship between organizational ideology and formal structure. *American Sociological Review, 42*(2), 208-219.

Kauer, D., Waldeck, T. C. P. z., & Schäffer, U. (2007). Effects of top management team characteristics on strategic decision making. Shifting attention to team member personalities and mediating processes. *Management Decision, 45*(6), 942-967.

Kelle, U. (1998). *Empirisch begründete Theoriebildung. Zur Logik und Methodologie interpretativer Sozialforschung* (2 ed.). Weinheim: Deutscher Studienverlag.

Kelle, U., & Kluge, S. (1999). *Vom Einzelfall zum Typus. Fallvergleich und Fallkontrastierung in der qualitativen Sozialforschung.* Opladen: Leske + Budrich.

Ketchen Jr, D. J., Thomas, J. B., & McDaniel Jr, R. R. (1996). Process, content and context. Synergistic effects on organizational performance. *Journal of Management, 22*(2), 231-257.

Kieffer, G. D. (1989). *The strategy of meetings.* New York: Warner.

Kiesler, S., & Sproull, L. (1982). Managerial response to changing environments. Perspectives on problem sensing from social cognition. *Administrative Science Quarterly, 27*(4), 548-570.

Kilduff, M., Angelmar, R., & Mehra, A. (2000). Top management-team diversity and firm performance. Examining the role of cognitions. *Organization Science, 11*(1), 21-34.

Kirsch, W. (1969). Die Unternehmensziele in organisationstheoretischer Sicht. *Zeitschrift für betriebswirtschaftliche Forschung, 21*, 665-675.

Kirsch, W. (1970). *Entscheidungsprozesse, Band 1: Verhaltenswissenschaftliche Ansätze der Entscheidungstheorie.* Wiesbaden: Gabler.

Kirsch, W. (1971). *Entscheidungsprozesse, Band 3: Entscheidungen in Organisationen.* Wiesbaden: Gabler.

Kirsch, W. (1991). *Unternehmenspolitik und strategische Unternehmensführung* (2 ed.). Herrsching: Verlag Barbara Kirsch.

Kirsch, W. (1992). *Kommunikatives Handeln, Autopoiese, Rationalität. Sondierungen zu einer evolutionären Führungslehre.* München: Verlag Barbara Kirsch.

Kirsch, W. (1993). *Wegweiser zur Konstruktion einer Theorie der strategischen Unternehmensführung* (unveröffentlichtes Arbeitspapier). München.

Kirsch, W. (1994). *Die Handhabung von Entscheidungsproblemen. Einführung in die Theorie der Entscheidungsprozesse* (4 ed.). Herrsching: Verlag Barbara Kirsch.

Kirsch, W. (1996). *Wegweiser zur Konstruktion einer evolutionären Theorie der Strategischen Führung.* München: Verlag Barbara Kirsch.

Kirsch, W. (1997a). *Kommunikatives Handeln, Autopoiese, Rationalität. Sondierungen zu einer evolutionären Führungslehre* (2 ed.). München: Verlag Barbara Kirsch.

Kirsch, W. (1997b). *Strategisches Management. Die geplante Evolution von Unternehmen.* München: Verlag Barbara Kirsch.

Kirsch, W. (1997c). *Wegweiser zur Konstruktion einer evolutionären Theorie der Strategischen Führung* (2 ed.). München: Verlag Barbara Kirsch.

Kirsch, W. (1998). *Die Handhabung von Entscheidungsproblemen. Einführung in die Theorie der Entscheidungsprozesse* (5 ed.). Herrsching: Verlag Barbara Kirsch.

Kirsch, W., Esser, W.-M., & Gabele, E. (1979). *Das Management des geplanten Wandels von Organisationen.* Stuttgart: Schäffer-Poeschel.

Kirsch, W., & Maaßen, H. (1990). *Managementsysteme. Planung und Kontrolle* (2 ed.). München: Verlag Barbara Kirsch.

Kirsch, W., & Mayer, G. (1976). Die Handhabung komplexer Probleme in Organisationen. In W. Kirsch (Ed.), *Entscheidungsverhalten und Handhabung von Problemen* (Vol. 13, pp. 99-219). München: Universität München.

Kirsch, W., & Trux, W. (1989). Strategisches Management. In N. Szyperski (Ed.), *Handwörterbuch der Planung* (pp. 1924-1935). Stuttgart: Poeschel.

Kirshner, D., & Whitson, J. A. (1997a). Editor's introduction to situated cognition. Social, semiotic, and psychological perspectives. In D. Kirshner & J. A. Whitson (Eds.), *Situated cognition. Social, semiotic, and psychological perspectives* (pp. 1-16). Mahwah, New Jersey: Lawrence Erlbaum Associates, Inc.

Kirshner, D., & Whitson, J. A. (1997b). *Situated cognition. Social, semiotic, and psychological perspectives*. Mahwah, New Jersey: Lawrence Erlbaum Associates, Inc.

Klages, H. (1971). *Planungspolitik*. Stuttgart, Berlin: Kohlhammer.

Klimecki, R., Probst, G. J. B., & Eberl, P. (1994). *Entwicklungsorientiertes Management*. Stuttgart: Schäffer-Poeschel.

Klimoski, R., & Mohammed, S. (1994). Team mental models. Construct or metaphor? *Journal of Management, 20*(2), 403-437.

Knight, D., Pearce, C. L., Smith, K. G., Olian, J. D., Sims, H. P., Smith, K. A., et al. (1999). Top management team diversity, group process, and strategic consensus. *Strategic Management Journal, 20*(5), 445-465.

Knyphausen-Aufseß, D. z. (1995). *Theorie der strategischen Unternehmensführung. State of the Art und neue Perspektiven*. Wiesbaden: Gabler.

Kogut, B., & Zander, U. (1992). Knowledge of the firm, combinative capabilities and the replication of technology. *Organization Science, 3*(3), 383-397.

Komorita, S. S., & Kravitz, D. A. (1983). Coalition formation. Social psychological approaches. In P. Paulus (Ed.), *Basic group processes* (pp. 179-203). New York: Springer.

Koners, U., & Goffin, K. (2007). Managers' perceptions of learning in new product development. *International Journal of Operations & Product Management, 27*(1), 49-68.

Krippendorff, K. (1980). *Content analysis. An introduction to its methodology*. Beverly Hills: Sage Publications.

Krogh, G. v. (1998). *Knowing in firms*. London: Sage Publications.

Krogh, G. v., & Roos, J. (1995). *Organizational epistemology*. New York: Palgrave Macmillan.

Krogh, G. v., & Venzin, M. (1995). Anhaltende Wettbewerbsvorteile durch Wissensmanagement. *Die Unternehmung, 49*(6), 417-436.

Krüger, W. (2002). *Excellence in Change. Wege zur strategischen Neuerung*. Wiesbaden: Gabler.

Kvale, S. (1995). The social construction of validity. *Qualitative Inquiry, 1*(1), 19-40.

Langfield-Smith, K. (1992). Exploring the need for a shared cognitive map. *Journal of Management Studies, 29*(3), 349-368.

Lant, T. K. (2002). Organizational cognition and interpretation. In J. A. Baum (Ed.), *The Blackwell companion to organizations* (pp. 344-362). Oxford: Blackwell.

Lant, T. K., & Mezias, S. J. (1990). Managing discontinuous change. A simulation study of organizational learning and entrepreneurship. *Strategic Management Journal, 11*(4), 147-179.

Lant, T. K., Milliken, F. J., & Batra, B. (1992). The role of managerial learning and interpretation in strategic persistence and reorientation. An empirical exploration. *Strategic Management Journal, 13*(8), 585-608.

Lant, T. K., & Shapira, Z. (2000). *Organizational cognition. Computation and interpretation*. Mahwah, NJ: Lawrence Erlbaum Associates.

Larson, J. R., & Christensen, C. (1993). Groups as problem-solving units. Toward a new meaning of social cognition. *British Journal of Social Psychology, 32*(1), 5-30.

Lau, D. C., & Murnighan, J. K. (1998). Demographic diversity and faultlines. The compositional dynamics of organizational groups. *Academy of Management Journal, 23*(2), 325-340.

Laughlin, P. R. (1980). Social combination processes of cooperative problem-solving groups on verbal intellective tasks. In M. Fishbein (Ed.), *Progress in social psychology* (Vol. 1, pp. 127-155). Hillsdale, NJ: Erlbaum.

Laughlin, P. R., & Earley, P. C. (1982). Social combination models, persuasive arguments theory, social comparison theory, and choice shift. *Journal of Personality and Social Psychology, 42*(2), 273-280.

Laughlin, P. R., & Hollingshead, A. B. (1995). A theory of collective induction. *Organizational Behavior and Human Decision Processes, 61*(1), 94-107.

Lave, J. (1988). *Cognition in practice. Mind, mathematics, and culture in everyday life*. Cambridge: Cambridge Univesity Press.

Lave, J., & Wenger, E. (1991). *Situated learning. Legitimate peripheral participation*. Cambridge: Cambridge University Press.

Lawrence, B. S. (1997). The black box of organizational demography. *Organization Science, 8*(1), 1-22.

Learned, E. P., Christensen, C. R., Andrews, K. R., & Guth, W. D. (1965). *Business policy. Text and cases*. Homewood, IL: RD Irwin.

Lee, T. W. (1999). *Using qualitative methods in organizational research*. Thousand Oaks: Sage Publications.

Levine, J. M., Resnick, L. B., & Higgins, T. E. (1993). Social foundations of cognition. *Annual Review of Psychology, 44*, 585-612.

Levinthal, D. A., & March, J. G. (1993). The myopia of learning. *Strategic Management Journal, 14*(Winter Special Issue), 95-112.

Lincoln, Y. S., & Guba, E. G. (1985). *Naturalistic inquiry*. Newbury Park, London, New Delhi: Sage Publications.

Lindblom, C. E. (1959). The science of „muddling through". *Public Administration Review, 19*(2), 79-88.

Lindblom, C. E. (1964). Contexts for change and strategy. *Public Administration Review, 24*(3), 157-158.

Lindblom, C. E. (1965). *The intelligence of democracy*. New York, London: Free Press.

Lorange, P., & Vancil, R. (1977). *Strategic planning systems*. Englewood Cliffs: Prentice Hall.

Louis, M. R. (1980). Surprise and sense making. What newcomers experience in entering unfamiliar organizational settings. *Administrative Science Quarterly, 25*(2), 226-251.

Lovaglia, M., Mannix, E. A., Samuelson, C. D., Sell, J., & Wilson, R. K. (2004). Conflict, power, and status in groups. In M. S. Poole & A. B. Hollingshead (Eds.), *Theories of small groups. Interdisciplinary perspectives* (pp. 139-184). Thousand Oaks, London, New Delhi: Sage Publications.

Luhmann, N. (1984). *Soziale Systeme. Grundriß einer allgemeinen Theorie*. Frankfurt a. M.: Suhrkamp.

Lyles, M. A., & Schwenk, C. R. (1992). Top management, strategy and organizational knowledge structures. *Journal of Management Studies, 29*(2), 155-174.

Lyles, M. A., & Thomas, H. (1988). Strategic problem formulation. Biases and assumptions embedded in alternative decision-making models. *Journal of Management Studies, 25*(2), 132-145.

Madhavan, R., & Grover, R. (1998). From embedded knowledge to embodied knowledge. New product development as knowledge management. *Journal of Marketing, 62*(4), 1-12.

Madsen, D. B. (1978). Issue importance and group choice shifts. A persuasive arguments approach. *Journal of Personality and Social Psychology, 36*(10), 1118-1127.
Maitlis, S. (2005). The social processes of organizational sensemaking. *Academy of Management Journal, 48*(1), 21-49.
Maitlis, S., & Lawrence, B. (2003). Orchestral manoeuvres in the dark. Understanding failure in organizational strategizing. *Journal of Management Studies, 40*(1), 109-140.
Malik, F., & Probst, G. J. B. (1981). Evolutionäres Management. *Die Unternehmung, 35*(2), 121-140.
Mandl, H., Friedrich, H. F., & Hron, A. (1988). Theoretische Ansätze zum Wissenserwerb. In H. Mandl & H. Spada (Eds.), *Wissenspsychologie* (pp. 123-160). Weinheim: Psychologie-Verlags-Union.
Mannheim, K. (1958). *Mensch und Gesellschaft im Zeitalter des Umbaus*. Darmstadt: Wissenschaftliche Buchgesellschaft.
March, J. G. (1997). Understanding how decisions happen in organizations. In Z. Shapira (Ed.), *Organizational decision making* (pp. 9-32). Cambridge: Cambridge University Press.
March, J. G. (1999). *The pursuit of organizational intellligence*. Oxford: Blackwell.
March, J. G., & Simon, H. A. (1958). *Organizations*. New York: Wiley.
Markoczy, L., & Goldberg, J. (1995). A method for eliciting and comparing causal maps. *Journal of Management, 21*(1), 305-333.
Mason, E. S. (1939). Price and production policies of large scale enterprises. *American Economic Review, 29*(2), 61-74.
Mathieu, J. E., Goodwin, G. F., Heffner, T. S., Salas, E., & Cannon-Bowers, J. A. (2000). The influence of shared mental models on team process and performance. *Journal of Applied Psychology, 85*(2), 273-283.
Mayring, P. (2002). *Einführung in die qualitative Sozialforschung. Eine Anleitung zu qualitativem Denken* (5 ed.). München: Psychologie Verlags Union.
Mayring, P. (2004). Qualitative content analysis. In U. Flick, E. v. Kardorff & I. Steinke (Eds.), *A companion to qualitative research* (pp. 266-269). London, Thousand Oaks, New Delhi: Sage Publications.
Mayring, P. (2007). *Qualitative Inhaltsanalyse. Grundlagen und Techniken* (9 ed.). Weinheim und Basel: Beltz.
Maznevski, M. L. (1994). Understanding our differences. Performance in decision-making groups with diverse members. *Human Relations, 47*(5), 531-552.
McGrath, J. E. (1984). *Groups. Interaction and performance*. Harlow - Essex: Prentice Hall.
McGrath, J. E. (1991). Time, interactions, and performance (TIP). A theory of groups. *Small Groups Research, 22*(2), 147-174.
McGrath, J. E., & Tschan, F. (2004). Dynamics in groups and teams. Groups as complex action systems. In M. S. Poole & A. H. van de Ven (Eds.), *Handbook of organizational change and innovation* (pp. 50-72). Oxford, New York: Oxford University Press.
McKiernan, P., & Carter, C. (2004). The millennium nexus. Strategic management at the cross-roads. *European Management Review, 1*(1), 14-68.
Mead, G. H. (1934). *Mind, self, and society*. Chicago: University of Chicago Press.
Meindl, J. R., Stubbart, C. I., & Porac, J. F. (1994). Cognition within and between organizations. Five key questions. *Organization Science, 5*(3), 289-293.
Ménard, C., & Shirley, M. M. (2005). *Handbook of new institutional economics*. Dordrecht: Springer.
Miller, D. (1987). Strategy making and structure. Analysis and implications for performance. *Academy of Management, 30*(1), 7-32.

Milliken, F. J., & Vollrath, D. A. (1991). Strategic decision-making tasks and group effectiveness. Insights from theory and research on small group performance. *Human Relations, 44*(12), 1229-1253.
Minsky, M. (1975). A framework for representing knowledge. In P. H. Winston (Ed.), *The psychology of computer vision* (pp. 211-277). New York: MacGraw-Hill.
Mintzberg, H. (1973). Strategy-making in three modes. *California Management Review, 16*(2), 44-53.
Mintzberg, H. (1978). Patterns in strategy formation. *Management Science, 24*(9), 934-948.
Mintzberg, H. (1987). The strategy concept I. Five p's for strategy. *California Management Review, 30*(1), 11-24.
Mintzberg, H. (1990). Strategy formation. Schools of thought. In J. W. Frederickson (Ed.), *Perspectives on strategic management* (pp. 105-235). New York: Harper Business.
Mintzberg, H. (1994). *Rise and fall of strategic planning*. New York: Free Press.
Mintzberg, H., Ahlstrand, B., & Lampel, J. (2007). *Strategy Safari. Eine Reise durch die Wildnis des strategischen Managements* (2 ed.). Heidelberg: Redline Wirtschaft.
Mintzberg, H., & Lampel, J. (1999). Reflecting on the strategy process. *Sloan Management Review, 40*(3), 21-30.
Mintzberg, H., & McHugh, A. (1985). Strategy making in an adhocracy. *Administrative Science Quarterly, 30*(2), 160-197.
Mintzberg, H., Raisinghani, D., & Théorêt, A. (1976). The structure of 'unstructured' decision processes. *Administrative Science Quarterly, 21*(2), 264-275.
Mintzberg, H., & Waters, J. A. (1982). Tracking strategy in an entrepreneurial firm. *Academy of Management Journal, 25*(3), 465-499.
Mintzberg, H., & Waters, J. A. (1984). Researching the formation of strategies. The history of Canadian Lady, 1936-1976. In R. B. Lamb (Ed.), *Competitive strategic management* (pp. 62-93). Englewood Cliffs, NJ: Prentice-Hall.
Mintzberg, H., & Waters, J. A. (1985). Of strategies. Deliberate and emergent. *Strategic Management Journal, 6*(3), 257-272.
Mohammed, S., & Angell, L. C. (2004). Surface- and deep-level diversity in workgroups. Examining the moderating effects of team orientation and team process on relationship conflict. *Journal of Organizational Behavior, 25*(8), 1015-1039.
Mohammed, S., & Dumville, B. C. (2001). Team mental models in a team knowledge framework. Expanding theory and measurement across disciplinary boundaries. *Journal of Organizational Behavior, 22*(2), 89-106.
Mohammed, S., Klimoski, R., & Rentsch, J. R. (2000). The measurement of team mental models. We have no shared schema. *Organizational Research Methods, 3*(2), 123-165.
Mohammed, S., & Ringseis, E. (2001). Cognitive diversity and consensus in group decision making. The role of inputs, processes, and outcomes. *Organizational Behavior and Human Decision Processes, 85*(2), 310-335.
Moscovici, S. (1988). Notes towards a description of social representations. *European Journal of Social Psychology, 18*(3), 211-250.
Mowrer, O. H. (1947). On the dual nature of learning. A reinterpretation of 'conditioning' and 'problem solving'. *Harvard Educational Review, 17*(2), 102-148.
Müser, M. (2000). *Ressourcenorientierte Unternehmensführung. Zentrale Bestandteile und ihre Gestaltung*. Lohmar: Josef Eul Verlag GmbH.
Nadkarni, S., & Narayanan, V. K. (2007a). The evolution of collective strategy frames in high- and low-velocity industries. *Organization Science, 18*(4), 688-710.
Nadkarni, S., & Narayanan, V. K. (2007b). Strategic schemas, strategic flexibility, and firm performance. The moderating role of industry clockspeed. *Strategic Management Journal, 28*(3), 243-270.

Nag, R., Hambrick, D. C., & Chen, M.-J. (2007). What is strategic management, really? Inductive derivation of a consensus definition of the field. *Strategic Management Journal, 28*(9), 935-955.

Narayanan, V. K., & Fahey, L. (1982). The micro-politics of strategy formulation. *Academy of Management Review, 7*(1), 25-34.

Nees, D. B. (1983). Simulation. A complementary method for research on strategic decision-making processes. *Strategic Management Journal, 4*(2), 175-185.

Neidhardt, F. (1979). Das innere System sozialer Gruppen. *Kölner Zeitschrift für Soziologie und Sozialpsychologie, 31*(4), 639-660.

Neisser, U. (1976). *Cognition and reality.* San Francisco: W.H. Freeman.

Nelson, R. R., & Winter, S. G. (1982). *An evolutionary theory of economic change.* Cambridge: Harvard University Press.

Newman, D., Griffin, P., & Cole, M. (1989). *The construction zone. Working for cognitive change in school.* New York: Cambridge University Press.

Nicolini, D. (1999). Comparing methods for mapping organizational cognition. *Organization Studies, 20*(5), 833-860.

Nisbett, R. E., & Ross, L. (1980). *Human inference. Strategies and shortcomings of social judgement.* Englewoods Cliffs: Prentice Hall.

Nonaka, I. (1994). A dynamic theory of organizational knowledge creation. *Organization Science, 5*(1), 14-37.

Nonaka, I. (2005). Managing organizational knowledge. Theoretical and methodological foundations. In K. G. Smith & M. A. Hitt (Eds.), *Great minds in management* (pp. 373-393). Oxford: Oxford University Press.

Nonaka, I., & Konno, N. (1998). The concept of 'Ba'. Building a foundation for knowledge creation. *California Management Review, 40*(3), 40-54.

Nonaka, I., Krogh, G. v., & Voelpel, S. (2006). Organizational knowledge creation theory. Evolutionary paths and future advances. *Organization Studies, 27*(8), 1179-1208.

Nonaka, I., & Takeuchi, H. (1995). *The knowledge-creating company. How Japanese companies create the dynamics of innovation.* New York: Oxford University Press.

Norman, D. A. (1982). *Learning and memory.* San Francisco: W. H. Freeman and Company.

Norman, D. A. (1993). Cognition in the head and in the world. An introduction to the special issue on situated action. *Cognitive Science News, 17*(1), 1-6.

Nutt, P. C. (1984). Types of organizational decision processes. *Administrative Science Quarterly, 29*(3), 414-450.

Nystrom, P. C., & Starbuck, W. H. (1984). Managing beliefs in organizations. *Journal of Applied Behavioral Science, 20*(3), 277-287.

Olson, B. J., Bao, Y., & Parayitam, S. (2007). Strategic decision making. The effects of cognitive diversity, conflict, and trust on decision outcomes. *Journal of Management, 33*(2), 196-222.

Orlikowski, W. J. (1992). The duality of technology. Rethinking the concept of technology in organizations. *Organization Science, 3*(3), 398-427.

Orlikowski, W. J. (2000). Using technology and constituting structure. A practice lens for studying technology in organizations. *Organization Science, 11*(4), 404-428.

Ouchi, J. K., & Wilkins, A. L. (1985). Organizational culture. *Annual Review of Sociology, 11*, 457-483.

Papadakis, V. M., Lioukas, S., & Chambers, D. (1998). Strategic decision-making processes. The role of management and context. *Strategic Management Journal, 19*(2), 115-147.

Paroutis, S., & Pettigrew, A. (2007). Strategizing in the multi-business firm. Strategy teams at multiple levels and over time. *Human Relations, 60*(1), 99-135.

Pea, R. D. (1993). Practices of distributed intelligence and designs for education. In G. Salomon (Ed.), *Distributed cognitions. Psychological and educational considerations* (pp. 47-87). Cambridge: Cambridge University Press.

Pelled, L. H. (1996). Demographic diversity, conflict, and work group outcomes. An intervening process theory. *Organization Science, 7*(6), 615-631.

Pelled, L. H., Eisenhardt, K. M., & Xin, K. R. (1999). Exploring the black box. An analysis of work group diversity, conflict, and performance. *Administration Science Quarterly, 44*(1), 1-28.

Pettigrew, A. (1987). *The management of strategic change*. Oxford: Basil Blackwell.

Pfeffer, J. (1981). Management as symbolic action. The creation and maintenance of organizational paradigms. In L. L. Cummings & B. M. Staw (Eds.), *Research in organizational behavior* (Vol. 3, pp. 1-52). Greenwich, CT: JAI.

Piaget, J. (1926). *The child's conception of the world*. London: Routledge and Kegan Paul.

Piaget, J. (1952). *The origins of intelligence in children*. New York: International Universities Press.

Picot, A., Reichwald, R., & Wigand, R. T. (2001). *Die grenzenlose Unternehmung. Information, Organisation und Management* (4 ed.). Wiesbaden: Gabler.

Picot, A., & Scheuble, S. (2000). Die Rolle des Wissensmanagements in erfolgreichen Unternehmen. In H. Mandl & G. Reinmann-Rothmeier (Eds.), *Wissensmanagement. Informationszuwachs - Wissensschwund? Die strategische Bedeutung des Wissensmanagements* (pp. 19-37). München: Oldenbourg.

Polanyi, M. (1967). *The tacit dimension*. London: Routledge & Kegan Paul.

Poole, M. S. (1981). Decision development in small groups I. A comparison of two models. *Communication Monographs, 48*(1), 1-24.

Poole, M. S. (1983). Decision development in small groups III. A multiple sequence model of group decision making. *Communication Monographs, 50*(4), 321-344.

Poole, M. S., & Hollingshead, A. B. (2004). *Theories of small groups. Interdisciplinary perspectives*. Thousand Oaks, London, New Delhi: Sage Publications.

Poole, M. S., & Roth, J. (1989a). Decision development in small groups IV. A typology of group decision paths. *Human Communication Research, 15*(3), 323-356.

Poole, M. S., & Roth, J. (1989b). Decision development in small groups V. Test of a contingency model. *Human Communication Research, 15*(4), 549-589.

Popper, K. (1965). *Das Elend des Historizismus*. Tübingen: Mohr Siebeck.

Popper, K. (2002). *Logik der Forschung* (10 ed.). Tübingen: Mohr Siebeck.

Porac, J. F., & Thomas, H. (1990). Taxonomic mental models in competitor definition. *Journal of Management Studies, 15*(2), 224-240.

Porac, J. F., & Thomas, H. (1994). Cognitive categorization and subjective rivalry among retailers in a small city. *Journal of Applied Psychology, 79*(1), 54-66.

Porac, J. F., & Thomas, H. (2002). Managing cognition and strategy. Issues, trends and future directions. In A. Pettigrew, H. Thomas & R. Whittington (Eds.), *Handbook of strategy and management* (pp. 165-181). London, Thousand Oaks, New Delhi: Sage Publications.

Porac, J. F., Thomas, H., & Baden-Fuller, C. (1989). Competitive groups as cognitive communities. The case of Scottish knitwear manufacturers. *Journal of Management Studies, 26*(4), 397-416.

Porac, J. F., Thomas, H., Wilson, F., Paton, D., & Kanfer, A. (1995). Rivalry and the industry model of Scottish knitwear producers. *Administrative Science Quarterly, 40*(2), 203-227.

Porter, M. E. (1975). *Note on the structural analysis of industries*. Cambridge: Harvard Business School.

Porter, M. E. (1980). *Competitive advantage. Creating and sustaining superior performance.* New York: The Free Press.
Porter, M. E. (1981). The contributions of industrial organization to strategic management. *Academy of Management Review, 6*(4), 609-620.
Porter, M. E. (1985). *Competitive strategy. Techniques for analyzing industries and competitors.* New York: The Free Press.
Porter, M. E. (1997). *Wettbewerbsstrategie. Methoden zur Analyse von Branchen und Konkurrenten* (9 ed.). Frankfurt a. M.: Campus Verlag GmbH.
Powell, T. (1990). *Organizational skill. A neglected source of competitive advantage.* Paper presented at the Academy of Management Annual Meeting.
Prahalad, C. K., & Bettis, R. A. (1986). The dominant logic. A new linkage between diversity and performance. *Strategic Management Journal, 7*(6), 485-501.
Probst, G. J. B., & Büchel, B. S. T. (1994). *Organisationales Lernen. Wettbewerbsvorteil der Zukunft.* Wiesbaden: Gabler.
Putnam, L. L. (1986). Conflict in group decision-making. In R. Y. Hirokawa & M. S. Poole (Eds.), *Communication and group decision making* (pp. 175-196). Newbury Park, CA: Sage Publications.
Quigley, N. R., Tesluk, P. E., Locke, E. A., & Bartol, K. M. (2007). A multilevel investigation of the motivational mechanisms underlying knowledge sharing and performance. *Organization Science, 18*(1), 71-88.
Quinn, J. B. (1980). *Strategies for change. Logical incrementalism.* Homewood: Irwin.
Rajagopalan, N., Rasheed, A. A., & Datta, D. K. (1993). Strategic decision processes. Critical review and future directions. *Journal of Management, 19*(2), 349-384.
Rajagopalan, N., & Spreitzer, G. M. (1997). Toward a theory of strategic change. A multi-lens perspective and integrative framework. *Academy of Management Review, 22*(1), 48-79.
Rasche, C. (1994). *Wettbewerbsvorteile durch Kernkompetenzen. Ein ressourcenorientierter Ansatz.* Wiesbaden: Gabler.
Reger, R. K., & Huff, A. S. (1993). Strategic groups. A cognitive perspective. *Strategic Management Journal, 14*(2), 103-123.
Reger, R. K., & Palmer, T. B. (1996). Managerial categorization of competitors. Using old maps to navigate new environments. *Organization Science, 7*(1), 22-39.
Regnér, P. (2005). The pre-history of strategy processes. In S. W. Floyd, J. Roos, C. D. Jacobs & F. W. Kellermanns (Eds.), *Innovating strategy process* (pp. 23-32). Malden: Blackwell Publishing Ltd.
Reichenbach, H. (1938). *Experience and prediction. An analysis of the foundations and the structure of knowledge.* Chicago: University of Chicago Press.
Richardson, L. (1994). Writing. A method of inquiry. In N. K. Denzin & Y. S. Lincoln (Eds.), *Handbook of qualitative research* (pp. 516-529). Thousand Oaks: Sage Publications.
Roberto, M. A. (2004). Strategic decision-making processes. Beyond the efficiency-consensus trade-off. *Group & Organization Management, 29*(6), 625-658.
Rogers-Wynands, S. (2002). *Freilegung strategischen Managementwissens. Ein wissensdiagnostischer Ansatz.* Wiesbaden: Gabler.
Roloff, M. E., & Van Swol, L. M. (2007). Shared cognition and communication within group decision making and negotiation. In D. R. Roskos-Ewoldsen & J. L. Monahan (Eds.), *Communication and social cognition. Theories and methods* (pp. 171-195). Mahwah, New Jersey: Lawrence Erlbaum Associates, Inc.
Rothbart, M. K. (1981). Measurement of temperament in infancy. *Child Development, 52*(2), 569-578.
Rouleau, L., Allard-Poesi, F., & Warnier, V. (2007). Le management stratégique en pratiques. *Revue Francaise de Gestion, 174*(5, Special Issue).

Rumelhart, D. E. (1980). Schemata. The building blocks of cognition. In R. Spiro, B. Bruce & W. Brewer (Eds.), *Theoretical issues in reading comprehension* (pp. 33-58). Hillsdale, NJ: Erlbaum.

Rumelhart, D. E. (1984). Schemata and the cognitive system. In R. S. Wyer & T. K. Srull (Eds.), *Handbook of social cognition* (Vol. 1, pp. 161-188). Hillsdale, NJ: Erlbaum.

Rumelhart, D. E., & McClelland, J. L. (1986). *Parallel distributed processing. Explorations in the microstructure of cognition.* Cambridge, MA: MIT Press.

Rumelhart, D. E., & Ortony, A. (1977). The representation of knowledge in memory. In R. C. Anderson, R. Spiro & W. E. Montague (Eds.), *Schooling and the acquisition of knowledge* (pp. 99-136). Hillsdale, NJ: Lawrence Erlbaum Associates.

Rumelt, R. P., Schendel, D., & Teece, D. J. (1994). *Fundamental issues in strategy. A research agenda.* Boston, MA: Harvard Business School Press.

Ryle, G. (1949). *The concept of mind.* London: Hutchinson.

Sackmann, S. A. (1991). *Cultural knowledge in organizations. Exploring the collective mind.* Newberry Park, CA: Sage Publications.

Sagie, A., Elizur, D., & Koslowsky, M. (1995). Decision type, participative decision making (PDM), and organizational behavior. An experimental simulation. *Human Performance, 8*(2), 81-94.

Salomon, G. (1993). No distribution without individuals' cognition. A dynamic interactional view. In G. Salomon (Ed.), *Distributed cognitions. Psychological and educational considerations* (pp. 111-138). Cambridge: Cambridge University Press.

Salvato, C. (2003). The role of micro-strategies in the engineering of firm evolution. *Journal of Management Studies, 40*(1), 83-108.

Samra-Fredericks, D. (2003). Strategising as lived experience and strategists' everyday efforts to shape strategic direction. *Journal of Management Studies, 41*(Special Issue), 141-174.

Samra-Fredericks, D. (2004). Understanding the production of 'strategy' and 'organization' through talk amongst managerial elites. *Culture and Organization, 10*(2), 125-141.

Sandner, K. (1992). Unternehmenspolitik - Politik im Unternehmen. Zum Begriff des Politischen in der Betriebswirtschaftslehre. In K. Sandner (Ed.), *Politische Prozesse in Unternehmen* (2 ed., pp. 45-76). Berlin et al.: Physica-Verlag.

Schank, R. C., & Abelson, R. P. (1977). *Scripts, plans, goals and understanding. An inquiry into human knowledge structures.* Hillsdale: Erlbaum.

Scharpf, U. (1988). *Entscheidungsfindung im Gruppenprozess.* Konstanz: Hartung-Gorre.

Schatzki, T. R., Knorr-Cetina, K., & Savigny, E. v. (2001). *The practice turn in contemporary theory.* London: Routledge.

Scheele, B., & Groeben, N. (1988). *Dialog-Konsens-Methoden zur Rekonstruktion Subjektiver Theorien. Die Heidelberger Struktur-Lege-Technik, konsensuale Ziel-Mittel-Argumentation und kommunikative Flußdiagramm-Beschreibung von Handlungen.* Tübingen: Francke.

Schendel, D., & Cool, K. (1988). Development of the strategic management field. Some accomplishments and challenges. In J. H. Grant (Ed.), *Strategic management frontiers* (pp. 17-31). Greenwich, CT: JAI Press.

Schendel, D., & Hofer, C. (1979). *Strategic management. A new view of business planning and policy.* Boston: Little, Brown.

Schneider, S. C., & Angelmar, R. (1993). Cognition in organizational analysis. Who's minding the store? *Organization Studies, 14*(3), 347-374.

Schneider, U. (1996). Management in der wissensbasierten Unternehmung. Das Wissensnetz zwischen Mitarbeitern knüpfen. In U. Schneider (Ed.), *Wissensmanagement. Die Aktivierung des intellektuellen Kapitals* (pp. 13-48). Frankfurt: Frankf. Allg. Zeitung.

Scholl, W. (2004). *Innovation und Information. Wie in Unternehmen neues Wissen produziert wird.* Göttingen: Hogrefe.
Schreyögg, G., & Noss, C. (1995). Organisatorischer Wandel. Von der Organisationsentwicklung zur lernenden Organisation. *Die Betriebswirtschaft, 55*(2), 169-185.
Schüppel, J. (1996). *Wissensmanagement. Organisatorisches Lernen im Spannungsfeld von Wissens- und Lernbarrieren.* Wiesbaden: Gabler.
Schütz, A. (1960). *Der sinnhafte Aufbau der sozialen Welt. Eine Einleitung in die verstehende Soziologie.* Wien: Springer.
Schütz, A. (1962). *Collected papers. Volume I. Studies in social theory.* The Hague: Nijhoff.
Schwarz, M., & Nandhakumar, J. (2002). Conceptualizing the development of strategic ideas. A Grounded Theory analysis. *British Journal of Management, 13*(1), 67-82.
Schwarz, N. (1995). Social cognition. Information accessibility and use in social judgment. In E. E. Smith & D. N. Osherson (Eds.), *An invitation to cognitive science. Thinking* (Vol. 3, pp. 345-376). Cambridge, MA: MIT Press.
Schweiger, D. M., Sandberg, W. R., & Ragan, J. W. (1986). Group approaches for improving strategic decision making. A comparative analysis of dialectical inquiry, devil's advocacy, and consensus. *Academy of Management Journal, 29*(1), 51-71.
Schwenk, C. R. (1988). The cognitive perspective on strategic decision making. *Journal of Management Studies, 25*(1), 41-55.
Schwenk, C. R. (1989). Linking cognitive, organizational and political factors in explaining strategic change. *Journal of Management Studies, 26*(2), 177-187.
Schwenk, C. R. (1995). Strategic decision making. *Journal of Management, 21*(3), 471-493.
Seidl, D. (2007). General strategy concepts and the ecology of strategy discourses. A systemic–discursive perspective. *Organization Studies, 28*(2), 197-218.
Seiffert, H. (2001). *Einführung in die Wissenschaftstheorie 3. Handlungstheorie, Modallogik, Ethik, Systemtheorie* (3 ed.). München: C. H. Beck.
Shaw, M. E. (1964). Communication networks. In L. Berkowitz (Ed.), *Advances in experimental social psychology* (Vol. 1, pp. 111-147). New York: Academic Press.
Shaw, M. E. (1978). Communication networks fourteen years later. In L. Berkowitz (Ed.), *Group processes* (pp. 351-361). New York: Academic Press.
Shelly, R. K. (1997). Sequences and cycles in social interaction. *Small Group Research, 28*(3), 333-356.
Shotter, J. (1990). *Knowing of the third kind. Selected writings on psychology, rhetoric, and the culture of everyday social life.* Utrecht: ISOR, University of Utrecht.
Shrivastava, P., & Schneider, S. C. (1984). Organizational frames of references. *Human Relations, 37*(10), 795-809.
Sillince, J., & Mueller, F. (2007). Switching strategic perspective. The reframing of accounts of responsibility. *Organization Studies, 28*(2), 155-176.
Silver, S. D., Cohen, B. P., & Rainwater, J. (1988). Group structure and information exchange in innovative problem solving. In E. J. Lawler & B. Markousky (Eds.), *Advances in Group Process* (Vol. 5, pp. 169-194). Greenwich, CT: JAI Press.
Simon, H. A. (1947). *Administrative behavior.* New York: Macmillan.
Simon, H. A. (1957). A behavioral model of rational choice. In H. A. Simon (Ed.), *Models of man* (pp. 241-260). New York: John Wiley.
Simon, H. A. (1978). Rationality as process and product of thought. *American Economic Review, 68*(2), 1-16.
Simons, R. (1995). *Levers of control. How managers use innovative control systems to drive strategic renewal.* Boston: Harvard University Press.
Simons, R. H., & Thompson, B. M. (1998). Strategic determinants. The context of managerial decision making. *Journal of Managerial Psychology, 13*(1/2), 7-21.

Simons, T., Pelled, L. H., & Smith, K. A. (1999). Making use of difference. Diversity, debate, and decision comprehensiveness in top management teams. *Academy of Management Journal, 42*(6), 662-673.
Skinner, B. F. (1938). *The behavior of organisms. An experimental analysis.* New York: Appleton-Century-Crofts.
Sloan, A. (1972). *My years with General Motors.* Garden City, NY: Doubleday.
Smircich, L., & Stubbart, C. I. (1985). Strategic management in an enacted world. *Academy of Management Review, 10*(4), 724-736.
Smith, J. B. (1994). *Collective intelligence in computer-based collaboration.* Hillsdale, NJ: Lawrence Erlbaum Associates Inc.
Smith, K. G., Smith, K. A., Olian, J. D., Sims, J., Henry P., O'Bannon, D. P., & Scully, J. A. (1994). Top management team demography and process. The role of social integration and communication. *Administrative Science Quarterly, 39*(3), 412-438.
Sniezek, J. A., & Henry, R. A. (1990). Revision, weighting, and commitment in consensus group judgement. *Organizational Behavior and Human Decision Processes, 45*(1), 66-84.
Song, M., Calantone, R. J., & di Benedetto, C. A. (2002). Competitive forces and strategic choice decisions. An experimental investigation in the United States and Japan. *Strategic Management Journal, 23*(10), 969-978.
Sparrow, P. R. (1999). Strategy and cognition. Understanding the role of management knowledge structures, organizational memory and information overload. *Creativity and Innovation Management, 8*(2), 140-148.
Spelsiek, J. (2005). *Motivationsorientierte Steuerung des Wissenstransferverhaltens. Modellierung, empirische Analyse und Anreizsystemgestaltung.* Wiesbaden: Dt. Univ.-Verlag.
Spencer, B., Peyrefitte, J., & Churchman, R. (2003). Consensus and divergence in perceptions of cognitive strategic groups. Evidence from the health care industry. *Strategic Organization, 1*(2), 203-230.
Sproull, L. S. (1981). Beliefs in organizations. In P. C. Nystrom & W. H. Starbuck (Eds.), *Handbook of organizational design* (Vol. 2, pp. 203-224). Oxford: Oxford University Press.
Squire, L. R. (1987). *Memory and brain.* New York: Oxford University Press.
Stachowiak, H. (1973). *Allgemeine Modelltheorie.* Wien: Springer.
Stasser, G. (1999). The uncertain role of unshared information in collective choice. In L. L. Thompson, J. M. Levine & D. M. Messick (Eds.), *Shared cognition in organizations. The management of knowledge* (pp. 49-49). Mahwah, NJ: Lawrence Erlbaum Associates.
Stasser, G., & Davis, J. H. (1981). Group decision making and social influence. A social interaction sequence model. *Psychological Review, 88*(6), 523-551.
Stasser, G., & Stewart, D. (1992). Discovery of hidden profiles by decision-making groups. Solving a problem versus making a judgment. *Journal of Personality and Social Psychology, 63*(3), 426-434.
Stasser, G., & Titus, W. (1985). Pooling of unshared information in group decision making. Biased information sampling during discussion. *Journal of Personality and Social Psychology, 48*(6), 1467-1478.
Stasser, G., & Titus, W. (1987). Effects of information load and percentage of shared information on dissemination of unshared information during group discussion. *Journal of Personality and Social Psychology, 53*(1), 81-93.
Steiner, G. A. (1970). Rise of the corporate planner. *Harvard Business Review, 48*(5), 133-139.

Steinke, I. (1999). *Kriterien qualitativer Forschung. Ansätze zur Bewertung qualitativ-empirischer Sozialforschung.* Weinheim, München: Juventa.
Steinke, I. (2004). Quality criteria in qualitative research. In U. Flick, E. v. Kardorff & I. Steinke (Eds.), *A companion to qualitative research* (pp. 184-190). London, Thousand Oaks, New Delhi: Sage Publications.
Stempfle, J. (2004). Eine integrative Theorie des Problemlösens in Gruppen. Problemlösungsprozess und Problemlöseerfolg. *Gruppendynamik und Organisationsberatung, 35*(2), 335-354.
Stempfle, J., & Badke-Schaub, P. (2002). Kommunikation und Problemlösen in Gruppen. Eine Prozessanalyse. *Gruppendynamik und Organisationsberatung, 33*(1), 57-81.
Stewart, D. D., & Stasser, G. (1995). Expert role assignment and information sampling during collective recall and decision making. *Journal of Personality and Social Psychology, 69*(4), 619-628.
Strauss, A. L., & Corbin, J. (1996). *Grounded Theory. Grundlagen qualitativer Sozialforschung.* Weinheim: Psychologie Verlag Union.
Stubbart, C. I. (1989). Managerial cognition. A missing link in strategic management research. *Journal of Management Studies, 26*(4), 325-347.
Sturdy, A., Schwartz, M., & Spicer, A. (2006). Guess who is coming to dinner? Structures and uses of liminality in strategic management consultancy. *Human Relations, 59*(7), 929-960.
Sutcliffe, K. M., & Huber, G. P. (1998). Firm and industry as determinants of executive perceptions of the environment. *Strategic Management Journal, 19*(8), 793-807.
Swan, J. A. (1995). Exploring knowledge and cognitions in decisions about technological innovation. Mapping managerial cognitions. *Human Relations, 48*(11), 1241-1270.
Swann, W. B., & Read, S. J. (1981). Self-verification processes. How we sustain our self-conceptions. *Journal of Experimental Social Psychology, 17*(4), 351-372.
Swiontek, J. (1997). *Realität und Versprechen von Führungsunterstützungssystemen.* Frankfurt a. M. et al.: Lang.
Tajfel, H. (1982). Social psychology of intergroup relations. In M. R. Rosenzweig & L. W. Porter (Eds.), *Annual review of psychology* (pp. 1-39). Palo Alto: Annual Reviews Inc.
Taylor, S. E., & Crocker, J. (1981). Schematic bases of social information processing. In E. T. Higgins, C. P. Herman & M. P. Zanna (Eds.), *Social cognition. The Ontario symposium* (Vol. 1, pp. 89-160). Hillsdale, NJ: Lawrence Erlbaum Associates.
Tepper, S. J. (2004). Setting agendas and designing alternatives. Policymaking and the strategic role of meetings. *Review of Policy Research, 21*(4), 523-542.
Thiel, M. (2002). *Wissenstransfer in komplexen Organisationen. Effizienz durch Wiederverwendung von Wissen und Best Practices.* Wiesbaden: Dt. Univ.-Verl.
Thomas, D. C. (1999). Cultural diversity and work group effectiveness. An experimental study. *Journal of Cross-Cultural Psychology, 30*(2), 242-263.
Thomas, J. B., Clark, S. M., & Gioia, D. A. (1993). Strategic sensemaking and organizational performance. Linkages among scanning, interpretation, action, and outcomes. *Academy of Management Journal, 36*(2), 239-270.
Thomas, J. B., & McDaniel, R. R. (1990). Interpreting strategic issues. Effects of strategy and the information-processing structure of top management teams. *Academy of Management Journal, 33*(2), 286-306.
Thompson, L. L., & Fine, G. A. (1999). Socially shared cognition, affect, and behavior. A review and integration. *Personality and Social Psychology Review, 3*(4), 278-302.
Thompson, L. L., Levine, J. M., & Messick, D. M. (1999). *Shared cognition in organizations. The management of knowledge.* Mahwah, NJ: Lawrence Erlbaum Associates.

Tindale, R. S., Sheffely, S., & Scott, L. A. (1993). Framing and group decision-making. Do cognitive changes parallel preference changes? *Organizational Behavior and Human Decision Processes, 55*(3), 470-485.

Tuckman, B. W., & Jensen, M. A. C. (1977). Stages of small-group development revisited. *Group & Organization Studies, 2*(4), 419-427.

Tyler, B. B., & Steensma, H. K. (1998). The effects of executives' experiences and perceptions on their assessment of potential technological alliances. *Strategic Management Journal, 19*(10), 939-965.

Ulrich, H. (1984). *Management*. Bern, Stuttgart: Haupt.

van Cauwenbergh, A., & Cool, K. (1982). Strategic management in a new framework. *Strategic Management Journal, 3*(3), 245-264.

Vancil, R. (1976). Strategy formulation in complex organizations. *Sloan Management Review, 17*(2), 1-18.

Vinokur, A., & Burstein, E. (1974). Effects of partially shared persuasive arguments on group-induced shifts. A group-problem-solving approach. *Journal of Personality and Social Psychology, 29*(3), 305-315.

Virany, B., Tushman, M. L., & Romanelli, E. (1992). Executive succession and organization outcomes in turbulent environments. An organization learning approach. *Organization Science, 3*(1), 72-91.

Volkema, R. J., & Niederman, F. (1996). Planning and managing organizational meetings. An empirical analysis of written and oral communications. *The Journal of Business Communication, 33*(3), 275-292.

von Cranach, M., Ochsenbein, G., & Valach, I. (1986). The group as a self-active system. Outline of a theory of group action. *European Journal of Social Psychology, 16*(3), 193-229.

Vroom, V. H., & Yetton, P. W. (1973). *Leadership and decision-making*. Pittsburgh, PA: University of Pittsburgh Press.

Wall, F. (1999). *Planungs- und Kontrollsysteme. Informationstechnische Perspektiven für das Controlling. Grundlagen - Instrumente - Konzepte*. Wiesbaden: Gabler.

Waller, M. J., Huber, G. P., & Glick, W. G. (1995). Functional background as a determinant of executives' selective perception. *Academy of Management Journal, 38*(4), 943-974.

Walsh, J. P. (1995). Managerial and organizational cognition. Notes from a trip down memory lane. *Organization Science, 6*(3), 280-321.

Walsh, J. P., & Fahey, L. (1986). The role of negotiated belief structures in strategy making. *Journal of Management, 12*(3), 325-338.

Walsh, J. P., Henderson, C. M., & Deighton, J. (1988). Negotiated belief structures and decision performance. An empirical investigation. *Organizational Behavior and Human Decision Processes, 42*(2), 194-216.

Ward, J. C., & Reingen, P. H. (1990). Sociocognitive analysis of group decision making among consumers. *The Journal of Consumer Research, 17*(3), 245-262.

Ward, T. B., Smith, S. M., & Finke, R. A. (1999). Creative cognition. In R. J. Sternberg (Ed.), *Handbook of creativity*. Cambridge University Press.

Watson, W. E., Kumar, K., & Michaelsen, L. K. (1993). Cultural diversity's impact on interaction process and performance. Comparing homogeneous and diverse task groups. *Academy of Management Journal, 36*(3), 590-602.

Wegner, D. M. (1987). Transactive memory. A contemporary analysis of the group mind. In B. Mullen & G. R. Goethals (Eds.), *Theories of group behavior* (pp. 185-208). New York: Springer.

Wegner, D. M., Erber, R., & Raymond, P. (1991). Transactive memory in close relationships. *Journal of Personality and Social Psychology, 61*(6), 923-929.

Weick, K. E. (1965). Laboratory experiments with organizations. In J. G. March (Ed.), *Handbook of organizations* (pp. 194-260). Chicago: Rand Mc-Nally.
Weick, K. E. (1967). Organizations in the laboratory. In V. H. Vroom (Ed.), *Methods of organizational research* (pp. 1-56). Pittsburgh: University of Pittsburgh Press.
Weick, K. E. (1976). Educational organizations as loosely coupled systems. *Administrative Science Quarterly, 21*(1), 1-19.
Weick, K. E. (1979). *The social psychology of organizing.* New York: Random House.
Weick, K. E. (1993a). The collapse of sensemaking in organizations. The Mann Gulch disaster. *Administrative Science Quarterly, 38*(4), 628-652.
Weick, K. E. (1993b). Organizational redesign as improvisation. In G. P. Huber & W. H. Glick (Eds.), *Organizational change and redesign* (pp. 346-379). New York: Oxford University Press.
Weick, K. E. (1995). *Sensemaking in organizations.* Thousand Oaks, CA: Sage Publications.
Weick, K. E., & Bougon, M. G. (1986). Organizations as cognitive maps. Charting ways to success and failure. In H. P. Sims & D. A. Gioia (Eds.), *The thinking organization. Dynamics of organizational social cognition* (pp. 102-135). San Francisco: Jossey-Bass.
Weick, K. E., & Roberts, K. H. (1993). Collective mind in organizations. Heedful interrelating on flight decks. *Administrative Science Quarterly, 38*(3), 357-381.
Welge, M. K., & Al-Laham, A. (1992). *Planung. Prozesse - Strategien - Maßnahmen.* Wiesbaden: Gabler.
Welge, M. K., & Al-Laham, A. (1999). *Strategisches Management. Grundlagen, Prozess, Implementierung* (2 ed.). Wiesbaden: Gabler.
Wernerfelt, B. (1984). A resource-based view of the firm. *Strategic Management Journal, 5*(2), 171-180.
Whetten, D. A. (1989). What constitutes a theoretical contribution? *Academy of Management Review, 14*(4), 490-495.
Whitney, J. C., & Smith, R. A. (1983). Effects of group cohesiveness on attitude polarization and the acquisition of knowledge in a strategic planning context. *Journal of Marketing Research, 20*(2), 167-176.
Whittington, R. (1996). Strategy as practice. *Long Range Planning, 29*(5), 731-735.
Whittington, R. (2003). The work of strategizing and organizing. For a practice perspective. *Strategic Organization, 1*(1), 117-125.
Whittington, R. (2006). Completing the practice turn in strategy research. *Organization Studies, 27*(5), 613-634.
Whittington, R., & Cailluet, L. (2008). The crafts of strategy. Special issue introduction by the guest editors. *Long Range Planning, 41*(3), 241-247.
Whittington, R., Molloy, E., Mayer, M., & Smith, A. (2006). Practices of strategising/organising. Broadening strategy work and skills. *Long Range Planning, 39*(6), 615-629.
Wiersema, M. F., & Bantel, K. A. (1992). Top management team demography and corporate strategic change. *Academy of Management Journal, 35*(1), 91-121.
Williamson, O. E. (1975). *Markets and hierarchies. Analysis and antitrust implications. A study in the economics of internal organization.* New York: Free Press.
Williamson, O. E. (1985). *The economic institutions of capitalism. Firms, markets, relational contracting.* New York: Free Press.
Williamson, O. E. (1991). Strategizing, economizing, and economic organization. *Strategic Management Journal, 12*(Special Issue), 75-94.
Willke, H. (1996). Dimensionen des Wissensmanagements. Zum Zusammenhang von gesellschaftlicher und organisationaler Wissensbasierung. In G. Schreyögg & P.

Conrad (Eds.), *Wissensmanagement. Managementforschung 6* (pp. 263-304). Berlin: Gruyter, Walter de GmbH.
Willke, H. (2006). *Systemtheorie 1. Grundlagen. Eine Einführung in die Grundprobleme der Theorie sozialer Systeme* (7 ed.). Stuttgart: UTB.
Wilson, B. G., & Madsen Meyers, K. (2000). Situated cognition in theoretical and practical context. In D. H. Jonassen & S. M. Land (Eds.), *Theoretical foundations of learning environments* (pp. 57-88). Mahwah: Lawrence Erlbaum.
Wilson, D. C., & Jarzabkowski, P. (2004). Thinking and acting strategically. New challenges for interrogating strategy. *European Management Review, 1*(1), 14-20.
Wilson, J. M., Goodman, P. S., & Cronin, M. A. (2007). Group learning. *Academy of Management Review, 32*(4), 1041-1059.
Wilson, T. P. (1970). Conceptions of interaction and forms of sociological explanation. *American Sociological Review, 35*(4), 697-710.
Winter, S. G. (2003). Understanding dynamic capabilities. *Strategic Management Journal, 24*(10), 991-995.
Wolfe, J., & Jackson, C. (1987). Creating models of the strategic decision making process via participant recall. A free simulation examination. *Journal of Management, 13*(1), 123-134.
Wrona, T. (2005). *Die Fallstudienanalyse als wissenschaftliche Forschungsmethode* (No. 10). Berlin: ESCP-EAP Europäische Wirtschaftshochschule Berlin.
Wrona, T. (2006). Fortschritts- und Gütekriterien im Rahmen qualitativer Sozialforschung. In S. Zelewski (Ed.), *Fortschritt in den Wirtschaftswissenschaften. Wissenschaftstheoretische Grundlagen und exemplarische Anwendungen* (pp. 189-216). Wiesbaden: Gabler.
Wrona, T. (2008). Kognitive Strategieforschung. State of the Art und aktuelle Entwicklungen. In T. Wrona (Ed.), *Strategische Managementforschung. Aktuelle Entwicklungen und internationale Perspektiven* (pp. 41-84). Wiesbaden: Gabler.
Wrona, T., & Breuer, M. (2009). Die Analyse von Gruppenkognitionen im Rahmen der kognitiven Strategieforschung. In A. G. Scherer (Ed.), *Methoden in der Betriebswirtschaftslehre* (pp. 71-96). Wiesbaden: Gabler.
Wrona, T., & Breuer, M. (2008). *The emergence of organisational strategies from a cognitive perspective.* Paper presented at the Academy of Management Annual Meeting, Anaheim, CA.
Zack, M. H. (1999). Managing codified knowledge. *Sloan Management Review, 40*(4), 45-58.
Zack, M. H. (2003). Rethinking the knowledge-based organization. *Sloan Management Review, 44*(4), 67-71.
Zajac, E. J., & Bazerman, M. H. (1991). Blind spots in industry and competitor analysis. *Academy of Management Review, 16*(1), 37-56.
Zollo, M., & Winter, S. G. (2002). Deliberate learning and the evolution of dynamic capabilities. *Organization Science, 13*(3), 339-352.
Zuber, J. A., Crott, H. W., & Werner, J. (1992). Choice shift and group polarization. An analysis of the status of arguments and social decision schemes. *Journal of Personality and Social Psychology, 62*(1), 50-61.
Zucker. (1977). *The mutable self.* Beverly Hills, CA: Sage Publications.
Zysno, P. V. (1998). Die Klassifikation von Gruppenaufgaben. In E. Ardelt-Gattinger, H. Lechner & W. Schlögl (Eds.), *Gruppendynamik. Anspruch und Wirklichkeit der Arbeit in Gruppen* (pp. 10-24). Göttingen: Verlag für angewandte Psychologie.